Compiling for the .NET

Common Language Runtime (CLR)

John Gough

Prentice Hall PTR
Upper Saddle River, New Jersey 07548
www.phptr.com

Library of Congress Cataloging-in-Publication Data

Gough, K. John (Kevin John), 1942-
  Compiling for the .NET common language runtime (CLR) / J. Gough.
    p. cm. - - (.Net series)
  ISBN 0-13-062296-6
   1. Compiling (Electronic computers) 2.Operating systems (Computers) 3.
  Programming languages (Electronic computers) I. Title. II. Series.

  QA76.76.C65 G68 2001
  005.4'53 - -dc21   2001050077

Editorial/Production Supervision: *Laura Burgess*
Acquisitions Editor: *Paul Petralia*
Editorial Assistant: *Richard Winkler*
Marketing Manager: *Debby vanDijk*
Buyer: *Alexis Heydt-Long*
Cover Design Director: *Jerry Votta*

©2002 Prentice Hall PTR

Published by Prentice Hall PTR
Prentice-Hall, Inc.
Upper Saddle River, NJ 07458

Prentice Hall books are widely used by corporations and government agencies for training, marketing, and resale.

The publisher offers discounts on this book when ordered in bulk quantities.
For more information, contact Corporate Sales Department, phone: 800-382-3419;
fax: 201-236-7141; e-mail: corpsales@prenhall.com
or write: Prentice Hall PTR
          Corporate Sales Department
          One Lake Street
          Upper Saddle River, NJ 07458

Printed in the United States of America
10 9 8 7 6 5 4 3 2 1

ISBN 0-13-062296-6

Pearson Education LTD.
Pearson Education Australia PTY, Limited
Pearson Education Singapore, Pte. Ltd.
Pearson Education North Asia Ltd.
Pearson Education Canada, Ltd.
Pearson Educación de Mexico, S.A. de C.V.
Pearson Education — Japan
Pearosn Education Malaysia, Pte. Ltd.
Pearson Education, Upper Saddle River, New Jersey

Contents

3   Understanding the CTS   55

4   Mapping to the CLR   103

5   Building Abstract Syntax Trees   135

6   Evaluating Semantic Attributes   165

Foreword

Machines, virtual or physical, are at the heart of computing. We program by programming to a machine model. However, we rarely target the actual machine, but rather use the services of compilers (and interpreters—last-second compilers, really) to mediate between a higher level language and the language understood by the various machines we target.

To understand a particular machine, one can read about it. Or one can write some code at the level of the machine's language. Or one can imagine how a programming language of one's choice and liking would be best mapped to that machine. It is the latter approach that bears the richest fruit as it helps to combine a thorough understanding of a machine's architecture with a solid mental model of how to map the understood into the machine's world. (The one better way to learn all these things is to actually write the kind of book you are now holding in your hands!)

Not everyone is a compiler writer, but most programmers do write "little compilers" all the time—often without being aware of it. The serious developer does not want to sit on the proverbial cloud; it is necessary and beneficial to gain a thorough understanding of the workings of the underlying machine, even if the task of mapping one's language to that of the machine is left to a compiler written by someone else. It is thus most helpful to understand how such a compiler works, what can and cannot be expected of it, and how the underlying machine model affects everything one's programs do.

John Gough's book is a beautifully rounded yet sufficiently compact introduction to the writing of compilers that target the new .NET *common language runtime* (*CLR*). By drawing parallels with the well-known *Java virtual machine* (*JVM*), he makes the *CLR* accessible to those familiar with *JVM* concepts. By walking the reader through most aspects of an actual compiler for an actual language—Component Pascal—and by making that compiler available in source form, John enables a deep and thorough exploration of this fascinating subject. Although the *CLR* is a virtual machine in its current and foreseeable implementations, it is a machine nevertheless and working through John's book is one of the most effective (and, in my mind, enjoyable) ways to learn about it.

Few authors are as qualified as John is to write this book. His years of academic and practical contributions to the compiler construction discipline led to a series of production-quality compilers, including *Gardens Point Modula* (*gpm*), which was distributed commercially for many years. As a member of Project 7, John was deeply involved in the earlier phases of development that eventually led to the *CLR* as it is known today. The compiler project he describes in this book was his contribution to Project 7.

I thoroughly enjoyed reading John's book and certainly expect most readers to agree. I've known and worked with John for almost seven years now: There is a lot to be learned from his thorough embrace of theory and practice and his willingness and drive to have it all come to life in "real bits!"

Clemens Szyperski
Redmond, WA
August 2001

Introduction

This is a book about code generation for the Microsoft.NET *Common Language Runtime* (*CLR*). There are a number of different contexts in which such code generation might occur. The book covers all of these contexts in enough detail to permit code generators for *.NET* to be created.

Compilers, Dynamic Code Generators, and Program Instrumentation

The most obvious context in which *.NET* code needs to be generated occurs when an additional programming language is to be implemented for the runtime. In this case a new compiler must be written. Fortunately, the designers of *.NET* spent considerable effort in making the execution engine capable of efficiently implementing a wide range of different programming languages. During the early development stages of *.NET* a number of independent language implementation groups were invited to create compilers for the platform. This initiative became known as "*Project 7.*"

There are a number of other contexts in which the generation of code starts with some kind of program input. Most of these are normally not thought of as programming languages translation problems. An example is the generation of specialized processing code from user queries. The dynamic generation of code in such contexts may be the most effective attack on the problem. Once again the facilities of *.NET* facilitate such program architectures. In particular, the system provides an *Application Programming Interface (API)*[1] that allows *Common Intermediate Language* (*CIL*) to be emitted into a buffer, and the buffer transformed into a *program executable module* (*PEM*).

Another context in which the generation of *CIL* occurs is the creation of tools that *rewrite* program executables. Such tools include all kinds of program instrumentation, including profiling and other performance measuring tools.

Software engineers who are sensitive to the performance of their software or simply want to understand what that compiler is doing to their source code, will also find the book useful. The book provides a sound basis for understanding the execution model of *.NET*. Based on such understanding, rational decisions may be made in program design, and the performance consequences of alternatives designs predicted.

Virtual Machines as Compiler Targets

The Execution Model

Code generators for *.NET* emit *CIL*, either as text to a file for subsequent "assembly" or directly into a file or a memory buffer. The codes of *CIL* or sometimes just *IL* for short, are instructions for a virtual machine and are always executed indirectly by means of a *Just-in-Time Compiler* (*JIT*). The *JIT* translates the instructions of *CIL* into machine code for the particular computer on which the program is to be executed. Under normal circumstances this machine code is not saved to a file, and whenever the program is to be re-executed the *CIL* is "re-*JIT*-ed."

Program executable modules, called *assemblies*, are usually demand-loaded and are *just-in-time compiled* (*JIT*-ed) at the time of loading. At load time each assembly is subject to some level of checking. At the very least the *JIT* must be able to make enough sense of the instructions to generate machine code. At a much more stringent level, the execution engine is able to ensure that the assembly is *memory-safe*. The implications of memory safety are explored in some detail below. Here it suffices to note that assemblies that pass this level of "verification" are guaranteed to be free from many kinds of runtime errors.

In broad terms, program code in *CIL* may have different levels of guaranteed runtime safety. Programs that are intended to pass the checks of verification are said to be written in *verifiable code*. Verifiable code must conform to several strict requirements. Firstly, all dynamically allocated memory must be *managed data*. This means that all objects must be allocated from the garbage collected heap, and must be *self-describing*. The importance

---

[1] I am afraid that this book is going to use a lot of *three letter acronyms* (*TLAs*). Some of these even have more than three letters. To smooth the way, the book spells out all the *TLAs* in full in this introductory chapter.

of self-description is that the garbage collector must be able to discover the exact type of the object from inspection of the contents of the object. In addition, all operations on data must be performed in such a way that the verifier is able to statically prove that the operation is appropriate for the exact type of the object. Finally, all method calls must pass arguments that are provably conformant to the statically specified method signature. For most programming languages in common use not all programs can be translated into verifiable code. In such cases programmers who wish their programs to pass verification must restrict themselves to a subset of the language. Programming constructs that cause problems are such things as union types (untagged variant records) and pointer arithmetic. Some recent procedural languages, such as *C#*[2] and *Java*, are inherently type-safe and can always be translated into verifiable code, although in *C#* there is an option to use unsafe language constructs. For the rest there are two choices. A compiler may either produce unverifiable code, or may restrict users to the safe subset. Unverifiable code in *.NET* is sufficiently unrestricted that even programming languages such as *ANSI C* may be compiled.

As well as speaking of *managed data*, we also speak of *managed code*. Managed data, as defined above, is data under the control of the garbage collector. Managed code is simply code that is executed by the *CLR* as opposed to ordinary native-code execution.

The virtual machine for which *CIL* is the instruction set is an *abstract stack machine*. This means that the instructions for the machine take operands that reside on an evaluation stack. The instruction set consists of instructions that *push* operands on the abstract evaluation stack, instructions that operate on the top of stack operands, and instructions that *pop* operands off the stack and store them in memory or in local variables. The use of abstract stack machines to define the intermediate language for communication between compiler front-ends and back-end code generators is historically significant.

The use of virtual machines as intermediate forms in compilation has frequently been justified as a sensible factorization of the compilation task. The argument runs roughly as follows. If compilers for N different languages need to be created for M different machine architectures, then $M \times N$ complete compilers need to be written, debugged, tested, and so on. If, on the other hand, all compilers work through a common intermediate form, then just N front-ends and M back-ends need to be created. This is the *code reuse* argument.

Another reason to use a virtual machine as an intermediate form has to do with what we might call *semantic factorization*, as opposed to the *implementation factorization* just discussed. In this case the full richness of the source language is reduced to a simplified set of operations that are still able to express all the operations of the source. In effect, every source program is rewritten as instructions to the virtual machine that implements the simplified operation set. The rewritten program is then further compiled or interpreted. This route is almost invariably taken for logic programming languages, such as *PROLOG*, or any of the pattern matching functional languages, such as *Haskell*. It is important to

---

[2] *C#* is the recently announced Microsoft object oriented language. The name of the language is pronounced "C-sharp." *C#* is as close as one may get to the native language of the *.NET* platform.

recognize that virtual machines used in this way are specific for the source language that spawned them. The instruction set of the virtual machine is still far removed from the semantic level of the final hardware, but rather is midway between the source language and machine language. This is the *bridging the semantic gap* argument.

A final reason to use a virtual machine as an intermediate form has come into prominence in the last few years. This implies the use of the intermediate form as the distribution form for executable program content. To an extent, the attraction follows from the code reuse argument. Rather than compile a program for every possible user machine architecture, generic intermediate code in generated. Each machine architecture has an "installer" of some sort, which converts the intermediate form into the final executable content. This might be done either by offline translation or by just-in-time compilation, as practiced in *.NET* and most *Java Virtual Machine* (*JVM*) environments. An important advantage of such systems arises when the installer is trusted. In this case security checks may be carried out at installation time, and the system need not trust every code creation program. This is the *portability and security* argument.

Some History: From the P-Machine to .NET

The idea of using an intermediate form within a programming language compiler as a means of communication between the front-end and back-end dates back at least to the 1970s. The idea is quite straightforward. Language dependent front-ends compile and semantically check programs, passing an intermediate language representation of the program to the code-generating back-end. In an ideal situation the front-end would be entirely independent of the target hardware, while the back-end would be sensibly independent of the particular language in which the source program was written. In this way the task of writing compilers for N languages on M machine architectures is factored into $N+M$ part compilers.

Many of these intermediate language representations were based on abstract stack machines. One particular representation, *P-Code*, was invented as an intermediate form for the ETH Pascal Compilers, but became pervasive as the machine code for the *University of California San Diego* (*UCSD*) Pascal System. What had been noted by the *UCSD* people was that a program encoded for an abstract stack machine may be used in two ways: A compiler back-end may compile the code down to the machine language of the actual target machine; or an interpreter may be written that *emulates* the abstract machine on the target. This interpretative approach surrenders a significant factor of speed but has the advantage that programs are much more dense in the abstract machine encoding. Usually the intermediate form uses only one byte per instruction, which is why such intermediate representations are often referred to as *byte code* forms. In the case of *UCSD* Pascal the code was so compact that the compilers could be run on the 4k or so of memory available on the very first microcomputers. As a consequence of this technology high-level languages became available for the first time on microcomputers. As an added benefit, the task of porting a language system to a new machine was reduced to the comparatively simple task of creating a new interpreter on the new machine.

The use of abstract machines as intermediate forms for conventional compilers has also had its adherents. For example, previous Gardens Point compilers used a stack inter- mediate form (D-Code) for all of the languages and platforms supported by the system. Although most implementations are fully compiled, a special lightweight interpreted ver- sion of the system was written in about 1990 for the Intel *iapx86* architecture, allowing users with a humble IBM XT to produce the same results as the 32-bit UNIX platforms that the other implementations supported. As a measure of the complexity of the virtual machine emulator, the interpreter was about 1000 lines of assembly language, with the floating point emulator a further 1000 lines.

A largely failed attempt to leverage the portability properties of stack intermediate forms was the Open Software Foundation's **Architecture Neutral Distribution Form** (*ANDF*). The idea behind *ANDF* was to distribute programs in an intermediate form and complete the task of compilation during an *installation* step. The *ANDF* form was code for an abstract stack machine, but one with a slight twist. Generators of conventional intermediate forms, such as D-Code, know enough about the target's addressing constraints to be able to resolve (say) object field accesses to address offsets. In the case of *ANDF* the target is not yet determined at the time of compilation, so that all such accesses must remain symbolic. In the symbolic case, instead of saying "the integer at the address *top-of-stack plus 8*" one must say "the field named *foo* of the object of class *Bar* whose reference is currently on the top of the stack." It has been suggested that this incorporation of symbolic information into the distributed form was considered to be a threat to intellectual property rights by many software companies, which was a factor in the failure of the form to achieve widespread adoption.

In the late 1990s Sun Microsystems released their *Java* language system. This system is, once again, based on an abstract stack machine. And again, like *ANDF*, it relies on the presence of symbolic information to allow such things as field offsets to be resolved at de- ployment time. In the case of *Java* and the *JVM* the "problem" of symbolic content turned out to be a virtue. The presence of the symbolic information is what allows deployment- time and runtime enforcement of the type system via the so-called *bytecode verifier*. These runtime type safety guarantees are the basis on which applet security is founded. As things now stand, *JVM*s are available for almost all computing platforms, and *Java* tells a program portability story which transends almost all other approaches.

In mid-2000 Microsoft revealed a new technology based on a wider use of the world wide web for service delivery. This technology became known as the *.NET* system. The technology has many components, but all of it depends on a runtime which is object- oriented and fully garbage collected. The runtime processes an intermediate form that, like the *JVM*, is based on an abstract stack machine. Apart from this superficial level of commonality, the design of the two virtual machines is quite different.

Memory Safety and Verification

Memory Errors and Their Consequences

One of the design goals of modern operating systems is to enforce *memory isolation* between processes. In fact many people argue that "operating systems" that allow one process to overwrite memory belonging to another are not operating systems in any real sense of the term. Many readers will have long enough memories to recall the frustration of running programs that malfunction and overwrite system data. Typically, the outcome was a system reboot and lost data.

Thankfully we may now take memory isolation between processes as a given. However, there is another level of isolation between program parts that is important. The symptoms of the lack of isolation between components within a single operating system process are the subtle bugs caused by *memory errors*. Let us take just one scenario: An erroneous address computation allows an arbitrary memory location to be overwritten. If the user is lucky, the bad address will not be part of the legal address space of the current process and a runtime exception will be generated. The much more insidious possibility is that the error will overwrite some data structure and the error will pass untrapped for the moment. The secretly trashed datum may cause the program to later produce erroneous results. Equally, some later use of the trashed datum may cause the program to crash. These kinds of errors are particularly difficult to diagnose, since naive debugging does not help. Suppose the trashed datum is a variable V. The debugger may let you see that the crash happens because V has a bad value. Unfortunately no matter how much time is spent looking at the source statements that change V, the bug cannot be found because the bad value gets put in V by another part of the program that does not mention V in its source code.

The sources of such memory errors are myriad. Here is an incomplete list —

- accessing a deallocated memory location

- accessing a nonexistent array element

- treating a pointer of one type as another

- sending wrongly typed arguments to a function

To this catalog of infamy must be added the problems, related to the first list item, of *memory leaks*. In this case, rather than release memory too soon, memory fails to be released at all, and the program slowly eats its way through its address space.

Memory Safety... By Design

In a statically typed language, locations have a signature that typically declares that the location contains a value of a certain data type. The signature may also make certain other assertions about the location, such as that it is only accessible to code within certain modules, or that the value is read-only, and so on. These declarations are *invariants* of the location. In effect, the invariants are a contractual guarantee that the location will at all times contain only values that are valid for the declared type, as well as any other guarantees implied by the declaration.

We say that a program is memory-safe if the program does not violate the invariants of any location in memory along any reachable control path of execution. What we would like to be able to do is to mechanically determine whether a given program is memory-safe or not. As it turns out, this is a provably impossible task for arbitrary programs. Nevertheless, we may conservatively show that certain classes of program are memory-safe.

Under some circumstances we will not be able to prove that a program will not *attempt* to violate an invariant of some location. What we may be able to do instead, is to show that any such attempt will be trapped at runtime and therefore will not succeed. Usually we will be content with such a guarantee, since it logically does preserve the invariant in question, even if in a rather undesirable way.

One of the triumphs of modern programming language design and implementation is that we now understand how to design languages and runtimes for which every semantically correct *source* program may be compiled into a memory-safe *executable* program.

There are a number of mechanisms that are needed to ensure memory safety in this sense. Firstly, we may remove the possibility of accessing deallocated memory, and the twin problem of memory leaks, by relying on automatic garbage collection. Garbage collection reclaims memory when the memory is provably unreachable and leaves it alone otherwise.

Insistence on array bounds checking removes another potent source of memory errors. In this case, as with garbage collection, there is a moderate runtime cost for the added safety.

Finally, we need to ensure that references can only contain values that point to objects of the appropriate type. This requires a number of separate mechanisms. As a first step either the compiler or the runtime system must guarantee that every reference is correctly initialized. That is, every reference must either be initialized to point to an object of the expected type or must hold a value that will raise an exception if accessed. Traditionally some distinguished value **nil** is used for this purpose. In addition we must ensure that the correctly initialized values may only be replaced by other correct values. In many languages this last requirement may be *statically computable*. By statically computable we mean that the guarantee may be enforced at compile time, rather than having to rely on runtime checks and error trapping. Programming languages for which every datum has a statically computable type are said to be *statically typed*. In some literature, the notion of static typing is described as "strong typing."

In most cases these mechanisms are overkill, in the sense that skilled programmers have always been able to create memory-safe programs without needing all this help. Nevertheless, the interests of programming productivity and program safety argue powerfully for the use of these methods.

Memory Safety in .NET

The *.NET* system provides a framework for memory-safe programming. There are a number of different aspects of *.NET* that contribute toward this outcome.

It is wise at the outset to emphasize that the guarantee of memory safety only applies to programs that use verifiable code. Dynamically allocated data in verifiable code is garbage collected, and every *datum* is of a known type at runtime. This is a subtly different concept from the static typing discussed above. Static typing guarantees that a particular *variable*, "modA.foo" say, is of its declared type. In the case of verifiable code in *.NET* we must also be able to compute the types of the temporary values on the abstract evaluation stack. Consider a particular program point where two control paths join. At the join we must be able to compute the types of the stack elements, despite the fact that differently typed values may have been *pushed* on the stack along the two joining paths.

There is also an issue of trust here. It may be the case that a particular language, *C#* say, has the property that all valid programs are memory-safe. However, on what basis should the system believe that just because a program says that it was written in *C#* that it must be memory-safe? The program might have been compiled by a buggy compiler.[3] Or some evil person might have done a binary edit on the *PEM*, or the file might only *say* that it was compiled from *C#* when it was really compiled from *Doctor Destructo's Demon Dialect*. The possibilities are endless.

One other scenario deserves explicit mention. Suppose a compiler correctly processes a valid source program that calls a method from some other module. Subsequent to the compilation the library is rewritten, and the signature of one of the methods is changed. The correctly compiled code may now be memory-unsafe!

.NET resolves all these problems by a combination of load-time verification and runtime checking. The load-time verifier computes the types of all data used in the *CIL* code of a program. As hinted above this may involve significant computations based on the control flow graph of each method. The verifier checks that all uses of data are consistent with their declarations. This necessarily involves access to multiple assemblies. This is so because consistency of argument types between method callers and method callees may cut across *PEM* boundaries. The case of static data exported from modules requires similar treatment. As a bonus, the load-time verifier ensures that local variables of methods are never used unless they have been initialized along every control flow path that leads to the attempted use. This is a subtle and interesting problem that we spend some time on in Appendix A.

As well as the load-time verifier, there is also a command line utility verifier computes the `peverify` that verifies *PEM*s. This not only applies a pass/fail test to the *PEM*, but

---

[3]Of course, I am reluctant to admit that a compiler might be buggy, but reality is a harsh critic.

also give helpful diagnostics as to *why* and *where* a *PEM* failed verification. It will be argued later that `peverify` is the *.NET* compiler writer's best friend.

Finally, it might be noted that even for unverifiable code it is not true that "anything goes." Consider the following textual *CIL* sequence —

```
ldc.i4 42
ldc.r4 3.14159265
mul
```

In this code the first instruction pushes the 4-byte integer constant 42 onto the evaluation stack. The second instruction pushes a 4-byte real constant ("float") approximately equal to π. The third instruction asks for these two stack elements to be multiplied together. Notice that the instruction set does not specify the type of multiplication. The *JIT* is supposed to work out what kind of multiplication is required from the operands. But in this case it is an impossible task, since one operand is an "int32", while the other is a "float32". This code sequence should[4] be rejected by the *JIT*, even in unverifiable code.

The Running Example

Many of the code fragments taken to illustrate the points in this book are taken from the *Gardens Point Component Pascal* (*gpcp*) compiler. This is an open source compiler for the object oriented language *Component Pascal*. The book does not describe all of the code of the compiler, concentrating instead on those aspects that are relevant to code generation for *.NET*. Readers interested in those parts of the compiler that are not described here may download the complete source of the compiler. The compiler source is reasonably well annotated. The original compiler was written as part of Project 7. It is being maintained as an ongoing part of two projects. One makes the core language available as a vehicle for software development or for use as a teaching language. As part of this project the language is currently being integrated into Microsoft's Visual Studio 7. The other project uses *gpcp* as a vehicle for programming language research.

gpcp has several different code emitters. The one of interest to this book produces *CIL* while other emitters produce *Java* byte codes for the *JVM*. The differences between these two targets is itself an interesting sidelight that is discussed in the references.

Component Pascal is an object-oriented language, and is statically type-safe. This means that every legal *Component Pascal* program may be translated into verifiable *CIL*. The other main features of the language make it a reasonable match to the *.NET* framework. The language has single implementation inheritance and exercises most features of the

---

[4]It is possible that the *JIT* will not check the types of *both* of its operands and will blindly accept the example sequence. If it does, it is certain to get the result wrong, as the *IL* sequence makes no sense.

.NET runtime. As the name suggests, the language is a *Pascal* variant, being most closely related to *Oberon-2*. Compared to *C++*, *C#*, or *Java*, *Component Pascal* is a relatively small language. It has most of the loop and choice constructs of other languages, but avoids the additional complexities caused by such things as method overloading and user-defined infix operators.

Compared to *Oberon-2*, *Component Pascal* adds some additional annotations to method and type declarations that allow extra consistency checks to be performed at compile time. The purpose of these extra checks is to allow stronger guarantees of runtime behavior in a component programming environment. Like all *Pascal* variants, it is the default that arithmetic operations, type conversions and array indexing are overflow- and range-checked. The base language does not provide facilities for interface implementation. For this reason the base language is not able to access *all* of the facilities of the *CTS* without some syntactic extensions.

gpcp is written in *Component Pascal* and may recompile itself either on the *.NET* platform, or under the *JVM*. This ability of the compiler to "bootstrap" itself provides a preliminary sanity check on the correctness of the implementation. At the least it provides a check that the translation is correct for those language features that the compiler itself uses. Since a compiler is a relatively complex program, this sanity check applies to a large fraction of the source language.

While most of the discussion in the book uses *gpcp* as a running example, there are times when it is necessary to consider other languages. This is needed, for example, when we discuss the translation of constructs that *Component Pascal* does not contain. In such cases the book uses the language *C#* as the example language. As noted earlier *C#* is as close as one may get to the native language of *.NET*. *C#* exercises almost all of the features of verifiable code.

As it turns out there are a small number of language features in *Component Pascal* that are not easily implemented in *.NET*. The issues involved in programming around these limitations are addressed toward the end of the book, in Chapter 12. In that chapter there is also some discussion of some of the features of other languages that pose particular problems for *.NET*.

The Reference Model

For all of what follows, we assume a compiler architecture that separates into a number of *phases*. These phases are at least conceptually separated in time, and can be represented at various levels of granularity.

The arguments for the particular software architecture shown in Figure 1.1 are addressed later, and in the case of the early stages need not concern us. One of the points of making this phase separation is so that we may agree on what we will *not* discuss in this book. In particular, the various possible ways in which abstract syntax trees may be created need not concern us.

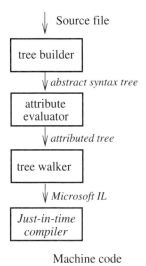

Figure 1.1: The reference architecture

Chapter 5 argues that the construction of an abstract syntax representation of the program to be translated is almost always the most sensible design choice. That chapter discusses the *form* of the **Abstract Syntax Tree** (*AST*) and the things it needs to represent. However we can gloss over the mechanism by which the source is parsed and the tree constructed. In essence, we assume that by some means or other an abstract syntax representation of the program has been produced. This is implied by the top box in Figure 1.1. The "output" of this phase is an *AST*.

The next step in the process is the computation of attributes of the nodes of the *AST*. These attributes include those that are required for semantic checking of the correctness of the source program, and also may include some that are required for code emission for the *.NET* system. The "output" of this phase is a *fully attributed AST*.

The third box in Figure 1.1 is the tree walking code-emitter. In essence, this phase involves a traversal of the *AST* during which the intermediate code is emitted. In the case of *gpcp* there are several different tree walkers. Each produces a different output language. The *.NET* tree walker traverses the tree and produces a *PEM* as output. The program executable encodes the *CIL*.

The final box in Figure 1.1 is the *JIT*. Under most circumstances the *PEM* that is output by the tree walker is produced offline and is written to a file. The connection between the third and fourth box in the figure may thus be quite indirect. In the usual offline creation scenario the two are separated in time. They may also be separated in space if, for example, the *PEM* is transmitted over the internet.

In any case the output of the final box is native code on the platform on which the *JIT* is running. The result of this translation is generally not saved, but is regenerated each time the *PEM* is reloaded. Some of the base class libraries are exceptions to this rule and are saved as native code to speed up loading.

Files and Procedural Interfaces

If we look inside the third box down in Figure 1.1, we have two different ways in which the desired functionality may be achieved. These two designs are shown in Figure 1.2.

On the left of the figure the box has been expanded out as a tree walker that emits *CIL* to a text file. In this case the text file is read by the *.NET IL*-assembler utility ilasm. This utility reads the text and produces the *PEM*. ilasm is a command line program that has options to produce either dynamically linked libraries (**.dll** files) or executable (**.exe**) files as output.

On the right of Figure 1.2 is a second possible expansion. In this case there is no text file, but instead calls are made through a procedural interface to the executable generation code. This call interface could be the *Reflection.Emit API*, which is supplied with *.NET*, or could be a custom interface that directly writes *PEM* files.

How is one to choose between these two styles of *PEM* generation? The advantages of the textual form of *CIL* are mainly those of convenience for the compiler writer. The textual form may be read and, if necessary, edited and reassembled during the development process. Suppose, for example, that you wish to try a different way of encoding some particular construct, or the verifier rejects your current code. In either case it is simplest to edit the *CIL* text by hand and resubmit to ilasm (and to peverify) to try out a variation. The recommendation of this book is thus to start out by producing the textual form of *CIL*.

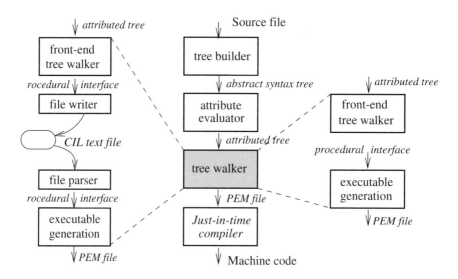

Figure 1.2: Two ways of expanding the tree walker

The advantages of producing program executables via a procedural interface come down to speed and flexibility. Firstly, and most importantly, the reading and writing of files in the production path through the textual interface all consume precious machine cycles and input-output bandwidth. By comparison, a procedural interface can be blindingly fast. Furthermore, if dynamic compilation is required, then there is no option but to use the procedural interface. *Reflection.Emit* allows either the writing of the output as a *PEM* file or the emission of the code as a preloaded assembly in memory. It is sensible to plan to move, at an appropriate stage of product development, from the textual to the procedural interface.

During the preliminary stage of development, when our recommendation is to use the textual interface and `ilasm`, it is still possible to make the process transparent. In other words it is not necessary to use separate commands to create the textual *CIL* and then to invoke `ilasm`. Instead, the compiler driver may spawn a new command line process and invoke `ilasm` on that process. This is the path that *gpcp* uses. In this case the overhead of reading and writing the text file is made worse by the overhead of process creation under many operating systems.

How to Read this Book

This book is intended to be read from the front to the back. Because of this, not all of the material relating to a particular topic occurs all in one place. For example, in Chapter 4 the important concept of *reference surrogates* is introduced, in connection with the implementation of certain kinds of assignment semantics on the *CLR*. The sometimes gory details of how the result is achieved are spread out over three code generation chapters, Chapters 7–9. This places the material in its logical context, but may be less helpful if this particular set of tricks is *all* that you wish to know at a particular reading. In such cases the index may help somewhat.

There are three main sections. The first section, Chapters 2–4, introduces background material on *CIL*, the *CLR*, and the *Common Type System (CTS)* that it supports. The last of these chapters tries to give some guidance in choosing the mappings from the constructs of your intended source language to the *CLR*. The second section deals with the compile-time representation of programs and the semantic analysis that is required prior to the emission of *CIL*. The final section, Chapters 7–11, deals with the emission of the intermediate language. The final chapter discusses some of the remaining issues, such as useful tricks for dealing with language features that do not easily find expression in *CIL*.

Assumed Knowledge

It has been assumed that the reader of this book will be familiar with the basic concepts of programming languages and their implementation. It is also assumed that the reader is familiar with the usual data structures and algorithm theory that would appear in the text for a typical second-level course in college.

It is helpful, but not essential, that the reader be familiar with the overall syntactic style, that is, the "look and feel," of an example of both of the major imperative language families, language *C* and language *Pascal*. It has not been assumed that the reader is familiar with either the new language *C#* or the language of the running example compiler *Component Pascal*. The *C#* examples are explained, as necessary, when they occur. Similarly for *Component Pascal*, any quirk of the language that is significant for a particular example is mentioned at the time. There is a broad overview of the language and its type system starting on page 121. This requires approximately four pages.

It is assumed that the reader is familiar with the basic concepts of object-oriented (OO) programming. A working knowledge of programming in any of the mainstream OO-languages should suffice.

Format and Style

Program fragments.   Program fragments occur with alarming frequency in this book. In general these programs are written in *Component Pascal*, *C#*, *ANSI C*, or *CIL*. In many cases the complete code of the example would be too large or too confusing. In such cases, the lines that are not relevant have been elided and replaced by ellipses (. . .).

In appropriate cases the style of fragments is a verbatim representation of what you would see on your computer monitor when viewing a program listing. In other cases, a so-called "publication format" has been chosen, in which keywords of the language are shown in lower case and bold. Here is the "Hello World" program in *Component Pascal* in the verbatim style —

```
MODULE Hello;
  IMPORT CPmain, Console;
BEGIN
  Console.WriteString("Hello CP World");
  Console.WriteLn;
END Hello.
```

And here is the same program in the publication format —

```
module Hello;
  import CPmain, Console;
begin
  Console.WriteString("Hello CP World");
  Console.WriteLn;
end Hello.
```

In reality, all keywords of *Component Pascal* are entirely in upper case. However, the combination of upper case *and* bold font is a bit overpowering, hence the style as shown.

In the case of *CIL* the program fragments are frequently annotated with commentary to help explain the code. In cases where the fragment is otherwise in verbatim style, the commentary is added in italic font, to distinguish it from any verbatim comments that might have been emitted to the *IL* file. Here is a brief example of the style, showing how a local variable is incremented in *CIL* —

```
ldloc.2              // push local #2 on stack
ldc.i4.1             // push int32 constant 1
add                  // add the two stack values
stloc.2              // store result in local #2
```

Finally, we sometimes want to abstract away the details of a particular piece of code but still indicate the purpose of the missing part in some way. In such cases, the program fragments use a *pseudocode placeholder*. Unlike other comment formats, where the comment has no semantic effect, the placeholder cannot be deleted without modifying the meaning (and well-formedness) of the fragment. Here is an example —

```
<push the array reference>
<push the index value>
ldelem.i4            // fetch the int32 element
ret                  // return as function result
```

In this case what is being shown is the way in which an array element is loaded onto the stack and returned as the function return value. From the point of view of this example we wish to abstract away the particular code sequence that has to be used to push the array reference onto the stack and the way in which the array index is computed. We also use pseudocode placeholders in source code fragments in which we do not wish to give details of a particular operation or expression evaluation. Here is one last example, this time in *C#* —

```
public static void DumpList(MyList theList) {
    while (<theList not empty>) {
        DumpItem(theList.Head());
        DumpList(theList.Tail());            // recurse!
    }
}
```

Grammar notation.   There are a few grammar fragments that are used throughout the book. These are presented as context-free grammars in a variant of the usual *Extended Backus-Naur Form (EBNF)*. The elements of the notation are *syntactic categories*, *terminal symbols*, and *metasymbols*.

Syntactic categories are nonterminal symbols of the grammar and are shown in roman font, often with mixed case. In any particular instance, the definition of the symbol may either precede or follow the used occurrences.

Terminal symbols consist of lexical categories, literal symbols, and keywords of the language being defined. Lexical categories, such as *identifier*, have descriptive names, and are shown in italic font. Keywords in the language being defined are shown in **bold** font. Literal symbols are shown in double quotes " and ".

Finally the metasymbols of the grammar are '[' and ']', '{' and '}', '(' and ')', and '|'. Square brackets are used to enclose optional phrases of the right-hand sides of productions. Curly braces are used to enclose phrases that may be repeated zero or more times. Ordinary parentheses are used as a grouping construct, while the *solidus* (the vertical bar) is used to separate alternative phrases.

Finally, the overall form of the grammar is a sequence of *productions*. Productions have the form of a syntactic category on the left-hand side and a phrase on the right-hand side, separated by the right-arrow symbol →, which is pronounced aloud as "produces." Figure 1.3 is a semiformal definition of the grammar of our *EBNF* dialect, defined in its own language.

```
      Grammar   →   { Production } .
   Production   →   NonTerminal "→" Phrase { "|" Phrase } "." .
  NonTerminal   →   roman-font-identifier .
     Terminal   →   italic-font-identifier | bold-font-identifier | quoted-literal .
       Phrase   →   Terminal | NonTerminal
                |   "(" Phrase { "|" Phrase } ")"
                |   "[" Phrase "]"
                |   "{" Phrase "}" .
```

Figure 1.3: Metagrammar for *EBNF* grammar notation

Sidebars.   Sidebars are used in a few places in the book, to take particular topics "out of line" of the normal discussion. It is intended that these might be skipped at a first reading if they are not of particular interest. The sidebars are enclosed in a border.

See Sidebar 1.1 for a definition of the diagrammatic format of class hierarchy schemas.

How to Use gpcp

As discussed above, the code generation examples are mostly taken verbatim from *gpcp*. In some cases there are obvious alternative ways of doing things, and these are discussed where they occur. This concentration on the details of just one implementation has both bad and good aspects. On the minus side, it means that a biassed impression may be gained of what is actually possible. However, compared to the alternative of discussing a number of different possibilities, none of which are implemented, we can claim the reader of the

SIDEBAR 1.1

CLASS HIERARCHY DIAGRAMS

Class hierarchy diagrams are shown using a format that shows the inheritance relationship between the various classes and also indicates other properties of each class. Here is an example of a class hierarchy diagram that appears later as Figure 5.3.

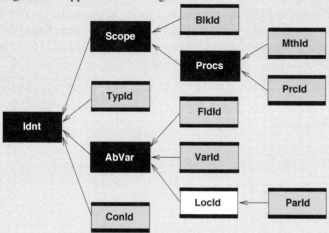

In this diagram, class types are shown as rectangles, with directed edges from each class to the parent from which it inherits. Solid lines are used to indicate implementation inheritance.

Abstract classes are shown shaded to black, as in the classes *Idnt, Scope, AbVar,* and *Procs* in the example. Final classes are shown lightly shaded, and classes that are extensible, like *LocId* in the example, are shown unshaded.

book has the following advantages: (1) you have a real, working example to play with; (2) if you want to try something different you can grab the *gpcp* source, hack on it, recompile the compiler, and see how your idea works.

There are a number of occasions where the text suggests exploring some experimental code generation alternative that *gpcp* does not use. A useful trick is to write a *Component Pascal* program that does something similar to the case that you wish to try. The structure of the procedures or types should be close to the effect that you want. The similar program is compiled through to textual assembly language, and the assembly code is then editted. The point is that the majority of the text will be exactly as you want it, and the rest can be modified to try out the experimental construct. This is an important technique for testing out constructs that are not verifiably type-safe. *gpcp* will only produce verifiable code, but you may manually introduce small changes to test different possibilities, while still being confident the the rest of the code will be well behaved.

The *gpcp* distribution comes with release notes and a "getting started" guide. These have detailed instructions for using the compiler. For our purposes here it is sufficient to note that the command line version of the compiler takes a number of command-line arguments to control its behavior. The compiler is able to produce output for the *JVM* as well as for the *.NET* runtime. The default when running on *.NET* is to produce code for *.NET*.

In default mode the compiler reads one or more source files, and produces for each source file a *PEM*. For source files that contain an entry point this will be an ".exe" file; otherwise it will be a ".dll" library. The compiler also persists a metadata symbol ".cps" file that holds information about the public interface of the module, the assembly language *CIL* ".il" file, and possibly a debugger symbol ".pdb" file for each input source file. Command line options can make the compiler create a listing ".lst" file even if there are no errors, or stop after semantic checking, metadata emission, or *IL* emission. The default behavior is to automatically invoke the assembler ilasm in a separate process, using a method described on page 211.

In principle, future versions need not use their own metadata format, as *.NET* has excellent built-in mechanisms for this. As will be discussed in Chapter 11, there are advantages in avoiding the textual assembly language step, at least in the case of mature compilers.

Notes on Chapter 1

The official documentation for the facilities of the *.NET* system is a necessary resource for anyone working on *.NET* programs. There is the choice of the documentation that comes as part of the Software Development Kit or the standards under development by *ECMA*. The *ECMA* standards documents are available from http://msdn.microsoft.com/net/ecma.

The grammar notation that is used here is called *"Extended"* BNF (*EBNF*) because it contains the constructs for optionality, repetition, and alternation. In effect, the right-hand sides of *EBNF* productions are regular expressions over the combined alphabet of terminal and nonterminal symbols. Plain *BNF* has productions with right-hand sides that are finite strings from the alphabet. The two formalisms have equal expressive power, but *EBNF* is more intuitive for most people. The notation was invented by Niklaus Wirth (the originator of *Pascal*) and was described in the interestingly titled paper "What Can We Do about the Unnecessary Diversity of Notation for Syntactic Definitions" from *Communications of the ACM*, 1977.

Those interested in the history of abstract stack machines can read a reprint of the original paper on P-Code by Uwe Ammann, which appeared as the chapter "Code Generation for a Pascal Compiler" in the book *Pascal, the Language and its Implementation* (D. W. Barron, Wiley, 1981). The *Pascal* compiler for which this was all designed was first described by Wirth in "The Design of the Pascal Compiler" in the journal *Software Practice and Experience*, Vol. 4, 1971.

The *UCSD Pascal* compiler, based on an interpreted virtual machine, was widely used from the late 1970s to the mid 1980s. It became available on the then newly introduced Apple computers in 1980. Ken Bowles at *UCSD* was the driving force behind the project. A good historical reference to the *UCSD* project is at the Jefferson Computer Museum, available on the web at `http://www.threedee.com/jcm/psystem/index.html`.

The original request for proposals from the Open Software Foundation for *ANDF* was dated April 1989. It appeared frequently in the references until about 1995, then disappeared from view.

The programming languages that were implemented as part of Project 7 include *Eiffel, Smalltalk, APL, COBOL, Python, Lightning Oberon, Component Pascal, Scheme, Mondrian,* and the advanced logic programming language *Mercury*.

An overview of the 10-year Gardens Point compiler project is given in K. John Gough, "Multi-language, Multi-target Compiler Development: Evolution of the Gardens Point Compiler Project" from the *Joint Modula Languages Conference*, JMLC1997, Linz, March 1997, and published as number 1204 in Springer's lecture notes in computer science.

The *Component Pascal* language was developed by Oberon Microsystems. The definitive reference to the language is the *Component Pascal Language Report* available from `http://www.oberon.ch/resources`. The same location contains some interesting information on the language rationale.

The complete code of *gpcp* is available from `http://www.plasrc.qut.edu.au/ComponentPascal`. Most of the examples discussed in the book are available for download from the site `http://www.SoftwareAutomata.com`, which has further material related to this book, as well as any corrections or late-breaking issues.

Understanding the Common Language Runtime (CLR)

2

This is the first of three chapters that deal with the characteristics of the *.NET* platform from the point of view of the language implementer.

This chapter deals with the *CLR* and its execution engine, the *Virtual Execution System* (*VES*). The *CLR* is the target for which we produce *CIL* code. As noted in the previous chapter, *CIL* code is actually executed by transformation to native code on the target machine. Usually the *IL* is transformed by a *JIT*. However, a correct *JIT* must produce native code that faithfully reproduces the observable state sequences that would be obtained by a hypothetical interpreter that directly executed the *CIL* instructions. Thus, from the point of view of the compiler writer, the semantic properties of the *CIL* instructions are the important factor, rather than the exact mechanism by which the semantics are implemented.

We thus have a separation of concerns. Our compilers must produce *CIL* that is a correct translation of their source programs. The *JIT* must transform these into semantically equivalent native codes on whatever machine supplies the final execution environment.

There are two aspect to the execution engine. First there is the instruction set that provides the basic infrastructure of program execution. This provides for data movement, arithmetic operations, procedure call and return, and so on, for a small set of primitive types. If this were all, we would be in the same position as with any other hardware machine model. In that case every language implementation would need to build its higher level primitives, data structures, and object model on top of the basic infrastructure.

The second aspect of the *CLR* is the rich *object model* of the *CTS*. The semantics of the *CTS* are built into the instruction set of *CIL*.

The first of these aspects of the *CLR* is the focus of this chapter. The object model of the *CTS* is the subject of the next chapter. In Chapter 4 we consider the issues involved in mapping the constructs of various programming languages to the facilities of the *CLR*. In that chapter we also consider a rich subset of the *CTS*, which together with certain conventions of use, forms the *Common Language Specification* (*CLS*). The importance of the *CLS* is that by adhering to this standard we may ensure that different *CLS*-compliant components will work together seamlessly. The *CLS* is thus the foundation of language interoperation in *.NET*. The *CTS*, in turn, is the foundation of the *CLS*.

In the present chapter, we describe the *CLR* in some detail. We shall also look at the structure of a program executable module (*PEM*), with its namespace, class, and method declarations. For the most part, we shall be using fragments of *C#* programs as examples, since this language has the most natural mapping to the structures of the *CTS*. We shall also look at a small number of *Component Pascal* examples for variety.

Initially, the major issue for any compiler writer targetting *.NET* is the mapping of the facilities of their source language onto the facilities of the *CLR*. We shall be in a position to address that issue by Chapter 4.

The Virtual Execution Engine

The Primitive Types

As noted in Chapter 1, the abstract machine of *CIL* is based around an evaluation stack. Values are pushed onto the stack, operated on by the instructions, and copied to program variables. The operands that may be placed on this stack are drawn from a small set of primitive types. These include the usual arithmetic and logical types, and various types of references. For the moment, we consider only the nonreference types.

The primitive types that are supported are given in Figure 2.1. The *CLS* column indicates whether the primitive type is part of the *CLS*. The *IL name* column gives the name of the type as it appears in textual *CIL*. Finally, the *suffix* column gives the two-character suffix that is used to qualify instructions in the instruction set. Thus "conv.r4" converts the top of stack value to the `float32` type, while "conv.u2" converts the top of stack value to `wchar` or `uint16`.

As well as the types listed, there are also signed and unsigned *native integer* types. These are not *CLS* types, but may be more efficient on machines that have word sizes other than 32 bits. We shall ignore these types in the rest of this book. There are also a few

C# type	CLS?	IL name	suffix	Comment
bool	√	`bool`	u1	Boolean type
char	√	`wchar`	u2	16-bit Unicode character type
float	√	`float32`	r4	IEEE 32-bit floating point type
double	√	`float64`	r8	IEEE 64-bit floating point type
sbyte	×	`int8`	i1	8-bit signed integer
short	√	`int16`	i2	16-bit signed integer
int	√	`int32`	i4	32-bit signed integer
long	√	`int64`	i8	64-bit signed integer
byte	√	`unsigned int8`	u1	8-bit unsigned byte
ushort	×	`unsigned int16`	u2	16-bit unsigned integer
uint	×	`unsigned int32`	u4	32-bit unsigned integer
ulong	×	`unsigned int64`	u8	64-bit unsigned integer

Figure 2.1: Primitive types in the *CLR*: Part 1

class types that are built in to the *CLR*. The first one of those that we meet will be the class *System.String*, without which we could not even write the "Hello World" program.

Note that, in Figure 2.1, not all of the primitive types are supported by the *CLS*. In particular, the *signed* integers of 16 bits or greater in length are in the *CLS*, while the corresponding *unsigned* integers are not. For the 8-bit data types the situation is reversed. The 8-bit unsigned integer type *byte* is *CLS* compliant, while the 8-bit signed integer type is not.

All of these primitive types may appear as fields in structures, as array elements, or as formal parameters of method calls. However, the *IL* instructions that manipulate the stack do not operate on all of these types. For example, there is no instruction to add together two 8-bit values. Instead, whenever the shorter types are loaded onto the stack, they are expanded by a set of *usual unary conversions*. The behavior is familiar from language *C*, where all signed integers shorter than **int** are promoted to **int** before any operations are applied to them.

As an example, if we have a local variable *ix* of **short** type, the expression *ix++* will be encoded, and executed, as shown —

```
.locals(int16 'ix')      // declare the local variable
    ...
    ldloc   'ix'         // load local and expand to int
    ldc.i4  1            // load 4-byte constant 1 value
    add                  // add two top-of-stack values
    stloc   'ix'         // store 16-bits of result to local
```

As we shall see later, we usually refer to local variables by their ordinal position in the declarations, rather than by using the name. However, the *IL* as shown is legal. It is worth noting that the same "add" instruction is used for all the unchecked addition operations that the *CLR* can perform. The *JIT* can work out, from its bookkeeping operations, whether the two top of stack elements are **int**, **long** or some real type; that is, a *floating point type*.

In general, integers shorter than 32 bits are sign-extended to the **int** type, while unsigned integers shorter than 32 bits will be zero-extended to **uint**. The 16-bit wide character type is also zero-extended to 32 bits, although the verifier will still know that it is a **char**.

The treatment of real values also involves unary conversions. Values of either *float* (IEEE 754 single precision) or *double* (IEEE 754 double precision) types are promoted to the *native float* type when they are pushed on the stack. The native float type is whatever type is most efficiently supported on the underlying machine. The type must be precise enough that a round trip conversion from *double* is exact. On the *Intel-x86* architecture the native float type would be the 80-bit temporary format used by the coprocessor.

All operations on real values use the native float format, with the store instructions performing appropriate narrowing conversions. For a majority of applications, it is admissible for real arithmetic to be carried out at the highest possible accuracy, with the final result converted to the required result type. For some numerical algorithms, however, it is critical that intermediate values in expression evaluations be of the specified precision. In the case of languages that guarantee this behavior, it is necessary to sprinkle narrowing conversions throughout typical floating point codes.

Execution State

The activation record.   The *state* of the execution engine relating to any method activation consists of two parts. There is an *activation record* that holds all of the per-activation data of the method, and the *evaluation stack*. When we need to represent the execution state diagramatically, we use the format of Figure 2.2. In the figure, the activation record is shown on the right, and the evaluation stack, which grows in the upward direction as data are "pushed," is shown on the left.

The activation record has two program accessible parts. These are a numbered collection of arguments to the method and a separately numbered collection of local variables. There may be zero or more arguments, and zero or more local variables. The number and

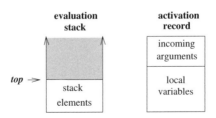

Figure 2.2: Method state showing activation record and evaluation stack

types of local variables are part of the definition of the method, just as the number and type of the formal arguments form part of the declaration of the method signature. Indeed, if debug information is to be persisted into the *PEM*, then the *names* of the locals and arguments appear in the definition and may be referred to by name in textual *CIL*.

The number and types of data in the activation record are fixed as part of the definition of the method. When a method is activated by a "`call`" instruction, then a new activation record is allocated, and certain mandatory initializations are carried out. Of course, in the case of recursive calls, each activation of a particular method gets its own activation record and hence its own copy of the variables.

Because *.NET* supports languages in which procedure call and return are strictly nested within any execution thread, the activation records will almost certainly be allocated on a *runtime stack*. Because of this, many descriptions of execution semantics of such languages refer to activation records as *stack frames*. We shall avoid use of this term entirely, strictly reserving the term *stack* for the evaluation stack and referring to activation records as activation records.

The numbering of locals and arguments is a *logical* numbering. Thus a local variable is allocated an index according to its position in the declarations, irrespective of whether it is a one-byte datum or a **struct** that extends over hundreds of bytes of memory.

The evaluation stack.   The operations that may be performed on the stack of the execution engine fit into three main categories. First, there are those that *push* values onto the stack. These are called "load" instructions in *CIL*. These instructions usually make the stack deeper by one value.

Next, there are instructions that perform operations on values that are already on the stack. These may either make the stack deeper or shallower, depending on whether the number of incoming values is larger or smaller than the number of outgoing values from the instruction. For example, as we have seen, the "`add`" instruction takes the two top stack elements and replaces them by the single result of the addition.

Finally, there are instructions that *pop* the top-of-stack element and store the value in some specified place. These are called "store" instruction in *CIL*.

There are actually a few extra instructions that do not fit into these three groups, including an instruction "`pop`", which simply discards the top-of-stack element. There is also an instruction "`dup`" that duplicates the top-of-stack element.

In Figure 2.2 the evaluation stack on the left of the diagram shows a top-of-stack pointer marked "*top*." However, there is no programmatic access to the value of the "stack pointer." As well there is no way of accessing any element of the stack other than the top one. In fact there is not even any way of nondestructively accessing the value of the top element. If we wish to copy a value from the top of the stack, but leave the stack unchanged, then we must duplicate the top of the stack, and store one copy.

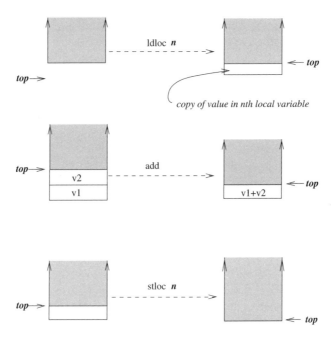

Figure 2.3: Stack transitions for load, add, and store instructions

It is important to realize that the stack of the execution engine is a *logical* stack. The elements of the stack are not any particular size, such as 32 bits, or 64 bits.[1] Thus each element of the stack may be one of the primitive types, or a reference, or even the value of a whole **struct**. The depth of the stack is thus the number of elements currently on the stack, without regard for type. It may be helpful to remember that *CIL* programs are executed by being transformed by a *JIT*. The stack elements do not have a particular size, because they do not exist at execution time. They only have a transient existence as value descriptors inside the *JIT*, during the processing of the assembly by the *JIT*.

In order to make these ideas clear, we shall consider a few instruction examples. We shall look in detail at the effect of these instructions on the state of the execution engine, and a typical scenario of use.

We have already seen an informal description of the effects of the "ldloc", "add", and "stloc" instructions. We show how these are represented in our diagramatic format in Figure 2.3. The stack grows upward in the page, and the current top of stack is marked. The stack on the left shows the state before the instruction is executed, the stack on the right is the stack afterward.

An important characteristic of an instruction in *IL* is the change in depth of the stack resulting from the execution. We shall call this number the *stack-Δ*, "stack-delta." For the three instructions in the figure the *stack-Δ* values are +1, −1, and −1, respectively.

---

[1]On the *JVM* stack elements are 32 bits, and pushing a **long** makes the stack deeper by 2!

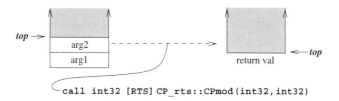

Figure 2.4: Stack transitions for a function call

Calling a static function.

When a static function is called, the arguments to the function are pushed onto the stack in order, and a "`call`" instruction is executed. The call instruction, in the assembler syntax, has the name of the function and its signature as part of the text. The effect of the instruction is to pop all of the arguments off the evaluation stack. If the function returns a value, then the return value is on the top of the stack at completion.

Suppose we have a function with the heading —

```
public static int CPDiv(int n, int d)
```

When a call to this funtion appears in *IL* the fully qualified name of the function will appear in a format that is explained later. For the moment it is sufficient to know that the textual *IL* to call this function will be —

```
call int32 [RTS]CP_rts::CPDiv(int32,int32)
```

The stack transition diagram is shown in Figure 2.4. We may note that as a general rule for calls of static functions, the *stack-*Δ will be (*number of return values – number of arguments*). For our example the *stack-*Δ is $(1 - 2) = -1$, as confirmed by the diagram.

Loading array elements.

As a final teaser example, we consider the loading of an array element. This is an instruction that really belongs later with the object model, but we will sneak a preview anyhow.

Let us suppose that we wish to load the eighth element of an array of characters. The eighth element will have index 7 in the array. We are not able to perform pointer arithmetic in verifiable code, so we instead push a reference to the array, push the index, then execute the "`ldelem`" (load-element) instruction. This instruction is specialized for the various kinds of element types. In our supposed case the element type is `wchar` type, which is manipulated as an unsigned two-byte quantity.

```
ldsfld wchar[] [A]B::C    // load ref. to wchar array
ldc.i4 7                  // push a literal 7 on stack
ldelem.u2                 // fetch character element
```

Figure 2.5: Stack transitions for an array element fetch

The array reference is presumed to be held in a static field C of the class B. The stack transition diagram for this case is shown in Figure 2.5. In this case the *stack-*Δ is -1, since the reference and the index are both popped by the instruction, with the fetched element being pushed onto the top of the stack.

The Base Instruction Set

There are about 220 instructions in *CIL*, of which about two thirds are base instructions. The remainder have to do with the object model and are treated in the section on the virtual object system (see page 55).

No attempt has been made here to explain the detail of every instruction. There are just too many instructions and too much fine print. At the stage of constructing a code generator, it will therefore be necessary to read the fine print from elsewhere. Here, the emphasis is on understanding the capabilities of the instruction set and getting the general idea. In the code generation chapters, we shall see some examples of the techniques that are used when the instruction set does not exactly match the semantics required for a particular programming language.

Load and Store Instructions

Pushing on the stack.   There are a number of different load and store instructions in *CIL*. The kinds of different data and the group of instructions that are used to load a datum onto the evaluation stack are given in Figure 2.6. These instructions generally take

Data kind	Opcode	Comment
static field	`ldsfld`	Op-arg: *Type Class::field-name*
instance field	`ldfld`	Op-arg: *Type Class::field-name*
local variable	`ldloc`	Op-arg: *local variable ordinal*
method argument	`ldarg`	Op-arg: *formal argument ordinal*
array element	`ldelem.*`	Suffix: specialized for element type

Figure 2.6: Data kinds and load instructions in *IL*

an instruction argument that spells out the details. In the case of the static and instance field loads, the argument is the type of the field and a fully qualified name of the field.

Local variables and formal arguments are loaded with the "ldloc" and "ldarg" instructions, respectively. These instructions take an ordinal as an argument, with locals and arguments separately numbered in order of declaration. There are three versions of these instructions. There is a specialized version for ordinals less than four. A typical instruction "ldarg.3" takes up only one byte in the *IL*. A "short" version of the instruction may be used if the ordinal fits in one unsigned byte. This instruction "ldloc.s *N*" takes up two bytes in the *IL*. Finally, the general version takes an *int32* ordinal, but takes up five bytes in the *IL*. The instructions "ldloc.3", "ldloc.s 3", and "ldloc 3" all have precisely the same effect at runtime, other than the different amount of program space occupied.

The numbering of formal arguments inside a method follows the order of declaration in the signature of the method. In the case of instance methods and virtual methods the receiver has the zero index and the explicit arguments are numbered starting from one. For static methods there is no receiver, and the explicit formal arguments number from zero.

The numbering of local variables defaults to the order of declaration in the .locals section of the method. There are ways to force variables to overlap in storage, but we shall ignore these until the "Defining Methods" section on page 93.

The instructions that load array elements are specialized for the element primitive type. The suffixes are listed in Figure 2.1 for the primitive types. Thus a load of an element of an array of unicode characters would use the "ldelem.u2" instruction, as shown in Figure 2.5. The only case additional to those for the primitive types in Figure 2.1 is the instruction that is used to load an element of reference type. For any array of references the instruction "ldelem.ref" is used. The verifier will be able to infer the type of the fetched element from the known type of the array reference. After the following instruction sequence —

```
ldsfld int32[][]  [A]B::C    // array of array of int32
ldc.i4 7                     // push a literal 7 on stack
ldelem.ref                   // top of stack is int32[]
```

the top-of-stack element is known to be of the declared element type. If you want to know how an array of arrays looks in memory, Figure 3.6, in the next chapter, gives an example.

Constants have their own load instructions, as shown in Figure 2.7. The *int32* numeric loads have specialized versions for the ten most commonly used integer constants, −1 to 8, using "ldc.i4.M1", "ldc.i4.0" through to "ldc.i4.8". There is a short integer version, "ldc.i4.s", which is used for *int32* constants that fit in one signed byte. There are also the usual type suffixes for the other primitive types.

Instructions to load *addresses* are needed whenever pointers must be passed to *byref* parameters in method calls. The instructions to do this are shown in Figure 2.8. These *address-load* instructions correspond to the *value loads* in Figure 2.6. In this particular case there are no special versions for the lowest numbered local variables and arguments,

Data kind	Opcode	Comment
numbers	ldc.*	Op-arg: *number*. Suffix denotes primitive type.
strings	ldstr	Op-arg: *literal string*.
null	ldnull	No argument is needed or allowed

Figure 2.7: Constant load instructions

Data kind	Opcode	Comment
static field	ldsflda	Op-arg: *Type Class::field-name*
instance field	ldflda	Op-arg: *Type Class::field-name*
local variable	ldloca	Op-arg: *local variable ordinal*
method argument	ldarga	Op-arg: *formal argument ordinal*
array element	ldelema	Op-arg: *Array element typename*

Figure 2.8: Data kinds and load address instructions in *IL*

but there are the "ldloca.s" and "ldloca" versions. Notice that the verifier is able to know the type of the pointers that are being loaded by the load-address instructions in every case. In the case of fields the instruction argument explicitly gives the type. In the case of locals and arguments it is known from the method signature. Finally, in the case of array element loads the type is known from the declared type of the array.

As well as being able to load addresses, we must also be able to dereference such addresses. The *load-indirect* instructions perform this task. There is only one instruction family "ldind.*", where, as before, the "*" character denotes a wildcard, as it would in a filename. This instruction takes a primitive type suffix. There is, as in the "ldelem.*" case, a "ldind.ref" instruction that indirectly loads a reference. Once again, it should be noted that since the bound type of the pointer is known, the type of the loaded datum is also known. These instructions all pop the address off the top of stack, pushing the indirectly referenced datum. All of the indirect loads thus have a *stack-Δ* of zero.

The final load instruction is "ldlen", which loads the length of the array whose reference is on the top of the stack. This instruction has a *stack-Δ* of zero.

Popping off the stack.   The store instructions follow the same pattern as the loads. These are summarized in Figure 2.9. These instructions take the datum on the top of the stack and store that value in the specified location. In the case of the "stelem.*" instruction family, the three top elements on the stack are the array reference, the index into the array, and the value to be stored. This instruction thus has a *stack-Δ* of −3.

The indirect stores take an address on the stack, with the datum to be stored above that. The instruction "stind.*" is specialized for destination types in the usual way.

Note that for all these store instructions, the destination type is not necessarily the same type as the top-of-stack type. Truncation of the value routinely occurs, because the

Data kind	Opcode	Comment
static field	stsfld	Op-arg: *Type Class::field-name*
instance field	stfld	Op-arg: *Type Class::field-name*
local variable	stloc	Op-arg: *local variable ordinal*
method argument	starg	Op-arg: *formal argument ordinal*
array element	stelem.*	Suffix: specialized for element type

Figure 2.9: Data kinds and store instructions in *IL*

operands on the stack have been subjected to the usual unary conversions. In languages in which range checking is required, an explicit, checked conversion is required to catch out-of-range values. Suppose, for example, that we have an integer value computed onto the top of the evaluation stack and need to store the result indirectly into a **short** destination operand. In the unchecked case, a indirect store instruction is all that is required. In the checked case, we must use *IL* along the following lines —

```
        <push pointer to destination>
        <compute value onto stack>
        conv.ovf.i2      // convert to int16 with overflow check
        stind.i2         // store 16-bits of result to local
```

Operate Instructions

There is a rich selection of instructions that operate on values on the top of the evaluation stack. These instructions take no operator arguments, since they implicitly take their operands from the top of the stack. Many of the instructions are polymorphic, with the actual operator chosen by the *VES* to match the operand type on the top of the stack.

Since *CIL* is intended for the implementation of a wide range of languages, there are instructions for a wide range of operations. There are also arithmetic instruction variants that check for signed or unsigned overflow, as there was with the "conv.*" instructions.

Arithmetic and logical instructions. We first consider the "add" family as an example of the pattern. The "add" instruction is polymorphic and, as noted earlier, performs integer, long integer, or real addition as required for the particular operands. There are also some permitted uses of the add instruction for pointer arithmetic in unverified contexts. These uses are discussed on page 73.

It may be noted that there are only three different possible additions, if we neglect the necessity for overflow detection. The unchecked addition of two 32-bit integers results in precisely the same bit-pattern whether the operands are signed or unsigned integers. However if we wish to detect arithmetic overflows, we must use different instructions for

Instruction	int32	int64	nfloat	*nfloat* is native *FP* format
add	√	√	√	unchecked addition
add.ovf	√	√	—	*signed* overflow check
add.ovf.un	√	√	—	*unsigned* overflow check

Figure 2.10: Applicability of *add* instructions

Instruction	int32	int64	nfloat	*nfloat* is native *FP* format
div	√	√	√	*signed* division
div.un	√	√	—	*unsigned* division
rem	√	√	√	*signed* remainder
rem.un	√	√	—	*unsigned* remainder

Figure 2.11: Applicability of *div* and *rem* instructions

the two cases.[2]   Figure 2.10 shows the applicability of the various addition instructions to the various stack data types. The variants with overflow checking do not apply to real operands. *IEEE* floating point arithmetic has its own ways of signalling and propagating out of range values, using *not-a-number symbols (NaNS)*.

Subtraction and multiplication instructions follow the same pattern as addition, but division and remainder are necessarily different. The quotient of two fixed point numbers really has a different binary result, depending on whether the numbers are signed or unsigned. We therefore have two different division and remainder instructions, as shown in Figure 2.11. There are no "*.ovf" versions of the division instructions. It is always an error to try to divide by zero.

It should be noted that the division instructions have *round toward zero* semantics, with a corresponding remainder operation. These are the traditional operations that are supported by most underlying hardware. If your language requires the mathematically better behaved *round toward* $-\infty$ semantics you will have to "do it by hand." The "Tailoring the Semantics" section (see page 256) gives some hints on how to do this.

There is just one numeric unary operator, "neg", which performs arithmetic negation. This instruction applies to all numeric types. In the case of integer types the instruction returns the 2's complement value. For the most negative value of the integer types there is no corresponding positive integer of equal magnitude, and the instruction returns the same value. There is no overflow-tested version of this instruction, so that if detection of this erroneous case is required, the following instruction sequence behaves as required —

---

[2]It may be noted that many hardware architectures are particularly unfriendly to overflow detection for unsigned arithmetic. The *Intel-x86* provides this, but most of the recent *RISC* architectures provide only signed overflow detection.

```
ldc.i4.0              // or ldc.i8 0 if required
<push value to negate>
sub.ovf               // subtract value from zero
```

Along with the arithmetic instructions, there is a full set of logical operations. All of these apply only to the whole number types. The bitwise Boolean instructions "and", "or", "xor", and "not" apply to *int32* and *int64* operands. There are also three shift instructions. These are all binary operations, with the value to be shifted pushed on the stack followed by the shift amount above that. The "shl" and "shr" instructions perform left and right shifts respectively, with the right shift being *arithmetic*. This means that the sign bit of the word is duplicated in the shift. A *logical right shift* is performed by the unsigned version, "shr.un".

In all cases the shift amount is an unsigned value. If the shift exceeds the word length, the result is undefined.[3] It follows that languages that require better-defined semantics than this will have to implement test and branch code as discussed on page 257.

Type conversions.   Type conversions between the various numeric types are performed by the "conv.*" family of instructions. The instructions are specialized for the result type, so we have "conv.r4" returning a *float*, "conv.u1" returning an unsigned byte, and so on. The convert instructions take a value on the top of the stack and leave a result on the top of stack that is a valid value in the destination type. Since the result is on the evaluation stack, it will be one of the primitive stack types, even if we have specified a narrower type as destination. The important thing is that for any type T, if the result of the conversion is written to a memory location of type T and then reloaded, the final value on the stack will be exactly the value immediately after the conversion. Consider the example of an *int32* value on the top of the stack. After "conv.i1" we will have a value that will be in the range $[-128 \ldots 127]$. This value will be able to be stored in an *int8* location and exactly retrieved.

For the conversions between integral (whole number) formats, the unchecked conversions begin by possibly truncating the value on the stack, followed by an appropriate sign or zero extension in the style of the usual unary conversions. In the case of conversions to real values, the value is converted to a real value of the requested type and then expanded to the native floating point type on the stack.

Conversions from real values to integer values truncate toward zero. Thus the result of applying "conv.i4" to 1.6 is 1, while applying the same operation to -1.6 results in -1. If the real value is too large for the integer format that is specified, the result is undefined.

Corresponding to every unchecked conversion to an integral destination type there is a checked conversion instruction "conv.ovf.*". These instructions raise an exception if

---

[3]This is to allow some freedom for the implementation. Some hardware platforms perform shifts using the low five or low six bits of the shift-amount register. In this case a shift by 65 would leave the same result as a shift by 1.

the value to be converted is too large for the destination type. We shall see examples of the use of these instructions in implementing *Component Pascal*'s overflow-checked narrowing coercions.

There are no overflow-checked conversion instructions with real destination types, and conversions to the real types are always nontrapping. If a value cannot be converted, as happens if a *double* with a magnitude greater than about 10^{38} is converted to *float*, the result is a not-a-number symbol (*NaNS*). If trapping behavior is required, each "conv.r*" instruction should be followed by a "ckfinite" check. This instruction throws an arithmetic exception if the real value on the top of the stack is a *NaNS* or an *IEEE* infinity. This instruction does not pop the checked value off the stack.

Finally, there are special versions of the checked conversion instructions that treat the incoming operands as unsigned. These have the name "conv.ovf.*.un". An example will make the use of these instructions clear. Applying the instruction "conv.i4" to a 32-bit whole number value will be a null operation. The instruction "conv.ovf.i4" will never trap on such a value. If we want to do a checked conversion from *uint32* to *int32*, we should use "conv.ovf.i4.un". This will throw an exception if the incoming value is greater than or equal to 2^{31}. Conversely, when converting from *int32* to *uint32* the ordinary checked conversion "conv.ovf.u4" will throw an exception if the incoming value is negative.

Branching and Jumping

The *CLR* provides a full repertoire of branching instructions. These are treated in several groups. There are the predicate instructions that compute Boolean values onto the stack. There are the conditional and unconditional branches. Finally, there is a table switch instruction that is used for **switch** or **case** statements.

Generating Boolean values.   There are just five instructions that generate Boolean results in the base instruction set. These instructions all take two operands on the top of the stack and return either **true** (a 1 of *I4* type) or **false** (a 0 of *I4* type). Figure 2.12 shows the operation of a typical instruction, "clt", *compare less than*. The instructions test for equality, less than and greater than, with the last two specialized for unsigned operands as well. This means that the other possible comparisons have to be generated by using identities such as those in Figure 2.13. As we shall see, these identities are only true for

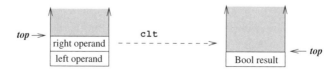

Figure 2.12: Compare less than instruction

$$\boxed{\begin{array}{l} \forall a, b : \; (a \neq b) \; = \; \neg(a = b) \\ \forall a, b : \; (a \leq b) \; = \; \neg(a > b) \\ \forall a, b : \; (a \geq b) \; = \; \neg(a < b) \end{array}}$$

Figure 2.13: Identities for integral comparisons

Operation	Instruction sequence
$lOp = rOp$	`ceq`
$lOp \neq rOp$	`ceq; ldc.1; xor`
$lOp < rOp$	`clt`
$lOp \leq rOp$	`cgt; ldc.1; xor`
$lOp > rOp$	`cgt`
$lOp \geq rOp$	`clt; ldc.1; xor`

Figure 2.14: All comparisons of two integral operands

ordered operands, such as whole number values and "proper" reals. The Boolean negation may be implemented by taking the *exclusive or* of the instruction result with an integer 1 value.[4]

For the moment we shall consider the applications of the five instructions to the integral types only. Figure 2.14 show how to generate all six possible comparisons of two integral values. The last four examples in the table have equivalent versions using the unsigned instructions "cgt.un" and "clt.un". As we shall see later, these unsigned comparisons are useful even in languages that do not have unsigned datatypes.

When these comparison operations are applied to real operands, the results are slightly complicated by the possibility that one or both of the operands are not normal floating point numbers. In short, the plain comparison instructions "ceq", "cgt", "clt" always return **false** if one or both of the values is a *NaNS*. In this case the values are said to be *unordered*. Other unnormalized numbers, such as the *IEEE* infinity values, are ordered and behave as expected.

If we wish to implement the other predicates, "$\neq$," "$\geq$," and "$\leq$," with correct behavior for unordered operands, then the use of the "ldc.1; xor" pattern of Figure 2.14 is not quite correct. As an example, if we wish to compute $a \leq b$ for two real operands, if one of the operands in a *NaNS* the "cgt" instruction will return 0, and the next two instructions will turn that into a 1. In these cases, we must make use of the fact that in the "c*.un" instructions the ".un" suffix means two different things. For integral operands it means "**un**signed", as elsewhere. For real operands it means "or **un**ordered", We thus get the correct behavior for the six possible tests as shown in Figure 2.15. The "not-equal"

---

[4]It is also possible to perform Boolean negation by comparing the original Boolean value with zero. It is unclear if there are advantages in using one method rather than another for this.

Operation	Instruction sequence
$lOp = rOp$	`ceq`
$lOp \neq rOp$	*see discussion in text*
$lOp < rOp$	`clt`
$lOp \leq rOp$	`cgt.un; ldc.1; xor`
$lOp > rOp$	`cgt`
$lOp \geq rOp$	`clt.un; ldc.1; xor`

Figure 2.15: All comparisons of two real operands

case requires some discussion. For all of the other tests we are asking if the operands have some particular ordering. In the "not-equal" case we really do want the test to return true if the operands are unordered. Thus even for *NaNS* it is always true that —

$$\forall a, b : \ (a = b) \ = \ \neg(a \neq b)$$

This is in contrast to the other operators. When comparing two real values, either or both of which are *NaNS*, it is simultaneously the case that $a < b$ is false *and* $a \geq b$ is false. This is why the last two identities in Figure 2.13 only hold for whole number types.

Labels and branches.   In textual *CIL* any statement may have one or more labels attached. Labels look like identifiers and must be distinct from all of the defined instructions and keywords of the assembler. Defining occurrences of labels are followed by a colon character. Used occurrences simply use the identifier. In binary *CIL* the target instructions of branches are specified as offsets into the instruction sequence. In order to make sense of this, the `ildasm` tool places a dummy label on every instruction in the disassembled code to make sure that all bases are covered.

We have spent some space on the Boolean comparison instructions, even though they are used rather less than the branch instructions that we now consider. As it turns out, the semantics of the conditional branches are defined in terms of the corresponding comparisons. But first, there are two variations on a unconditional branch instruction.

The instructions "`br` *label*" and "`br.s` *label*" unconditionally branch to the specified label. The second of these, the short form, must have a target that has a position offset within the signed 8-bit range in the binary *CIL*. For textual *IL* it is difficult to check this condition, so compilers that produce textual *CIL* generally play it safe and always use the long form.

There are two conditional branch instructions that take a single operand on the stack. All of the rest are binary and take two operands.

```
brfalse, brfalse.s   branch on false, zero or null
brtrue,  brtrue.s    branch on nonfalse or nonnull
```

These instructions may be applied to integral values on the stack and may also be used to test values of reference type for **null**. Another op-code, "brnull," is an alias for "brfalse." All of these instructions pop their operand from the stack.

The instruction "brtrue" branches for any nonfalse value and is thus the preferred way of encoding tests against zero. For example, the test —

if foo $\neq$ 0 **then goto** *label*

is encoded as —

```
<push foo on stack>
brtrue  label
```

rather than as the correct but ungainly —

```
<push foo on stack>
ldc.i4.0           // push zero
ceq                // test for equality
brfalse  label
```

The binary conditional instructions take two operands on the stack and compares them. If the specified condition is met, control branches to the specified label. Otherwise, control *falls through* into the immediately following instructions. All of these instructions have a *stack-*Δ of -2. In all cases, the left-hand operand is pushed first, followed by the right-hand operand, in the test —

lOp **test** *rOp*

The long versions of the binary conditional branches are shown in Figure 2.16, together with the semantically equivalent instruction sequence using the compare instructions. On most hardware the branches will not be implemented this way, but will be directly supported by native branch instructions. This figure is for signed integer types.

For the unsigned types, the equivalent choice of instructions is shown in Figure 2.17. In this case the "b*.un" versions of the instructions are used. The exception is the equality check, which is the same for signed and unsigned cases. The instruction "bne.un" only exists in the unsigned form. The signedness of the operands makes no difference to the integer tests, of course, but is important for the **un**ordered versions which come next.

For real types, the choice of instructions is governed by the desired behavior with unordered operands. Figure 2.18 shows the choice of instruction when it is required that unordered operands should fall through into the **false** successor. From discussion of the

Test	Instruction	Equivalent sequence
$lOp = rOp$	beq	ceq; brtrue
$lOp \neq rOp$	bne.un	ceq; brfalse
$lOp < rOp$	blt	clt; brtrue
$lOp \leq rOp$	ble	cgt; brfalse
$lOp > rOp$	bgt	cgt; brtrue
$lOp \geq rOp$	bge	clt; brfalse

Figure 2.16: Binary conditional branches, **int***NN* operands

Test	Instruction	Equivalent sequence
$lOp = rOp$	beq	ceq; brtrue
$lOp \neq rOp$	bne.un	ceq; brfalse
$lOp < rOp$	blt.un	clt.un; brtrue
$lOp \leq rOp$	ble.un	cgt.un; brfalse
$lOp > rOp$	bgt.un	cgt.un; brtrue
$lOp \geq rOp$	bge.un	clt.un; brfalse

Figure 2.17: Binary conditional branches, **unsigned int***NN* operands

Test	Instruction	Equivalent sequence
$lOp = rOp$	beq	ceq; brtrue
$lOp \neq rOp$	bne.un	ceq; brfalse
$lOp < rOp$	blt	clt; brtrue
$lOp \leq rOp$	ble.un	cgt.un; brfalse
$lOp > rOp$	bgt	cgt; brtrue
$lOp \geq rOp$	bge.un	clt.un; brfalse

Figure 2.18: Binary conditional branches, real operands

Boolean comparisons, it follows that instructions that are equivalent to a sequence that ends with a "brfalse" must take the "or **un**ordered" version of the compare instruction.

An example might make this clear. Suppose we wish to perform a $\geq$ test and fall into the **false** path on unordered operands. If we use the "bge" instruction, the equivalent "clt" comparison will return **false** on unordered operands. The second instruction in the expansion, "brfalse", will then succeed, incorrectly branching to the true successor label. If we instead choose the "bge.un" instruction, the "clt.un" that starts the expansion will return **true** for unordered operands. The second instruction in the expansion, "brfalse", will not then branch, correctly causing control to fall through into the false successor path.

There are certain restrictions on the target labels for all of the branch instructions. Branches may only branch within a single method body and cannot branch into or out of exception handler regions. The special instructions that are used for control flow in **try**, **catch**, **filter**, and **finally** blocks are discussed later.

In addition to the branch instructions, there is one *jump* instruction. This instruction, "jmp," takes a method descriptor as its argument and jumps between method bodies. It is used to construct *trampoline stubs*.

Table switch statement.

The implementation of **switch** or **case** statements requires an indexed, indirect branch. The *IL* instruction "switch" performs this function. We shall spend some space discussing the efficient implementation of dispatched branches in later chapters.

A typical format of this instruction in textual *IL* is —

```
        <instructions to push selector value on stack>
switch (          // start label table
        lb01,     // first label
        ...,
        lb07)     // last label
br      lb08      // branch to default label
```

Control falls through if the selector value is outside the range of the table—that is, if the selector is less than zero or greater than or equal to the table length. It is customary to follow the switch table, either by the default case or by an unconditional branch to the default case, as shown.

In binary *IL* the switch instruction is followed by an *uint32* value encoding the table length and the various branch offsets, in order, as *int32* values. Offsets are measured from the byte immediately following the "switch" instruction.

Miscellaneous Instructions

The miscellaneous instructions include calls and returns, and some nonverifiable instructions that manipulate untyped data. We deal first with the calls and returns.

The "call" instruction takes an instruction argument that gives the full signature of the method to be called. This instruction is used for calling static methods and for the nonvirtual call of instance methods. All arguments to the call must be pushed, in order, prior to the call. The pattern of a typical call sequence is shown in Figure 2.19. An example of a call to a static method showing the fully qualified name syntax is shown in Figure 2.21. The method receiver, if there is one, is pushed before the arguments. On page 27 we noted that the *stack-*Δ for a static call was equal to (*number of return values – number of arguments*). In the case of instance method calls, we must add an extra "argument" to account for the method receiver.

```
// int res = func(exp1, exp2);

locals(int32 'res')        // res is local number zero
  . . .
  <push to push exp1>
  <push to push exp2>
  call  int32 MyClass.func(int32,int32)
  stloc.0                  // store return value in res
  . . .
```

Figure 2.19: Typical call instruction sequence

The indirect call instruction, "`calli`," takes the arguments in order on the stack, with a function pointer on the top of the stack. The "`calli`" instruction is usually not verifiable. Delegates are a type-safe alternative to function pointers, as is described in the next chapter.

Function pointer values, or *procedure values* as they would be called in *Pascal*, are loaded onto the stack using the "`ldftn`" instruction. This instruction takes an instruction argument that is the name and signature of the function to call. This is only useful if the function pointer is to be stored in a variable somewhere. The *IL* sequence —

```
<push args>
ldftn void Console::WriteInt(int32,int32)
calli void (int32,int32)
```

has exactly the same effect as —

```
<push args>
call void Console::WriteInt(int32,int32)
```

We may declare a local variable or a field of a structure to be a function pointer type using the syntax —

method <*callConv*> <*signature*>

In this syntax <*callConv*> is the call convention, which includes markers such as "instance" and "`virtual`", while <*signature*> is the method signature. The signature has the same format as an explicit method call, but the method name is replaced by the pointer marker, "`*`." Thus a method that might have its function pointer value loaded using the instruction —

```
ldftn instance int32 MyClass::Foo(int32)
```

could then be stored in a location declared with the type —

```
method instance int32 * (int32)
```

This particular signature format is what would sometimes be called an *abstract declarator* in *ANSI C*.

Codes using function pointers are generally unverifiable, but we may make them more self-documenting by explicitly moving the **this** pointer of an instance call to the zeroth parameter position. Thus the type in the last declaration might equivalently have be declared —

```
method instance explicit int32 * (class MyClass, int32)
```

The **this** has been moved to the head of the formal parameter list, and all the other parameters have been moved down one place. This documents the type of the receiver, which would otherwise be absent from the signature. We discuss function pointers again in the next chapter.

Methods always terminate with a return instruction, "ret". This instruction is used for returning from pure procedures—that is, **void** functions—and is also used for returning from value-returning functions. In the value-returning case the value to return is pushed on the stack prior to the execution of the "ret". In correct *IL* the return value is the only value on the stack when the "ret" is reached.

The instruction "initblk" initializes a block of memory. The operands on the stack are the memory address of the start of the block, the value to be placed in each byte, and the number of bytes in the block. The value and size are both of unsigned type. This instruction implements the *memset* function of *ANSI C* efficiently. The instruction is never verifiable and has a *stack-*Δ of -3.

The instruction "cpblk" performs a block move of memory. The operands on the stack are the *destination address*, the *source address*, and the number of bytes to copy. The stack transition for the "cpblk" instruction is shown in Figure 2.20. The *stack-*Δ of this instruction is -3. The implementation may copy multiple bytes at a time, so it is assumed that the addresses are both on a suitable alignment boundary. This instruction is an efficient way of implementing the *memcpy* function of *ANSI C* or the entire assigments of structures or arrays in *Pascal*-family languages. The instruction is always unverifiable and so can only be used in unverified contexts. Since *gpcp* produces verifiable *IL* it cannot use this instruction but instead performs entire assignments using field by field copying.

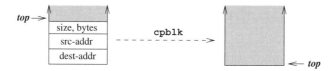

Figure 2.20: Stack transitions for "`cpblk`" instruction

Structure of an Assembly

The unit of deployment in *.NET* is the assembly. Assemblies are also the units of sharing within an execution environment. For the moment we may think of assemblies as being either dynamic link libraries or application executables. In either case an assembly is the unit of loading.

Individual assemblies may contain many classes and may contain multiple namespaces. Thus the size of an assembly may vary from just a few thousand bytes up to hundreds of thousands of bytes in the case of large libraries.

Assemblies are a packaging mechanism containing code of the classes that are included, along with the metadata for all of the facilities of the assembly. We shall not deal with all of the very rich detail of the design, but will simply note a few points that are of interest in almost all applications.

The metadata of the assembly contains all of the information that is needed for program introspection, version control, and if necessary, integrity assurance. The boundary of an assembly forms one of the possible abstraction boundaries, since the *CLR* controls which names defined inside the assembly are visible from the outside.

Usually, an assembly is a single file, but this need not always be the case. An assembly contains a manifest that may refer to several different files. Nevertheless, it is helpful to think of an assembly as being a "logical dll" even if it is spread over several files.

The default behavior of `ilasm` is to produce a single assembly from each file that it processes. We may therefore, at least initially, make the assumption that a single compilation unit will become a single assembly.

The textual structure of a compilation unit for `ilasm` consists of a number of class definitions. These class definitions are introduced with the keyword **.class**. Classes are optionally nested within *namespaces*, introduced with the keyword **namespace**. Namespaces may themselves be nested.

Classes contain definitions of fields and methods. These features are introduced with the keywords **.field** and **.method**. We shall look in detail at the structure of these definitions in the next chapter.

Visibility and Accessibility Declarations

Named entities in *CTS* have *visibility* and *accessibility* attributes. Visibility refers to the property of a name being visible or not visible in a particular assembly. Accessibility refers to the legality of access in a particular context. Top-level classes in the *CTS* have just two choices for visibility. Class names may be **public**, which means that the names are visible in other assemblies. Otherwise they are visible only within the assembly in which they are defined. This *assembly* visibility is the default for class names, but the keyword to obtain this behavior is **private**. All members of a class have the same *visibility* as their containing class. However, we may control the *accessibility* by attaching modifiers to individual member definitions.

When named entities are defined in *CIL*, they have a declared accessibility attribute. The possible categories of accessibility that a name may have are —

- **private** accessibility. Such a name is accessible only to code that belongs to the same class. In *C#* private names are declared using the **private** keyword.

- **assembly** accessibility. Such a name is accessible to all code inside the same assembly but is not accessible to code outside the assembly. Assembly accessibility is the default in *C#*. If a name is not marked by a accessibility attribute, then it has assembly accessibility.

- **public** accessibility. Such a name is accessible to all code in any assembly. Any other assembly may import the assembly and refer to its public names. In *C#* public names are declared using the **public** keyword.

- **family** accessibility. Such a name is accessible only to code of classes that extend the class in which the name is defined. This mode of accessibility is called **protected** in *C#*.

- **family or assembly** accessibility. Such a name is accessible to code of classes that extend the class in which the name is defined and is also accessible to all other code in the assembly in which the name is defined.

- **family and assembly** accessibility. Such a name is accessible to code of classes that extend the class in which the name is defined, but only if they reside in the same assembly as the definition of the name.

Some languages do not map cleanly onto the *CLR* facilities for controlling visibility. In such cases the compiler itself must enforce the required semantics, without the help of the runtime.

Names in CIL

In general, names in *CIL* are fully qualified by assembly, namespace and class name. An example, showing the components of a static method call instruction, is shown in Figure 2.21. This one instruction is almost the whole body of the *C#* version of the infamous "Hello World" program. In this case, the return type of the call is the simplest possible case, **void**. If the return type had been an imported, public type, then that type too would have duplicated the same "assembly, namespace, class" pattern. It may also pay to note that since namespaces may be nested, there may be more *dot-qualified* components in the name than appear in this example.

Used occurrences of names that are not qualified by assembly name must refer to names defined within the same assembly. Imported names must always be qualified by the assembly name.

Defining occurrences of names generally use only the simple name of the entity. The fully qualified name is generated from the context in which the definition appears. As an example, suppose that we are textually inside the definition of a class named *Bar*. We suppose that the definition of *Bar* is textually inside the definition of a namespace named *Foo*. Finally, we suppose that the namespace is defined within a compilation unit that will become part of the assembly *MyAssembly*. A declaration of a static field *fld* might appear as —

       public static int fld;

Code within another assembly will push this field onto the runtime stack by executing the instruction —

       `ldsfld int [MyAssembly]Foo.Bar::fld`   *// load static field*

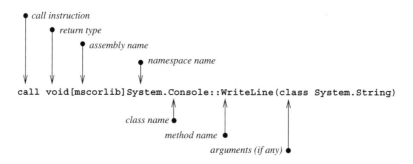

Figure 2.21: Method call syntax example

Some Examples

A "Hello World" walkthrough.   The *C#* version of the canonical "Hello World"
program looks as follows —

```
class HelloWorld {
  public static void Main() {
    System.Console.WriteLine("Hello C# World");
  }
}
```

When this is compiled with the command line compiler `csc`, and the resulting *CIL* file is
disassembled, the result is as shown in Figure 2.22. In this figure, some of the disassembly
comments have been stripped out, and line numbers inserted. Long lines have been split

```
.assembly extern mscorlib {}                             // line 1
.assembly hellocs {}                                     // line 2
.module hellocs.exe                                      // line 3
.class private auto ansi HelloWorld
        extends [mscorlib]System.Object                  // line 4
{
  .method public hidebysig static void Main() il managed
                                          // method heading ... line 6
  {
    .entrypoint                                          // line 8
    .maxstack   8                                        // line 9
      ldstr   "Hello C# World"                           // line 10
      call    void [mscorlib]System.Console::
                      WriteLine(string)                  // line 11
      ret                                                // line 12
  } // end of method HelloWorld::Main                    // line 13

  .method public hidebysig specialname rtspecialname
          instance void .ctor() il managed               // line 15
  {
    .maxstack   8                                        // line 17
      ldarg.0                                            // line 18
      call    instance void [mscorlib]System.Object::.ctor()
                                    // call .ctor of super ... line 19
      ret                                                // line 20
  } // end of method HelloWorld::.ctor
} // end of class HelloWorld
```

Figure 2.22: Disassembly of *C#* "Hello World"

over two lines to fit in the page width. Nevertheless, the source exactly as it appears in the figure is legal input to ilasm.

The *hellocs PEM* consists of a single class declaration and contains just two method declarations. As we shall see in more detail later, all code resides inside classes in the *CLR*.

The listing begins with declarations of other assemblies that this *PEM* relies on. In this case only the *mscorlib* assembly is required to gain access to the *System* classes. At line 2, the name of this assembly is defined, and line 3 defines the file name of the *PEM*.

The first method is the *Main* method that is the entry point for applications written in *C#*. *Main* is overloaded, so that if the application takes no command line arguments, no argument list is needed in the method signature. Compared to the *C#* source, there is an extra attribute that appears between ".method" and "Main()". This describes the name overloading rule for the language. The rule for *C#* is "*hide by signature*", which is the default rule for the *CTS*. The heading finishes with the tokens "il managed" declaring that the method is managed code.

The method begins by declaring, at line 8, that this is an application entry point. There can only be one such declaration in an assembly. Note that the name *Main* has special meaning to *C#* but has no particular significance to ilasm. The method that contains the entry point may thus take whatever conventional name is used in the source language. The preamble ends by declaring, at line 9, that this method has a maximum stack depth[5] of 8.

The working *IL* of the method is just three lines. At line 10 the literal string is pushed onto the evaluation stack with the "ldstr" instruction. The second instruction is a static call to the *WriteLine* method of the *System.Console* class of the *mscorlib* assembly. Recall the format of calls, as described in Figure 2.21 on page 44. The final instruction, at line 11, terminates the method by returning.

In the *C#* source, the code did not declare a constructor for the *HelloWorld* class. Nevertheless, the compiler has created a default no-arg constructor. All constructors have the special name ".*ctor*". Unlike *Main*, this name does have special significance to the runtime. If the *C#* source had explicitly declared a constructor for the class the constructor would have been named *HelloWorld*(). No matter, the constructor would still be called .*ctor* in the *CIL*.

Another "Hello World" walkthrough.   The *Component Pascal* version of the canonical "Hello World" program looks as follows —

```
MODULE Hello;
  IMPORT CPmain, Console;
BEGIN
  Console.WriteString("Hello CP World");
  Console.WriteLn;
END Hello.
```

---

[5] In fact, the compiler lied, since the maximum stack depth is just one in this case. We say more about this later, in the "Method Definitions" section (see page 217).

The *CIL* resulting from submitting this source to *gpcp* is shown in Figure 2.23. In this figure, as before, some of the assembler comments have been edited out, and listing line numbers have been inserted. Long lines have been split over two lines to fit in the page width.

```
.assembly 'Hello' {}                                        // line 1
.assembly extern RTS {}                                     // line 2

.namespace Hello                                            // line 4
{
.class public sealed Hello                                  // line 6
  {
.method public specialname rtspecialname static void
                .cctor() il managed                         // line 8
    {
      ret                                                   // line 10
    } // end of .cctor method

.method public static void '.CPmain'
                (string[]) il managed                       // line 13
    {
.entrypoint                                                 // line 15
      ldarg.0                                               // line 16
      stsfld class string[] [RTS]ProgArgs::argList          // line 17
.line 4 'Hello.cp'
      ldstr  "Hello CP World"                               // line 19
      call   wchar[] [RTS]CP_rts::strToChO(string)          // line 20
      call   void [RTS]Console::'WriteString'(wchar[]) // line 21
.line 5 'Hello.cp'
      call   void [RTS]Console::'WriteLn'()                 // line 23
      ret                                                   // line 24
    } // end of method .CPmain
  }
}
```

Figure 2.23: *CIL* of *Component Pascal* "Hello World"

The structure of the *CIL* is similar to the previous example, although the overall structure of the module needs to be mapped onto the various entities of the *CLS*. The whole of the module forms a namespace, which in this case has the same name as the module. Within the namespace a "synthetic static class" is defined, to encapsulate all of the static features of the module. This synthetic class has the same name as the module also.

The *.assembly* declarations are different to those in the previous case. We do not import *mscorlib*, as that is implicitly imported by the current version of ilasm. However, all modules compiled by *gpcp* reference an assembly named *RTS* that contains some runtime support code.

There are a number of detailed differences that are worth noting. First, within the code are some ".line" directives, which pass source line number information into the *PEM* for the debugger. The code does not define an instance constructor for the synthetic static class *Hello.Hello*, but does define a *class constructor* for it with the special name *.cctor*. In this example, the class constructor is empty and returns immediately at line 10.[6]

The module body statements of *Component Pascal* are treated differently in *.NET* depending on whether or not the module will become a dynamic linked library or an application. If the module imports the system module *CPmain*, the module is compiled into an application and defines an entry point that is always called ".CPmain". If *CPmain* is not imported, the module becomes a library, and the module body code appears in the class constructor that is run just once at module load time. An assembly may need a class constructor *and* an entry point, if there are static features of the class that need to be initialized at load time.

In *C#* there is nothing equivalent to the import of *CPmain* that signals the type of *PE* file that the compiler ought to produce. Instead, a command option to the compiler determines whether the file becomes a library or an application. As may be expected, it is an error to try to compile a file into an application if the file does not contain an appropriate *Main* method.

The detail of the *gpcp* entry point *IL* has some differences from the *C#* version. The first action of any *Component Pascal* module that imports *CPmain* is to take the incoming command line argument array and store it in a convenient location in the runtime support system (*RTS*). The support module *ProgArgs* allows the argument strings to be counted and retrieved. Lines 16 and 17 take the incoming argument (possibly **nil**) and store it in static field *ProgArgs::argList* in the *RTS* assembly.

The body of the module written by the programmer starts in the fourth line of the source. The translation of this line starts at line 19 of the *CIL* listing. As in the previous case, the literal string is pushed onto the stack, using a "ldstr" instruction. The next line calls a system support method that transforms the native string into a character array. *Component Pascal* has no true string type, so routines such as *Console.WriteString* take character arrays as argument. The two console routines are then called, ending the method.

Compilation Unit Structure

Each compilation unit consists of zero or more namespace definitions, possibly nested. Class definitions may occur inside or outside these namespaces. We have seen an example of each in the two "Hello World" examples.

---

[6]The *CLR* expects every *object type* to have at least one constructor. However, synthetic static classes do not define objects and cannot be instantiated.

Figure 2.24 is an example of a *C#* source file with multiple class declarations. In this particular case, these classes have only static features. The more general case is treated in the section on the virtual object system (see page 55). This code is a fragment of the code of the *Component Pascal* runtime support. It includes the definition of the static variable in which the command line argument of applications are stored. From the command line, this file would be compiled by the command —

```
csc /t:library /debug DummyRTS.cs
```

The debug option ensures that local variable names are preserved in the assembly. When the resulting *DLL* is disassembled, the structure of the assembly is revealed as shown in Figure 2.25. In this example all of the instructions of all of the methods have been edited out, so as to highlight the structure. We shall look at the *IL* of some of the methods later. However, the line numbering in the figure reflects the lines of the unedited *CIL*.

```
// This is file "DummyRTS.cs"
public class Console
{
    public static void WriteLn() {
        System.Console.WriteLine();
    }

    public static void WriteString(char[] str) {
        int len = str.Length;
        for (int i = 0; i < len && str[i] != '\0'; i++)
            System.Console.Write(str[i]);
    }
} // end of public class Console

public class ProgArgs
{
    public static System.String[] argList = null;

    public static int ArgNumber() {
        if (ProgArgs.argList == null)
            return 0;
        else
            return argList.Length;
    }
} // end of public class ProgArgs
```

Figure 2.24: *C#* file with two static classes

```
.assembly extern mscorlib { }
.assembly DummyRTS {}
.module DummyRTS.dll

.class public auto ansi Console
                extends [mscorlib]System.Object {      // line 5
  .method public hidebysig static void
                            WriteLn() il managed      // line 7
  { ... } // end of method Console::WriteLn

  .method public hidebysig static void
            WriteString(wchar[] str) il managed {      // line 12
    .locals ([0] int32 len,                            // line 14
            [1] int32 i)                               // line 15
    ...
  } // end of method Console::WriteString

  .method public hidebysig specialname rtspecialname
                instance void .ctor() il managed      // line 41
  { ... } // end of method Console::.ctor
} // end of class Console

.class public auto ansi ProgArgs
                extends [mscorlib]System.Object {      // line 49
  .field public static class string[] argList          // line 51
  .method public hidebysig static int32
                        ArgNumber() il managed          // line 52
  { ... } // end of method ProgArgs::ArgNumber

  .method public hidebysig specialname rtspecialname
                static void .cctor() il managed        // line 68
  { ...   } // end of method ProgArgs::.cctor

  .method public hidebysig specialname rtspecialname
                instance void .ctor() il managed      // line 75
  { ...   } // end of method ProgArgs::.ctor
} // end of class ProgArgs
```

Figure 2.25: *CIL* for *C#* file with two static classes

In this example in the *CIL* we see that we have two classes, which are not grouped inside a namespace. Each of these classes is defined as extending the default object supertype, which has the fully qualified name[7] [mscorlib]System.Object, as seen at

---

[7]In current releases of *.NET* the preferred way to refer to the *System.Object* and *System.String* types is by the keywords **object** and **string**. Future releases of the runtime may insist on this.

line numbers 5 and 49. As we would have expected from the *C#* "Hello World" example, the compiler has supplied a default constructor for each of the classes. These constructors do nothing except call the supertype constructor.

However, there is something new in the *ProgArgs* class. This class has an initialized static field. Such initializations are executed at assembly load time and thus form part of the code of the class constructor. The constructor, as mentioned earlier, has the special name *.cctor*. In this particular instance the explicit initialization in Figure 2.24 is redundant, as static fields that are of object type will be initialized to **null** implicitly. In some coding standards such an explicit initialization is expected and thus ends up in the class constructor.

The code of the class constructor to initialize this particular static field is particularly simple. Here is the *IL* —

```
ldnull                                        // line 70
stsfld    class string[] ProgArgs::argList    // line 71
ret                                           // line 72
```

Branching code examples.   The *IL* of the *ArgNumber* function is rather more interesting. This is the first example that we have seen that included some flow of control instructions. The *IL* of the function appears in Figure 2.26. The first thing to note about

```
//   public static int ArgNumber() {
//       if (ProgArgs.argList == null)
//           return 0;
//       else
//           return argList.Length;
//   }

.locals ([0] int32)          // anonymous local variable 0       line 54
        ldsfld    string[] ProgArgs::argList                     // line 55
        brtrue.s lb01                                            // line 56
        ldc.i4.0                                                 // line 57
        stloc.0                                                  // line 58
        br.s      lb02                                           // line 59
lb01:   ldsfld string[] ProgArgs::argList                       // line 60
        ldlen                                                    // line 61
        conv.i4                                                  // line 62
        stloc.0                                                  // line 63
lb02:   ldloc.0                                                  // line 64
        ret
```

Figure 2.26: *IL* of the *ArgNumber* function

the encoding of this function is that it declares a local variable that does not appear in the source code of Figure 2.24. This local variable, local '0,' is used to merge the function result along the two control paths, sinking the separate returns in Figure 2.24 into a single return of the local variable value. It is not necessary to treat multiple return statements in this way, and indeed *gpcp* would use a different method.

The next thing to note is the way in which the test for **null** is encoded. In order to understand line 56 it is necessary to know two facts. The **null** value is encoded as zero, and the "brtrue" instruction takes "true" to mean any nonzero value. If the value in the static field is **null**, then a zero is loaded on the stack at line 57, and stored in the local variable at line 58. If the value is non-**null**, the array reference is loaded on the stack at line 60, and the length is taken from the array reference at line 61. The "ldlen" instruction is a built-in operation on arrays, which returns the number of elements in the array.

The appearance of the "conv.i4" at line 62 appears perplexing. The "ldlen" instruction pushes a result of the unsigned native integer type. This type will be at least 32 bits in precision. The conversion to int32 will modify the value only if the actual array length is greater than 2×10^9, in which case the result will be wrong anyhow. As of the *Beta* release of *.NET*, the verifier does not object to the omission of this explicit conversion.

Another simple example of a branching construct is the *IL* generated from the *Console.WriteString* static method. In this case we have a loop. The *IL* of this example is shown in Figure 2.27. The per-character loop extends from label "lb05" to the conditional branch instruction on line 37.

There are a couple of things to note about this loop. This is a post-tested loop, with the test for loop termination appearing only at the end. The loop begins at line 22 with an unconditional branch to the test code that starts at line 31. The control flow will most probably immediately jump back to line 23. In Chapter 9 alternative ways of laying out such loops are discussed.

The termination test of this loop involves a logical conjunction and is implemented by *short-circuit evaluation*. This means that the Boolean evaluation is terminated as soon as the result is known. Thus the first part of the test $i \geq len$, at line 33, jumps straight out of the loop if the result is true. Only if the first test is false does control fall through into the second test. Also note that the sense of the first test is reversed compared to the source code, which tests $i < len$. The first test is reversed, because it is a test for jumping *out* of the loop, while the test in the source is the condition for *continuing* the loop. The second test is not reversed in sense, since it is the condition for taking the backward edge to label "lb04" to continue the loop.

```
//  public static void WriteString(char[] str) {
//      int len = str.Length;
//      for (int i = 0; i < len && str[i] != '\0'; i++)
//          System.Console.Write(str[i]);
//  }

.locals ([0] int32 len,                                      // line 14
         [1] int32 i)                                        // line 15
        ldarg.0                 // load argument str             line 16
        ldlen                   // get array length               line 17
        conv.i4                                              // line 18
        stloc.0                 // store in len                  line 19
        ldc.i4.0                                             // line 20
        stloc.1                 // set i to zero                 line 21
        br.s   lb03             // jump to test                  line 22
lb05:   ldarg.0                                              // line 23
        ldloc.1                                              // line 24
        ldelem.u2                                            // line 25
        call void [mscorlib]System.Console::Write(wchar)    // line 26
        ldloc.1                 // load i and increment       // line 27
        ldc.i4.1                                             // line 28
        add                                                 // line 29
        stloc.1                 // store new value of i       // line 30
lb03:   ldloc.1                                             // line 31
        ldloc.0                                             // line 32
        bge.s lb04              // test i ≥ len                  line 33
        ldarg.0                                             // line 34
        ldloc.1                                             // line 35
        ldelem.u2                                           // line 36
        brtrue.s lb05           // test str[i] ≠ 0               line 37
lb04:   ret                                                // line 38
```

Figure 2.27: *IL* of the *WriteString* procedure

Notes on Chapter 2

This chapter has not given details of the complete instruction set of *CIL*. There is a complete list of instructions in Appendix B, but it is probably necessary to refer to one of the online manuals to get sufficient detail on the semantics of all of the instructions.

If you have access to the Software Development Kit, it is certainly worth compiling a few simple programs at this time. If you choose to write *Component Pascal* programs, then you may view the *IL* file with an editor to see how your program turned out. If you use the *C#* compiler, you do not have the choice of producing textual *IL*. You may view the output by using the "disassembler" program "ildasm". This program produces its output by default in a friendly, browsible *graphical user interface (GUI)*. It is also possible, using the "/out=*filename*" switch, to persist the output to a file. One of the really attractive features of this program is it ability to "round-trip" assemblies. This means that a file may be disassembled using ildasm and then reassembled using "ilasm" to recreate a new *PEM* with the same semantics. This property is a pretty strong guarantee that ildasm is not leaving anything important out.

If you like, you may try disassembling some code that started off as *IL* out of *gpcp*. If you compare the disassembler output you will see that the assembler has inserted a few default values that *gpcp* does not bother to write out to the *IL* file.

It is not recommended that the managed *C* compiler "cl" be used as a routine source of *IL* examples for those new to the framework. The problem is that this compiler emits a very large amount of output that has to do with interfacing to the unmanaged world of the native libraries. The *IL* is of good quality, and is an interesting contrast to *C#*, but it is just a little confusing trying to find the real *IL* amid all the literal data declarations.

Understanding the Common Type System (CTS)

This chapter deals with the object model of the common language runtime, the *CTS*. It is this shared framework that enables different languages to work together at a higher level than the binary compatibility that traditional *COM* uses.

By sharing the same object model it is possible for components written in one language to inherit behavior from components written in another. Rather than just being able to call library functions written in another language, in the *.NET* framework components may pass objects to one another and extend each others capabilities.

The Virtual Object System

We may classify all types in *.NET* into two categories, as shown in Figure 3.1. There are the **value types**, including the built-in scalar types, and user defined enumerations and structures. The **reference types** include all pointer types and object references.

Reference types have the fundamental property that assignments of such values has alias semantics. If we copy a reference and modify the datum to which the reference refers, then both references will refer to the modified datum. Value types, by contrast have value

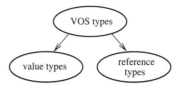

Figure 3.1: *CTS* types are either value types or reference types

semantics for assigment. If we make a copy of a value structure and modify one copy, the other copy is unchanged.

There is another useful categorization of types in the *CTS*, which is the separation between *self-describing* types and *non-self-describing* types. The difference is fundamental. If we have an instance of a self-describing type then the value carries with it some denotation of the *exact type* of the value. Values of a non-self-describing type are nothing more than a bunch of bits. For example, there is no sure way of telling whether a particular value in a memory word is a signed or an unsigned integer. In a statically typed language the compiler will be able to ensure that only values of the declared type are placed in the word, but there is no way we can tell the type from the bit-pattern.

In the *CTS*, only the object types are self-describing. These are a subcategory of the reference types, described below.

Value Types

The subdivision of value types is shown in Figure 3.2. At the level of granularity that we consider, there are four kinds of value types. The two leftmost leaves in the figure are built-in types, while the two on the right are user-defined.

The built-in types.   On the left of Figure 3.2 are the scalar types. These have no substructure, and have special encodings in *CIL*. The scalar types include all of the primitive types shown in Figure 2.1—that is, all of the arithmetic types, together with the Boolean and character types.

As we shall see later, some reference types carry type information with their values. These are the *self-describing* types. Other references may be of a known type as a result

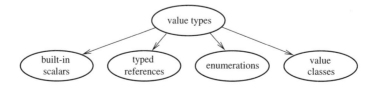

Figure 3.2: Hierarchy of value types in the *CTS*

of invariant properties that are enforced by the compiler. When such references need type information to be attached to their values, we use *typed references*. Typed references are value types that aggregate a reference and a type denotation. There are special instructions in *IL* for creating these special values and extracting their components.

Value classes.   Value classes are aggregate types, but are not self-describing. Assignment of value classes has value semantics. In *C#*, declaration of **struct**s results in value classes appearing in the *IL*. Value classes may be used when the full capabilities of the object types is not required. The creation and manipulation of values of a value class have much lower resource use than is the case for object types.

Here is a first example in *C#* —

> **public struct** ValCls { **public int** i,j,k; }

The resulting textual *CIL* is shown in Figure 3.3. Although in *C#* we use different keywords to define a **struct** or a **class**, in *CIL* they are both classes. The distinction between these two kinds of class is carried by the *value* attribute in the class definition. Notice that the class has been given the *sealed* attribute, and has been given the base class [mscorlib] System.ValueType. This system type is the supertype of all value classes.

```
.class value public auto ansi sealed ValCls
        extends [mscorlib]System.ValueType
{
   .field public int32 i
   .field public int32 j
   .field public int32 k
} // end of class ValCls
```

Figure 3.3: Disassembly of **struct** definition

In *CIL* value classes must always be declared as inheriting from *System.ValueType* and must always have the **sealed** attribute. That is to say, value types cannot be further extended.

Every value type has an associated *boxed type*. The boxed type is an object type and carries type information with the value. In truth, it is the associated boxed type that really inherits from *System.ValueType*.

It is possible to declare methods that are bound to value types. These may be either static or instance methods, but cannot be virtual methods. Instance methods bound to a value class have a **this** argument, which will always be a reference to the actual receiver value. This reference carries no type information, since value classes are not self-describing. In fact, so far as the *VES* is concerned, the **this** argument may even be **null**. As

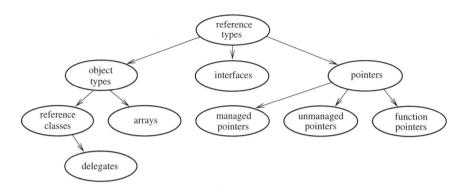

Figure 3.4: Hierarchy of reference types in the *CTS*

we shall see, this would be impossible for a virtual method, since the *VES* needs to access the *self-description* of the **this** value[1] in order to dispatch the right method.

Instance methods of value classes do not need to extract type information from their receiver, since an instance method is attached to an exact class. Within an instance method, the type with which the code is dealing is known to the compiler.

Reference Types

Most of what is popularly thought of as object-oriented behavior results from the characteristics of the reference types, and more specifically the object types.

In the *CTS*, the reference types form a rich hierarchy, as shown in Figure 3.4. There are three subdivisions of the reference types. These are the *object types*, *interface types*, and *pointer types*.

Arrays and reference classes are object types. Object types are self-describing and are complete types. Completeness implies that knowing an object is of some particular exact object type completely specifies the features of the object. As we shall see in the next section, knowing that an object is of some interface type provides only a partial specification of the features of the object.

Array object types. An array's *type* is determined entirely by its *element type*, and at runtime has an attribute that specifies the length. Line 17 of Figure 2.27 was an example of the use of the "ldlen" instruction to extract the array length from the array reference.

It is useful to be clear that in the *CTS* two arrays are the same type if they have the same element type. Furthermore, array types do not have names but take their names from

---

[1]This would read better for *OO* languages in which the receiver is called **self**. "... the *VES* needs to access the self-description of the **self** value ..."

the name of their element type. If we wish to refer to (any) "**array of** *String*" in *IL*, in a method signature for example, we will use the type denotation "**string** [ ] ". In *IL*, as in *C#*, an array is specified by naming the element type and following the name by a pair of empty brackets, '[]'.

In *C#*, and in the *CTS*, arrays of the same element type are assignment compatible. This *structural compatibility* of array types is not the semantic model that some programming languages use. For example, in *Pascal*-family languages arrays are named, and two differently named arrays are distinct, even if they have the same element type and length. Thus —

```
type
      Foo = array 8 of CHAR;
      Bar = array 8 of CHAR;
```

are different types and are not assignment compatible. This behavior is called *name compatibility*. In effect, two types are compatible if they share the same (fully qualified) type name. It follows that languages that require name compatibility for arrays must rely on the compiler to enforce the restriction, since neither the *CTS* nor the verifier will do so.

Support for the creation and indexing of one-dimensional arrays is built into the *VES*. Much of the documentation refers to these one-dimensional arrays as *vectors*. The instruction "newarr" creates a new one-dimensional array. As we saw on page 27, the "ldelem.*" family of instructions loads array elements, and the corresponding "stelem.*" family assigns values to array elements.

Multidimensional arrays are not directly supported by the instruction set. There are methods in the *System.Array* class that allow for the creation of arrays of different dimensionality, with element counts that do not necessarily start at zero. The same class also defines methods for accessing and manipulating values of such array types. As at the *Beta* release of *.NET* these methods are not inlined and exact some performance penalty. An alternative is to use arrays of arrays instead. This is the required semantics for *Pascal*-family languages anyway. In *C#* terms this corresponds to using the second line below, rather than the first —

```
int [,]    foo = new int [8,4];
int [] []  bar = new int [8] [];
for (int i = 0; i < 8; i++) bar[i] = new int [4];
```

Unfortunately, adopting the second form in *C#* requires providing an explicit initializer loop, as seen in the third line of the code fragment. Of course, in languages in which this is the way in which multidimensional arrays are declared, the compiler would emit constructor code without requiring any user intervention.

Depending on the way in which the multidimensional arrays have been implemented, the code for accessing elements is also different. Suppose we have the following code, accessing the two arrays —

```
foo[2,3]   = 17;      // true two-dim int array type
bar[2][3]  = 19;      // array of array of int type
```

The disassembly of this code, shown in Figure 3.5, demonstrates the special syntax that is used for access to the *System.Array* types. In the first implementation, lines 1–5, all the work is performed by a call of an instance method, *Set*, with a special signature. The receiver is the array reference, and the three arguments are the two array indices and the value to be assigned.

```
// foo[2,3]  = 17;              // true two-dim int array type
ldsfld    int32[0...,0...] Hello::foo            // line 01
ldc.i4.2                                         // line 02
ldc.i4.3                                         // line 03
ldc.i4.s 17                                      // line 04
call      instance void int32[0...,0...]::Set(int32,
                                              int32,
                                              int32)   // line 05
// bar[2][3] = 19;              // array of array of int type
ldsfld    int32[][] Hello::bar // push static field bar      line 06
ldc.i4.2                       // push first index           line 07
ldelem.ref                     // get reference              line 08
ldc.i4.3                       // push second index          line 09
ldc.i4.s 19                    // push int32 value           line 10
stelem.i4                      // store the array element
```

Figure 3.5: Disassembly of multidimensional array accesses

The second implementation navigates the data structure, using the one-dimension array instructions of *IL*. Figure 3.6 shows the runtime layout. The variable *bar* is a reference to an array of eight references to separate four-long arrays of integer type. We begin by pushing the static field *Hello::bar* at line 6. This field has type "int32[][]". We push

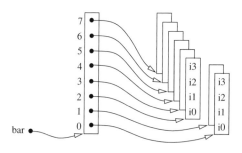

Figure 3.6: Runtime layout of array of arrays

the first array index at line 7 and load the element at line 8. It will be recalled that the "ldelem" instruction is specialized for the various array element types. In this case the array element is a reference so we use the instruction "ldelem.ref". To finish, we push the second index, then the element value, and finally perform the assignment using the "stelem.i4" instruction. Note that this instruction has a *stack-Δ* of -3.

If the "call" of *Set* at line 5 of this example, and corresponding "calls" of *Get* are inlined by the *JIT*, the first array access method should be faster than the second.[2] Furthermore, it may be noted that a true two-dimensional array requires a single object allocation, while an array of arrays requires many. In our example, the array of arrays structure requires nine separate objects to be allocated.

Array covariance.

Array covariance.   Before leaving arrays, a word on array covariance. Suppose that T_1 is a subtype of some type T. In the *CTS* an array of the type "**array of** T_1" is considered to be assignment compatible with a location that has the declared type "**array of** T". This property is called *array covariance*.

There are two immediate consequences of this rule. First, it is necessary for the *VES* to type-check every array element assignment. Secondly, it places a small but significant hole in the type system.

Suppose that an "**array of** T_1" has been assigned to a location of type "**array of** T". Code that has access to the wider array—that is, the "**array of** T"—would normally expect to be able to assign any variable of type T to any element position in the array. However, this is illegal, since there may be other, original references of type "**array of** T_1" that point to the same array. From the point of view of the original references the sudden appearance of an element of type T in the array would violate their invariants. This danger is removed by the *VES* performing a type check on every array element assignment.

The overhead of a type check is relatively small. The consequences for the type system are arguably more far-reaching. Suppose it is your task as a software engineer to write a library, with a method that takes an argument of array type. For the sake of concreteness, let us assume that it is a method that adds a new element to the array. Under normal circumstances it would be reasonable to assume that it was possible to write such a method, and statically guarantee that it was free from type errors. Unfortunately this is not the case. If a user of the library quite legally passes an array of a subtype to your method, the method will fail with an array element assignment exception.

Of course, array covariance did not appear in the *CTS* by accident. This behavior is specified in some languages, *Java* for example. If the *CTS* did not allow array covariance it would be difficult to implement such languages efficiently. In any case some people believe there are circumstances in which array covariance leads to somewhat more convenient code. At core, these are religious matters, and as compiler writers it is our job to implement the language, not argue the religion.

---

[2]The converse is also true. If the calls are not inlined, the first method will be significantly slower.

Class object types.   Reference classes are the types from which the *CTS* gets its characteristic object-oriented flavor. Reference classes are self-describing and complete. Such classes declare that they inherit from exactly one supertype and may also implement zero or more interfaces. The built-in class *System.Object* is the sole exception to this rule, as it is the root of the class hierarchy and does not inherit from any other type.

Variables that are declared to be of some reference object type may be assigned a value of any assignment compatible type. References to objects of a subtype are assignment compatible with variables of the supertype. This form of assignment compatibility can be guaranteed at compile time in statically typed languages. Consider the following scenario. Two variables have been declared as follows —

public A a;	// *A is a class object type*
public B b;	// *B is a class object type*
...	
a = b;	// *assign value in b to a*

The compiler can check the relationship between the types *A* and *B*. If *A* is a supertype of *B*, then the assignment is known to be correct. The value in variable *b* need not be of exact type *B*, but if it is a subtype of *B* then it is necessarily also a subtype of *A*.

If *A* is a subtype of *B*, then the assignment is statically incorrect. It is possible that the assignment might be dynamically correct, if the exact type of *b* happens to be a sufficiently narrowed subtype of *B*. However, the assignment would then require a runtime type check, which would appear as an explicit narrowing cast in the source —

a = (A) b;	// *assign value in b to a*

Finally, the types *A* and *B* might be unrelated. In that case the assignment is known to be incorrect statically, and incorrect dynamically also.

At this point it is worth noting that type-check casts of the kind in the last example are also able to be checked statically. When a value of static type *B* is cast to some other class object type *A*, we have three possibilities. The cast might actually be widening, in which case no check is needed. If the cast is narrowing, then the runtime check needs to be performed and might either succeed or fail. Finally, if the types *A* and *B* are unrelated, we may conclude that the runtime check will always fail, and a compile-time error will be signalled. As we shall see later, it is not possible to reach such strong conclusions in the case of type-check casts to interface types.

Here is the *IL* syntax for class definitions. This syntax applies to both value and reference classes. Value classes are recognised by the fact that they extend *System.Value-Type*; all others are reference classes.

$$
\begin{array}{rcl}
\text{ClassDecl} & \rightarrow & \textbf{.class} \text{ ClassHeader "\{" \{ MemberDecl \} "\}" .}\\
\text{ClassHeader} & \rightarrow & \{ \text{ ClassAttr } \} \textit{ ident } [\textbf{ extends } \text{TypeRef }]\\
& & [\textbf{ implements } \text{TypeRef } \{ \text{ ',' TypeRef } \}] .\\
\text{MemberDecl} & \rightarrow & \textit{<Member Declaration>} .
\end{array}
$$

Classes may be defined with a rich repetoire of attributes to control visibility and other characteristics. Here we shall only mention the attributes that apply to top-level classes. The case of nested classes is somewhat more detailed.

The attributes listed in Figure 3.7 may be used, with the indicated semantics. The first group of attributes in the figure control visibility. Top-level classes may only have public or assembly visibility, which are denoted by the keywords **public** and **private** respectively. All members of the class take their *visibility* from this declaration. The modifiers that the members include in their definitions can only control the member's *accessibility*.

The next group of attributes control the semantics of inheritance, and instantiation. A class that is declared to be **interface** is not an object class at all but is an interface class. These are described in a later section.

A class that is declared to be **abstract** cannot have an instance created. If a class has one or more abstract methods, then it is necessarily an abstract class. However, abstract classes need not have any abstract methods, or indeed any methods at all. A **sealed** class cannot be extended further. All virtual methods of a sealed class will be final, although it is not clear that they need to be declared that way. It is possible for a class to be both **abstract** and **sealed**. Logically, such a class can neither be instantiated nor extended. Such a class

Attribute	Effect
private	(Default) This class and its members will not be visible outside of this assembly. Cannot be used with **public**.
public	This class and its members will be visible outside of this assembly. Cannot be used with **private**.
abstract	This class cannot be instantiated.
interface	This class is an interface definition.
sealed	This class cannot be further extended.
ansi	This class uses *ANSI* marshalling for character strings. This is the default behavior.
autochar	This class uses platform-specific marshalling of character strings.
unicode	This class uses unicode marshalling for character strings.
auto	The layout of this class is determined automatically.
explicit	An explicit layout will be given for this class.
sequential	The class is laid out sequentially.

Figure 3.7: Class declaration attributes

can only contain static features, and might be used to implement *static classes* for those languages that have such things.

The third group of attributes in the figure control the way in which character strings are marshalled across a managed-to-unmanaged call boundary. The **ansi** attribute is the default.

The final group of attributes control the layout of features in the memory image of instances of the class. The default layout is **auto**, which leaves the layout up to the runtime. There are circumstances in which objects are passed to and from unmanaged code. In such cases the layout expected by the *VES* must correspond to the native layout used by the unmanaged code. The other two layout attribute values allow control of this characteristic. Explicit layout is considered further in Chapter 4.

Class members.   Classes have *members*, sometimes also called *features*. In the *CTS* there are four kinds. These are *fields*, *methods*, *properties*, and *events*. Method declarations are dealt with in some detail in "Defining Methods" (page 93).

Fields may be either instance fields or static fields. Every object of a particular class type has its own copy of the instance fields. Static fields are shared, and may be thought of as residing inside a runtime class descriptor that is unique for each self-describing class. In the *IL* there are different instructions for accessing the values of static and instance fields. Static fields are declared with the **static** attribute. If **static** is not specified, the field will be an instance field.

As well as the **static** attribute that determines the basic kind of field, fields have other attributes that control accessibility, mutability, and some special name markers. These additional predefined attributes for fields are shown[3] in Figure 3.8. Accessibility was discussed on page 43. In the figure the first group of attributes control the accessibility of the field, as described. The **privatescope** accessibility was not discussed previously. This mode allows the compiler complete control over access, since the datum can only be accessed by using the field definition token. This feature supports static local variables of functions in language *C* or **own** variables in *ALGOL*. It may be thought of as a structured form of name mangling.

Fields that are marked **literal** do not occupy space in the object but appear in the metadata. Only static fields may be literal, and they must have an explicit value in their definition. Fields that are marked **initonly** are used for fields that are given a value at load time, and are never changed thereafter. **Initonly** fields may only be given a value by the code of an initializer. However, an attempt to change an **initonly** field is a verification error rather than a runtime error. This means that marking a field as **initonly** is only effective in verified contexts.

The final group of attributes mark names as having special significance to various tools, or to the runtime system. For example, the names of the access methods for properties are marked with the **specialname** attribute.

---

[3] Attributes that control serialization and marshalling have been omitted from this discussion.

Attribute	Effect
assembly	This field is only accessible within this assembly.
family	This field is only accessible in this class and in subclasses of this class.
famandassem	This field is accessible in this class and its subclasses but only within this assembly.
famorassem	This field is accessible in this class, its subclasses, and throughout this assembly.
private	This field is only accessible within this class.
privatescope	This field is only accessible within the assembly, and then only by using the field definition token.
public	This field is publicly accessible.
literal	This static field is a literal value.
initonly	This field may only be assigned in constructors.
specialname	The name has special significance to tools.
rtspecialname	The name has significance to the runtime.

Figure 3.8: Field declaration attributes

Properties provide an additional mechanism, other than fields, for associating named data values with classes or with object instances. In languages such as *C#* properties are declared as part of classes. Properties have names, and have associated *getter* and *setter* methods. In *C#* properties are accessed by name, using the usual field-access syntax. However, since properties may be defined to have only a *setter* method or only a *getter* method, properties may be write-only or read-only. If both methods are defined, the property allows both reading and writing. Every used occurrence of a property name in a source program translates into a call to the associated accessor method in the *IL*. From a theoretical point of view, properties provide a mechanism for enforcing invariants on values. Since all accesses to the property value must pass through the access methods, the bodies of the methods are the place to enforce assertions. For example, if some checking code is put inside a *setter* method, it is guaranteed that no code may change the value without passing the check. The same argument applies to code-instrumentation. If instrumentation is placed in the property access methods, it is guaranteed that *all* accesses to the value will be intercepted.

The access methods may be static, instance, or virtual methods. They may work by simply getting or setting the value of an associated, private *backing field* or may compute their values on the fly. Of course, the backing field must be **private**; otherwise we could not be sure that the value was not accessed explicitly, thereby evading the discipline of the accessor methods. The case of virtual methods for property access is particularly important, since method overriding may then be used to add additional checks to existing property access code.

At runtime the *VES* neither knows nor cares about properties. All accesses are encoded as conventional calls to the *getter* and *setter* methods. Thus languages that do not have special syntax for properties can still access the values. However, properties have a special status in the metadata and thus have special syntax in *CIL*. Figure 3.9 is typical code of a property. In this case the property is read-only, but has an additional method for incrementing the property value. In practice the private *count* field would be initialized by the constructor, which is not shown in the figure. In a cross-language environment, programs that do not understand properties will ignore the metadata and call the two methods directly.

```
.class public Counter
    .method virtual instance specialname public int32 get_Count ()
      {                                    // the getter method
          ldarg.0                          // push this value
          ldfld int32 'count'              // fetch the private field
          ret                              // return the result
      }

    .method virtual instance public void  Increment ()  {
          ...                              // increment the count field
      }

    .property int32 Count ()  {       // the property declaration
          .backing int32 count ()
          .get instance int32 get_Count ()
          .other instance void  Increment ()
      }
} // end of public class Counter
```

Figure 3.9: *IL* example of property definition

Events are the last of the four kinds of member that a class may contain. Events are a special kind of object reference that are distinguished in the metatdata because of their role in the *event-handling model* of the virtual object system. Events are references to a particular specialization of delegate types, which are the subject of the next section.

Delegate types.   Delegates may be thought of as a type-safe mechanism for implementing the "*function pointers*" of language *C*. In *Pascal*-family languages, the equivalent construct is the *procedure variable*. In contrast to the direct implementation of function pointers described earlier, delegates are type-safe and verifiable. Unlike traditional function pointers in most languages, delegates may be used for both static and dispatched methods.

Delegate types, as may be seen from their position in the hierarchy of Figure 3.4, are implemented as a kind of reference class. Each instance of a delegate encapsulates a datum that denotes the method that has been assigned to the instance. In the case of instance methods it also encapsulates an object reference that will be the **this** of any invocation. If the delegate instance has been assigned a static method, the encapsulated object reference will be **null**.

The key to the verifiability of delegates derives from the fact that delegates are entirely opaque structures. There are no operations on delegates except for a constructor and methods to invoke the encapsulated function. Furthermore, the code of even these few methods is supplied by the runtime, rather than by the compiler. The runtime is able to guarantee that the encapsulated function has the correct signature, because it checks this itself within the hidden constructor code.

As a first example, the declaration of a delegate type to encapsulate a function that takes two parameters of type "double" and returns "double" may be achieved by the *IL* in Figure 3.10. The signature of the constructor is always the same. The first argument is of some object type, while the second is of type **unsigned native int**. On current 32-bit machines the function pointer value will be an **int32**, but future compatability and the verifier require the native type here. The *Invoke* method is the method that is called to activate the encapsulated function. The signature of this method must match the signatures of the functions that will be assigned to the delegate.

```
.class public auto sealed DoubleToDouble
                extends [mscorlib] System.MulticastDelegate {
    .method public specialname rtspecialname instance
                void .ctor(object,   unsigned native int)  runtime managed {}
    .method public virtual instance
                float64 Invoke(float64, float64)  runtime managed {}
} // end of class DoubleToDouble
```

Figure 3.10: A simple delegate declaration

Notice that all delegate types must be declared to be **sealed**, and they signal their special semantics by extending the class *System.MulticastDelegate*.[4] The fact that the implementations of the two methods are supplied by the runtime, rather than by explicit *IL*, is shown by the empty bodies of the methods and the *runtime-managed* denotation. The only additional methods that a delegate may possess are used for asynchronous calls. In such cases the two additonal methods are called *BeginInvoke* and *EndInvoke*.

When the constructor is called it is passed two data. First on the stack is the receiver object for the delegated calls, and a function pointer is on the top. For a static procedure, the first datum is **null**. Suppose, for example, that we wish to create an instance of the delegate type declared in Figure 3.10. We wish to encapsulate the function *Math.Power*.

---

[4]The name of the class that is extended is a historical relic. Originally the *Delegate* class was used for delegates, and an extension, the *MulticastDelegate* class, was used for events. In the final version the extended class must be used as the base class for both (ordinary) delegates and the *event* types that we discuss next.

The *C#* source code might have gone —

```
DoubleToDouble x = new DoubleToDouble(Math.Power);
```

Figure 3.11 shows how this would be translated into *IL*, in the case that the variable *x* is a static field.

```
  . . .
  ldnull                              // no encapsulated receiver for static method
  ldftn    float64 Math::'Power'(float64, float64)
  newobj   instance void ThisMod.DoubleToDouble::.ctor
                                   (object, unsigned native int)
  stsfld   class ThisMod.DoubleToDouble ThisMod::'x'
  . . .
```

Figure 3.11: Constructing a static delegate value

If the delegate is to be bound to a particular object, then that object is specified at the time of delegate construction, and the encapsulated method will be an instance or virtual method of the object's type. In *C#* the syntax for such an assignment is similar to the static case. The compiler recognizes the instance method and generates the alternative code.

As an example, suppose we wish to use a delegate to attach a no-args method *Count* to an object *TargetObj*. Presumably whenever the delegate is invoked, we wish for some field of the target object to be incremented. The source syntax might be —

```
NoArgDelegate x = new NoArgDelegate(targetObj.Count);
```

where it is assumed that the appropriate delegate type is named *NoArgDelegate*. Figure 3.12 shows typical resulting *IL*. Once again we have assumed that the delegate reference is held in a static field of the class *ThisMod*.

```
  . . .
  <push reference to targetObj>                  // receiver for invocation
  ldftn    instance void Target::'Count'()
  newobj   instance void ThisMod.NoArgDelegate::.ctor
                               (object, unsigned native int)
  stsfld   class ThisMod.NoArgDelegate ThisMod::'x'
  . . .
```

Figure 3.12: Constructing a delegate value with an instance method

In this example, if the method *Count* had been a virtual method of the type of the target object, then the produced code would have needed to be slightly different. In that case, the *v-table* of the object is accessed at the time that the delegate is constructed. Figure 3.13 shows the variant code. Notice the "dup" instruction. We need to duplicate the object reference, since one copy is passed to the delegate constructor and one copy is used up by the "ldvirtftn" instruction.

```
    . . .
    <push reference to targetObj>                    // receiver for invocation
    dup
    ldvirtftn    instance void Target::'Count'()
    newobj   instance void ThisMod.NoArgDelegate::.ctor
                               (object, /unsigned native int/)
    stsfld   class ThisMod.NoArgDelegate ThisMod::'x'
    . . .
```

Figure 3.13: Constructing a delegate value with a virtual method

We have now seen how delegates are declared and instantiated. It remains only to see how they are invoked. In most languages a call to a function pointer or procedure variable has the same syntax as a function call, but with the variable designator expression replacing the name of the function. In *IL*, in order to invoke the encapsulated function, we need to make a virtual call to the *Invoke* function of the delegate. The pattern is —

```
    <push reference to delegate object>
    <push arguments to invocation>
    callvirt  instance retType DelegateClass::Invoke( <args>)
```

where *retType* is the return type of the encapsulated functions. For our second example, the instance of a *NoArgDelegate* held in a static field *x*, the *IL* would just be —

```
    ldsfld   class ThisMod.NoArgDelegate ThisMod::'x'
    callvirt instance void ThisMod.NoArgDelegate::Invoke()
```

Notice that the reference that we push is a reference to the delegate. There is no mention of the object receiving the encapsulated *Count* method. The receiver object is frozen inside the delegate at the time of instantiation.

Event types.   Event types are delegates with some additional semantics. The declaration of an event type in *IL* is identical to the declaration of an ordinary delegate type. Both extend *System.MulticastDelegate*. In the case of ordinary delegates some of the inherited functionality is not used. As before the internal structure is opaque.

The essential semantic difference between delegates and multicast delegates is that multicast delegates use the built-in support for *lists* of delegates. When the *Invoke* method of an event is called, *all* of the encapsulated methods on the list are invoked. The base class of delegates has methods for combining multicast delegates together, and for removing delegates from the list. When the *Invoke* procedure of a multicast delegate is activated, the delegates on the list are called in the order that they were linked. If the encapsulated methods are value-returning functions, the call of *Invoke* returns the return value of the last delegate to be called. The return values of all but the final delegate are discarded.

Under normal circumstances events are implemented by a *backing field* of the appropriate type. This field will be declared **private** to preserve its integrity, and will only be acessible via method calls in the *IL*. The reasoning is the same as for the private backing fields used for property implementation.

Compilers for languages that support this event-handling model define methods to register and deregister delegates on their multicast variable. These methods wrap the underlying methods of *System.MulticastDelegate* so as to expose simple *add* and *remove* procedures specific to each event member of a class. The wrappers take a single argument that is the new delegate to add or remove, and are hard-coded to link to their specific event backing field. Suppose that a class has a public member named "`reaction`" of some event type *BlahHandler*. The add and remove methods will be generated by the compiler, in addition to any methods of the class that are declared by the user. The skeleton code is shown in Figure 3.14. The *add_reaction* method adds a new delegate to the multicast delegate currently held in the private field *reaction*. It does so by calling the static *Combine* method of the *System.Delegate* class. The *remove_reaction* method is almost precisely the same, except that it calls the static *Remove* method of *System.Delegate*. It should be noted that these two methods are declared in *System.Delegate*, even though they may only be called on objects of classes that extend *System.MulticastDelegate*. It is possible to call *Combine* directly; indeed it is necessary to do so if linking to an event datum that is a local variable.[5] The public nature of the event in this example is embodied in the **public** declaration for the add and remove methods, while the backing field remains private. The two methods are declared to be **synchronized** since the linking and unlinking must be performed atomically. Remember that the common context in which event handling is required is one of multithreading.

The final few lines in Figure 3.14 show how information about the event is passed into the metainformation through `ilasm`. These lines declare the semantics of the add and remove methods for the metadata.

Interface types.
Interfaces are *fully abstract types*. Interfaces declare abstract methods and may possibly define static methods and fields. However, they cannot have instance fields or nonabstract instance methods. Classes may declare that they implement particular interfaces. If they do so, they enter into a contract to supply methods to implement

---

[5] Why? Well for languages without nested procedures there is no way that an "`add_*`" wrapper method could manipulate the local variable of another procedure.

```
.field private class BlahHandler 'reaction'   // the backing field
...                                            // any user methods
.method public specialname instance void add_reaction(
            class BlahHandler) il managed synchronized {
    ldarg.0                                    // destination ref
    ldarg.0
    ldfld    class BlahHandler ThisClass::'reaction'
    ldarg.1                                    // delegate to add
    call     class [mscorlib]System.Delegate
             [mscorlib]System.Delegate::Combine(
                        [mscorlib]System.Delegate,
                        [mscorlib]System.Delegate)
    castclass BlahHandler                      // cast to dest. type
    stfld    class BlahHandler ThisClass::'reaction'
    ret
}
...                                            // remove_reaction is similar
.event BlahHandler reaction {
    .addon instance void ThisClass::
                        add_reaction(class BlahHandler)
    .removeon instance void ThisClass::
                        remove_reaction(class BlahHandler)
}
```

Figure 3.14: Wrapping the linking and unlinking methods

all of the nonstatic methods declared in the interface. Abstract classes that implement interfaces may leave methods **abstract**, but concrete classes must define or inherit concrete implementations for all of the methods in the interface.

Variables that are declared to be of some interface type may be assigned values of any type that implements the interface. Unlike the case with class object types, it is not always possible to be able to guarantee correctness of such assigments at compile time. Consider the following scenario. Two variables have been declared as follows —

public A a;	// A is an interface type
public B b;	// B is a class object type
...	
a = (A) b;	// assign value in b to a

In the corresponding example with class types, on page 62, the compiler was able to statically check the relationship between the types *A* and *B*. In this case things are not so simple. If class *B* is statically known to implement interface *A*, then the assignment is known to be correct. This follows since, even if the exact type of *b* is a subtype of *B*, it will inherit the obligation to implement *A*. The problem occurs if *A* and *B* are apparently unrelated. In the class object case we could reject the code as certain to fail. However, in the case of interfaces, if class *B* is not sealed, then the exact type of *b* might be some subtype of *B*, validly implementing the interface *A*. Casts to interface types are thus seldom able to be rejected at compile time and mostly remain as runtime type checks in the *IL*.

Interfaces are not complete types in the sense defined earlier. If we know the exact type of an object, then we know about all of the accessible features, including fields and methods. On the other hand if we only know that an object implements a particular interface, then we have only partial knowledge. We may be sure that the object has a set of methods that may be invoked, but we do not have any static guarantee about any other features. In the *.NET* system we may find out about the other features using *runtime introspection* with the reflection *API*, but this does not help at compile time.

Interfaces are defined in *IL* with the same syntax as classes. However, the class definition must contain the **interface** attribute. Interfaces cannot declare that they inherit from any class but may declare that they implement any number of other interfaces. Of course, interfaces do not actually implement anything, since they cannot define instance methods. The effect of an interface *I* declaring that it implements a particular interface *J* is to ensure that any class implementing *I* transitively inherits the obligation to implement *J* as well.

An interface may only define fields that are static. Methods in an interface definition must be either **static**[6] or be **abstract public**. Figure 3.15 is a very simple example of an interface, expressed in *CIL*. In this case there is a single method. Presumably classes that implement this method will pass on the strings to some kind of voice synthesizer, so that the program can chatter on to the user. In practice such an interface would probably need some kind of class constructor to initialize the synthesizer engine, and so on.

```
.class public interface abstract Talkative {
    .method public virtual abstract void speak (string)
    {}
} // end of interface Talkative
```

Figure 3.15: A very simple interface example

Classes that contract to implement an interface have a number of ways to supply the required methods. Suppose that a class *A* declares that it implements an interface *I*, which contains a method *Foo*. Class *A* may —

- provide a so-called *"MethodImpl"* that declares that *Foo* is implemented by some named public method with a matching signature

[6]In fact if the class is to be *CLS* compliant, there can be no static methods other than the class constructor ".cctor".

- provide the definition of a public method named *Foo* with the required signature

- have a parent that implements *I* and defines a public method *Foo* with the right signature

- have a parent that that does not implement *I* but defines a public method *Foo* with the right signature anyway

- leave the slot empty if *A* is declared **abstract**

These rules are applied in order, in case several apply. If no rules apply, then it is a load-time exception.

It may be noted that the first rule gives a way of avoiding ambiguity if a class implements two interfaces and each defines an equally named method. In this case two methods may be defined with different names to implement the separate semantics of the two contracts. Separate *MethodImpls* are then used in the *IL* to associate each method with its contractual obligation.

Managed and unmanaged pointers.   So far we have discussed only references to objects. Such references are totally *opaque*. The only operations on such values are assignment to type-compatible locations, and their use to gain access as a handle to the referenced object. As well as object references, there are other some kinds of references. The other kinds of references are the *pointers*.

We have already discussed function pointers briefly in the previous chapter, on page 40. The three other kinds of pointers are —

- **managed pointers**. These are created by taking the address of an object field or a managed array element. They may point to the address one beyond the end of a managed array.

- **transient pointers**. These are created by taking the address of a datum, including local variables and parameters. Transient pointers can only exist on the evaluation stack. A location cannot be declared to be of this type.

- **unmanaged pointers**. These are the traditional pointers of languages such as *C*. They may be used to hold arbitrary addresses, but such use usually results in unverifiable code and may threaten memory safety. Pointer arithmetic is permitted on such values.

Local variables and parameters may be declared to be of a managed pointer type. In *IL* such a declaration is of the form *TypeName &*. Fields of objects, array elements, and static fields can never be declared to be of managed pointer type.

Unmanaged pointers may be declared anywhere that an integer may be declared. In fact, so far as the *CLR* is concerned, unmanaged pointers *are* just unsigned integers of an appropriate size. Nevertheless, it is good practice to declare such data as being bound to a particular type by using the *IL* declaration form *TypeName* *. Unmanaged pointers should never be allowed to point into the garbage-collected heap, as such use may compromise memory safety.

Perhaps the key pointer kind is the transient pointer, since all pointers that have values derived by use of the "ld*a" (load address) instructions start their lives as transient pointers. When a transient pointer is assigned to a managed pointer location, the value becomes a managed pointer. If it is assigned to an unmanaged pointer location, then the value becomes an unmanaged pointer. In particular, when a transient pointer on the stack is passed as an actual parameter to a method that expects a reference parameter, the value becomes a managed pointer.

Managed pointers may point either to the garbage-collected heap or elsewhere in memory. For example, the address of a class object field will clearly be in the heap, while the address of a local variable will be in the activation record of the current method. Managed pointers are reported to the garbage collector, so that the collector may find all references to the heap. The collector will be able to discover which pointer values are in the heap and which point elsewhere in memory.

Managed and unmanaged pointers may be combined with integers in certain ways. Integers may be either added or subtracted from pointers, returning a pointer of the same kind but almost certainly scoring a "fail" from the verifier. Pointers may be subtracted from each other, resulting in an integer. Here is an experiment to try. Compile the following legal but boring *Component Pascal* program with the "/nocode" flag. This will result in an *IL* file, but no executable.

```
MODULE Hack;
  IMPORT CPmain, Console;
  VAR arr = ARRAY 4 OF INTEGER;
BEGIN
  Console.WriteInt(arr[0], 1); Console.WriteLn;
END Hack.
```

Inside the *IL* file, the code to push the arguments of the call of *Console.WriteInt* will look like this —

```
ldsfld int32[] Hack.Hack::'arr'
ldc.i4.0
ldelem.i4          // push arr[0]
ldc.i4.1           // push 1, then call...
```

Now hack on the "Hack.il" file with your favorite editor, replacing the loading of the array element in the first three lines of the fragment with the following *IL* —

```
ldsfld int32[]  Hack.Hack::'arr'
ldc.i4.1
ldelema int32              // address of arr[1]
ldsfld int32[]  Hack.Hack::'arr'
ldc.i4.0
ldelema int32              // address of arr[0]
sub                        // subtract the pointers
```

Now assemble this file with ilasm, and run it. The program writes out 4, showing that the default integer type takes up four bytes. Maybe on future 64-bit machines this program will say 8 instead. If the stand-alone verifier is now run over the executable using "peverify /il Hack.exe", then the verifier will tell you exactly what it mistrusts about this program, and why.[7]

The Object Instruction Set

In the last chapter, we dealt with the base instructions of *IL*. In this section we shall look at the remainder of the instructions. These instructions implement the object model of the *CTS*. Since the base instruction set is complete, in principle all of the instructions of the object instruction set could be synthesized from sequences of instructions in the base set. However, keeping the instructions separate provides two benefits. First of all, the user does not need to know the details of object layout, which are abstracted away in the *CTS* model. Secondly, because the object instructions carry symbolic information with them, the task of verification of correct usage is made feasible.

Loading and Storing Data

We have already seen most of the instructions for manipulating fields and array elements. Figures 2.6 to 2.9 include all of these instructions. However, we collect them together here in Figure 3.16 for convenience. We have instructions to load and store instance fields, static fields, and array elements. In the case of instance fields a reference to the object is on the top of the stack, and the class that defines the field is specified in the instruction argument. The exact type[8] of the object must always be the specified class or an extension of the class. In the code generation chapters we refer to the reference to the object as the *object handle*.

It is an important detail that the class that is specified must be the class that *defines* the field. If the field is inherited from some supertype, then the class name of the supertype

---

[7]This process of writing a type-safe program and then modifying the *IL* is a useful experimental technique. The compiler produces all of the "boilerplate" code required, allowing short experimental code sequences to be substituted with minimal effort.

[8]The term *exact type* is used in much of the *CTS* documentation to mean the type of the precise class of which the object is an instance. This is to distinguish the cases in which a reference to the *type* of an object would mean "that type or any subtype of that type."

Data kind	Opcode	Comment
instance field	ldfld	Op-arg: *Type Class::field-name*
static field	ldsfld	Op-arg: *Type Class::field-name*
array element	ldelem.*	Suffix: specialized for element type
instance field	stfld	Op-arg: *Type Class::field-name*
static field	stsfld	Op-arg: *Type Class::field-name*
array element	stelem.*	Suffix: specialized for element type

Figure 3.16: Load and store instructions in object set

must qualify the reference. This is different to the *JVM*, which is happy to accept any qualifying class in which the particular field is visible.

In the case of static fields there is no reference on the stack, and the class that defines the field is specified in the instruction argument. Thus "ldfld" has a *stack-Δ* of 0, while "ldsfld" has a *stack-Δ* of 1. Static fields have an empty *object handle*, in our code generation jargon.

Array element loads and stores expect a reference to the array and an array index to be on the stack. In the code generation chapters we refer to this pair of values as the *array object handle*. In the case of element store instructions, the value to be stored is on top of the handle. Figure 3.17 represents the stack transitions for an array store.

Corresponding to the load instructions in Figure 3.16 we have instructions that load addresses of fields and elements. The value pushed on the stack is a transient pointer. These pointers may be dereferenced either for loading or storing with the load indirect, "ldind.*", and store indirect, "stind.*", instructions. Of course these instructions are also used to dereference pointers passed as reference parameters. All of these instructions are shown in Figure 3.18.

The load and store instructions that have a type suffix are "ldelem.*", "stelem.*", "ldind.*", and "stind.*". Usually these suffixes are the two-character type tags such as "i4". However, all of these instructions also have a form "*.ref", used for accessing references.

Figure 3.17: Storing an array element

Data kind	Opcode	Comment
static field	`ldsflda`	Op-arg: *Type Class::field-name*
instance field	`ldflda`	Op-arg: *Type Class::field-name*
array element	`ldelema`	Op-arg: *Array element typename*
pointer target	`ldind.*`	Suffix: specialized for target type
pointer target	`stind.*`	Suffix: specialized for target type

Figure 3.18: Load address, load and store indirect instructions in object set

Loading Type Descriptors

At runtime, types are described by instances of the *System.Type* class. Obtaining access to these objects is the mechanism on which all *program introspection* depends. Once we have the *System.Type* object, we are able to call the methods of the *System.Reflection* classes to ask about the type. The loading of *System.Type* objects onto the stack is therefore the key primitive operation.

Two contexts arise. We may know the name of the class and wish to push the corresponding *System.Type* object on the stack. This corresponds to the expression evaluation on the right-hand side of the *C#* assignment —

```
System.Type t = typeof(<type name>);
```

Alternatively, we may have an object reference, and wish to perform introspection on the dynamic type of the object. This case corresponds to the expression evaluation on the right-hand side of the *C#* assignment —

```
System.Type t = obj.GetType();
```

If we know the name of the type, we use the "`ldtoken`" instruction to fetch the corresponding *runtime type handle*. From this handle we may get the *System.Type* object by a call to the *GetTypeFromHandle* method of the *System.Type* class. The *IL* is shown at the top of Figure 3.19. If we have an object reference, then we must call the *GetType* method inherited from *System.Object*. The *IL* is shown at the bottom of Figure 3.19.

Using Types to Direct Control

For many people, the essence of object-oriented programming is that behavior may be specialized according to the *class* of an object. In principle this may be done two ways. We may have denotations for method calls for which the actual method that is invoked depends on the exact type of the *receiver object*. Alternatively, we may have type-test predicates that select the flow of control. In *.NET*, both mechanisms are supported.

```
// Get Type object for statically known type
    ldtoken  <type-name>                         // get runtime type handle
    call class System.Type
        System.Type::GetTypeFromHandle(    // get System.Type object
            value class System.RuntimeTypeHandle)
    ...

// Get Type object for object on stack
    <push object reference>
    call instance class System.Type
        System.Object::GetType()               // get System.Type object
    ...
```

Figure 3.19: Pushing a *System.Type* object on the stack

Type tests.   There are two type-test instructions in *CIL*. The first of these is "cast-class". This instruction is used for *type assertions*. A typical usage of this instruction looks like this —

```
<push object reference on the stack >
castclass    class [asm]MyClass        // assert type of object
...                                     // top of stack is MyClass
```

The type definition that appears in the instruction may be either the name of a class or the name of an interface type. If the cast fails, an *InvalidCastException* exception is thrown. If the cast succeeds, the value left on the stack is guaranteed either to be of the designated class (or one of its subclasses) or to implement the designated interface, as the case may be. The verifier understands the semantics of this instruction and will treat the top of stack value as the designated type downstream of the assertion. The *stack-*Δ for this instruction is 0.

Of course, it is often known statically that the cast will succeed. Typically an explicit cast is placed in the source code so that the compiler will allow selection of members of the asserted type or assignment to a location of a narrower type. The corresponding "castclass" instruction in the *IL* will keep the verifier happy, and also check that the programmer was telling the truth!

In should be noted that it is valid to perform a type assertion on a **null** value. In such cases the assertion always succeeds, leaving a **null** value on the top of the stack.

The other type-test instruction is the instance test "isinst". This instruction is similar to "castclass", to the extent that it takes an object reference on the top of stack and returns an object reference of the designated type. However, in this case, if the value cannot be cast to the designated type the instruction pushes **null** on the stack, rather than throwing an exception. Once again the verifier understands the semantics, so the returned value is treated as being of the designated type downstream of the test.

It may be noted that this test is rather different from all of the other predicates that *IL* supplies. The others all return a Boolean value—that is, a 0 or 1 of type *int32*. This instruction returns either a **null**, for **false**, or a non-**null** value of known type, for **true**. This does not cause a problem, since the "brfalse" and "brtrue" instructions branch on **null** and non-**null** as well as on 0 and 1.

This instruction may be used to implement type tests in a fairly obvious way. A more interesting use is for the *regional type guard* of *Component Pascal*. In this language, the form —

> **with** *ident* = *Type1* **do** . . .   (* *ident is known to be of Type1 here* *)
> | *ident* = *Type2* **do** . . .   (* *ident is known to be of Type2 here* *)
> **else** . . .
> **end**

uses the type of the variable to select the branch of the statement to execute. It performs selection in the same way that the corresponding ordinary **if** statement would do —

> **if** *ident* **is** *Type1* **then** . . .
> **elsif** *ident* **is** *Type2* **then** . . .
> **else** . . .
> **end**

However, there is one important difference. Within each branch of the **with**, the *guarded region* as it is called, the selected identifier is known to be of the designated type. Thus no further casting of the identifier is required within each guarded region. This is why the statement is called a *regional type guard*.

The "isinst" instruction allows an elegant implementation of this construct. Figure 3.20 gives the complete *IL* for the code fragment shown above. In this figure, the source code has been interspersed as comments, to mark the source position in the *IL*. Additional local variables have been declared, one for each of the type guards.

The implementation of the statement begins by pushing the selected identifier. The "isinst" test is applied to this value, and the result duplicated. One copy of the result is saved into the corresponding temporary, and the other copy is tested to see if it is **null**. If it is, control branches to the next test; otherwise the code of the guarded region is executed. Within each guarded region applied occurrences of the selected identifier are replaced by accesses to the appropriate temporary variable.

In theory, if the selected identifier was a local variable of a procedure, it would not be necessary to define the typed temporary variables. This is because the verifier is able to track the types of local variables within control flow such as this. The verifier does not or

```
    .locals(class Type1 t1, class Type2 t2)    // declare some temporaries
         ...
//    with ident = Type1 do
              <push ident on stack>
              isinst class [asm]Type1                // do first type test
              dup                                    // duplicate the result
              stloc.0                                // save one copy in t1
              brfalse    lb01                        // branch on null
              ...                        // first guarded region, use t1 for ident here
              br         lb03                        // branch to end
//    |  ident = Type2 do
    lb01: <push ident on stack>
              isinst class [asm]Type2                // do second type test
              dup                                    // duplicate the result
              stloc.1                                // save one copy in t2
              brfalse    lb02                        // branch on null
              ...                        // second guarded region, use t2 for ident here
              br         lb03                        // branch to end
//    else
    lb02  ...                            // else part code
//    end
    lb03: ...
```

Figure 3.20: *IL* code for **with** statement fragment

cannot track the types of other possible identifier kinds, such as arguments and static fields, so for generality the construct must be implemented with a temporary variable as shown.

Virtual methods. Virtual methods provide a way of attaching different behavior to each type in a type hierarchy. As noted earlier, instances of object types are self-describing. You may think of the self-description as being implemented by a hidden field of every object that points to a shared *runtime type descriptor*. Every object of the same type will reference the same descriptor and will contain all of the information that is the same for all instances. Among other things the runtime type descriptor must have the hook that allows runtime introspection on the type. It must also contain any information that the garbage collector needs to safely collect objects of the type.

However, from the point of view of mediating behavior, the most important information in the runtime type descriptor is the *virtual method dispatch table*, or *v-table* for short. The *v-table* consists of an indexed array of *slots*, each of which contains a method pointer. Each slot of the *v-table* is associated with a particular method name and signature. In order to invoke a virtual method, the method name and signature are resolved (possibly at compile time) to a *v-table* slot index. At runtime the *VES* takes the reference to the **this** and follows the hidden reference to the *v-table*. The *VES* pulls out the method pointer in the chosen slot of the *v-table* and invokes that method.

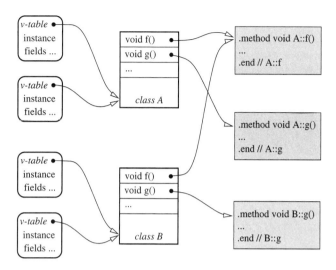

Figure 3.21: Objects with methods f() and g()

Consider Figure 3.21, which shows four objects, two each of two related types, *A* and *B*. Each object contains the instance data for that particular object and a reference, called *v-table* in the figure, that references the runtime type descriptor for that particular object. Each runtime descriptor has a *v-table* with just two methods, called *f* and *g*, shown in the figure. The *v-table* for class *A* selects A::f() and A::g() to implement the two behaviors. For class *B*, for behavior *f*, the *v-table* selects the same method A::f(), as did class *A*. For behavior *g*, the *v-table* of class *B* selects its own method, B::g(). Presumably *B* is a subtype of *A* and has inherited the *f* behavior unchanged, but has overridden the *g* behavior.

Calling virtual methods. Virtual methods are declared *virtual* in the *IL* and must obey a number of other rules that are discussed later. They are invoked by first pushing the receiver onto the evaluation stack. The actual parameters, if there are any, are pushed next in order. The method is then invoked, using the "callvirt" instruction.

In the case of a virtual call the *stack-Δ* is "*number of return values – number of ingoing values*". The ingoing number is the number of arguments plus one extra to account for the receiver "argument". As noted earlier, inside the method the **this** will always be arg-0.

The operation argument to "callvirt" has the same general structure as a call to a static or (nonvirtual) instance method. Typical examples of the three cases are —

call void [RTS]Console::'WriteInt'(**int32,int32**)   // *static call, stack-Δ = –2*
call instance float64 [LitValue]LitValue.value::'real'()   // *instance call, stack-Δ = 0*
callvirt instance int32 [Symbols]Symbols.Idnt::'parMode'()   // *virtual call, stack-Δ = 0*

In the case of an instance call, the name of the method in the instruction argument is exactly the name of the method that will be invoked. In the case of a virtual call the name in the instruction argument is the name of the method qualified by the static type of the reference. Of course, the exact type of the reference that will become the receiver may be a subtype of the static type. In this case, the actual method that is invoked will be whatever method is in the corresponding slot of the *v-table* of the exact type.

The "`callvirt`" instruction is also used for invoking interface methods. In such cases the name of the method in the instruction argument will be qualified by the name of the interface "class."

Virtual methods in *.NET* do not have to be invoked with "`callvirt`". It is legal to call such a method using the static call instruction, "`call`". If this is done, there is no dispatch via the *v-table*. Instead, the exact named method will be invoked. This particular ability is useful under at least two circumstances. First, if the compiler is able to statically know the exact type of a reference, then the use of the static call instruction will save time, since it is more efficient in most implementations. Secondly, if a method needs to call the virtual method that it overrides—that is, a method wants to make a **super** call, then it must use the static call instruction.

Creating Objects

There are two instructions that are used for creating new objects. These are "`newarr`", which creates a new one-dimensional array, and "`newobj`", which does everything else.

One-dimensional arrays are created by the "`newarr`" instruction. This instruction takes a type as instruction argument and expects a length value, of unsigned type, on the top of the stack. The instruction returns a reference to the new array on the top of the stack. The array will index from zero and will be initialized to zeros of the appropriate type.

The type appearing as the argument to the instruction may be a built-in type, such as *int32* or *wchar*, or it may be any other type, including value types. Figure 3.22 is the *IL* to create the array of arrays structure of Figure 3.6. The code begins by allocating the reference array of eight elements. The instruction argument to the call of "`newarr`" is **array of int**, so the array that is created has type **array of array of int**. All of the elements of this one-dimensional array will be initially **null**. This is the object on the left of Figure 3.6.

The code now executes the **for** loop that allocates the eight one-dimensional arrays with element type **int**. The body of the loop pushes the array reference and the element index, then allocates the sub-array with another "`newarr`" instruction. In this case the array is an **array of int**. The new element is assigned to the array by the "`stelem.ref`" instruction.

The code ends by incrementing the loop counter and testing the continuation condition for the loop. If the continuation condition is met, control jumps back to the loop label "`lb01`".

```
// int [] []   bar = new int [8] [] ;
// for (int i = 0; i < 8; i++) bar [i] = new int [4] ;

        ldc.i4.8                    // push array length
        newarr int []               // an array of int[]
        stsfld int [] [] A.'bar'    // store the reference array
        ldc.i4.0                    // start the for loop
        stloc 'i'                   // initialize i to begin
lb01:                               // the loop header label
        ldsfld int [] [] A.'bar'    // load the reference array
        ldloc 'i'                   // load the array index
        ldc.i4.4                    // push array length
        newarr int                  // an array of 4 ints
        stelem.ref                  // store int[] elem in int[][] array

        ldloc 'i'                   // fetch loop counter
        ldc.i4.1                    // push a literal one value
        add                         // add to the counter value
        dup                         // duplicate the new value
        stloc 'i'                   // save the updated counter
        ldc.i4.8                    // push a literal eight value
        blt lb01                    // test for end, or goto loop
```

Figure 3.22: *IL* to create array of arrays structure

The other object creation instruction, "newobj", performs two functions. First, it allocates space for the new object, and then it invokes the object constructor that is designated by the intstruction argument. A typical use of this instruction is —

ldstr "Assertion failure at Symbols.cp:315"
newobj instance void [mscorlib] System.Exception::.ctor(**string**)

In this example the argument to the constructor is pushed on the stack before the "newobj" instruction. The constructor is an instance method, but the receiver for the call is created by the first phase of execution of the instruction. This example creates an exception object, with an optional information string. The next instruction is almost certainly going to be "throw", as we shall see in the "Exception Handling" section (see page 95).

Instructions for Value Types

There are a number of instructions that handle value types in managed code. These instructions initialize objects, load and store value objects on the evaluation stack, and copy the fields of a value object. There are also instructions to box and unbox value objects. In order to see how value classes are copied and passed as various kinds of parameter, we shall look at some typical uses.

Initializing and copying value objects.

Data aggregates, such as arrays and classes, may declare that they have fields of value class types, and local variables of such types may be declared. In each case the space for the object is allocated when the encapsulating object or activation record is allocated. However, we may need to initialize or reinitialize the value of such value data. The "initobj" instruction does this. It expects the address of the value object on the stack, and initializes the bound object. A typical idiom for initializing a local variable of value class type would be —

```
.locals (value class [asm]Nsp.T 'vct')
   . . .
   ldloca 'vct'
   initobj value class [asm]Nsp.T
```

The "ldloca" instruction pushes the address of the local variable onto the stack. The value is a transient pointer. There is also an instruction for copying the contents of value objects, "cpobj". This instruction may be used for assigment of entire values, although as we shall see in the following example, most compilers use a "ldobj stobj" sequence instead.

Loading and storing.

The "ldobj" and "stobj" instructions load and store value objects from the evaluation stack. It should be remembered that in *.NET* an abstract stack value may be a complete value object. The "ldobj" instruction expects an address on the stack, while the "stobj" instruction expects the value to be stored on the top of the stack with the destination address immediately below that.

An example shows most of the variations of loading and storing value classes. One such example is the short *C#* program in Figure 3.23. This program declares a **struct** named *ValCls*, which will be implemented as a value class. The class has two static methods, each with two formal parameters of the value class type. One method, *ValRef*, has a first parameter that is passed by value, and a second parameter passed by reference. The other method, *RefOut*, has a first parameter that is passed by reference, and a second that is also passed by reference, but marked with the **out**[9] attribute. Both methods simply copy the value of their first parameter to the second.

The program defines a second class with an entry point. The *Main* method calls the two instance methods, so that we may see how value class objects are passed as value and reference parameters.

The *Params* class declares two objects of value class type. These two objects, unlike the case with reference class objects, do not require any explicit initialization. If these two

---

[9]In *C#* an **out** formal parameter is a reference parameter with special behavior. The marker indicates that the parameter only carries information out of the method. This allows optimization of the call in situations that require marshalling.

```
public struct ValCls {
    public int i;
    public int j;
    public static void ValRef(ValCls inV, ref ValCls outV) {
        outV = inV;
    }
    public static void RefOut(ref ValCls inV, out ValCls outV) {
        outV = inV;
    }
}

public class Params {
    ValCls a;                                  // no new needed for value class
    ValCls b;                                  // no new needed for value class
    public static void Main() {                       // program entry point
        ValCls.ValRef(a, ref b);
        ValCls.RefOut(ref a, out b);
    }
}
```

Figure 3.23: Manipulating value objects in *C#*

variables had been declared as local variables of the *Main* method, then we would have had to initialize them explicitly with a call of **new**. Any such initialization calls will appear in the *IL* as inline occurrences of the "initobj" instruction.

The disassembly of the class with the entry point is shown in Figure 3.24. Here it may be seen that the first call, to the static method *ValRef*, passes its first parameter by value and its second by reference. The first actual parameter, *a*, is pushed onto the evaluation stack by a "ldsfld" (load static field) instruction. This is a value rather than a reference copy. The second actual parameter, *b*, is passed by reference, by having its address pushed by the "ldsflda" (load static field address) instruction.

The second call, to the static method *RefOut*, passes both of its parameters by reference. In both cases the addresses are pushed by the "ldsflda" instruction. Note that the same instruction is used to push the address of both ordinary reference (**inout**) and **out**-mode parameters.

The implementation of the value class is shown in Figure 3.25. In this figure we may see that for the method *ValRef* the reference parameter, marked **ref** in *C#*, is marked with an ampersand & in the *IL*. In the method *RefOut* both of the formal parameters are marked as reference, but the second parameter is also marked with the **out** attribute.

In order to assign a value of value class type, we always begin by pushing the address of the destination object. In the first method we do this by pushing the second parameter,

```
.class public auto ansi Params extends object
{
  .field private static value class ValCls a
  .field private static value class ValCls b
  .method public static void Main() il managed
  {
    .entrypoint
    ldsfld      value class ValCls Params::a
    ldsflda     value class ValCls Params::b
    call        void ValCls::ValRef(value class ValCls,
                                    value class ValCls&)
    ldsflda     value class ValCls Params::a
    ldsflda     value class ValCls Params::b
    call        void ValCls::RefOut(value class ValCls&,
                                    value class ValCls&)
    ret
  } // end of method Params::Main
} // end of class Params
```

Figure 3.24: Passing value objects as parameters

which is a transient pointer to the destination actual parameter. Since the first formal parameter is a copy of the actual value object, the "ldarg.0" instruction pushes the value. The assignment is then performed by a "stobj" instruction.

In the second method, as before, we begin by pushing the destination address, which is held in the second parameter. In this case however the first formal parameter is not the source value, but is a pointer to the source. We therefore push the address, using a "ldarg.0" instruction, but we must then use a "ldobj" instruction to push the bound object value. As in the first case, the value is assigned by a "stobj" instruction.

It might be noted that, throughout this example, the unqualified name of the class may be used, as it is local to the same assembly.

Boxing and unboxing.

Boxing and unboxing.   Although we are able to create pointers to data of value types, these are not object references and are not self-describing. In order to be able to call virtual methods on value types, we must *box* the type. When we want to retrieve the value, we must then *unbox* the object. These are built-in primitives of the execution engine.

The instruction "box" takes a pointer to a value type and returns a reference to an object with a copy of the value instance embedded in it. The instruction takes an operator argument of the name of a value type. The object is treated by the verifier as being of type *System.Object*. The original pointer may point into the garbage-collected heap, if the value instance is a field of an object, or may be a local variable or argument, or even a static

```
.class value public auto ansi sealed ValCls
       extends [mscorlib]System.ValueType
{
  .field public int32 i
  .field public int32 j
  .method public static void
          ValRef(value class ValCls inV,
                 value class ValCls& outV) il managed {
     ldarg.1                       // push destination address
     ldarg.0                       // push incoming value
     stobj       ValCls            // store at destination address
     ret
  } // end of method ValCls::ValRef

  .method public static void
          RefOut(value class ValCls& inV,
          [out] value class ValCls& outV) il managed {
     ldarg.1                       // push destination address
     ldarg.0                       // push source value address
     ldobj       ValCls            // fetch source value
     stobj       ValCls            // store at destination address
     ret
  } // end of method ValCls::RefOut
} // end of class ValCls
```

Figure 3.25: Making copies of value class parameters

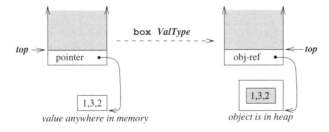

Figure 3.26: Evaluation stack before and after executing *box*

field of a class. The boxed object will certainly be in the heap. Figure 3.26 shows the relationship between the stack before and after execution of the instruction. In the figure it has been assumed that the value type is a value class that encapsulates three integers.

The "unbox" instruction takes a reference to a boxed value object and returns a managed pointer to the embedded value. The value is not copied and is still in the heap. Since

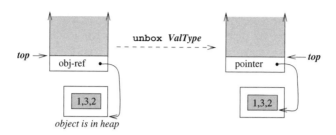

Figure 3.27: Evaluation stack before and after executing *unbox*

the garbage collector is aware of all managed pointers, this poses no problem. Figure 3.27 shows the relationship between the stack before and after execution of the instruction. In the next chapter, we shall examine an alternative strategy to this built-in facility, in which compiler-defined, named box classes are created for value classes.

Typed references.   There are a small number of instructions that are used for manipulating typed references. You will recall from the discussion of Figure 3.2 that typed references are opaque aggregates for attaching type information to references. These facilities are used for dealing with dynamically typed data.

Typed references are created by pushing a pointer to the data and executing the "mkrefany" instruction. The pointer may be either managed or unmanaged. The instruction has the type name as a operation argument. The result is a typed reference on the stack. This instruction is not verifiable if the verifier cannot prove that the pointer actually points to data of the nominated type.

The two components of a typed reference are a type token and the address of the data. These may be retrieved by the "refanytype" instruction, which returns the type token, and "refanyval", which returns the pointer contents as a managed pointer. Both of these require the typed reference on the stack. In the case of "refanytype" the instruction has no operator argument; "refanyval" must nominate the type expected.

Defining Methods

Methods contain the executable code of a program and are the callable units of *CIL*. All such callable units are called "methods" in *IL*, whether they are static or dispatched procedures, and whether they are value returning functions or proper procedures. There are four different kinds of method declarations that are used in *IL*. These are *method declarations*, *method definitions*, *method references*, and *method implementations*.

The syntax for method declarations is —

MethodDecl   →   **.method** MethodHead "{" { MethodBodyItem } "}"
MethodHead   →   { MethodAttr } [CallConv] TypeRef *DottedName*
                              '('[Parameter { ',' Parameter }] ')' { ImplAttr } .

The method body items are the instructions and any directives associated with the implementation of the method body. The return type of the method together with the list of types of the parameters form the *signature* of the method.

Method declarations have a method head, but have no method body items. These are used for declaring the name and signature of a method so it may be used at a call-site. Method declarations are also used to declare abstract methods.

Method definitions are the main interest of this section. These define the name and signature of a method, and also give the body items that define the operational behavior of the method at runtime.

Method references are references to methods whose definition lies in another module or assembly. These are resolved to some concrete method at runtime.

A method implementation or *MethodImpl* associates a particular method body with some method declaration. In particular, a *MethodImpl* may be used to specify that a particular method should be used to implement a specified abstract method in the implementation of some interface type.

The method heading, as shown in the syntax, consists of method attributes, optional call convention markers, a return type, the method name, a parenthesized parameter list, and implementation attributes.

Method Attributes

There are many different method attributes that are predefined. These include all of the accessibility attributes that are used for fields, repeated here in Figure 3.28. The various accessibility attributes have the same meaning and effect as when used on field declarations.

Attribute	Effect
assembly	This method is only accessible within this assembly.
family	This method is only accessible in this class and in subclasses of this class.
famandassem	This method is accessible in this class and its subclasses but only within this assembly.
famorassem	This method is accessible in this class, its subclasses, and throughout this assembly.
private	This method is only accessible within this class.
privatescope	This method is only accessible within the assembly, and then only by using the method definition token.
public	This method is publicly accessible.

Figure 3.28: Method declaration accessibility attributes

Attribute	Effect
abstract	This method is abstract and must be declared abstract.
virtual	This method is virtual.
static	This method is static, and does not have a receiver
final	This method cannot be overridden in subclasses.
hidebysig	Hide by signature.
newslot	This method does not override any other method.
specialname	The name has special significance to tools.
rtspecialname	The name has significance to the runtime.

Figure 3.29: Further method attributes

Other attributes apply just to methods. These specify the form of the method, whether static or virtual, and so on. They also give some additional information that may be used by the compiler for checking for correctness. These additional attributes are shown in Figure 3.29. Methods may be exactly one of *static*, *instance*, or *virtual*. Static methods do not have a **this** pointer. They are associated with a particular class, rather than an **instance** of a class. Plain (that is nonvirtual) instance methods are associated with an object instance that becomes the **this** pointer of the call. However, the particular method that is invoked is determined statically from the name and signature of the call. Virtual methods are associated with an object instance that becomes the **this** pointer of the call. However, unlike instance methods, the particular method that is invoked by the call is determined from the *v-table* attached to the **this** pointer. As noted, methods that are declared to be virtual may be called either through the *v-table* or statically.

If a method is declared to be abstract, then it must also be declared virtual. Such a method heading can only be part of a method *declaration*, rather than a complete method definition. We may declare that a virtual method is *final*. In this case the method cannot be overridden in any subclasses of the present class. This is a useful annotation, since it often allows the compiler to optimize calls to such methods. This marker is also used in cases where the overriding of a particular method might lead to the breaking of invariants in the present class. The *hidebysig* attribute specifies that methods only obscure inherited methods of the same name if the signatures match. This attribute is the default and is ignored by the runtime. Finally, the *newslot* attribute declares that this method does not override an equally named inherited method.

Call Conventions

The call convention of the method header specifies how the method is to be invoked. The most common of these are shown in Figure 3.30. It is not strictly necessary to specify the *instance* marker in method definitions, since it may be deduced from the other attributes. However, it is always necessary in method references at call sites, since the method attributes are absent in that location.

Attribute	Effect
instance	This method has a **this** pointer.
explicit	Only used directly following **instance**, the **this** appears explicitly in the parameter list.
varargs	This method uses the varargs convention.
others	Various native call convention markers.

Figure 3.30: Various call convention attributes

Implementation Attributes

Implementation attributes follow the parameter list of the method declaration. Most commonly the attributes are just *il managed*, but there are several other possibilities. The most likely attributes are shown in Figure 3.31. The *il managed synchronized* combination has been seen in connection with the "`add_*`" and "`remove_*`" methods of events, which necessarily contain critical sections. The constructor and *Invoke* methods of delegates provide examples of the *runtime-managed* combination.

Attribute	Effect
il	This method body is specified by *IL*.
runtime	The method body is supplied by the runtime.
native	The method body is native code.
managed	This method is managed.
unmanaged	This method is unmanaged.
synchronized	This method must be executed in a single thread, and should block other callers.

Figure 3.31: Various method implementation attributes

Signatures

The signature of a method consists of the return type (or **void** in the case of a proper procedure) and the ordered list of parameter types and modes. Each element of the parameter list has optional modes and an optional identifier.

$$\begin{aligned} \text{Parameter} &\rightarrow \text{[ParamAttributes] Type } [\mathit{identifier}]\,. \\ \text{ParamAttributes} &\rightarrow \text{'[in]'} \mid \text{'[out]'} \mid \text{'[opt]'}\,. \end{aligned}$$

The **in** and **out** attributes may only be used with parameters of reference type and do not form part of the signature so far as matching is concerned. They are hints to the compiler so that efficient marshalling may be attempted in cases of remote calling. The optional name is simply a convenience in textual *IL*; `ilasm` will map such occurrences of names to the ordinal numbers used in the *PEM*.

The **opt** attribute indicates that the parameter is optional from the point of view of the source language. The *CLR* will still expect to receive a value, but that value may be supplied by a tool rather than by code in the source program.

The types that appear in parameter lists indicate whether the corresponding parameter is passed by value or by reference. Reference parameters that are managed pointers have the type followed by the ampersand character "&". The type itself consists of a type reference followed by zero or more array markers "[]".

Method Pointers

Method pointers may be created by the "`ldftn`" and "`ldvirtftn`" instructions. Some uses of the "`ldftn`" instruction were discussed on page 40 in the previous chapter.

Locations intended to hold function pointers may be declared bound to functions with a specified signature. Uses of such data are seldom verifiable. Function pointer values are scalar types, holding just an address, possibly the entry point of the method. For languages that allow nested procedure declarations, such pointers are inadequate, since they are not associated with the activation of an enclosing method.

The "`ldvirtftn`" instruction takes a reference to an object on the top of the stack and returns a pointer to the virtual function bound to the exact type of the object. The operator argument is the same as for a virtual call of the same method. Thus the code sequence —

```
<push receiver>
<push args>
<push receiver>
ldvirtftn    returnType MethClass::methName(<arg type list>)
calli    returnType(<arg type list>)
```

calls exactly the same method as —

```
<push receiver>
<push args>
callvirt    returnType MethClass::methName(<arg type list>)
```

Of course, the point of creating a function pointer is to store it in some location or pass it as a parameter to some call. If the function pointer in the above example was to be stored in a local variable, the location could be declared with the location signature —

```
.locals(... ,
        method returnType*(<arg type list>) 'mpnm',
        ...  )
```

Note the use of the abstract declarator format. The signature of the concrete method is copied, but with the qualified name of the method replaced by the star character '*'.

Overriding and Overloading

Whenever a new method is introduced it is necessary to consider the effect of the new declaration on the accessibility of any other equally named method. There are two separate mechanisms at work: *overriding* and *overloading*.

Overriding.   In the object model of the *CTS* virtual methods are inherited from the supertype of each class. Suppose that we wish to dispatch a virtual method with a particular name and signature on some particular receiver object. Let us further suppose that several of the ancestor types of the exact type of the receiver object define a matching procedure. The dispatch mechanisms of the *CLR* will ensure that the matching method from the exact type will be invoked, or if there is no such method, the matching method from the closest ancestor will be invoked. This does not mean to say that some kind of search is performed at runtime. At class load time the values in the *v-table*s are organized in such a way that the effect of the lookup algorithm is obtained by a simple lookup in the *v-table* of the receiver object.

The summary effect of the resolution algorithm is that whenever a new virtual method is defined it hides any equally named method with the same signature. This *overriding* behavior is one of the pillars of object-oriented programming.

Note that this particular behavior is specific to the dispatch of virtual methods. If methods are simply (nonvirtual) instance methods, or are invoked by the "call" rather than the "callvirt" instruction, then the hiding does not occur. To be specific, consider a class *SubC* that extends a class *SuperC*, where both classes declare a virtual no-arg void method *Foo*. Let us suppose that that we have a reference that is statically of type *SuperC*. The *IL* instruction —

```
callvirt instance void ThisNameSpace.SuperC::'Foo'()
```

will invoke either *SuperC::Foo* or *SubC::Foo* depending on whether the exact type of the reference is *SuperC* or *SubC*, respectively. However the two instructions —

```
call instance void ThisNameSpace.SuperC::'Foo'()
call instance void ThisNameSpace.SubC::'Foo'()
```

will call precisely the named methods without regard to the exact type of the reference.

So far as the *CTS* is concerned, any definition of a matching method in a subclass replaces the inherited method in the corresponding slot of the virtual method table of the subclass. Such a definition does not make the inherited method inaccessible for statically bound invocations. Whether or not any particular source language has some syntax for exploiting this capability of the *CTS* is another matter entirely.

It is important to recognize that overriding occurs based on the entire name and signature of the method. If two methods are defined that have the same name and parameter list, but differ in return value, then they will occupy separate slots in the *v-table*. Both *C#* and *Java* would reject programs which try to do this, although it is a common feature of languages that permit *return type covariance*. In a later chapter we shall explore ways of programming around this restriction in the *CTS*.

Overloading.   If two methods of a class have the same name but different signatures, then the method name is said to be *overloaded*. Some people believe that overloading is inherently evil and prefer languages that outlaw the practice. Others argue that overloading is convenient and unharmful. Still others take the middle ground and believe that overloading is admissible for constructor methods but nowhere else. This is another deeply religious issue. However, the plain truth is that many widely used languages require overloading, and hence overloading must be efficiently supported by the *CLR*.

In principle, it is the job of the compiler to resolve any applied occurrence of a method name to one exact name-and-signature combination. This may be a nontrival exercise in the presence of implicit type coercions, and the rules vary from language to language.[10]

Both *C#* and *Java* allow overloading but only on the number and type of the parameters. Overloading on the basis of the return type of the method is not allowed in either of these languages, even though the *CTS* is able to support this. *Component Pascal* does not permit overloading but curiously does permit covariance of return type for overridden methods.

So far as the *CLR* is concerned, methods are matched on the basis of the complete name-and-signature. The possibility of having different methods for which the simple name is overloaded follows directly.

A more interesting question is whether standard libraries ought to define methods that require users to resolve overloaded simple names. Certainly the *.NET* answer to this question is "yes," with the standard class libraries having many sets of overloaded methods. This particular choice poses difficult questions for users of the libraries that code in languages that do not support overloading. Some attempts to answer these questions are discussed in Chapter 10.

---

[10] And, in the case of *Java*, between preliminary and final definition of the same language.

Method Bodies

The method body is a sequence of method body items. These include instructions, labels, and various directives. Most of these will be dealt with in other sections of this book. Figure 3.32 is a summary of the most common method body items. The *.entrypoint* directive states that this method is the entry point of the application. Only one such method may be so marked in the whole assembly. In a *C#* program the method would be named *Main*.

A *.locals* declaration introduces one or more local variables. The syntax is —

LocalDecl → **.locals** '(' LocalSignature { ',' LocalSignature } ')' .

A complete discussion of the syntax and options for local variable declaration is given on page 219. In the same section there is a discussion of how the maximum stack height may be computed. It is fortunate that both the maximum stack declaration and the locals declaration may be placed anywhere within the method body. *gpcp* computes the maximum stack height during emission of instructions to the *IL* and declares additional temporary local variables during the code emission process. For compilers that write out their code this way, the values are not known until emission is complete for a particular method.

Body Item	Description
.entrypoint	This method is the application entry point.
.locals	Declares local variables for this method.
.maxstack	Specifies the maximum stack height.
.line	Specifies a source line number.
instruction	An *IL* instruction.
label	A code label in the *IL*.

Figure 3.32: Various method body items

Exception Handling

The *CLR* provides facilities for many different structured exception-handling models. With the present exception of what have been called *resumption models*, the *CLR* supports the implementation of exception handling in most languages. This support comprises two parts. First, there are instructions and directives in *CIL* for the primitive operations of throwing and catching exceptions. Secondly, there is a base type in the *CTS* from which all exceptions classes should directly or indirectly derive.

In this context we use the word *exception* to mean any abnormal execution state. Entry into the abnormal state may have been requested by program code or by a check performed by the *VES*. Some languages allow source programs to explicitly raise exceptions using some dedicated syntactic construct. Other languages require that the compiler test certain assertions and explicitly raise an exception in the event that the test fails. For example, in most *Pascal*-family languages it is an error if a **case** statement does not select any case, and the statement does not have an **else** clause. In both of these cases the *IL* of the program will have an explicit use of the "throw" instruction. The *VES* responds to a very large number of program errors by raising an exception of some type or another. Failure of class casts, indexing out of bounds on arrays, attempting to divide by zero, or attempting to load an assembly that cannot be found are just some of these.

Whenever a thread of control is in an exceptional state, there is an object called *the exception object* that plays a special role. In the case of explicit executions of "throw", the exception object is explicitly constructed by a call of "newobj" with an appropriate constructor method. A typical idiom would be —

```
        brtrue lb01                                        // skip if assertion is true
        ldstr "Assertion failure at Symbols.cp:315"
        newobj instance void [mscorlib]System.Exception::.ctor(string)
        throw
    lb01:
```

The Basics

The underlying basis of the exception-handling model of *CIL* is a **try ... catch ... finally** structure, with semantics similar to those of *C#* or *Java*. Instructions that appear within a **try** block are said to be in a *protected block*. If any exception is raised in this code, or an unhandled exception is raised in code called by the code of the protected block, then execution of the protected block is stopped, and the *VES* searches for a *handler*. Before any handling action is taken, any **finally** code associated with the protected block is executed.

The *VES* checks the scope of the declared handlers within the current method, to see if the protected block to which they apply covers the instruction that raised the exception. If such a handler is found, then that handler is selected; otherwise the search continues in the calling method.

Handlers may be filtered or unfiltered. An unfiltered handler accepts any exception that is raised, and control enters the code of the handler with the exception object being the sole object on the evaluation stack. The code of the handler must pop this reference before it calls "leave".

There are two kinds of filtered handler. The most used kind is declared to accept some particular class of exception object. When such a handler is selected the *VES* performs a type check on the current exception to see if it is the nominated type, or a subtype of that type. If that is the case, the code of the handler is entered, with the exception object on the evaluation stack so that the code may do further tests on the object.

It is also possible for a program to declare explicit tests on the exception object with code in a **filter** block. The code of this block finishes by pushing a Boolean on the stack to indicate whether the handler block should be entered. In the event that a filtered handler declines to handle an exception, the search for a handler resumes as before.

Programs may also define **finally** blocks. These blocks are guaranteed to always be executed after completion of the **try** block, even if the execution terminated abnormally. These are typically used to ensure that resources are reclaimed before execution is abandoned.

There are three different formats that may be used to define the various regions of a structured exception handler. At runtime the exception handling regions are defined by tables associated with each method. These tables denote the limits of the various regions in terms of their offsets from the method entry point. This is the way in which exception handling appears in the disassembler output. It is also possible to define the regions in terms of labels, rather than offsets. Finally, it is possible to write *CIL* in a structured way, with keywords and braces delimiting the scope of the various blocks. This is the only approach that we will use in the examples here.

Defining the Blocks

A grammar of structured exception-handling block (*SehBlock*) in *IL*, for the structured format that we consider, is as follows —

SehBlock	→	TryBlock SehClause { SehClause } .
TryBlock	→	**.try** "{" *instructionSequence* "}" .
SehClause	→	**catch** typeRef "{" *instructionSequence* "}"
	|	**filter** *label* "{" *instructionSequence* "}"
	|	**finally** "{" *instructionSequence* "}"
	|	**fault** "{" *instructionSequence* "}" .

Such a structured exception handler block may occur within any instruction sequence, leading to nested exception-handling regions. We shall deal with each of these types of handler clauses in order.

The .try block.   A try block is a sequence of instructions enclosed within braces, following the keyword **.try**. Control may only exit from a try block by an exception being thrown or by the special instruction "leave". In particular, it is not possible to branch either into or out of a try block, and it is not possible to return out of a try block by a "ret" instruction.[11]

The "leave" instruction takes a label as instruction argument. The label is the destination to which control transfers, possibly after a **finally** block is executed. The evaluation

---

[11] Of course, it is quite possible to write a *C#* program that "returns" out of a try block. If you check the resulting *IL* however, you will find that the return has been translated into a "leave" instruction that jumps to a "ret" outside of the block.

stack must be empty when the "leave" is executed. This means that value-returning functions may need to store their return values in a local variable. Figure 3.33 shows a typical idiom, for a function returning a Boolean value.

```
.locals(bool 'retVal')          // local to hold return value
    . . .
.try {
        . . .
        <compute return value on stack>
        stloc 'retVal'          // save result value in local
        leave lb01              // jump to label lb01
} catch [mscorlib]System.Exception {
        . . .
}
lb01:
        ldloc 'retVal'          // fetch the function result
        ret                     // now return the function result
```

Figure 3.33: Returning a value from inside a **try** block

The catch block.

In most languages, the **catch** block is the mechanism for handling exceptions. The definition of a catch block nominates the type that the handler is able to handle.

$$SehClause \quad \rightarrow \quad ...$$
$$| \quad \textbf{catch } typeRef \text{``\{'' } instructionSequence \text{``}\}\text{''}.$$

The *VES* will perform filtering on the exception objects to ensure that the block is entered only with objects of the nominated type.

Control enters the catch block with the exception object on an otherwise empty evaluation stack. The code of the block is responsible for ensuring that this object is popped from the stack before control exits the block. As with a **try** block, control may only leave a catch block by raising another exception or by executing "leave".

Here are two examples of using the catch block to achieve similar semantics, but originating from differing styles of encoding in the source language. In *C#*, a handler that performs different recovery actions based on the type of the exception object would be encoded with multiple **catch** clauses, as shown in Figure 3.34.

In *IL*, the multiple catch clauses map directly into separate type-filtered catch clauses. Figure 3.35 shows the structure. Notice that each catch block must finish with a "leave" instruction. The exception object on the stack at the entry to each catch block must be popped within the block.

```
try {
    . . .                     // body of try block
} catch (TypeA x) {
    . . .                     // x is known to have type TypeA
} catch (TypeB x) {
    . . .                     // x is known to have type TypeB
} catch (TypeC x) {
    . . .                     // x is known to have type TypeC
}
```

Figure 3.34: try with multiple **catch**es in *C#*

```
.try {
    . . .                     // body of try block
    leave exitLb
} catch TypeA {
    . . .                     // x is known to have type TypeA
    leave exitLb
} catch TypeB {
    . . .                     // x is known to have type TypeB
    leave exitLb
} catch TypeC {
    . . .                     // x is known to have type TypeC
    leave exitLb
}
exitLb:
```

Figure 3.35: try with multiple **catch**es in *IL*

The *Component Pascal* dialect accepted by *gpcp* has a single **rescue** handler per procedure. Thus, any selection on exception object type must be explicit in the source language handler. Semantics similar to Figure 3.34 may be achieved in *gpcp* with the source fragment in Figure 3.36.

In this case the *IL* contains a single catch clause, filtered in this case on the exception base type *System.Exception*. Inside this, **catch**, a sequential type-selection structure, tests the type of the exception object. Figure 3.37 sketches the structure in the *IL*.

There is a slight semantic difference in the *Component Pascal* case. In the *C#* example if no **catch** is selected the search for a handler continues in the caller. In the *Component Pascal* case, it is an error for no case to be selected. If the exact *C#* semantics are required, the **with** statement in Figure 3.36 must end with **else** *RTS.throw*(x) to rethrow the same exception in the context of the caller.

```
begin
    . . .                           (* body of "try" block *)
rescue (x)                          (* local x has type System.Exception *)
    with x  :   TypeA do
        . . .                       (* x is known to have type TypeA *)
    | x  :   TypeB do
        . . .                       (* x is known to have type TypeB *)
    | x  :   TypeC do
        . . .                       (* x is known to have type TypeC *)
    end  (* with *)
end  (* proc *)
```

Figure 3.36: **rescue** with type selection in *gpcp*

```
.try {
    . . .                     // body of try block
    leave exitLb
} catch [mscorlib] System.Exception {
    stloc 'x'                 // store in local variable x
    ldloc 'x'                 // push exception object
    isinst TypeA              // test for object of TypeA
    brfalse lb01
    . . .                     // x is known to have type TypeA
    leave exitLb
lb01:
    ldloc 'x'                 // push exception object
    isinst TypeB              // test for object of TypeB
    brfalse lb02
    . . .                     // x is known to have type TypeB
    leave exitLb
lb02:
    ldloc 'x'                 // push exception object
    isinst TypeC              // test for object of TypeC
    brfalse lb03
    . . .                     // x is known to have type TypeC
    leave exitLb
lb03:
    . . .                     // with statement trap here
}
exitLb:
```

Figure 3.37: **rescue** with explicit type selection

The filter block.   In languages in which it is necessary to select handlers on criteria other than the type of the exception object, the **filter** clause may be used. In this structure an *IL* code label is nominated in the declaration —

SehClause   →   ...
      | **filter** *label* "{" *instructionSequence* "}".

The code of the filter consists of two logical parts. These are the filtering logic and the handler proper. When an exception is raised in a block protected by a **filter** clause, control is passed to the designated label, with the exception object on the evaluation stack. The filtering logic that follows the designated label is responsible for popping the exception object from the stack. It must also decide whether the handler should be entered, and push a Boolean result onto the stack. The filtering code returns using the special "endfilter" instruction, with just the Boolean result on the stack. The handler code itself has the same constraints as a **catch** block and has the exception object on the stack at entry, as usual.

In the defining syntax, the instruction sequence following the **filter** keyword is the *IL* of the handler. The code of the filter may be anywhere within the same method and cannot overlap with any **try** block. The instructions of the filter would typically be parked at the end of the method, following the return instruction that terminates normal control flow.

Filtered handler blocks would be used when information other than type determines the applicability of a particular handler. A typical idiom would define some extension of *System.Exception* with some additional fields set by the class constructors. The filtering logic would retrieve the exception object, perform whatever computation was required on the new fields, and push an appropriate Boolean.

The finally block.   A **finally** clause contains code that is executed at the end of a **try** block, whether the block is terminated normally or exceptionally. The block must end with the special "endfinally" instruction, with an empty stack.

SehClause   →   ...
      | **finally** "{" *instructionSequence* "}".

A **finally** clause is thus entered under two circumstances. If the exit from the **try** block was normal—that is, the "leave" instruction was executed—then the instructions of the handler are executed and control continues to the label designated in the "leave". If the exit was exceptional, then the instructions of the handler are executed, and the search for a **catch** handler either begins, or continues.

Notice that the execution of the **finally** clause does not affect the state of the exception handling. The clause *observes* the state of the exception system but does not *handle* any exception.

The fault block.   A **fault** clause is used if some special action must be taken when an exception is detected, but not otherwise. If the associated **try** block was completed by the "leave" instruction, the **fault** clause is skipped.

$$SehClause \quad \rightarrow \quad ...$$
$$| \quad \textbf{fault} \text{ "\{" } instructionSequence \text{ "\}"}.$$

As is the case for the **finally** clause, this clause *observes* the exception state but does not modify it. The clause must end with the "endfault" instruction, which is a synonym for "endfinally".

Notes on Chapter 3

There is a huge amount of material on the *CTS* that simply has to be left out of a chapter of this kind. Hopefully what has been included is enough to get started, with the documentation filling in the finer detail on a demand-driven basis.

Languages that do not directly have the notions of properties and events can still access properties and events in the framework, through the method call pathway. Chapter 10 gives some further discussion of this issue. There is also another, *indexed* form of property that has not been mentioned in the current chapter. These *indexed properties* are included in the discussion in Chapter 10.

An interesting taxonomy of exception-handling semantics was given by Drew and Gough in "Exception Handling: Expecting the Unexpected" in the journal *Computer Languages* (Vol. 38, No. 8), 1994. The paper reviews the world immediately before the *try, catch* model achieved its current dominance.

A number of example programs relating to the material in this chapter are available from the Software Automata web site referenced in the notes from Chapter 1.

Mapping to the Common Language Runtime (CLR)

As the previous two chapters have indicated, the *CLR* provides a rich variety of features from which we may construct the runtime behavior of our target languages. In general there are multiple ways of achieving any particular operational behavior, so it is necessary to make some choices.

The most immediate choice is whether or not to emit verifiable code. Certainly, it is advantageous to be verifiable, if the target language is sufficiently constrained to allow this. If this choice is made, then we may have more confidence in the correctness of our code, and users will have greater guarantees of runtime safety.

In this chapter, as well as considering the verifiable option, we shall be looking at some of the techniques that are used if the unverifiable-code choice is made. In particular, we shall explore the world of explicit object layout and unmanaged pointers. This is the region of the *CLR* where some of the features of *ANSI C* will take us.

Even in the case of verifiable code, there is still a further choice to be made. A subset of the features of the *CLR* has been specified by Microsoft as the domain of language interoperation. This is the *Common Language Specification*, the *CLS*.

The Common Language Specification

The *CLS* is an agreed subset of the features of the *CLR*. The *CLS* defines the set of built-in types that may be used and the features of the *CTS* that may be used. There are certain conventions of use that are defined also. The idea is a simple one. If a compiler emits code that can *consume* all of the features of the *CLS*, then we say the compiler is a *CLS consumer*. Programs that are compiled by a *CLS*-consuming compiler can access all of the functionality of all *CLS*-compliant libraries. Conversely, compilers that emit code that is *CLS*-compliant can be sure that all *CLS*-consumer languages can interwork with their product.

As well as being a *CLS* consumer, we may define several other possible relationships with the specification. As noted, *CLS* consumers are able to access and use all of the features of the *CLS* that are made available from other language processors. At the production end of the process, we might distinguish between two levels of achievement. *CLS* producers simply guarantee that their output is *CLS* compliant. Such a producer can be sure that every *CLS*-consuming tool may correctly interwork with the code that it produces. Notice that this guarantee does not imply that the producer is able to emit *every* single feature of the *CLS*. Instead it guarantees that every single feature that it *does* emit will be *CLS*-compliant. The other possible producer relationship is the *full producer* relationship. Such a compiler not only guarantees that its output is *CLS* compliant but defines a mechanism for generating *every* feature of the *CLS*.

The constraints of the *CLS* are constraints on the features of the software that are exposed at the language interoperation boundaries. They do not constrain the *CLR* features that are used *inside* the modules of the program. For example, the *signed* 8-bit integer type is not a *CLS* type. This does not mean that (for example) *Component Pascal* programs cannot use the signed 8-bit type *BYTE*. What it does mean is that programs may not expose formal parameters of this type in exported interfaces that are marked as *CLS* compliant.

The *CLS* is very far from being a "least common denominator" of the common *.NET* languages. There are a rich variety of features, so that *CLS* compliance is a significant goal for a compiler to set. Being a *CLS* producer is a relatively modest goal. It is the "entry price" to the language interoperation game. If your compiler does not guarantee this, then you cannot be sure that other *CLS* tools can work with your output.

To be a *CLS* consumer is a more ambitious goal. Many languages lack constructs to correspond to all of the features of the *CLS*. For example, languages that do not have the notion of interface implementation will not have any native mechanism to access this feature of the *CLS*. There are several possibilities. We might give up the goal of being a *full CLS* consumer and just use the bits that map naturally onto our source language. Alternatively, we might extend the source language to access the missing features. This is the approach that *gpcp* uses. *Component Pascal* has no notion of interface implementation, but a language extension allows *gpcp* programs to interwork with this feature. There is no mechanism to *define* interfaces in the extended language, but programs may declare that their types *implement* one or more interface types that are imported from a *CLS*-compliant library. In this way we may achieve full *CLS* consumer status while making minimal changes to the base language.

Mapping Features to the CLR

The initial design task, when considering implementing a *.NET* compiler, is to map the constructs of the source language onto the *CLR* features. This decision, together with the desired relationship with the *CLS*, determines pretty much all of what follows after.

In most of this book we emphasize the production of verifiable code. The running example compiler produces verifiable code, and it is in this area that producing code for the *CLR* diverges from conventional native-code targets. Nevertheless, producing unverifiable code is a valid option, and it is necessary in order to achieve certain kinds of functionality. The next section considers the features of the *CLR* that may be used in unverifiable code.

As a practical choice, the approach that is adopted here to demonstrate the features of unverifiable code is, wherever possible, to start with some verifiable *IL*. The code is then manually modified to show the new feature, reassembled, and tested. This is much simpler than trying to produce complete *IL* programs manually.

Unverifiable Code

Explicit object layout.   The possibility of using explicit layout of classes allows us to take the same level of control of type representation that we would have in a native-code compiler. The key to all of this is to define value classes with the **explicit** attribute.

```
.class public value explicit sealed FourReals
            extends [mscorlib]System.ValueType {
    .pack 4
    .size 32
}
```

This code defines a value class, named *FourReals*. Instances of the class will be 32 bytes in size and will be placed on a quad-byte boundary at runtime. In code that uses the *FourReals* type, we may take the address of an instance and perform pointer arithmetic to access the interior of the structure. We call such a value class with no declared structure a *memory blob*.

It is useful to note one thing right away. By using this feature of the *CLR*, we have obtained complete control over access to the memory of instances. What we have lost, apart from verifiability, is cross-machine *portability*. Conventionally, compilers that target multiple runtimes need some kind of *configuration information* that specifies the hardware constraints of the chosen target machine. Do floating point *doubles* need to be on an octo-byte boundary? What is the natural size of the integer registers? And so on. One of the attractions of the *CLR* is that we do not need to care for such details ... unless we go to explicit layout.

We shall consider two separate applications of explicit layout. The first is the use of explicit layout to implement value arrays. You will recall that the built-in arrays of the *CTS* are object types. Array instances are dynamically allocated from the garbage-collected heap and are self-describing. If we must have or choose to have, value arrays, then we may use explicit layout. Consider the *Modula-2* declaration —

```
type FourReals = array [0..3] of REAL;
var theArray :   FourReals;
```

We may implement this array type on the *CLR*, using a 32-byte memory blob. For current *Intel-x86* machines we should probably choose quad-byte alignment. For purposes of readability we may choose to retain the source-program type name into the *IL*. That is where the example class at the top of the section came from.

Whenever we need a variable of this type, we declare an appropriate field of the value class. The static variable in the declaration would appear in the *IL* as —

```
.class public sealed ModBody extends object {
  .field public static value class FourReals 'theArray'
    . . .
}
```

We may declare instance fields of other classes as being of this value class type and may declare local variables and formal parameters of this type. Here is an example of a procedure with a local variable of the array type —

```
procedure Foo();
  var localArray :   FourReals;
begin . . .
```

For this example, the *IL* for the method will simply declare a local variable of the value class type. In the example we use the optional **init** tag on the declaration to ensure that the local is initialized to zero on entry —

```
.method assembly static void 'Foo' () il managed {
  .locals init (value class FourReals 'localArray')
    . . .
}
```

Using this design, space for the array will be allocated as part of the activation record of the method. This space will be automatically reclaimed when the method terminates.

In the next section we shall see how to access the contents of explicit memory blobs. At this stage we simply note that if a compiler implements value arrays in this way, the built-in array bounds-checking mechanisms no longer apply. In such designs the code must do its own array bounds checking.

In *gpcp*, where all arrays are implemented by verifiable reference types, a procedure like *Foo* would have had to allocate an array on the heap in the method prolog. Just for the record, the *IL* in this case would look as follows —

```
.method assembly static void 'Foo' () il managed {
   .locals init (float64 [] 'localArray')
      ldc.i4.4                      // push length
      newarr float64                // create array
      stloc.0                       // store in local
      ...
}
```

With the *gpcp* design the local array is *explicitly* allocated in the *IL*, even though it is *implicitly* allocated in the source code. In that case, the reference to the array will be part of the activation record of the method and will disappear when the method completes. The dynamically allocated array will not be reclaimed until the garbage collector finds it.

As a second example of the use of explicit layout of classes, we consider the implementation of untagged **union** types. Untagged unions are the familiar union type from *C*, but correspond to tagless *variant record* types in *Pascal*-family languages. In some applications of union types there is some data external to the union that signifies which variant of the union is *active*. In many other cases unions are used to deliberately circumvent the type system.

Consider the following *ANSI C* type declaration —

typedef union{**double** d; **struct** { **int** lo,hi;} i;} TrickWord;

This type overlaps a single floating point double location with two (32-bit) integers. We may implement this in *IL* by defining a value class that not only has explicit layout, but also specifies the offset of each field. Here is the *IL* —

```
.class public value explicit sealed TrickWord
            extends [mscorlib]System.ValueType {
   .pack 4
   .field [0] public float64 'd'                    // field offset 0
   .field [0] public int32 'lo'                     // field offset 0
   .field [4] public int32 'hi'                     // field offset 4
}
```

It may be wise to note that if this structure is intended to allow the two words of the floating point value to be accessed independently, the meaning of the two integer fields will depend on the implementing hardware architecture. On a so-called *little-endian* machine like *Intel-x86*, the "i.hi" field will hold the most significant word, including the sign bit. On a *big-endian* machine architecture, the "i.lo" field will hold the most significant word. The example is more convincing in *Pascal*. In that case the syntax for "variant records" does not require the declaration of the inner **struct**, and the field names all appear at the same lexical level. Here is the union type declared in *Modula-2*.

```
type TrickWord = record case (* no tag *) : BOOLEAN of
                   | TRUE  : d     : REAL;
                   | FALSE : lo,hi : INTEGER;
                 end (* case *)
               end (* record *)
```

Unmanaged pointers.
Whenever explict layout of classes is used, we must use pointer manipulation to access the interior of the class instances. These address computations will always generate unmanaged pointers.

As a first example, let us consider indexing over the four floating point numbers in the *FourReals* type defined above. As before we may experiment with such code by generating verifiable *IL* using *gpcp* and modifying the file with a text editor. The relevant parts of the source are —

```
TYPE    FourReals = ARRAY 4 OF REAL;
VAR     rx4        : FourReals;
...
FOR idx := 0 TO 3 DO WriteReal(rx4[idx]) END;
...
```

The corresponding parts of the *IL* file are shown in Figure 4.1. In this figure, the manually inserted code is marked in the comments. At the top of the listing we have inserted the definition of the explicit layout class, exactly as we saw it earlier. The declaration of the static field "rx4" replaces the previous declaration, which was for one of the built-in array types.

The code that accesses the array begins by loading the address of the memory blob. We must index into the instance by computing the offset. In this case the elements are eight bytes apart. Thus we must take the index, multiply it by the element size, then add it to the base address. As expected, we load and store the elements using the load- and store-indirect instructions.

For the case of value classes used to implement arrays, we are compelled to use address arithmetic. The runtime cannot know that the interior of the class should be accessed as an array, since we have given the runtime no such information. All that we have told the

```
.namespace M4
{
.class public sealed explicit value FourReals          // new
               extends [mscorlib]System.ValueType {    // new
  .pack 4                                               // new
  .size 32                                              // new
  }                                                     // new

.class public sealed M4 {
.field assembly static value class M4.FourReals 'rx4'  // new
.field assembly static int32 'idx'
    ...
    ldc.i4.0   // initialize loop counter
    stsfld int32 M4.M4::'idx'
lb1:           // FOR loop header label
    ldsflda float64 M4.M4::'rx4'                        // new
    ldsfld int32 M4.M4::'idx'                           // new
    ldc.i4.8                                            // new
    mul                                                 // new
    add                                                 // new
    ldind.r8                                            // new
    call void M4.M4::'WriteReal'(float64)
    ldc.i4.3   // loop exit test
    ldsfld int32 M4.M4::'idx'
    ldc.i4.1
    add.ovf    // increment counter
    dup
    stsfld int32 M4.M4::'idx'
    bge lb1    // branch to loop header
```

Figure 4.1: Pointer arithmetic accessing data blob

runtime is the alignment and size. The situation with explicit classes with declared fields is somewhat better. In this case the runtime is able to load and store fields exactly as it would do for an automatically packed class. The following experiment demonstrates the possibilities. We define an ordinary value class with nonoverlapping fields —

```
TYPE    Funny = RECORD
                   i0,i1,i2,i3,i4,i5,i6,i7 : BYTE;
                   r : REAL;
                END;
```

When we compile a program that uses this type, we may go in and set explicit offsets on the fields, so that "r" and "i0" are at the same offset. Apart from the fact that the type has now become a union type, the code that accesses the fields is unchanged.

Here is the skeleton of the class declaration, as modified. The modifications are all insertions and are shown **bold** in the listing —

```
.class value sealed explicit Funny
               extends [mscorlib]System.ValueType {
.field [0] assembly int8 'a0'
.field [1] assembly int8 'a1'
       . . .
.field [7] assembly int8 'a7'
.field [0] assembly float64 'r'            // now overlaps a0..a7
       . . .
}
```

When a program using this type fetches field "r", say, the code that accesses the field works exactly as it would for the unmodified class. From the point of view of the *JIT*, code must be generated to fetch the datum at the offset stored in the class description for that field. The only difference is the runtime was *told* what the offset was going to be, instead of being allowed to work it out for itself. In fact if you avoid really dangerous modifications, such as overlapping fields of references types with fields of other types, the verifier will still give the code a passing grade.

Function pointers.   We have referred briefly in the previous chapters to the facilities in the *CLR* for function pointers (on page 40), and method pointers (on page 92). These facilities allow for a direct implementation of language *C* function pointers, or *Modula-2* procedure variables, in unverified implementations.

The implementation is relatively straightforward. Data of function pointer type have location signatures that are the same as the signature of a concrete function of that type. The infrastructure that emits signatures for functions may also create the signature strings that are required for handling function pointers. Thus the *C* function pointer type with abstract declarator —

> **int (*) (int, int)**

would be equivalent to the *IL* location type of the static field —

> **.field static method int32 * (int32, int32)** 'fPtr'

Such a location would have a value, of some function "Add", say, assigned by the *IL* code —

```
ldftn int32 Module::'Add'(int32, int32)
stsfld method int32 * (int32, int32) ThisCls::'fPtr'
```

A pointer of this type would be called by first pushing the two arguments, as for a direct call of the procedure value, then executing the call-indirect instruction —

```
ldsfld method int32 * (int32, int32) ThisCls::'fPtr'
calli int32 (int32, int32)
```

Notice that the call instruction does not have the "*" marker in its operand argument.

In the case of pointers to instance methods, the preferred style would be to define the location using the **explicit** marker in the call convention. As discussed on page 40, this better documents the purpose of the type. The code associated with an instance method might be defined by —

.field static method instance explicit int32 *
                          (**class** MyMod.MyClass, **int32**, **int32**) 'fPtr'

A value might be assigned to this method pointer type by code similar to —

```
ldftn  instance int32 MyMod.MyClass::'Add'(int32, int32)
stsfld  method instance explicit int32 *
               (class MyMod.MyClass, int32, int32) ThisCls::'fPtr'
```

When this function pointer is called, it is necessary to push the receiver of the method, followed by the two integer actual parameters. Finally, the value might be called by code of the form —

```
ldsfld method instance explicit int32 * (class MyMod.MyClass, int32, int32)
calli int32 (class MyMod.MyClass, int32, int32)
// or use – calli instance int32 (int32, int32)
```

Notice that the uncommented call uses the implicit static call convention. We might just as easily have called the function pointer by means of a "calli" instruction, using the **instance** call convention. In that case we would not have used the explicit signature showing the receiver object reference in the zero-position of the formal parameter list. The important thing is to ensure that the call convention, taken together with the return type and formal argument list, indicates the correct *stack-Δ*.

Finally, the case of virtual methods is almost identical to the instance case above. It should be remembered that the indirect call of a function pointer that is implemented by the "calli" instruction is an ordinary static call. The "virtual" magic that performs type-directed dispatch is incorporated into the "ldvirtftn" instruction. It is this instruction that indexes into the *v-table* of the object and extracts an ordinary function pointer. The example code given immediately above for the instance method case may be applied directly, with the substitution of "ldvirtftn" for "ldftn".

Conformant arrays and "alloca."   A major difference between the *Pascal*-family languages and the *C*-family is that in *Pascal*-family languages the length of an array is part of the type definition. Many languages with this particular characteristic allow arrays of any length to be passed as arguments to formals declared as *conformant arrays*—that is, arrays with element type but no length specified. When such arrays are passed by value, it is necessary to create a copy of the array in either the calling or called procedure. It is possible to do all of this using dynamically allocated arrays, as we shall see later. However, for languages that map arrays onto value structures it is undesirable to do so. In such cases, it is possible instead to expand the activation record of one of the procedures and perform a block copy.

The implementation details are useful for all languages that allow expansion of the activation record. This includes language *C* with its *alloca* and *memcpy* functions. In order to motivate the discussion, we shall nevertheless concentrate on the case of conformant arrays.

In *Modula-2* it is possible to declare that a formal parameter of a procedure is of some fixed-length, named array type. It is also possible to declare that a formal parameter is of the type **array of** T, where T is the element type of the array and could be any type denotation, including another array type. Such a formal parameter is called a conformant array, or equivalently an *open array*. Inside the procedure with the conformant array, it is possible to obtain the index of the last element of the actual parameter array, so that iteration over the array is possible (and so that the compiler may implement index bounds checking.)

Whenever such arrays are passed, an additional, hidden parameter is passed as well, to specify the array upper bound. Value-mode conformant array parameters need to be copied at the call, while reference-mode parameters require no copying. In either case, within the procedure the formal must be accessed indirectly, since the offset of the array base within the activation record cannot be computed at compile time.

With value-mode conformant arrays it is logically possible to perform the parameter copy either in the calling procedure or in the called procedure. We consider just the case where the called procedure performs the copy as part of the procedure entry prolog. Figure 4.2 shows the activation record immediately before and after the copying of a value conformant array. The example activation record has two formal parameters. At the call, in the "before" picture, the formal parameter points to the actual parameter array. The second actual parameter, in this case, *elNm*, states that the actual array has eight elements. In the procedure prolog it is therefore necessary to expand the activation record by $elNm \times elSz$, where *elSz* is the size in bytes of the array element type. The activation record is expanded, and the actual array is copied to the newly allocated area. Finally, the formal parameter is "warped" to point to the array copy.

The implementation of this plan in *CIL* introduces at least two *IL* instructions that are unique to the world of unverifiable code. The instruction "`localloc`" expands the activation record. The size is pushed on the stack, and the instruction returns a pointer

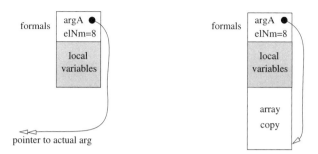

Figure 4.2: Activation record before and after copying a conformant array

to the allocated area. The instruction "`cpblk`" takes three stack operands and performs a memory to memory copy. The number of bytes to copy is on the top of the stack. Below that is the source address, and below that again the destination address.

Figure 4.3 shows the *IL* code of the prolog of a procedure that uses this design to copy a value open array. In this example, the pointer to the actual parameter is in argument position #0, while the array length value is in argument position #1. We compute the array size from the length and the known element size. It is necessary to define two temporary local variables. One holds a copy of the array size, while the other will hold a pointer to the newly allocated region.

The activation record is expanded, and the actual value is copied using the block copy instruction. Finally, the formal argument is overwritten, so as to point to the copy of the array. Throughout the rest of the procedure, the formal parameter is accessed in exactly the same way as if it was a reference parameter.

In the case of multidimensional conformant arrays it is necessary to pass as many additional, hidden parameters as there are array dimensions. These values, analogous to the "elNm" value in the previous example, are the element counts for each dimension in some agreed order. In the case of an n-dimensional array, the size of the memory blob required to hold the array copy will be —

$$size = elSz \times \prod_{j=0}^{n-1} elNm_j$$

where *elSz* is the element size in bytes, and *elNm$_j$* is the number of elements in the jth dimension. The *elNm$_j$* values are required, not just for computing the copy size in the prolog, but for array indexing throughout the procedure. The byte offset of a typical element is computed by the algorithm —

$$tmp := index_0;$$
for $j := 1$ **to** $n - 1$ **do** $tmp := tmp * elNm_j + index_j$ **end**;
$offset := tmp * elSz;$

```
.method public static void 'Foo' (int32* 'argA',
                                   int32  'elNm') il managed {
.locals (int32  'cpSz',          // size of copy region
         int32* 'nPtr')          // address of new region
// start of prolog
        ldarg.1                  // size value is arg #1
        ldc.i4.4                 // push the element size
        mul                      // compute region size
        dup                      // duplicate the size
        stloc.0                  // save region size in 'cpSz'
        localloc                 // expand the activation record
        dup                      // duplicate the address
        stloc.1                  // save address value in 'nPtr'
        ldarg.0                  // pointer to actual is arg #0
        ldloc.0                  // push saved region size
        cpblk                    // copy the actual now!
        ldloc.1                  // push saved address value
        starg.0                  // formal now points to copy
// end of prolog
        . . .
```

Figure 4.3: Copying a value conformant array parameter

where $index_j$ is the jth array index and, as before, $elNm_j$ is the number of elements in the jth dimension.[1] For statically sized arrays, only multiplication by constants would be required. Figure 4.4 shows how the address computation would expand out, in line, for the three-dimensional array of **double** case. The goal of the code is to push the offset onto the evaluation stack.

It is worth working through this code with some care, since it demonstrates a technique that we have not shown before. Notice that there is no sign of the temporary variable *tmp* in this code. One might view the code as implementing the definition of offset by unrolling the loop for the case $n = 3$. At all times the value corresponding to *tmp* is on the evaluation stack and never needs to be moved off-stack to a local variable.

After the index-0 value is pushed, the initial value of the variable *tmp* is on the top of the stack. The next step is to take *tmp*, multiply by *eNm1*, and add the index-1 value. At the end of this computation, the new value of *tmp* is again on the top of the stack. Next, we multiply by *eNm2* and add the index-2 value. At the end of this computation, the final value of *tmp* is on the top of the stack. As a final step, we multiply the value by the known element size, which is eight in this case.

---

[1] This formula assumes the *C* and *Pascal* layout for arrays. The *FORTRAN* case is different again.

```
.method public static void 'Foo'(float64* 'argA',
                                 int32 'eNm0',
                                 int32 'eNm1',
                                 int32 'eNm2') il managed {
    . . .
// start of offset computation
    <push index #0>
    ldarg.2                          // push eNm1 length value
    mul
    <push index #1>
    add
    ldarg.3                          // push eNm2 length value
    mul
    <push index #2>
    add
    ldc.i4    8                      // push the constant element size
    mul                              // offset is now on top of stack
// end of offset computation
    . . .
```

Figure 4.4: Offset computation for 3D conformant array

Verifiable Code

In order to map the features of a language to verifiable code on the *CLR*, a few constraints need to be observed. First, it may be necessary to reduce the scope of the language by the removal of constructs that are necessarily unsafe. For example, there is no clear way in language *C* of implementing unchecked type casts between pointer and integral types. Similarly, although as noted above, union constructs based on explicit class layout *can* be verifiable, in general this will not be the case. Completely general unions allow pointer types to be overlapped with integral types, and this is never verifiable. As a final example of problematic constructs, source languages that allow the expression of explicit pointer arithmetic also cannot be translated in a verifiable way.

As well, there are certain other mapping constraints. For example, languages that have value semantics for arrays do not have the option of using the memory blobs of page 105. This is because the pointer arithmetic associated with array access will always be unverifiable. Therefore in such cases arrays will have to be implemented by using the built-in reference types of the *CTS*. We look at the detailed issues involved in implementing value semantics by reference types in the next section.

In a later chapter, we return again to the question of implementing certain constructs that have semantics that are not naturally supported by the *CLR*. Chapter 12 looks at some of the tricks that may help with things like covariant return types, multiple inheritance, parametric polymorphism (or *generics*, as it is more often called), and structural compatibility of types.

Value semantics with reference types.   Let us first clear up a definitional issue. When we speak of a type having *value semantics*, or alternatively *reference semantics*, what exactly do we mean, and how can we tell what it is that we have?

In this book we use the practical definition that a type has *reference semantics* if, after we perform an assignment between two values declared to have that type, subsequent mutation of the copy also mutates the original. This is the case, for example, with the reference classes of *C#* or *Java*. If it is the case that mutation of a copy of a structure does not modify the original, then we say that the type has *value semantics*.

Typically scalar types—that is, types consisting of a single value of limited size—are value types. Languages that have *structured* value types usually have provisions for *entire assignment* of values of the type. In such an assignment all components of the value are copied to the new location. It is also typical for languages with structured value types to not require the explicit initialization of values of the type.

As an example, *C#* has both kinds of structured types, both of which are aggregate types with named fields. Variables declared to be of some **struct** type in *C#* will be implemented by a value class. When a variable is declared to be of this type, the memory allocated to the value may be statically allocated or allocated in the activation record of a method. Variables declared to be of some **class** type will be implemented as a reference class, with the *reference* allocated statically or in the activation record. However, the variable will be initially **null**. The class object itself does not become allocated until an explicit call of **new** is executed. There is no copy instruction for a reference object in *C#*. The best we can do is to provide an optional "clone" operation.

Notice that these initialization rules make sense for the *CTS*. Value types are not self-describing, so creation of a value class instance requires no operations other than the allocation of a correctly sized blob of zeroed memory. Object creation, on the other hand, requires much more work. The memory has to be allocated from the garbage-collected heap, and the parts of the object that give access to the static fields, the *v-table*, and the introspection capabilities must be initialized.

Most *Pascal*-family languages allow entire assignments of both arrays and record types. Note that this is enabled by the type compatibility rules for these languages, in which two array types are not assignment compatible unless they are of the same length as well as of the same element type.

The important point to understand is that although we may have to *implement* a type using a reference type, this does not mean that we cannot achieve value semantics. The case of arrays makes a good example to explore the issues. Suppose that we agree that arrays in our source language will be implemented as *CLR* reference arrays. Consider the following *Pascal* types —

```
type    Arr8    = array 8 of INTEGER;
        PAr8    = pointer to Arr8;

var     a1,a2   : Arr8;
        p1,p2   : PAr8;
```

Notice that when we represent these constructs in *IL*, the identity of the array types will be lost. There is no such thing as different integer array *types* in the *CTS*. There is only "int32[]", which we shall have to use for integer arrays of any length. The variable declarations in the example will be translated into *IL* as though they had been declared in *C#* in the following way —

```
int32[]    a1 = new int32[8];
int32[]    a2 = new int32[8];
int32[]    p1;     // no initialization
int32[]    p2;     // no initialization
```

Here is a paradox. The two distinct types, **array of** *INTEGER* and **pointer to array of** *INTEGER*, have precisely the same representation at runtime. Both of these are represented at runtime as the *CTS* reference array type. The different semantics of the two types are achieved by the *different translations into IL of assignment and initialization*.

For example, let us assume that in the code with the example *Pascal* declarations, we have two assignments —

```
begin
  new(p1);      (* allocate a new array *)
  p2 := p1;     (* assign the pointer types *)
  a2 := a1;     (* assign the array types *)
  ...
```

The two assignments will have very different *IL*. The assignment of the pointers will, well, copy the pointers. The array assignment will copy the *contents* of the array. The *IL* will correspond to *C#* code with an explicit, element-by-element copy —

```
{
  p1 = new int32[8] (* allocate new array *)
  p2 = p1; (* assign the pointer types *)
  for (int i = 0; i < 8; i++) a2[i] = a1[i];
  ...
```

As we have already noted, a declaration of the pointer type will not require initialization in the *IL*. Array types, on the other hand, will require the emission of an explicit allocation in *IL*. In the case of static arrays the initialization will be placed in the class constructor,

".cctor". Local variables of array type will need an explicit allocation and initialization in the method prolog.

In this book we refer to reference types that are used to implement types that have value semantics in the source language as **reference surrogates**. The possibility that types with value semantics will have to be implemented by reference surrogates has an important effect on the infrastructure needed to generate code. In native-code contexts we might have predicates in the code emitter module that ask, "Is this type a reference type?" In the present case we have two separate predicates: "Does this type have reference semantics?" and separately, "Does this type have a reference implementation?" The two questions will not always have the same answer. We simply have to understand, at every point, which of these two different questions is relevant.

In non-object-oriented languages it is probable that all record types may be implemented by means of value classes in the *CTS*. However, for languages with dispatched virtual methods it will be necessary to implement record types by reference classes—that is, by means of reference surrogates. In such cases any entire assignment will need to be performed by field-by-field copying. Further, if some fields are themselves of value types that are implemented as reference surrogates, then recursive calls to copying methods may be necessary. In the general case, what looks like a simple value copy in the source language may need to be implemented by what amounts to a *deep copy* in the *CTS*. In an unverified context the whole type could be implemented by a flat aggregate of memory blobs, and the entire assignment would just be a call to the unverifiable copy-block "cpblk" instruction.

Interlanguage safety of reference surrogates.   The use of reference surrogates to implement value records requires some care in a multilanguage environment. Value records necessarily have immutable type, even if they are implemented by means of an extensible class instance.

Consider a class that has a field of some reference surrogate type. Within the original language there is no way of referring to the reference field. However, from the point of view of (say) a *C#* compiler reading the metadata for the aggregate type, the reference field is just another reference. In particular it would appear legal to overwrite the reference field with a new value that references an object of a subtype of the original type. Such a possibility would play havoc with the semantics of the original program, even though it does not threaten memory safety.

Fortunately, in the case of record types the *CLR* has sufficient expressive power to ensure proper behavior. The simple precaution of marking reference surrogate fields as **initonly** ensures that these fields cannot be overwritten. For one-dimensional array types the same principle applies. The reference surrogate field in the encapsulating class may be marked as **initonly**, thereby ensuring the immutability of the allocated object reference.

Unfortunately, there does not appear to be any mechanism to ensure the safety of arrays of arrays. Within the confines of the language that defines multidimensional arrays in this way, the surrogate references to the lower-dimension array objects are invisible,

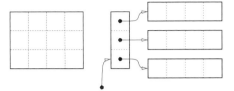

Figure 4.5: Abstract and runtime views of same 2D array

and hence safe. However, a language that sees all of the runtime implementation details would be capable of breaking the abstraction. Consider the two-dimensional array shown in Figure 4.5. The abstract view of the array is the 3×4 rectangular region of memory at the left of the figure. On the right is the representation of the same array at runtime, using reference surrogates. The danger now is that program code that deals directly with the runtime representation might legally perform some manipulation of the references. For example, the reference array might be changed so that the zeroth and first references point to the same one-dimensional array. The effect on a source program that sees only the abstract view would be perplexing, to say the least. Every time the program wrote to the "[0,2]" element of the array, unaccountably the "[1,2]" element would change its value also.

Tagged variant types. We have already mentioned the *untagged variant types* of which the *ANSI C* union type is typical. The prospects for implementing this functionality in verifiable code are slight, unless there happen to be no references in any of the variants. The situation with tagged variants is rather more hopeful.

It may be observed that the new generation of object-oriented languages, such as *C#*, *Java*, *Oberon-2*, and *Component Pascal*, do not have a union construct. The reason that unions are absent is because single inheritance can achieve the same effect in a more efficient and type-safe way. This observation gives a hint as to how to implement tagged unions in the *CTS*.

Variant types are union types in which at any one time only one member of the union, called the *active variant*, is valid. In the case of tagged variants, the active variant is determined by the value of the tag. The usual idiom for processing variants is to extract the tag value and use that as the selector in a **case** or **switch** statement. The switch will have one branch for each member of the union. All of this is rather reminiscent of the situation with concrete subtypes of an abstract type. Every instance of the type is of some particular *exact type*, corresponding to the active variant in the union case. In the subtype case, at least in *.NET*, we may process variants by selecting on an explicit tag or using type-tests on the object.

So here is a prescription for implementing tagged variants. Each variant becomes a separate concrete extension of an abstract type. The abstract type will contain any fields common to all variants and will also hold the tag. A constructor method will map the tag values to the various subtypes. Consider the following typical *Modula-2* type declaration —

type   VarRec =   **record**
                       share :   INTEGER;
                       case tgFld :   BOOLEAN **of**
                       | TRUE : rlFld : REAL;
                       | FALSE : arFld : **array** [0..7] **of** CHAR;
                       end
                  end

In this declaration there is a shared field *share* of integer type and a variant tag of Boolean type, named *tgFld*. The variant part of the type has two variants selected by the Boolean tag. The "true" variant has a single field of floating point real type, named *rlFld*. The "false" variant contains an array of eight characters, named *arFld*. A type-safe implementation of this structure in *IL* is shown in Figure 4.6. Note carefully that abstract classes and their

```
.class public sealed abstract 'VarRec' {
    .field public int32 'share'
    .field public initonly bool  'tgFld'
}

.class public sealed 'VarRec$1' extends 'MyMod.VarRec' {
    .field public float64 'rlFld'
    .method public instance void '.ctor'() {
       ldarg.0                         // fetch this reference
       ldc.i4.1                        // set tag to TRUE
       stfld boolean 'tgFld'           // store to initonly ok!
    }
}

.class public sealed 'VarRec$2' extends 'MyMod.VarRec' {
    .field public initonly wchar[] 'arFld'
    .method public instance void '.ctor'() {
       ldarg.0                         // fetch this reference
       ldc.i4.0                        // set tag to FALSE
       stfld boolean 'tgFld'           // store to initonly ok!
       ldarg.0                         // fetch this reference
       ldc.i4.8
       newarr wchar                    // allocate 8-long array
       stfld wchar[] 'arFld'           // store to initonly ok!
    }
}
```

Figure 4.6: Implementation of example variant record

extensions are always reference classes. Hence the value type *VarRec* will be implemented by the two extensions of the reference class *MyMod.VarRec*. Note also that the second variant has a field that is itself a reference array.

The two constructors set the tag field as part of their execution. The tag field is declared **initonly**, so that the tag can never be inconsistent with the immutable type of the object. Similarly, in the second variant the array reference is declared **initonly**, so that the array can never be deleted or have its length modified. Naturally, the constructors have permission to set the initial values to these fields.

This particular mapping of variant records is entirely type-safe and conforms to the strict semantics of *Modula-2*. Unfortunately, a very large proportion of legacy code that uses such constructs relies on the ability to manipulate variant records that are at least temporarily in invalid states. For example, almost all legacy compilers will permit a value to be assigned to the tag field, in spite of the fact that such an assignment renders the value invalid. In the *CTS* it is impossible to change the exact type of an object once it has been created. It is therefore probable that any compiler that maps variant records using the proposals of this section will also have to insist on total conformance to the exact semantics of the source language. In particular, any attempt to change the active variant of an existing value will have to be translated into code that creates an entirely new object of the correct type and replaces the reference to the old object with a reference to the new. In this context the fact that the value type has a reference implementation is a saving grace. It means that the variants may be exchanged atomically by the overwriting of the reference. The reference is an artifact of the implementation and is inaccessible to the source program. It is therefore not possible for the source program to create an alias of the object.

The Component Pascal Choices

About Component Pascal

Component Pascal is an OO *Pascal* variant. Its predecessors are *Oberon-2*, *Modula-2*, and the original *Pascal*. Of these languages *Oberon-2* is the immediate parent, and *Component Pascal* is almost strictly a superset of that language. The embedded imperative language has expressive power similar to other *Pascal* dialects. Compared to *Oberon-2*, the language adds some additional annotations to types that aim to increase the compile time guarantees of type safety.

The built-in types and structured statements of the language are similar to other *Pascal* dialects or, for that matter, any other contemporary imperative language. There are the usual assignment, procedure call, and loop constructs that one would expect.

This section makes no attempt to describe the whole of the language. The features that are covered are those ones for which the issue of mapping to the *CLR* is a matter of necessary deliberation.

Types. *Component Pascal* allows the declaration of **array**, **record**, and **pointer** types. It has a bitset type, **set**, which is restricted to base types that allow mapping onto words of the underlying implementation platform. Array types have fixed length, and arrays of differing length are not assignment compatible. Pointers may only be bound to record and array types, although variable-size "open" arrays are permitted here. There are no union or variant record types, nor are there subrange or enumeration types. Because pointers cannot be bound to other types, it is almost always possible to omit the explicit pointer dereference operator "^". Thus if *p* is of pointer-to-record type, we may write "a.b" rather than the semantically equivalent "a^.b" that would have been necessary in traditional *Pascal* dialects.

The language allows for the definition of **procedure** types, which are roughly equivalent to *ANSI C* function pointers. A typical procedure type declaration might be —

> **type** RealFunc = **procedure** (x :   REAL) : REAL;

This states that the procedure type *RealFunc* takes a value mode, real (floating point double) parameter and returns a result also of real datatype. Variables, record fields, and formal parameters may all be declared to be of a procedure type. When values of procedure type are assigned, assignment compatiblity requires that the two procedure types have the same signature. This is an example of *structural equivalence*, rather than the *name equivalence* that is demanded for type compatibility elsewhere in the language.

Record types are declared with the usual *Pascal* syntax with one addition. These types are extensible and may be declared as extending a single base type. A typical example might be —

> **type** ExtendedType = **record** (BaseType) *<field declarations>* **end**;

ExtendedType is the name of the record type being declared here, and the typename in the parentheses, *BaseType*, is the record type that is being extended. Record types that are not explicitly declared as being extensible are sealed, so in the example the parent type must have been declared as —

> **type** BaseType = **extensible record** *<field declarations>* **end** ;

As well as being declared to be **extensible**, records may also be declared to be **abstract**.

If we want to declare pointer types that point to these two example record types, typical syntax would be —

> **type** ETypePtr = **pointer to** ExtendedType;
> **type** BTypePtr = **pointer to** BaseType;

These pointer types capture the "extends" relationship from their bound record types so that *ETypePtr* extends *BTypePtr*. Values of the extended pointer type are able to be polymorphically assigned to locations declared to be of the base pointer type.

Procedures. Procedures and functions are declared using the usual *Pascal* syntax. Here is an example of a proper procedure—that is, one that does not return any value. This procedure is named *Foo* and declares a single local variable of integer type named *ix* —

```
procedure Foo (<formal parameter declarations>) ;
  var ix :   INTEGER;
begin
  <statements>
end Foo;
```

Note that the name of the procedure is repeated at the end, as a useful marker for compiler error recovery.

Formal parameters may be declared to have one of four modes. The default is *value* mode, but there are also *in, out* and *var* modes. Here is a procedure heading with one formal parameter of each mode —

```
procedure Foo(a:T; var b:T; in c:T; out d:T);
```

Parameter a is of type T and has value mode. Parameter b is of type T and has *variable* (*inout*) mode. The actual parameter will be passed by reference. Parameter c has *in* mode. The actual parameter will be passed by reference and is read-only within the procedure. The actual must be initialized prior to the call of this procedure. Parameter d has *out* mode. The actual parameter will be passed by reference in this case also, but need not be initialized prior to the call. It is an error if there is not a verifiable assignment to this formal along every path in the control flow that reaches any procedure return point.

The actual parameter that is passed to a value mode formal may be the value of any expression. An actual parameter that is passed to an out mode or inout mode formal must be a mutable variable. An actual parameter that is passed to an in-mode formal must be a "variable," but may denote a constant or read-only location.

As well as these ordinary procedures and functions, *Component Pascal* allows procedures to be bound to particular record or pointer-to-record types. These *type-bound procedures* correspond to dispatched methods in other *OO* languages. Here is the heading of the declaration of a procedure that is bound to the *BaseType* record type described earlier —

```
procedure (in p :   BaseType)Mthd() :   BaseType, new, extensible;
```

Unlike other *OO* languages, the *name* of the method receiver is able to be defined. In this example, the receiver is named p, and the method takes no other parameters. The method returns a value of type *BaseType*. The method is declared as being **new**—that is, it does not override any equally named method from a supertype. It is also declared as being **extensible**—that is, it is able to be overridden in extensions of *BaseType*. Here is such an overriding method, bound to the type *ExtendedType* —

```
procedure (in x :   ExtendedType) Mthd()  :   ExtendedType;
```

In this example we do not use the **new** attribute, since the method does override an inherited method. We do not use the **extensible** attribute either, thereby declaring that this method is final. As a matter of fact, since *ExtendedType* is sealed, the method could not be extended anyhow. Notice that in this example the overriding method returns a subtype of the return type of the method that it overrides. We say that this method has a *covariant return type*.

Type-bound procedures may be bound to either record or pointer types. Receivers of pointer type are always passed by value. In the case of record types, the receiver mode must be either *in* or *var* mode. It follows that in all cases methods will have a receiver value that is a reference.

A curiosity of the syntax of *Component Pascal* is that methods are declared at the outer level of the module, not lexically within the declaration of the type to which they are bound. In the case of a set of concrete types that extend an abstract base type, this allows the corresponding equally named methods to be grouped together in the source code. We are thus able to group methods of the same *name* together, rather than grouping methods of the same *class* together as happens in *C#*. Sometimes this is very convenient, and at other times, less so.

Procedures (but not methods) may be declared nested within other procedures and methods. These procedures have access to the local variables and formal parameters of their enclosing block. Such a nested procedure cannot be the value assigned to a location of procedure type.

OO features.
As well as the possibility of binding methods to extensible types, there are a few other manifestations of object orientation in the language. First, assignment of references to extensible types is polymorphic in the usual way. The related language *Oberon-2* defined semantics for polymorphic assignment of record types (using *projection semantics*), but this has been removed from *Component Pascal*.

There is a type-test predicate. One may say —

```
if expression is SomeType then ...
```

with the expected semantics in the case of subtypes. There is also the *regional type guard* previously described in detail on page 79. Finally, there is a type assertion construct that roughly corresponds to the checked type casts of other languages. The syntax —

```
expression(<some type name>)
```

asserts that the exact type of *expression* will be of the designated type, or a subtype of that type. If the compiler is not able to statically verify that the assertion is true, a runtime test will be required. If the test fails, the program raises an exception. These assertions are often used in the interior of designator expressions, such as —

```
ptrObj.boundTp(TypeDesc.Record).baseTp.Diagnose()
```

The assertion is that the *boundTp* field of *ptrObj* will have type *TypeDesc.Record*. Having passed this test we are then able to select the *baseTp* field and call the *Diagnose* method. Presumably, the other possible types for the *boundTp* field do not have a *baseTp* field, so the compiler would reject the designator if the type assertion were not present.

Module structure.   Modules in *Component Pascal*, as in *Modula-2*, are the compilation units with which the compiler deals. Modules form the domains of program analysis and define the boundaries at which identifier visibility is controlled. All outer-level, named entities in a module are private to that module unless they are explicitly marked as exported. Types, variables, procedures, and manifest constants may be *private*—that is, not exported. They may be *public*—that is, exported to any other module that explicitly imports the module. Finally, variables may be exported in *read-only* mode. In the case of public record types individual fields may be marked as private, public, or read-only. Naturally, the read-only restriction only applies within importing modules. Within the defining module such read-only data are completely accessible.

Naturally, there are some required consistency conditions. For example, exported procedures may not have formal parameters or a return type of a nonexported type. Furthermore, if an extensible record type is exported, then any extensions of the record type must be equally visible. A similar rule applies to extensible methods.

The gpcp Mappings

The first decision that needs to be made in any design is how the structure of compilation units with which the compiler deals will be mapped into assemblies, modules, namespaces, and classes in the *CLR*. Until this is done, we may not begin to think about how to map our own language's visibility markers to those of the *CLR*.

In the case of *Component Pascal* the module is the unit of naming control. Modules are the boundaries through which we have import/export control. Unlike *Modula-2*, in *Component Pascal* a compilation unit may only contain a single module. The *gpcp* design choice is to map a module into a single namespace and compile that into a single *CLR* assembly. Both the assembly name and the namespace name are taken from the module name.

Within a module, record types are mapped into *CLR* classes of various kinds, and there is a *synthetic static class* defined to hold the static procedures and data of the module. This class cannot be instantiated or extended.

Types, variables, and procedures at the outer level of the module are declared in the source program with visibility markers. These declare whether the object is exported or not or, in the case of types or variables, possibly exported in *read-only* mode. These markers map onto the attributes for visibility and accessibility in the *CLR*.

Types that are exported are declared to have "public" visibility in *IL*. Types that are not exported become classes that are private to the assembly. A similar rule applies to procedures and variables. Exported entities have public accessibility, while nonexported entities are declared with "assembly" accessibility. Variables and fields of records that are exported in read-only mode are treated as though they were public. This implies that the guarantee of integrity that the read-only marking denotes is only enforced by the compiler rather than the runtime. It would have been possible to implement every such field and variable as a property of the associated class and declare a "get_*" but no "set_*" method for each such property. If this had been done, the runtime itself would have enforced the constraint. This would have been a heavier-weight, but still viable, alternative design.

Mapping types.   The record types of *Component Pascal* need to be mapped in some way to the **class** constructs of the *CTS*. But what kinds of of records should be mapped to what kinds of class? *Component Pascal* does not make a declarative distinction between value and reference aggregate types. Record types *always* have value semantics, and pointer types *always* have reference semantics.

The *gpcp* choices are as follows. Named record types that are neither extensible nor extensions of another type are implemented as value classes. If a program declares a pointer to such a record type, then the pointer type is implemented as a reference class with a single field of the type of the value class. This reference class is an explicit *boxed* occurrence of the embedded value class. It has at least one advantage over the automatically boxed classes manipulated by the "box" and "unbox" instructions. In this case we may access the fields of the boxed value without unboxing. Procedures that are bound to such a record type are implemented as (nonvirtual) instance methods of the value class. Procedures bound to a type that is any pointer to the record are implemented as (nonvirtual) instance methods of the explicit boxed class. Consider the source file shown in Figure 4.7. This program declares a record type and a pointer to the record type. The record type has a single field of wide character type.

There are two type-bound procedures declared on this record type. One, *Foo*, takes the record type as its receiver. The other, *Bar*, takes the pointer to the record as its bound type. Because the two are in principle bound to the same underlying record type, the names exist in the same namescope and must be distinct. In the interests of brevity, both methods are declared with empty bodies.

Since the record type is inextensible and does not extend any other type, this type will be implemented as a value class. The procedure *Foo* will be implemented as a instance

```
MODULE ValCls; IMPORT CPmain;

  TYPE  RecTyp = RECORD c : CHAR END;
        PtrTyp = POINTER TO RecTyp;

  PROCEDURE (IN r : RecTyp)Foo(),NEW; END Foo;
  PROCEDURE (r : PtrTyp)Bar(),NEW; END Bar;

END ValCls.
```

Figure 4.7: Declaration of inextensible record type

method on this value class. A companion boxed reference class will be declared for this value class. This class will be sealed, as a reflection of the inextensibility of the bound type that it represents. The procedure *Bar* will be implemented as an instance method on this reference class. The *IL* that *gpcp* produces from this source is shown in Figure 4.8. In this figure the various constructors and copy methods have been removed to save space.

```
.namespace ValCls
{
  .class value sealed RecTyp
        extends [mscorlib]System.ValueType {
    .field public wchar 'c'
    .method assembly instance void 'Foo'() il managed {
       ret
    } // end of method Foo
  } // end of class RecTyp

  .class sealed Boxed_RecTyp {          // Actually, pointer to RecTyp
    .field public value class ValCls.RecTyp 'v$'
    .method assembly instance void 'Bar'() il managed {
       ret
    } // end of method Bar
  } // end of class Boxed_RecTyp
}
```

Figure 4.8: Implementation of inextensible record type

Note that the boxed class, *Boxed_RecTyp*, has a single field of the *RecTyp* type. In all such cases the name of the field that encapsulates the boxed value is called "v$".

There is an interesting artifact of this design. Methods bound to the record type, and to the *pointer* to the record type, are bound to the same underlying type in the source semantics but are bound to separate types in the implementation. It seems curious, but no ambiguity can arise. Suppose that we have a program variable of the pointer type, named p, say. Consider the two method invocations —

```
p.Foo();            // implicit dereference of p
p.Bar();            // direct call on pointer type
```

In the first case there is an implicit dereference of the pointer type of p to match the (record) type of the receiver of *Foo*. In the second case the receiver type of *Bar* is the same type as p. These two calls will appear in the *IL* as —

```
call   instance void ValCls.ValCls::'Foo'()
call   instance void ValCls.Boxed_RecTyp::'Bar'()
```

Another small point about this particular design choice is that modules that export a record type as a value record must also define and export the boxed type, even if the module does not declare a pointer to the record. The point is that multiple importing modules may independently define pointer types that are bound to the same exported record type. These modules must agree on the name of the boxed type, so the module that exports the record must define and name the type.

Enough about the inextensible records. What of extensible records? It turns out that there is little choice. Extensible record types may have extensible type-bound procedures. These have to be implemented as virtual methods in the *CTS*. We appear to have no choice but to implement such records as reference classes.[2] This means that extensible records in *Component Pascal* are always implemented by reference surrogates. If a pointer is declared to such a record type, then it will be implemented as the same reference class. As was discussed in the previous chapter, with reference surrogates two types may map into the same type in the *CTS*, with the semantic difference being reflected in the different translations of assignments.

If we consider a small variation on the previous example, we declare the record type as extensible, thereby ensuring that the implementation will be by a reference class. Figure 4.9 has the modified source code. In this case the procedure declarations have been left unchanged. The two procedures are still inextensible and hence will be implemented as instance methods. Of the two procedures, one is still bound to the record type, and the other to the pointer to the record. The resulting *IL* is shown in Figure 4.10. As expected, there is only one class here. The two procedures have mapped into methods bound to the same reference class.

The *IL* in the figure has been shortened by the removal of the constructor method and also the copy method. It is necessary to have a copy method, since the language allows

---

[2]That is, we have no choice unless we are prepared to explicitly define the whole machinery of method dispatch ourselves. This rather extreme alternative is necessary for some languages that feature multiple inheritance.

```
MODULE RefCls; IMPORT CPmain;

   TYPE   RecTyp = EXTENSIBLE RECORD c : CHAR END;
          PtrTyp = POINTER TO RecTyp;

   PROCEDURE  (IN r : RecTyp)Foo(),NEW; END Foo;
   PROCEDURE  (r : PtrTyp)Bar(),NEW; END Bar;

END RefCls.
```

Figure 4.9: Declaration of extensible record type

```
.namespace RefCls
{
   .class RecTyp {
     .field assembly wchar 'c'
     .method assembly instance void 'Foo'() il managed {
         ret
     } // end of method Foo

     .method assembly instance void 'Bar'() il managed {
         ret
     } // end of method Bar
   } // end of class RecTyp
}
```

Figure 4.10: Implementation of extensible record type

entire assignments of inextensible record types. Of course, *RecTyp* is extensible and hence may not be assigned directly. However, a sealed extension of *RecTyp* might be defined in another module and then assigned. Since the private fields of *RecTyp* would be inaccessible in the importing module, the copy method for the extended type must be able to recursively call the copy method of its supertype.

One final design point. Suppose an anonymous record type is defined by the syntax **pointer to record … end**. There is no point in defining a separate value type and associated boxed type in this case, since it is impossible to declare unboxed occurrences of this type. In this case it makes sense to implement the type as a reference class and save a bunch of bits in the executable.

The choices for arrays are rather simpler. Arrays are implemented by reference surrogates. Multidimensional arrays are implemented as arrays of arrays, as has been discussed earlier. The consequences of this design for the assignment of entire arrays and the passing of arrays by value are explored in Chapter 9.

Mapping procedures.

Mapping procedures.   Modules in *Component Pascal* may have ordinary procedures at the outer level. These procedures are not associated with any class or type in the source language. Nevertheless, they are implemented as static methods belonging to the synthetic static class discussed earlier. The mode annotations on formal parameters are easily mapped. Reference parameters of all kinds map into reference parameters in the *IL*. Formals marked as **in** or **out** carry the corresponding attribute in the method definition.

There is one curious consequence of the use of reference surrogates. Suppose that we declare a procedure that takes two parameters of the same array type. We shall assume that the first has value mode, while the second has (**var**) reference mode. The declaration might be —

> **procedure** Foo(a : **array of** CHAR; **var** b : **array of** CHAR);

In the *IL* both parameters will have the same type! Since the arrays will be implemented by reference surrogates, we do not have to take an address to get a reference to the array. The reference is all that we have! This is an echo of the observation in the last section that for types that are implemented by reference surrogates, the record type and a pointer to the record type are not distinguished in the *IL*. The declaration of our example procedure will be —

> **.method assembly static void** Foo(wchar[] 'a', wchar[] 'b')

In the case of the first parameter the incoming parameter will be a *clone* of the actual array specified in the program. In the case of the second parameter the incoming parameter will just be a copy of the surrogate reference.

Type-bound procedures are mapped into instance and virtual methods in a very straightforward fashion. The various annotations map onto attributes of the method declaration, as shown in Figure 4.11.

Source annotation	IL *attributes*
abstract	abstract virtual
new, extensible	newslot virtual
extensible	virtual
new	instance
<none>	final virtual

Figure 4.11: Mapping procedure annotations to method attributes

The last two table entries deserve some explanation. If a procedure is **new** but not extensible—that is, both new and final—then it is implemented as a nonvirtual instance method. This avoids cluttering up the *v-table* needlessly.[3]

---

[3]There is actually a small exception here if the language is extended to allow the implementation of interfaces. If a procedure supplies the implementation for an interface method, then it must be marked **virtual**. This rule applies even if the method is both **new** and **final**.

If a procedure is neither new nor extensible, then it must be implemented as a virtual method, since it overrides another method. However, since it is nonextensible, it may be declared to be final. Even in cases where methods are declared to be virtual, there are circumstances that permit such methods to be called statically, as is discussed on page 253. Marking methods final whenever possible facilitates this.

Since in *IL* all methods are declared at the same lexical level, it is necessary to decide what to do about nested procedures. All such procedures are emitted into the same scope, as are their enclosing procedure or method. Thus a procedure nested inside a method will become a static method of the same class, while a procedure nested inside an outer level procedure will become a static procedure of the synthetic static class. To eliminate any ambiguity in the namespace, nested procedures have mangled names formed from the names of all the enclosing methods. The accessibility of all such nested methods is declared to be **private**.

Problem areas.   There are a small number of language features in *Component Pascal* that do not map easily into the constructs of *IL*. Some of these, such as methods with covariant return types and structural compatibility of procedure types, have elegant workarounds that are discussed in Chapter 12.

There are other problems that defy easy solutions. Possibly the most intractable of these is how to allow nested procedures to access the local variables and parameters of their enclosing blocks. This is the *uplevel addressing problem*. There are two traditional mechanisms that are used in native-code implementations: static links and display vectors. Neither of these is applicable here. One solution to this problem is to perform static program analysis to determine exactly which local data are accessed in this way. All of these "uplevel addressed variables" are passed as additional hidden, reference-mode parameters to the nested procedures that require such access. This works. However, the solution is exceptionally ungainly, since it requires the additional hidden parameters to be passed along *all possible call paths* that lead from an outer procedure to an inner one that accesses nonlocal data. An alternative attack that requires more effort in the compiler, but is more elegant at runtime, is explored in detail in the final chapter.

gpcp performs initialization analysis to ensure that all local variables are properly initialized before use. The level of conservatism of the algorithm matches that of the initialization analysis of the *IL* verifier. There is one small glitch with parameter passing. The execution engine does not necessarily take any notice of the "[in]" and "[out]" attributes on reference parameters. Suppose that a local variable has its first use as the actual parameter passed to an **out**-mode formal parameter in a method call. So far as *Component Pascal* is concerned, the call itself supplies the variable initialization. However, since the verifier does not take any notice of the attribute, it will object to the taking of the address of an uninitialized local variable. The solution is reasonably cheap. Such cases are detected during static analysis, as described in Appendix A, and a dummy assignment of a suitable zero value to the local is made to keep the verifier happy.

Extensions for interoperation.   As well as operating within the *.NET* framework, it is intended that programs compiled by *gpcp* should be full consumers of *CLS*conformant libraries. This poses a small number of problems for the design, since there are some *CLS* features that have no counterpart in *Component Pascal*. The approach adopted has been to add extensions to the syntax of the language to allow these additional features to be accessed.

An example may make the approach more clear. *Component Pascal* has no equivalent to interface implementation. However, it is desirable to allow *Component Pascal* to define types that implement *CLS*-defined interface types. Thus *gpcp* defines syntax that allows record declarations to contract to implement any number of interfaces. There is no facility (in the current version) for the *definition* of interface types, but such types defined elsewhere may be implemented. Note that as well as a syntax addition, this choice requires that the compiler understand the semantics of the implementation contract. For example, the compiler will return an error if the source program fails to implement all of the methods in an interface contract.

Other extensions to facilitate consumption of the *CLS* are a "protected" access modifier for imported names and support for imported enumeration types. In both cases the compiler allows the use, but not the definition, of data with these properties. The compiler also allows the definition of **event** types, with syntax similar to the definition of procedure types. There are new built-in procedures for registering and deregistering call-back procedures for declared events. This allows *Component Pascal* programs to perform standard event handling in the *CLR*.

Component Pascal does not have facilities to raise or handle exceptions, but any program utilizing the *CLS* must be prepared to receive an exception in response to a method call. In this case, the runtime support of *gpcp* defines the *NativeException* type and a procedure that allows an exception value to be constructed with a string argument. A syntactic extension allows an optional single **rescue** clause to be defined at the end of any procedure. This rescue clause will be encoded as a **catch** clause in *IL*, one that expects an incoming *System.Exception* object on the stack. The rescue clause nominates a name for the exception object, so that within the clause the program is able to perform further type tests on the exception if that is necessary. This appears to be the minimal implementation of exception handling that is sufficiently expressive to work with the *CLS*. Some discussion of the *gpcp* exception-handling model was given on page 99.

The final issue discussed here is access to constructor methods. *Component Pascal* does not have explicit constructors, relying instead on a standard procedure. This procedure, **new**, is used to create all object instances. Calls of **new** translate in the *IL* into calls to the no-arg constructor of the object class. This built-in facility is insufficient for *CLS* classes that do not have a public no-arg constructor, or that rely on the constructor method to set "initonly" fields. The solution adopted in *gpcp* is to treat a constructor of type T in the *CLS* as a static function returning T in *Component Pascal*. Such constructors are supplied with a *miranda*[4] name by which they may be referenced within the using program. Of course, the compiler will know, as it must, whether an apparent function call is actually a constructor invocation, since the one translates into a "`call`" instruction and the other into a "`newobj`" instruction.

Notes on Chapter 4

Idioms in gpcp.   There are a small number of idioms in *gpcp* that have do to with programming style rather than some deep property of the language. For example, the compiler does not have a single linked list in its code, instead relying on expansible lists that expand using an *amortized doubling* algorithm. Sidebar 4.1 has more details.

Another idiom is the use of the visitor pattern, particularly over symbol tables. There are lots of symbol tables attached to various scope descriptors in the abstract syntax representation, and we often want to do processing equivalent to the idea —

> **for** <*every identifier i*> **do** i.Op() **end**

where *Op* is some specific operation to be applied to each entry in the table. The compiler defines a visitor type for this purpose and defines new operations as required for all kinds of useful purposes. Further details of this technique are found in the "Using the Visitor Pattern" section (see page 192).

Finding out more.   The mappings of various constructs in *gpcp* are easily investigated by submitting test cases to the compiler. In the case of other languages the same approach may be used to explore the choices that have been made, possibly with the assistance of `ildasm`.

With *C#* the mappings are immediate, with the *CLR* semantics very closely matching the *C#* defintions. The *Visual Basic 7* compiler is a good source for finding out how to use the typed reference facilities in the *CLR*.

The managed extensions to *Visual C++* are also a good source of example code, particularly for interoperation with the unmanaged code in the libraries. Unfortunately, the disassembled code from this style of compiler is much harder to interpret than the compilers that exclusively produce managed code.

---

[4]Named after 1966 US Supreme court decision (*Miranda v. Arizona*), stating that plaintiffs who cannot afford an attorney must have one appointed for them.

SIDEBAR 4.1

MAKING EXPANSIBLE LISTS BY AMORTIZED DOUBLING

One of the most prevalent data structures in *gpcp* is the expansible indexed list. Most places in which such indexes are used would have used linked lists in a more conventional setting. In almost every circumstance the featured structure uses less memory and consumes fewer machine cycles than a linked list would.

Expansible arrays may be indexed in the same way as ordinary arrays and have an *Append* operation, which adds a new element to the top of the array. The implementation consists of a record type with three fields. This record is implemented as a value class in the *CLS*. Consider an expansible array of some datatype, T. The fields are a pointer to an array of T of unspecified length, named a, which is initially **nil**. There are two integer fields, named *tide* and *high*. *tide* is a public, read-only field which denotes the logical number of elements in the array. At any time the valid array elements are in positions 0 to *tide*-1. *high* is a private field which denotes the number of element positions in the currently allocated array to which a points. This is the maximum value of *tide*. When *tide* $=$ *high* it is time to expand the underlying array.

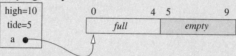

These arrays automatically adjust their length as additional elements are needed. The magic is all in the *Append* code —

```
procedure Append(s :  TSeq; e :  T);
  var tmp : pointer to array of T; idx :  INTEGER;
begin
  if s.a = nil then new(s.a, 4);
  elsif s.tide = s.high then
    tmp := s.a; s.high := s.high*2; new(s.a, s.high);
    for idx := 0 to s.tide-1 do s.a[idx] := tmp[idx] end;
  end;
  s.a[tide] := e; INC(s.tide);
end Append;
```

Whenever necessary, the array doubles its length and copies the elements from the old array to the new. As the array grows in size the allocation of more memory becomes less frequent, compensating for the fact that the copying becomes more expensive. The occasional high cost of array expansion and copying is amortized over all of the other insertions that occur at negligible cost. In the *CLR* the sequence type will be implemented as a value class, while the array will be a dynamically allocated, managed object.

This data structure has a special appeal in circumstances in which the lists only expand. If elements need to be deleted, copying of the whole array will generally be required.

Building Abstract Syntax Trees

5

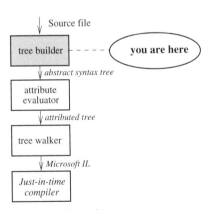

As a first step in the compilation of each program, using our reference architecture we must construct an **Abstract Syntax Tree** (*AST*). This data structure is the key representation of the program being compiled and is the data structure on which most of our computation takes place. This chapter discusses how the form of this data structure should be designed for each language, and how an instance of the data structure is built for each program written in the language. Chapter 6 deals with the computation of attributes on the *AST*, as a preliminary to the emission of code.

As mentioned in the introduction, we wish to avoid detailed discussion of tree construction in this book. This is because there is very little that one may say about this topic that is specific to *.NET*. Nevertheless, we do say a little bit about it, simply to make the book relatively self-contained.

Although we avoid the details of tree *construction*, we need to consider the *design* of the tree representation. We need to do this for two separate reasons. First, we need to be able to support the various kinds of traversal that are required for code emission. In addition, we need to make sure that there is a place in the nodes of the tree for all of the attributes that we need to compute.

This chapter thus deals with the design of the data structures that the later phases of the compilation will use. The book takes a particular point of view about the *right* way to do this. Of course there are alternative design philosophies that also work, but since we want to be definite about the examples, we need to have a concrete design.

Before we launch into the details, it may be worth taking a step back and thinking about why we call these data structures *abstract* syntax trees. The point is there is nothing "abstract" about the trees that we build. Let us keep in mind that these are trees that represent *abstract syntax* and not *abstract trees* that represent syntax.

For programming languages with a text representation there are invariably elements of the (concrete) syntax that are present to allow the text to be parsed unambiguously. Consider the structure of binary operators in expressions. The essential structure—that is, the abstract syntax—of a binary expression reduces to the fact that it has an *operator identification* and *two subexpressions*. We need say nothing at all about operator precedence, parentheses, and so on, because the only purpose of such rules is to help the parser figure out where the subexpressions begin and end in any particular case.

Scanning and Parsing

Why Building an Abstract Syntax Tree Is Always Best

For some simple languages it is possible to write a compiler with an architecture that is sometimes called a *single pass compiler*. The notion of counting "passes" in a compiler is somewhat problematic, because it is based on historical designs in which the compiler repeatedly read in one file and wrote out another. Due to memory constraints the complete transformation from source to object code was as laborious as a blacksmith shaping a block of metal with many small blows. However, what is meant by contemporary uses of the phrase is that the compiler reads the source file only once, does not create any intermediate files, and produces its output *incrementally*. Such compilers read a little input, write a little output, read some more input, write some more output, and so on. This is not the approach that is advocated here.

The problem with incremental compiling is that it relies on the property that the early "chunks" of output never need any whole-of-module information. This can lead to significant contortions on the part of both language designers and language implementers. Consider the case of a language that permits mutually recursive procedures and strictly checks conformance between actual and formal arguments in procedure calls. Within a single module one of a mutually recursive pair must appear first, and its embedded call to the procedure that has not yet been seen has to be handled somehow. We might simply assume that the call is correct, resolving to kill the compilation with an error message if the already emitted code for the call turns out, after all, to have been incorrect. However, this strategy fails on perfectly legal programs when the encoding for the first call needs to include code for implicit type promotion of arguments (from "int" to "double", say). Instead what we need is the arbitrary addition of syntax to the language to allow "forward" declarations of particular procedures. Figure 5.1 shows what this looks like for a generic *Pascal* dialect.

```
program foo;
    ...
    procedure Bar(i : integer); forward;
    ...
    procedure Foo(c : char);
    begin
        ... ; Bar(x); ...
    end;
    ...
    procedure Bar(i : integer);
    begin
        ... ; Foo(y); ...
    end;
    ...
end.
```

Figure 5.1: *Pascal* code with forward declaration

Early language *C* implementations used an equally ugly trick, in which the forward function appeared in an `extern` definition. This allowed the compiler to enter the function details in the symbol table and then generate correct code for the call to this function. Of course the real declaration of the function might have turned out to be `static` rather than `extern`, so the compiler had to be ready to replace the first definition with the later declaration.

All this *can* be made to work, at least in the case that the language implementer feels free to modify the syntax of the source language at will!

The forward declaration problem, together with a host of similar difficulties, will simply disappear if we build an *AST* representation of the whole compilation unit. If we do this, we may perform arbitrary traversals of the *AST* or the symbol tables, computing needed attributes in any consistent order. This capability brings considerable freedom with it. If it appears that some additional attribute might be useful at some late stage of compiler development, then you may be sure that you may evaluate it from the *AST*.

In cases for which the language semantics are specified by an attribute grammar formalism, the order in which attributes are evaluated (and the number of traversals that are required to compute all attributes) is decided by the compiler-building tool. Such tools necessarily build a complete *AST*.

One of the historical arguments against *AST*-based representations was the rather wanton use of memory resources that such designs entail. The amount of space used by an *AST* depends to some extent on the number of attributes that are directly stored in a node, rather than being recomputed as needed or included by reference. Nevertheless, figures of 10 to 20 bytes of memory per byte of lightly commented source code are typical. Given the memory resources of contemporary development environments, this should not be a constraint.

In short, there is no reasonable argument against an *AST*-based architecture even for the simplest languages. The flexibility and even execution speed of the approach always win the day.

Specifying Abstract Syntax

The essence of abstract syntax is that it specifies the canonical properties of a particular language construct. Furthermore, it is usually the case that the abstract syntax is more intuitive than the concrete syntax. For example, it is easy to understand the overall structure of the abstract syntax of expressions, with binary, unary, and leaf nodes. By contrast the structure of the concrete syntax for typical expression languages has multiple levels of precedence, leading to a confusing proliferation of syntactic categories (nonterminal symbols) that have no meaning in the abstract syntax. The appearance of *expression*, *simpleExpression*, *term*, *factor*, and *primary* says more about the constraints of the particular parser technology than it says about the underlying structure of expressions.

We may thus expect that formalisms for expressing abstract syntax are significantly simpler than those used for concrete syntax.

Here we use a simple, semiformal grammar for expressing abstract syntax. It is an informal notation based on the "*IDL*" notation used for specifying the abstract syntax of language *Ada* in the early 1980s. The notation expresses relationships between three kinds of entities: *node-types*; *node-class-types*; and *typed attributes*. Node-class-types are simply collections of node-types. Node-types are declared to have named attributes, and each of these has a declared datatype. The datatypes may be node-class-types or node-types, or are of some externally defined datatype such as *String*.

A simple example probably makes this more clear than the description. Here is the abstract syntax for an expression representation —

```
EXPR    ::= Binary | Unary | IdLeaf | Leaf
Binary ==> operator : OpEnum,
             leftOp   : EXPR,
             rightOp  : EXPR;
Unary  ==> operator : OpEnum,
             child    : EXPR;
IdLeaf ==> ident     : SymTabEntry;
Leaf   ==> value     : ConstDesc;
```

In this example there are four kinds of expressions. Binary expressions have an operator attribute of some externally defined enumeration type. They also have two other *structural* attributes that are the left and right operands. These are both of expression type, corresponding to the left and right subexpressions of the expression. Unary expressions have an operator attribute, again of enumeration type, and a single subexpression attribute. Identifier leaf expressions have a single attribute, which is a symbol table entry, while a different leaf node type has a value attribute which is a constant descriptor.

The *EBNF* grammar for *IDL* allows one other kind of "type" in an attribute declaration. Attributes may be declared to be of some type, or may be defined to be a *sequence* of some type —

Class-definition	→	*class-id* ':: =' *node-id* { '|' *node-id* }';' .
Node-definition	→	*node-id* '==>' Attribute-def { ',' Attribute-def } ';' .
Attribute-def	→	*attr-id* ':' Type .
Type	→	*class-id* | 'seqOf' *class-id* | *externally-defined-type* .

The justification for using a formalism such as *IDL* is that it allows the properties of the abstract syntax to be expressed abstractly, without any regard for the actual data structures that will eventually need to be used to realize the trees. In principle the conversion of the *IDL* into concrete type declarations in the compiler is a separate step, sometimes called *data reification*.

If the *AST* is to be realized in an object-oriented language, then the idea of using a separate data reification step may seem a bit like overkill. The translation of *IDL* into an *OO*-language is immediate. *IDL* "node-class-types" become abstract base classes, with each of their "node-types" being a subclass derived from the base. Attributes of node-types become instance fields of the concrete class that realizes the node-type. Attributes of sequence type are implemented by the list construct of your choice. There is little else to add. In the event that an object-oriented implementation is contemplated, it is probably justifiable to skip the *IDL* step and go straight to the concrete types.

In the case of implementation frameworks that are not object-oriented, it is necessary to adopt a slightly more laborious approach. For statically typed but non-object-oriented languages the only form of supported polymorphism applies to union types, or in *Pascal* terminology *variant records*. In such languages a datum declared as a pointer to a union type may legally reference an instance of any one of the possible variants. In such an implementation framework the translation from *IDL* is less obvious. In effect, every node-class-type is implemented as a reference to some union type. Each of the node-types belonging to the node-class becomes one of the variants of the union. Of course, in such cases each instance of the union type must have a type tag that orchestrates tree traversal using a "**case** tag **of**" construct or an equivalent **switch** statement. In the object-oriented framework the equivalent navigation of the trees may be controlled either by (virtual) method dispatch based on the class of the tree node or by the use of a type-case selection statement. We shall see examples of each style later.

From Concrete Syntax to Abstract Syntax

The actual process of building an *AST* for a particular program is the task of the scanner and parser of the compiler. There are a number of different possible approaches here and a considerable choice of tools to assist.

In the case of *gpcp* the compiler uses a recursive descent parser, with a rather dubious history. An attributed grammar for *Component Pascal* was processed by the parser generator *COCO/R*. This particular version of the tool produced a parser and scanner written in *Modula-2*. This parser was modified by hand from *Modula-2* to the closely related *Component Pascal*.

A word of warning should be given to anyone wishing to delve into the *gpcp* parser module. *Component Pascal* has some syntactic ambiguities, particularly in the syntax for designators. A typical problem is that in the middle of parsing a designator, if a left parenthesis is the next token, then it is not known whether the token is the start of the argument list of a procedure call, or whether it is the start of a type assertion (narrowing cast). Since these two constructs have different abstract syntax, a decision needs to be made. Difficulties of this kind are not unusual with real languages. There are essentially two different approaches to tackling such problems. In the first instance the abstract syntax might be modified by the definition of some kind of "union" node. Later, during semantic analysis, when the correct interpretation of the construct is known, a tree-to-tree transformation can replace the tree fragment with a node of the appropriate kind. The other approach, and the one chosen by *gpcp*, is to perform enough type analysis during parsing that a query to the symbol table can decide on the correct interpretation of the next phrase.

The general question of how much of the *AST* attribute evaluation to perform during tree building is an interesting one. The question is discussed further in "Evaluating Expression Type" (see page 173).

Designing the Abstract Syntax

The remainder of this chapter uses the design of the abstract syntax used by *gpcp* as its main example. For other languages the design will turn out differently, but the *process* of design will be the same. It is therefore worth working through the discussion of design alternatives, even if you cannot use the final result directly. The detail of the *AST* is also used in the later chapters.

What Kinds of Nodes Are There?

For a typical imperative programming language we have four different kinds of *descriptor* nodes in the *AST*. These are **expression descriptors**, **statement descriptors**, **type descriptors**, and **identifier descriptors**. Each of these descriptor types corresponds to a node-class-type in *IDL*. We have already seen a simplified version of the way in which the various expression node-types derive from the expression node-class-type. The other descriptor types have a similar structure, with a number of derived node-types.

In a statically typed language, each datum and expression has a type that is statically computable. It is a reasonable point of view in such cases to think of *static type* as being the most fundamental of attributes. Since a language like *Component Pascal* has a variety of ways of defining types, we would expect to have different specializations of the abstract type descriptor for each of the ways in which a type may be declared. Thus we have descriptors for array types, pointer types, and so on.

In languages with named entities we need a means of binding names to definitions. In most languages these bindings are permanent, and we handle the possibility that names may become hidden and then once again become visible by a separate *scope control* mechanism. We expect therefore to have separate specializations of the identifier descriptor structure for variables, procedures, named constants, and all of the other kinds of program entities that can have names.

Finally, if our language is *statement-oriented*, we shall specialize the statement descriptor class for each kind of statement that the language definition admits. Note that not all of the languages that one might think of as statement-oriented truly have this underlying structure. Some languages, by contrast, are *expression-oriented*, and every "statement" is actually an expression evaluation. In the case that an expression is evaluated solely for its side effects we consider the expression as having the type "**void**." Or maybe, as in the case of language *C*, it is legal to compute a nonvoid expression and then silently discard the result. In any case, for such languages we would need only three base descriptor class-types, rather than four.

Choosing the Descriptor Structure

In the last section it was implied that the choice of node-types for each node-class-type was determined in some natural fashion by predetermined properties of the language. Well, now we need to take a bit of a harder look at the real decisions that have to be made.

The situation is complicated by a number of factors. First, there is a question of *granularity*. Do we want to define distinct node-types that share the same abstract syntax?

Consider the case of **while** loops and **repeat** loops. Both of these loops have an abstract syntax with just two features: There is a *selector expression*, and there is a *loop body*. In a correct program the selector expression will turn out to have Boolean type, while the loop body will be a sequence of statements. It looks therefore as though we may use a single node-type to represent the two loop kinds in the *AST* and use a tag to tell which is which when we really need to know. For some of the semantic checking we shall treat all nodes of loop type in the same way. In other traversals, such as emitting the final code, we will need to use an **if ... then ... else** structure predicated on the tag value.

At the other end of the scale, we need to decide whether or not to invent distinct node-types for every subsubvariation of a particular structure. In *IDL* all nodes belonging to a particular node-class are at the same derivation level. However, in the implementation we may choose a more deeply nested structure. An example may make this clear. Typically we might expect to have identifier descriptors for *types, variables, named constants, procedures, functions, methods,* and *modules.* For the moment let us just consider the variables. If we have a single node-type for all variable identifier descriptors, then we can easily say

if *theId* **is** *IdDesc.Variable* **then ... end**

But then we have to decide what attributes such a node would have in the abstract syntax. The trouble is that static variables, static fields, instance fields, local variables, and procedure arguments all require different attributes. For an OO implementation we can resolve this at the implementation level by defining an inheritance hierarchy in which there is an abstract variable type with subtypes, and maybe even sub-subtypes. We shall see some examples of this in the practical code.

Similarly, we need to decide whether a proper procedure (in *C* terms, a function returning **void**) gets a different node-type from a value-returning function.

In any case the point to be made here is that design decisions have to be made about the sharing of abstract syntax between different node-types and the possibility of creating deep inheritance hierarchies to share attributes between related nodes.

During the development of *gpcp*, the design started off with a fairly flat structure with, for example, separate node-types for static and automatic variables. When it turned out that the code was littered with tests for nodes belonging to *sets* of node-types, the design was refactored. The current design defines an abstract variable descriptor and various subtypes, as shown in the inheritance diagram of Figure 5.2. In the diagram, *Idnt* is an abstract base class, from which all identifier descriptors are derived. This includes variables and several other kinds. *AbVar* is an abstract class from which all variable identifier nodes are derived. The directly derived identifier node-types are *VarId*, which is used for static variables and fields; *FldId*, which is is used for instance fields; *LocId*, which is used for local variables; and finally *ParId*, which is used for procedure parameters (arguments). *FldId, VarId,* and *ParId* are all final classes, while *LocId* is extensible.

The abstract classes on which all of the other descriptors are based are exported by a module *Symbols.* The four sets of derived classes are defined in modules *IdDesc, TypeDesc,*

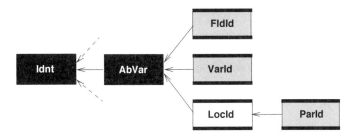

Figure 5.2: Variable descriptor hierarchy in *gpcp*

ExprDesc, and *StatDesc* respectively. The *Symbols* module also exports sequence types for each of the abstract classes. All these sequences are implemented as dynamic arrays and are expanded using amortized doubling, as described on page 134.

Type Descriptors

In *Component Pascal* we have the following kinds of types: built-in types; array types; record types; pointer types; and procedure types. There is also a descriptor for an "opaque" type, which is a type about which we know nothing except the name. Opaques are a convenient placeholder for types for which we do not yet have a definition.

Compilers for *.NET* will often need to have internal structures to describe types and attributes that exist in the *CLS* but do not exist in the source language of the compiler. The particular issues involved are discussed in some detail in Chapter 10. In the case of *gpcp* there are type descriptors for enumerations, and also a number of attribute values that *Component Pascal* cannot define but must be able to access.

In the event, we end up with six different kinds of type descriptor, all of which are final, and all of which directly derive from an abstract base class named *Type*. The abstract base type contains fields that are common to all concrete types. In principle there are two such attributes —

```
Type ==> kind : INTEGER,   // an enumeration tag, used as a selector
         idnt : Idnt;      // a reference to the identifier descriptor
                           // or nil if the type is anonymous
```

The *kind* field is used so that it is possible to perform selection with a **case** statement, rather than having to use virtual dispatch everywhere. In a well-formed program the *idnt* field can only be **nil** or hold an *Idnt*, which must be an instance of the *TypId* subclass.

In practice, there are a number of other common fields in the abstract descriptor. These are used for various housekeeping tasks, such as marking nodes as having been visited during type resolution.

The simplest of the derived classes are those for base types and opaques. The only basetypes are the built-in types such as the integer and real types, characters, and the *ANYREC* and *ANYPTR* types. Base types have a single additional attribute, *tpOrd*, that is used as an enumeration tag.

Opaques begin their lives with just one attribute, the type name. This is accessed from the inherited *idnt* field. Opaques need just one attribute of their own. Once the type becomes resolved to some known type, we use the *resolved* attribute to point to the now-known type, so that references to the opaque may follow the reference to the actual type. This attribute is **nil** while the type is not yet resolved.

Pointer type descriptors.

Pointer types are similarly simple. The only attribute that a pointer type needs is a denotation of the type to which the pointer is statically bound. We thus have a single attribute, *boundTp* of type *Symbols.Type*. In a correct *Component Pascal* program pointers can only be bound to array or record types. Nevertheless, we allow the attribute to be any kind of type descriptor during tree building and only enforce the restriction later, as part of semantic checking.

Array type descriptors.

Array types in *Component Pascal*, as in most *Pascal* dialects, may be declared with some fixed length. Arrays of different length are considered to be different types. Formal procedure arguments of array type may be declared without specifying a length, and it is possible (and common) to declare a **pointer** to an array with no length. Arrays without a specified length are called *open arrays*.

Arrays are thus declared with two attributes: *length*, which is of integer type; and *elemTp*, which is a type reference. Notice that, in keeping with the *Pascal* tradition, multidimensional arrays occur only as one-dimensional arrays, the element type of which is another array type.

As discussed in the previous section, a design decision needs to be made in such cases. It would be possible to declare separate concrete classes for open and fixed length arrays, both deriving from an abstract array class. The alternative design choice, the choice made in *gpcp*, is to use a single *Array* descriptor class and simply set the length attribute to zero in the open array case. There is no overwhelming reason to choose one design over another in *.NET*. In the *JVM* environment, however, there is a strong incentive to minimize the total number of separate classes, as each ends up as a separate class file in the file system. In any case if the first option (separate descriptors) were to be taken, then it would be a mistake to derive both array classes directly from *Symbols.Type*. This is because we will frequently need to be able to test simply if a descriptor is *any* kind of array. With the design suggested we would be able to do a type test of the descriptor against the abstract array superclass.

Record type descriptors.

Record type descriptors require a large number of attributes. In our mapping of *Component Pascal* to the *CLS*, record types may be implemented either as reference or value classes in the *CTS*. It is probably wise to choose abstract syntax for record descriptors that is general enough to express all of the structure of classes in the *CLS*. That way we may be sure that we can represent all of the semantics of imported *CLS* classes.

Class types in the *CLS* may have at least three different kinds of declared features. Classes have instance fields, methods that are bound to the type, and static features. We might further subdivide the static features into static fields, static methods, and static constants, but there are arguments to not do so.

We might also note that classes define a lexical scope. If we meet a syntactic construct of the following form —

$$designatorExpression.identifier$$

then we must perform the following processing. Find the binding of *designatorExpression* in the current namescope. If the designator binds to an abstract variable, then select the type descriptor attribute of the variable identifier. If the designator binds to a type identifier, then select the type descriptor attribute of that type identifier. In either case we must now bind the *identifier* name in the namescope defined by the selected type. If the designator was bound to a variable, then the identifier must bind to an instance field or method. If the designator was bound to a type identifier, then the identifier must bind to a static field or method.

This suggests that our type descriptor needs some kind of symbol table attribute but need not define separate namescopes for static and instance lookups. It may also be noted that some languages permit the syntactically confusing practice of allowing static features to be qualified on object instances as well as being qualified on the class name.

Finally we note that classes need attributes to describe their inheritance structure. In *Component Pascal* this consists of just one supertype, while in the *CLS*, as in *C#*, we must provide for a single supertype and a *list* of interfaces.

The structure of the abstract syntax for record types thus needs at least the following features —

```
Record ==> kind       : INTEGER,      // inherited from Type
           idnt       : Idnt,         // inherited from Type
           baseTp     : Type,         // the supertype
           bindTp     : Type,         // see discussion
           symTb      : SymbolTable,  // feature namescope
           fields     : seqOf Idnt,   // instance fields
           methods    : seqOf Idnt,   // instance fields
           statics    : seqOf Idnt,   // static features
           interfaces : seqOf Idnt;   // implements list
```

As well as these structural attributes, we will need some semantic attributes, such as a set of flags that say whether the class is final or extensible, and so on. We will also need some code attributes to hold such things as the mangled names used in the *PEM*.

There are a couple of wrinkles that are peculiar to *Pascal*-family languages. In such languages we maintain the distinction between records and pointers to records. Suppose now we discover a type error during semantic checking, and we wish to give a helpful diagnostic such as "type error: formal type was *Foo*, actual arg was type *Bar*". Now consider how the type name is to be generated. If the type is a named type, we follow the *idnt* reference in the type descriptor and pull out the name. Simple. Now if the type is an anonymous pointer to a named type we may follow the *boundTp* reference, get the name, and generate the string "*POINTER TO bound-type-name*". Still simple. What, however, if our type descriptor is an anonymous record type?

In this case we would like to have an additional attribute that is a reference leading back from the anonymous record type to the pointer type that binds it. This structural attribute is called *bindTp*. Notice that such an attribute is only applicable to anonymous types. Consider the following *Pascal* declaration fragments —

type	BarPtr	=	**pointer to record ... end**;
	FooRec	=	**record ... end**;
	FooPtr1	=	**pointer to** FooRec;
	FooPtr2	=	**pointer to** FooRec;

Notice that the *named* record type *FooRec* does not have a unique binding pointer type. In fact named record types may have zero, one, or many binding pointer types. An anonymous record type has at most one binding pointer type, so in this case the *bindTp* attribute is well-defined and may be used to generate the explicit diagnostic name "*BarPtr^*", which is *Pascal*-talk for "the type pointed to by *BarPtr*."

Procedure type descriptors.

Procedure type descriptors are also relatively complicated in *Component Pascal*. This will not necessarily be the case for other languages, many of which will not even need such a construct.

Procedure type descriptors, for those languages that need them, hold information about the signatures of procedures. That is, they record the list of formal arguments and their types, a return type and, in the case of type-bound methods, a receiver type as well. In some languages such information can only be associated with the declaration of named procedures. In such cases we might say that only *procedures* have signatures, and we should associate the signature information with the abstract syntax for each procedure. For such languages signature information should be an attribute of the identifier descriptor of each procedure.

Languages that have facilities for declaring **procedure types**, or function pointer types as they would be called in some languages, need to be able to specify signature information that belongs to the type rather than to a particular procedure. In such cases we are forced to invent abstract syntax for procedure types. As the next section indicates, once we have defined procedure type descriptors, we may reuse the design to hold the signature information for procedure identifiers as well.

From the point of view of the structure of the abstract syntax, we might argue that there are four kinds of procedure types in languages like *Component Pascal* or *C#*. Procedures may be *value returning functions* or *proper procedures*—that is, functions returning **void**. Independently, procedures may be *static* or be bound to a particular *receiver* datatype. Again we have the choice between separate subclasses deriving from an abstract procedure type class or a single class with distinguished values of attributes to indicate the finer detail.

In the event, *gpcp* uses a single descriptor. There are attributes for return type and receiver type, and the four possibilities outlined above are encoded in the four possible patterns of **nil** and non-**nil** in these two fields.

From the point of view of generating the code to call some procedure, we need also to distinguish between *instance methods* and *virtual methods*. However, this distinction is not a structural difference. In either case we need the same receiver type attribute. At most we need a flag in some appropriate code attribute in the identifier descriptor.

The abstract syntax for procedure types has the following *IDL* —

```
Procedure ==> kind     : INTEGER,   // inherited from Type
              idnt     : Idnt,      // inherited from Type
              retType  : Type,      // nil for proper procedures
              receiver : Type,      // nil for static procedures
              formals  : seqOf ParId;
```

The formal parameter list is a sequence of the same *ParId* descriptors that appear deep in the variable identifier hierarchy of Figure 5.2. This is another design compromise. If the procedure type descriptors were used only for procedure types, this may as well have been a sequence of type descriptors rather than a sequence of parameter id descriptors. However, since we use the same type descriptor nodes for concrete procedures, we need the *names* of the parameters as well as the types. Thus we must have a list of identifier descriptors rather than a list of type descriptors. Of course, when we use a procedure type descriptor associated with a procedure type (rather than the type of a procedure), we have no names for the parameters. The paradox of dealing with identifier descriptors that have no identifier is a small price to pay for the economy of design.

As noted before, there is often a need for additional, nonstructural attributes in the abstract syntax. In the current case, whenever we generate a *call* instruction in the *CIL*, we need to know how the height of the abstract stack will have been affected. In order to do this we need to know the number of arguments to the call and the number of return values. The number of arguments is not just the length of the *formals* sequence, since we must add one for the receiver if there is one. The number of return elements is either zero or one, but may be two in the case of the *JVM*, which counts 32-bit slots rather than logical stack elements. In any case *gpcp* declares two integer code-attributes, *argN* and *retN*, for these two numbers.

Enumeration type descriptors.   Enumerations are more complicated than might be suspected. This is because they need to define a named scope so that the source language construct *TypeName.enumId* may be resolved to its literal constant value. Enumerations must therefore have some kind of symbol table attribute in which to implement the scoped lookup. In the event, the descriptor also has an identifier *sequence* attribute, so that the enumeration constants may be traversed in order of declaration.

```
Enum ==> kind    : INTEGER,      // inherited from Type
         idnt    : Idnt,         // inherited from Type
         symTb   : SymbolTable,  // member namescope
         statics : seqOf Idnt;   // list of members
```

Identifier Descriptors

The abstract syntax for identifiers needs to describe the structure of the various kinds of things that may be given a name in our programming language. Different languages have different lists, but *Component Pascal* is fairly typical. It has names for variables, record fields, types, constants, procedures, methods, and modules. We have already pointed out some of the fine structure of variable identifier representation.

Looking at the list, we may note a couple of organizing principles. Firstly we note that with the exception of modules, every identifier has some statically computable datatype. This suggests that we might define a *type* attribute in the abstract base type from which all other identifiers are derived. This attribute would be unused in the module identifier case.

A second organizing principle follows from the observation that there are identifiers that define a namescope and those that do not. Procedures, methods, and modules define namescopes, while the others do not. This suggests that we could define another abstract base type from which all of the identifiers that define scopes are derived. We are led to the structure shown in Figure 5.3.

In this figure *Scope* is the abstract superclass for all descriptors that open a new namescope. *ConId* and *TypId* are the descriptors for literal constants and types respectively, while *BlkId* is the descriptor type for modules. The descriptors for procedures and methods are *PrcId* and *MthId*. Both of these derive from an abstract procedure type, *Procs*.

The abstract syntax for the base descriptor type, *Idnt*, is given by —

```
Idnt ==> kind    : INTEGER, // an enumeration tag
         type    : Type,    // datatype of identifier
         defScp  : Scope,   // defining scope
         <various lexical attributes ...>
```

The attribute *defScp* in the abstract syntax for *Idnt* denotes the defining scope. This attribute may be a *BlkId* that denotes a module, either the module currently being defined or an

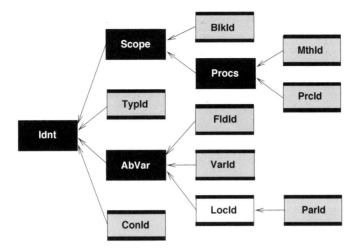

Figure 5.3: Complete identifier descriptor type hierarchy in *gpcp*

external module that defines imported identifiers. The attribute will denote a procedure or method in the case that the identifier is defined in a nested scope.

Lexical attributes.

All identifier descriptors have *lexical attributes* that denote various lexical properties of the identifier. These include the source position of the declaration, so that errors relating to the identifier may be reported. In *gpcp* they also include the hash bucket index that is used as a unique key in the symbol tables, as described in "Symbol Tables and Scope Representation" (see page 161).These attributes exist for all identifiers, so they are defined in the abstract *Idnt* type. They are not shown in any of the following *IDL* in the interests of brevity.

Constant and type identifier descriptors.

Type identifier descriptors have no attributes other than the ones inherited from the abstract type *Idnt*.

```
TypId ==> kind   : INTEGER,   // inherited from Idnt
          type   : Type,      // inherited from Idnt
          defScp : Scope;     // inherited from Idnt
```

Constant descriptors are not much more complicated. Apart from the inherited attributes, there is an attribute *conExp*, which denotes the defining expression. It is an error if this expression does not statically evaluate to a literal value.

```
ConId ==> kind   : INTEGER,   // inherited from Idnt
          type   : Type,      // inherited from Idnt
          defScp : Scope,     // inherited from Idnt
          conExp : Expr;      // the constant expression
```

Variable identifier descriptors.

Variable identifier descriptors.   Variable descriptors have a relatively rich substructure, as noted earlier. The abstract variable designator *AbVar* does not add any attributes but allows type tests to select all variable designators.

Local variables and the parameter designators derived from them have an integer field that holds the variable ordinal number, *varOrd*. This is really a code attribute, but for both the *.NET* and *JVM* intermediate forms, local variables are selected by ordinal number. Parameter identifiers have an additional semantic attribute that denotes the parameter mode, whether **in**, **out**, or **var**. This attribute is set by the tree builder. The *parId* node is used for method receivers as well as formal parameters.

The *VarId* variant of variable designators is used for both static variables, which are bound to a module, and for static fields of classes. One additional attribute is added for this type, which denotes the type designator of the binding class in the static field case. This field is unused for static variables, since the binding module is already denoted by the *defScp* attribute that is inherited from *Idnt*. For languages such as *C#* or *Java* all static data is inside classes, and there are no static variables as they occur in *C++* and *Component Pascal*.

Scopes and module identifiers.

Scopes and module identifiers.   The abstract *Scope* descriptor type is the base type of all those descriptor types that open new namescopes. It adds a single additional attribute to the *Idnt* type. This is a symbol table attribute.

```
Scope ==> kind   : INTEGER,     // inherited from Idnt
          type   : Type,        // inherited from Idnt
          defScp : Scope,       // inherited from Idnt
          symTb  : SymbolTable; // the defined namescope
```

The descriptor type that is used for modules, *BlkId*, derives from the *Scope* descriptor. Module descriptors are used for two kinds of things. They may describe the module currently under compilation, or they may describe an imported module from which the current module needs to access facilities. The same descriptor structure is used for both, with the enumeration tag *kind* being used to distinguish the two cases. In fact, *BlkId* does not make any use of two of the inherited attributes from *Idnt*. Modules do not have a type and in *Component Pascal* do not have a defining scope either. Some languages, notably *C#* and *Modula-2*, do allow nested namespaces and would use the *defScp* attribute in *BlkId*.

When a *BlkId* is used to denote an imported module, it needs no other structural attributes. However, when it is used for the module under compilation it needs structural attributes to hold, among other things, the statement sequences that make up the initialization and finalization code of the module.

Here is the simplified abstract syntax for *BlkId* —

```
BlkId ==> kind     : INTEGER,      // inherited from Idnt
          type     : Type,         // inherited but unused
          defScp   : Scope,        // inherited but unused
          symTb    : SymbolTable,  // inherited from Scope
          modBody  : Stmt,         // initialization code
          modClose : Stmt,         // finalization code
          procs    : seqOf Procs;  // procs defined here
```

The module body and module close sections are single statements that may turn out to be statement sequences. The *procs* attribute is a sequence of abstract procedure descriptors. This sequence will hold all of the procedures and methods defined in the module. It is convenient to keep all the procedures on this list, since it allows iteration over all defined procedures and modules.

Procedure and method identifier descriptors.
As shown in Figure 5.3, there are separate descriptors for procedure and method identifier descriptors. Each of these is derived from a common abstract descriptor type, *Procs*. All of the structure that is common to all procedures is factored into the abstract type.

Here is the abstract syntax for the *Procs* descriptor —

```
Procs ==> kind    : INTEGER,      // inherited from Idnt
          type    : Type,         // inherited from Idnt
          defScp  : Scope,        // inherited from Idnt
          symTb   : SymbolTable,  // inherited from Scope
          body    : Stmt,         // code of procedure body
          rescue  : Stmt,         // exception handler code
          except  : LocId,        // the caught exception
          bndTyp  : Type,         // bound type of procedure
          nestPs  : seqOf PrcId;  // nested procs, if any
```

The descriptor has attributes for the code of the procedure and its optional exception handler (rescue) clause. There is also a placeholder for the local variable that will be assigned the caught exception within the handler.

The *bndTyp* attribute denotes the record type to which the procedure is bound. In a pure *Component Pascal* environment this attribute would only be needed for methods, since procedures are not associated with a particular class. However, since we wish to access the facilities of the *CLS*, it is necessary to make the abstract syntax of procedures expressive enough to denote imported static procedure. Such procedures do have a binding class type, in the same way methods do.

Finally, for *Pascal*-family languages we need to be able to represent the nested structure of procedure declarations. This is achieved, in this design, by adding an attribute for the sequence of nested procedures. Note an oddity of *Component Pascal* here. In this language, procedure declarations may be nested inside procedures or methods, but method declarations cannot be nested. Because of this, we may declare this attribute as a sequence of *PrcId* rather than a sequence of the abstract superclass *Procs*.

PrcId descriptors add only one attribute, which is an ordinal used to denote the descriptors of the built-in standard procedures such as *NEW* and *INC*. For user-declared procedures this attribute has the "not standard" value.

Similarly, the *MthId* descriptor has only two additional attributes. Here is the abstract syntax for the *MthId* descriptor —

```
MthId ==> ...                    // attributes inherited from Procs
         mthAtt : SET,           // method attribute flags
         rcvFrm : ParId;         // formal receiver descriptor
```

One additional attribute is a set of flags denoting, among other things, whether the method is abstract, extensible, and so on. The other attribute denotes the receiver name, mode, and type. This reflects the semantics of the *Oberon-2*-family languages. In these languages the **this** has a user-defined (maybe even meaningful) name, and mode. This provides some interesting semantics. For example, if the receiver has **in** mode, then the compiler will prevent any mutation of the receiver in the body of the method.

Given the rather small differences between the procedure and method descriptor syntax, the question naturally arises as to whether we need two separate descriptors. We might just as well have added the three extra fields to the *Procs* descriptor and made it concrete rather than abstract. Nevertheless, there are a number of places in the code in which the processing of procedures and methods is quite different. With separate descriptor types it is possible to define the processing in separate virtual methods and to use dispatch on the descriptor type to select the appropriate case, increasing program clarity.

Expression Descriptors

Expression descriptors are used to denote the various expression types that occur in our source programs. We might make the descriptor structure either more or less rich. Some previous Gardens Point compilers had experimented with very deep inheritance hierarchies for expression abstract syntax. In the extreme every different operator has its own node-type in the abstract syntax. This is an interesting approach, since it allows tree traversals to be almost completely free of conditional code. Instead all the semantics of the traversal are buried in the different code of the (virtual) methods for each node-type. Nevertheless, this leads to a large number of different classes in the implementation and almost certainly more code overall.

The design for *gpcp* started off with a much more minimalist approach, with essentially three node-types, one each for binary operators, unary operators, and tree leaves. During the early stages of development it appeared that some additional structure would simplify the architecture. The problem is that separating nodes on the basis of their *arity* ignores the real issues of different attributes. Consider the case of unary nodes. If we use the definition that any expression node with just one subexpression is a unary node, then both negation and field selection are unary nodes. One takes an expression of numerical datatype and negates its value. The other takes an expression that denotes an object and selects some named field of that object. Clearly the attributes needed for the abstract syntax are significantly different, as one requires no other attribution, while the other will need an attribute of *FldId* type.

In the released implementation *gpcp* has the expression descriptor class hierarchy shown in Figure 5.4. In this figure *LeafX* is an extensible descriptor type with two extensions. *IdLeaf* is used for expressions consisting of a single identifier, while *SetExp* is used for set-valued expressions. *UnaryX* is another extensible descriptor with two extensions. *IdentX* is used for unary expressions with an identifier attribute, such as field selection. *CallX* is used for procedure and method calls. There is only one descriptor type for binary expressions.

A general question that arises in the design of abstract syntax for expressions is whether or not there are expressions of other arities. For example, in language *C* and its derivatives there is the *ternary* expression form —

$$(exp_1?exp_2 : exp_3)$$

As well, we may represent procedure and function calls as expressions of variable arity. Consider a typical call syntax such as —

$$designatorExpression\ (argList)$$

We may consider this to be an expression form of arbitrary arity, or we might consider it simply to be a unary expression with an auxiliary attribute of sequence type. In *gpcp* the

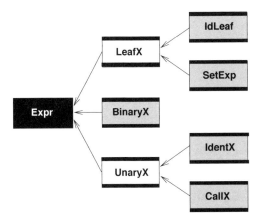

Figure 5.4: Complete expression hierarchy in *gpcp*

second of these two choices has been made, which is why the *CallX* node appears as a specialization of the *UnaryX* node.

The abstract syntax for all expression designators has a field for the computed data-type of the expression. There is also a tag which is used to denote the actual node operator. After all, *gpcp* has 29 different binary "operators" that share the use of the *BinaryX* descriptor. These shared attributes are defined in the abstract superclass *Expr*. There are also some lexical attributes, used for error reporting. These are omitted from the following *IDL*.

Leaf expression nodes.
Unspecialized leaf nodes are used for literal constants. Apart from the inherited attributes there is only one additional attribute, *value*, which is of an externally defined type —

```
LeafX ==> kind   : INTEGER,     // tag inherited from Expr
          type   : Type,        // inherited from Expr
          value  : LitValue;    // constant value union
```

The value union type is a tagged object capable of denoting any numeric or string-valued literal. This type is defined in a utility module that is capable, for example, of performing arithmetic on these values, as is required for constant folding during semantic analysis.

The *IdLeaf* specialization of *LeafX* is used for leaf expressions that have an identifier attribute, such as references to entire variables. Compared to a literal leaf node, this type needs one additional field, which is the identifier descriptor that the leaf denotes —

```
IdLeaf ==> kind   : INTEGER,     // tag inherited from Expr
           type   : Type,        // inherited from Expr
           value  : LitValue,    // inherited but unused
           ident  : Idnt;        // qualified identifier
```

The final leaf descriptor variation is used for set constructors. Set constructors define bit-patterns by listing the elements of the corresponding set. Such constructors have the concrete syntax —

'{' [*element* { ',' *element* }] '}'

where elements are either integer-valued expressions or are ranges of values that are expressed in the form "$exp_1 .. exp_2$" and denote all of the set elements from exp_1 up to exp_2.

Clearly, this is really a structure of variable arity, with an attribute that is a sequence of expressions. Looking ahead, we foreshadow that an expression range will be represented by a suitably tagged *BinaryX* descriptor. Here is the descriptor abstract syntax for set-constructor expressions —

```
SetExp ==> kind   : INTEGER,      // tag inherited from Expr
           type   : Type,         // inherited from Expr
           value  : LitValue,     // inherited from LeafX
           varSeq : seqOf Expr;   // set element expressions
```

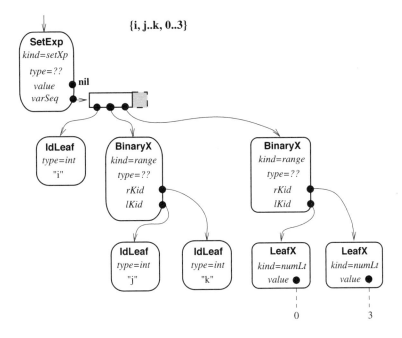

Figure 5.5: Example *AST* for a set expression

In this particular case the inherited *value* attribute does find a use. After semantic analysis of the element expressions, all of the constant parts of the set are folded down to a single literal constant value in the *value* attribute. At one extreme a completely constant set will end up with an empty element sequence and a non-**nil** value field. At the other extreme a set with no constant elements will have an unmodified element sequence and a value attribute that is still **nil**.

Figure 5.5 is an example of the *AST* that results from a simple set expression. In this case, the set is $\{i, j..k, 0..3\}$.[1]

Unary expression nodes.   As shown in Figure 5.4, the *UnaryX* descriptor is a concrete node-type and has two specializations. The unspecialized node is used whenever there is no additional attribute associated with the operation. This is the case for the explicitly unary operators, such as arithmetic or logical negation. The abstract syntax simply defines a single subexpression attribute —

---

[1] Set values are just bit-patterns, and sets are constructed at runtime by adding elements to the set one by one. If some or all of the elements of the set are constants, we can save runtime by computing the constant part of the bit-pattern at compile time as part of semantic analysis. For a sneak preview of what the *AST* of the example set expression looks like *after* semantic analysis, see Figure 6.7.

```
UnaryX ==> kind    : INTEGER,  // tag inherited from Expr
           type    : Type,     // inherited from Expr
           kid     : Expr;     // the subexpression
```

The two specializations are used for procedure and function calls, and for named selection respectively.

The *CallX* node adds an attribute that is a sequence of expressions to denote the argument list of the call —

```
CallX  ==> kind    : INTEGER,    // tag inherited from Expr
           type    : Type,       // inherited from Expr
           kid     : Expr,       // inherited from UnaryX
           actuals : seqOf Expr; // arguments of the call
```

The *IdentX* node is used when a unary node requires an identifier attribute. The specialization adds an attribute of *Idnt* type to the base *UnaryX* type —

```
IdentX ==> kind    : INTEGER,  // tag inherited from Expr
           type    : Type,     // inherited from Expr
           kid     : Expr,     // inherited from UnaryX
           ident   : Idnt;     // the selecting identifier
```

When this node is used for field selection, the identifier attribute will hold a *FldId* or *VarId*, depending on whether it is an instance field or static field. When the node is used to denote a type assertion, equivalent to a type-cast in *C#*, the identifier will be a *TypId* denoting the name of the type.

The binary expression node.
Binary expression nodes are simple. There are no specializations. The structure consists of two subexpressions and denotes the operator by the inherited *kind* attribute. Here is the abstract syntax —

```
BinaryX ==> kind : INTEGER,  // tag inherited from Expr
            type : Type,     // inherited from Expr
            lKid : Expr,     // left subexpression
            rKid : Expr;     // right subexpression
```

These nodes are used, as expected, for the binary operators in expressions. Some of these uses are less obvious than others. For example, array indexing uses a binary expression node. The array designator is the left subexpression, while the index expression is the right subexpression. A number of the built-in functions have function call form in the concrete syntax but are resolved to inline binary expressions in the attributed *AST*.

Consider a "call" to the built-in function *MAX(e1, e2)*. Initially, this construct will be represented in the *AST* by a *CallX* node. The *kid* field will be an *IdLeaf*, while the *actuals* sequence will have length-2 and encode the two argument expressions. During tree attribution, when the true identity of the "call" is discovered, the tree will be replaced by a *BinaryX* node with *kind = maxOf*.[2] Figure 6.5 in the next chapter shows this transformation.

Abstract Syntax for Simple Statements

Statement descriptors denote program statements in the abstract syntax. As indicated earlier, some statements with different semantics may be able to share node structures. The complexity of the descriptors varies from the very simple to the quite complex. We shall not deal with the details of all of these but will discuss three or four very simple examples in this subsection and two of the more complex examples in the next.

All statement descriptors derive from the *Stmt* base type. This abstract base class has no attributes other than a tag attribute and some lexical information. The tag, *kind*, denotes the statement kind, while the lexical information is required so that it is possible to emit source line-number information to the *PEM*.

Some languages have syntax for structured statements in which the production right-hand sides refer to the syntactic category *StatementSequence*, while other languages use a single statement or expression evaluation as the recursive category. *Component Pascal* is of the first kind. Language *C* and its derivatives and early *Pascal* dialects are of the second kind. In such cases, there is always some kind of *compound statement* that collects a sequence of statements into a single statement. In *C*, statements are grouped by braces "{" and "}", while in original *Pascal* it was the **begin, end** construct. Nevertheless, in the design of the abstract syntax we may use either kind of representation for either kind of language, as a matter of convenience.

In the event, the abstract syntax used by *gpcp* uses single statements and defines a compound statement called *Block* that has no counterpart in the concrete syntax —

```
Block ==> kind : INTEGER,      // tag inherited from Stmt
          body : seqOf Stmt; // sequence of statements
```

The descriptor for an empty statement is even simpler, with no new attributes at all.

The abstract syntax of procedure call and return statements is also rather simple. In each case the only attribute is an expression. In a return statement the expression will either be **nil**, if the return is from a proper procedure, or the expression that is returned after evaluation, if the return is from a value-returning function. For a procedure call statement, the expression will necessarily be of *CallX* type and will have *kind = prCall*.

Finally, in this section we consider assignment statements. The *Assign* descriptor has an abstract syntax with two subexpressions —

---

[2]Of course if both of the arguments turn out to statically resolve to constants, then the tree will be replaced by a leaf node denoting either **true** or **false**.

```
Assign ==> kind : INTEGER,   // tag inherited from Stmt
           lhsX : Expr,      // left-hand side designator
           rhsX : Expr;      // right-hand side value
```

The left-hand side expression will be some kind of designator, while the right-hand side expression will denote the value that is assigned.

A Few Harder Examples

Choice statements. There are two choice statements in *Component Pascal*. The **if** statement has a structure with a repeating **elsif** and optional **else** part. This is fairly conventional structure, with the possibility of repeated predicate evaluations at runtime. The **with** statement is rather less common and, confusingly enough, is unrelated to the use of the same keyword in *Modula-2*. This statement is a "type-case" construct. Figure 5.6 shows a typical use of the **with** statement. In this figure *ptr* is a variable, and $T1$, $T2$, and $T3$ are names of types.

```
WITH ptr : T1 DO
        statement sequence 1
| ptr : T2 DO
        statement sequence 2
| ptr : T3 DO
        statement sequence 3
ELSE
        statement sequence 4
END;
```

Figure 5.6: Typical use of the **with** statement

This statement, at runtime, tests the type of the *selection variable*, effectively using the same test as

$$\textbf{if } \textit{ptr} \textbf{ is } T1 \textbf{ then}$$

If the variable *ptr* is of type $T1$ or any of its subtypes, then statement sequence 1 is executed and the **with** terminates. If not, the next predicate is evaluated, with effectively the same test as

$$\textbf{elsif } \textit{ptr} \textbf{ is } T2 \textbf{ then}$$

and so on.

It might appear that this adds no new semantics beyond what might be expressed with an **if**. However this is not the case. This statement is a *regional type guard*. Once a predicate has been satisfied, the selected variable is known to be of the predicated type.

This means that within the conditional statement sequence there is no need to use type assertions (narrowing casts) to access features of the predicated type. There is another important difference, which is that in the case of the **if** statement, if there is no **else** and no predicate is satisfied, then the statement terminates silently. For the **with** statement, failure to select one of the branches raises an exception.

In summary, the differences between these two statements are semantic rather than structural. We certainly need to generate quite different code for the two cases, but we may use the structural similarity to share the same abstract syntax for the two cases. Here is the abstract syntax used by *gpcp* for the shared *Choice* descriptor —

```
Choice ==> kind   : INTEGER,      // tag inherited from Stmt
           preds  : seqOf Expr,   // sequence of predicates
           blocks : seqOf Stmt;   // sequence of statement
```

The two new attributes are the sequence of predicate expressions and the sequence of corresponding selected statements. Notice that these two sequences must be of the same length, taking into account the trivial predicate associated with the **else** case. Recall also that statement sequences in the source are encoded as a single compound statement (*Block*) type in the abstract syntax. The last attribute therefore, in general, denotes a *sequence* of statement sequences.

Choice nodes arising from **with** statements have predicates that, apart from the last, are encoded as *BinaryX* nodes with an **is** operator. The nodes arising from **if** statements can have arbitrary expressions of Boolean type on the predicate list.

Figure 5.7 shows a diagram of the *AST* arising from the code example in Figure 5.6. Only the first and last predicates are shown in this figure.

Case or switch statements.

The statement type with the greatest structural complexity in *Component Pascal* is the **case** statement. This provides multiway branching functionality, roughly equivalent to that provided by the **switch** statement in *C*-family languages. Figure 5.8 has the concrete syntax of this statement.

Compared to a **switch** statement,[3] the only significant structural difference is the greater generality of the *SelectSet* structure, which replaces the list of labels used in language *C*. In the present case, the select set may consist of one or more values in a comma-separated list. These values may be expressions that statically evaluate to simple scalar values or may be ranges expressed in the form *e1 .. e2*. This mechanism allows contiguous ranges of selector labels to be compactly stated, for example using —

```
| 1 .. 4 : statementSequence;
```

---

[3] Here we are comparing with structured uses of **switch**. We conveniently ignore the fact that in *C* it is possible to create switch statements that have almost arbitrary control flow. Mercifully, neither *Java* nor *C#* allows such unstructured use.

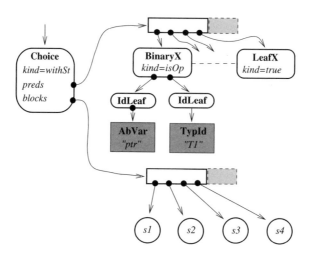

Figure 5.7: Abstract syntax from Figure 5.6

CaseStatement	$\rightarrow$	**case** Expression **of** CaseList **end** .
CaseList	$\rightarrow$	[Case { "|" Case }] [**else** StatementSequence] .
Case	$\rightarrow$	[SelectSet ":" StatementSequence] .
SelectSet	$\rightarrow$	Element { "," Element } .
Element	$\rightarrow$	Expression
	|	Expression ".." Expression .

Figure 5.8: Concrete syntax of **case** statements

where in *C* one would need to say —

```
case 1: case 2: case 3: case 4 : {
    statementSequence; break;
}
```

It will be shown in Chapter 9 that we may advantageously use *ranges* of selector values in the encoding of switch structures. With this in mind, we can choose abstract syntax that is capable of representing ranges, with the idea of merging adjacent labels that select the same statement sequence. We begin by defining a helper structure that denotes a selection —

```
Triple ==> minR  : INTEGER, // minimum of range
           maxR  : INTEGER, // maximum of range
           index : INTEGER; // StatSeq selected
```

The idea is that we will place the statement sequence for each case in a list of statement sequences and refer to the selected case by giving the index of the sequence in the list.

During tree building every *Element* in the concrete syntax is translated into a *Triple* in the abstract syntax. In the event that an element is a singleton value, the *minR* and *maxR* attributes will be the same value. Looking ahead we can see that the rule for permitting merging of triples is that the ranges are contiguous and they have the same index value.

Using this helper, we now give the abstract syntax for *Case* —

```
Case ==> kind   : INTEGER,        // tag inherited from Stmt
         select : Expr,           // selector expression
         blocks : seqOf Stmt,     // case code blocks, in order
         elsBlk : Stmt,           // default statement sequence
         labels : seqOf Triple;   // ranges index block sequence
```

In this structure, the *labels* list indexes into the *blocks* sequence. As hinted above, during semantic checking of the *AST*, we would expect the *labels* list to be shortened as triples are merged. However the *blocks* list will maintain both its length and its initial ordering.

Symbol Tables and Scope Representation

Symbol tables allow our software to map from the character strings used to denote identifiers in a source program into the unique entity that the identifier represents in a particular program context. The same identifier may refer to many different entities in different parts of the same program. The binding of a particular name therefore depends on two elements: the source string; and the *lexical scope* in which the string occurs.

All but the simplest languages need to represent lexical scope explicitly. Incremental compilers sometimes use a single symbol table and add and remove items from the table as local scopes are entered and left, but this is unusual. For the architecture that is favored here, scopes need to have persistent representation, since access to local symbol table information is required in each phase. We need to be able to go back to a particular scope at any time and ask, "What is the association of identifier *x* in this scope?" Nevertheless, in the interest of efficiency it is important to perform the mapping from character string to symbol-table key once only. It is also important to remember that not all languages place all *kinds* in the same namespace. In *ANSI C*, for example, type tag names for **struct** and **enum** types are in a distinct namescope, while functions, **typedef** names, and variables all share a separate, nestable scope hierarchy.

The choices for symbol tables and scope representation in *gpcp* are fairly typical practice. Within the lexical scanner, strings are entered into a hash table that maps every such string into an ordinal number. As we shall see, it is important that the algorithm guarantees that every distinct string will be allocated a unique *hash key*, as the ordinals are called. Program entities that define namescopes—that is, procedures, modules, and record types—all have an attribute of symbol-table type. The symbol tables are represented by binary trees, using the hash ordinal as key. This design choice ensures that the large number of scopes that contain very few declared names are represented in a space-efficient fashion. Similarly, the occasional densely populated scopes are still reasonably efficient, with the randomness of the hash function ensuring that the trees will always be well-balanced. The only real disadvantage of this design is that it has an absolute requirement that the hash key of every namestring be unique. This requirement, in turn, requires the hash table algorithm to be one of the *closed hash algorithms*. The alternative *open hash algorithms* will, when necessary, allocate additional strings to the same hash key, using some kind of overflow data structure. Unfortunately, while open hashing algorithms just run more slowly when the table fills up, the closed algorithms have rigid limits and respond with a catastrophic overflow error. In *gpcp* the hash table size is configurable from the command line, from a moderate default up to a very, very large size. In principle it would be possible for a compiler to trap the overflow and perform an automatic retry with a larger table. Some other Gardens Point compilers work in this way, but *gpcp* just fails with a diagnostic message to the user suggesting the setting of a larger table size.

Inside most compilers there will be two types of name lookup that are used within any particular namescope. There are circumstances in which the binding must be within exactly the local scope. In other circumstances a name needs to be bound within an indefinitely deeply nested hierarchy of scopes starting at the current scope. The hierarchical lookup is, of course, no more than a series of local lookups on a sequence of related symbol tables. However, external access to both the local and hierarchical versions of the lookup needs to be provided.

With the lexical rules of most languages, whenever a name is introduced in a scope, it must only be distinct from others declared in the same scope. Declarative occurrences of names are thus usually associated with local lookups. With most language semantics, *used occurrences* of names require resolution in the hierarchy of scopes, starting with the local context. In *gpcp* a hierarchical lookup is associated with a context that is described either by a scope object, such as a procedure, or is described by the namescope of a record type. In each case, the descriptor of the context contains a symbol-table attribute and contains another attribute that denotes the parent in the hierarchy. For a procedure, the lexical parent will be the scope in which the procedure itself was declared. For a record type the lexical parent is the descriptor of the base type that the current record extends. In either case it is only after an unsuccessful search has traversed its way to the root of the hierarchy that we may declare that the identifier use is erroneous.

It is important to take careful note of the semantics of your particular language, so as to know which kind of lookup is required in any instance. In *Component Pascal*, for example, any new field defined in a record type must have a name that is different from the name of every other visible field. This includes names of visible fields that have been inherited from the supertypes. The situation with type-bound procedure (method) names is quite different. In this latter case a locally introduced method may have the same name as an inherited method. Such name overriding is, after all, the whole essence of virtual dispatch. These different semantics suggest that different symbol table lookups are required to check for the correctness of the definitions of the two different kinds of type members. In *gpcp*, in fact, a slight trick is used to achieve these semantics. A uniform, local-scope check is performed at the time that newly defined members of either kind are inserted into the record namescope. This happens during tree construction. Later, during type resolution, the namespaces are flattened by propagating the names of fields, but not methods, down to the symbol tables of their inheritors. Name clashes between inherited and local fields are discovered at that time. Other designs are clearly possible.

There are similar, subtle issues involved when languages have features allowing for imported scopes to be opened up. For example, the line —

```
using SomeNamespace ;
```

in a *C#* program opens up the named namespace, so that the classes defined in the space are directly visible *unqualified*. An example may make this more clear. Normally the namespaces from the assembly "mscorlib" are visible without having to be named on the command line with a "/r:name" option. Thus, in the following fragment —

```
using System;
    . . .
    Console.WriteLine(...);
    System.Console.WriteLine(...);
```

we may refer to the *Console* class directly, rather than having to use the *fully qualified* name as in the final line. For this example, the fully qualified name still works and binds to the same class.

The semantics of **using** in *C#* cannot be implemented by simply "unpacking" the classes of the specified namespace into the outer namescope of the module being compiled. The imported classes are placed in a scope that, in effect, surrounds the file-level scope of the compilation unit. Thus if the compilation unit defines its own class called *Console*, then the first call in the previous fragment will not work anymore. In that case the local class *Console* takes precedence over the same name in the scope opened up by the **using** declaration.

We have seen that a single **using** declaration places identifiers in a namescope that surrounds the file-level scope of the compilation unit. What now if a program has two or more **using** declarations? Do each of the declarations create another layer in some kind of "onion-skin" model, or do all of the names become placed in one shared, surrounding scope? Consider the following critical test. Two namespaces are imported in one or other order, but both define a class with the same name and that name is used in the program. Now, which of the following happens: (a) the program will not compile because of the name clash; (b) the program compiles and the used occurrence binds to the class in the first (or the last) namespace to be imported; or (c) neither class is visible in unqualified form?[4]

---

[4]Don't guess! Either check the language specification or write a test program.

Any one of these semantic rules is relatively simple to achieve. Semantic rule (b) can be achieved with an onion-skin structure with one or other order of layering around the file scope. However, all three behaviors are possible using a single surrounding scope. The differences arise from the strategy that is adopted when an insertion is refused by the table. If such a refusal provokes an error, then we have rule (a). If the refusal is silently ignored (or the second insertion overwrites the first), then we get the two versions of rule (b). Finally, if we respond to a refusal by making a list of all disputed names, and remove them all at the end of the importation step, then we have rule (c).

What is the take-home message of this rather long digression? Well, there are subtle issues to resolve here, and it is *essential* to understand the exact semantics of your source language before you blunder into a design that is "obvious, simple, and *wrong*."

Notes on Chapter 5

The *IDL* that we have used for defining abstract syntax is a semiformal version of the notation invented for language *Ada* in the early 1980s. The acronym stands for "interface definition language." Since that time it has become common to refer to *any* interface definition notation as "*IDL*," whether or not it derives from the original notation. Tools for processing language *Ada* programs shared a particular abstract syntax form called *DIANA* for "Descriptive Intermediate Attributed Notation for *Ada*."

The generation of compiler front-end components from specification is widely practiced, although handwritten parsers are still sometimes seen. The tools "lex" and "yacc" and their more modern derivatives are probably the most used. Originally part of the *UNIX* toolkit, these programs are now available on all computing platforms.

The *COCO/R* tool for generating recursive descent parsers is due to Hanspeter Mössenböck. There are versions that produce parsers written in *Oberon-2, Modula-2, ANSI C, Java*, and perhaps other languages. A rather different approach to front-end construction allows not only the parser and scanner but all semantic attribution to be produced from specification. My personal favorite toolset here is *Eli*. Information about *COCO/R* can be found at http://cs.ru.ac.za/homes/cspt/cocor.htm, while the *Eli* homepage is http://www.cs.colorado.edu/~eliuser.

Evaluating Semantic Attributes

6

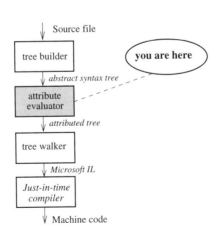

Source file

tree builder → you are here

abstract syntax tree

attribute evaluator

attributed tree

tree walker

Microsoft IL

Just-in-time compiler

Machine code

Having constructed an *AST*, we now need to evaluate the attributes of the tree. For the most part, these attributes are computed during one or more traversals of the tree. A few attributes may be evaluated during graph traversals (of type graphs, for example) or are evaluated over symbol tables.

The attributes that we compute are usually different in kind from the *structural attributes* that define the "shape" of the tree. Although there are no sharp boundaries, it is helpful to think of these attributes as belonging to two different categories. First, there are *semantic attributes*, such as the datatype of every expression, and then there are various *code attributes*. Code attributes are attributes used in the generation of code. These may have no counterpart in the semantics of the language. For example, it is necessary to determine how a particular datatype in the source language maps onto the *CTS* type system. Such an attribute has no meaning to the source language, although making the right choice may determine whether or not the correct source language semantics may be achieved.

Apart from any syntactic errors that the parser may have discovered, most of the burden for checking correctness of the source program rests with the semantic attribution. It is for this reason that most of the node types in the *AST* need to have lexical attributes. When errors are discovered during parsing, the text position that is reported is the current scanner position in the input stream, or maybe the position of the previous token. With the deferred reporting that occurs during semantic attribution, we must extract the position information from the tree node and send that off to the error reporting mechanism. There are a few subtleties here, and design decisions are required. As an example, suppose that we meet the declaration of an abstract method for a type that has not declared itself to be abstract. We would like to give a message that reminds the user that only abstract types may have abstract methods. But to what source position should the message attach? Should the message point to the start of the type declaration, where the keyword **abstract** is missing, or to the method heading, where the trouble became apparent? Remember that these positions might be hundreds of lines apart. The choice in *gpcp* is to attach the message to the type declaration, while spelling out the name of the method that caused the problem. Aside from error reporting, lexical attributes are used in the emission of line information to the *IL* for the debugger.

One of the semantic attributes to consider computing at this stage in the compilation is the safe initialization of local variables. This is a condition that the verifier checks, to ensure that every local variable is initialized along every path that leads from the start of the method to the first use of the variable. It is possible to satisfy the verifier by simply automatically initializing all locals to an appropriate zero value, but we may do much, much better by performing a small amount of dataflow analysis. The details are spelled out in Appendix A.

Some of the technical language that is used in the context of tree attribution is defined in Sidebar 6.1.

Reading Metadata

Even in the simplest programs, the information in the *IL* will come from more than one place. Look at the *IL* for the two versions of "Hello World" that appeared in Figures 2.22 and 2.23. In the first there is a reference to "[mscorlib] System.Console::Write-Line" and in the second to "[RTS] Console::WriteString". How did the compiler know that those were the *CLR* names of the library methods? Did the compiler trust that

SIDEBAR 6.1

SOME DEFINITIONS FOR TREE ATTRIBUTION

Attributes are computed during traversals of the tree. We divide attributes into three kinds. *Intrinsic*, or sometimes *lexical*, attributes are placed in the tree nodes during tree building. The alternative name makes some sense, since lexical properties, such as the source position corresponding to a particular *AST* node, are predetermined, rather than being the subject of computation.

Synthesized attributes of a node are computed from other attributes belonging to the children of the node. Such attributes are typically computed as a postorder traversal of the tree unwinds.

Derived attributes of a node are computed from other attributes belonging to the parent of this node or attributes that belong to the sibling nodes of this node. Such attributes are typically computed during a recursion down the tree.

An important special case is attributes that may be computed during a single top-down, left-to-right traversal of the tree. Such attributes are said to be *L*-attributed. Attributes of this kind may be either derived or synthesized. The important consequence of this property is that such attributes may be evaluated, on the fly, during top-down construction of the *AST*.

In most discussions of this framework what we have called *derived* attributes are called "inherited" attributes. The problem is that we have already used this term to denote an attribute field of an *AST* node that is defined in the node's supertype. We need to avoid phrases such as "this inherited attribute (field) holds a synthesized attribute (value)." In this context, name overloading would be far too confusing, so we shall avoid it.

the source program had the correct signature for these methods or did it check somewhere? In both cases the compiler read *metadata* that gave the proper names and allowed complete checking of the method signatures. In the *C#* program the line —

> **using** System;

gave unqualified access to the facilities of the *System* namespace of the *mscorlib* assembly. The metadata of this assembly is imported into every *C#* program compilation.

In the *Component Pascal* example, the static methods of the *Console* class are made visible by the second line of the program —

> **import** CPmain, Console;

In this case the compiler read a *symbol file* that told the compiler that the facilities of *Console* are to be found in the *runtime system assembly* (*RTS*).

With both *C#* and *Component Pascal* we say that files are compiled *separately* but not *independently*. That is to say, when a particular file is compiled, the compiler has access to metadata specifying the relevant public interfaces of all of the modules and libraries that it depends on. Such access allows the interfaces between compilation units to be stringently checked at compile time, even in the presence of separate compilation.

Compile Time and Runtime Consistency Checks

Traditionally metadata is used during compilation to ensure that multipart programs agree on the types and signatures of the public interfaces of the separately compiled parts. For example, if a module is being compiled with imports from two previously compiled modules and those two modules both reference some third module, we would like to ensure that the two imports were each compiled against the same interface definition for the third.

It is a quite separate problem to ensure that at deployment time the interfaces of the actual components are the same ones that the compiler was told about. For those systems that can check such things, configuration errors might be detected at link-edit time, for linked applications, or at load time in the case of dynamically loaded libraries.

Thus we have two aspects of interface conformance. We would like to use our metadata to ensure that interfaces are consistent at compile time. We would also like to ensure that each interface encountered at runtime is the same as the one that was promised at compile time.

Unfortunately, *interface* conformance is not the whole of the "version consistency problem." It is entirely possible that two versions of a module may have precisely the same public interface but different *behavior*. In such cases client programs may work with one version but not with the other.

The *.NET* framework provides extremely powerful mechanisms for solving all three aspects of the version consistency problem. At compile time we may access the metadata of existing assemblies to ensure that separate modules are compiled against correct and consistent definitions of the public interfaces.

At runtime method calls are bound based on the complete name and signature of the methods. If there is an inconsistency between the method signature against which a call was compiled and the actual signature of the method in the loaded assembly, a *MissingMethodException* will be thrown. Similar checks apply to member access generally, with appropriate exceptions in the event of violations. Thus the *CLR* itself guarantees consistency between compile time expectations and runtime reality. It is possible to perform equivalent consistency checking offline, by using the standalone verifier tool "`peverify`".

The final issue is that of enforcing *behavioral* consistency. This is a difficult problem, since on any one system different applications may require different versions of the same "shared" library. Such possibilities are the genesis of what has been called "*DLL hell*." The *.NET* framework attacks the problem by providing mechanisms for attaching *strong names* to assemblies. A strong name is a cryptographically enforced guarantee that a particular assembly has a specified originator and version number. Multiple versions of strongly named assemblies may be placed in the *global assembly cache* (*GAC*), and programs using the assembly may specify that they require one particular version or some range of acceptable versions. This capability is called "side-by-side execution."

Metadata: Where to Find It

In the *.NET* framework there are essentially three choices for the mechanism by which metadata is made known to the compiler. The traditional method used for languages of the C family is the use of *header files*. These header files are usually text files produced by human programmers. The effect of including these header files is to inject a series of external declarations into the text of the compilation unit, usually during a separate pre-processing step. *Pascal*-family languages since *Modula-2* have used *symbol files*, usually in some binary format. These symbol files are produced automatically as a side effect of module compilation. It is usual for these symbol files to have some kind of cryptographic fingerprint associated with them, making it possible to automatically check that different modules are referring to precisely the same interface. Finally, the *.NET* framework embeds metadata into its *PEM*s in a way that allows the compiler of importing modules to extract whatever information is required for correct interfacing.

These different designs have different objectives to some extent. In the case of header files the objective is simply to ensure consistency. Modules that include the same header file see the same interface. Although header files are conventionally used in this way, the underlying file inclusion mechanism may be used in much more general and unstructured ways.

The symbol file mechanism has broader objectives, in that it provides a way to auto-matically check that different modules sharing the facilities of some other module have all been compiled against the same interface definition. The presence of this extra information also allows for "smart recompilation." If the compilation of a modified module leads to an unchanged cryptographic checksum, we may be sure that the interface has not changed, and dependent modules need not be recompiled. Note that these consistency checks attack only the *syntactic* aspect of the versioning problem. The use of symbol files with checksums guarantees that interfaces match, ensuring that the compiler has correct type and signature definitions for imported facilities. In the event that two versions of a module have different behavior but the same interface, symbol file mechanisms do not and cannot help.

The embedded metadata in program executables in *.NET* is able to supply all of the interface information required by the compiler. This information may be extracted either at compile time, or even at runtime, using the facilities of the *System.Reflection* libraries. In principle, it is possible to use the *PEM* metadata to provide the same information that a separate symbol file would do. The option of applying strong names to assemblies provides the opportunity to go much further and solve all aspects of the versioning problem.

Choosing a Metadata Mechanism

In the case of languages that have built-in mechanisms for sharing metadata, as in the case of *ANSI C* header files, there is probably very little choice but to go with the tradition. For other languages there is a choice. Choosing to use the metadata facilities of the *.NET* framework has much to recommend it. In particular, all of the advantages of the powerful version control mechanisms of *.NET* become accessible to the language implementation. The alternative of using separate metadata (symbol) files is also a viable choice and is the one used by the current release of *gpcp*.

If the choice is made to use the *.NET* metadata framework, then certain consequences follow. The problem that needs to be solved is that the built-in facilities for metadata in *.NET* assemblies do not necessarily provide *all* of the information that is required for any particular language. Consider as an example the problem of array type names in *Pascal*-family languages. Recall that in the *CLR*, array types are defined by the name of their element type. There are no built-in facilities for giving either a name or a statically specified length to such a type. We conclude that using the built-in metadata facilities of *.NET* for other languages will require enhancement of the metadata by the use of *custom attributes*. Custom attributes are discussed in detail beginning on page 299.

Now it is time to make the choice. One may use a traditional metadata mechanism and have to invent some other way of accessing the version control facilities of *.NET*. Alternatively, one may use the metadata mechanisms of *.NET* and design whatever enhancements are required, in the form of custom attributes.

In any case in the remainder of this chapter it is presumed that metadata for external resources has been read in by some means or another. It is also assumed that type and identifier descriptors have been constructed to represent the imported objects in the abstract syntax.

Type Resolution

For some languages it is necessary to perform some kind of type resolution prior to attribution of code. This may happen, for example, because the language permits types to be used before they are declared.

Most procedural languages allow the declaration of recursive data structures. The rules vary, however. *Pascal* only allows the particular idiom in which a pointer may be declared bound to a type that is not yet declared. As minimal mechanisms go, this one is inspired. Consider the following code fragment —

```
type
    FooPtr = pointer to FooRec;
    SomeRc = record
                 i,j : FooPtr;
             end;
    FooRec = record
                 next : FooPtr;
                 ...;
             end;
```

When the declaration of the pointer type is discovered, a pointer type descriptor may be constructed with the bound type attribute left unresolved. Note, however, that the bound type does not need to be known for the runtime representation size of the type to be determined. The size will be whatever the size of the address type is known to be. It follows that upon meeting a declaration of some other type, such as *SomeRc* in the example, the only undeclared types that can be encountered are pointers. Thus the runtime size of all types is computable at parse time, facilitating incremental compilation.

C has a different constraint. Named types that occur as *typedef* names may only recurse through the use of the tag names of *tagged types* such as structs.

In such simple cases it is possible to avoid a separate type resolution step by simple, *ad hoc* backpatching. However, this will not do for languages that allow more general forms of forward reference.

Component Pascal allows arbitrary forward references to type names within a single declarative scope. The only constraint is that all types must be declared before the first procedure declaration is met. This is an interesting choice. The constraint guarantees that all type names and structures are resolved before any code has to be generated, even in the case of incremental compilers. On the other hand, type resolution is algorithmically more complex. Furthermore, the whole strategy depends on the fact that in this language the declaration of the methods of a type are textually separated from the declaration of the fields of the type.

The design choice in *gpcp* is to invoke a separate type resolution step when the parser detects the end of the first part of each declarative section. This algorithm illustrates two separate characteristic patterns of attribution. We start by launching a visitor pattern in the symbol table, using the method to be described in "Using the Visitor Pattern" (see page 192). The other pattern is a depth-first graph traversal on the type graph. The visitor pattern finds all identifier descriptors in the symbol table and invokes the *Resolve*() method on the *type* attribute of the identifier. Notice that type resolution is done incrementally, scope by scope, before construction of the tree for the whole module is complete. Much of the semantic checking of type declarations happens during this step.

Perhaps this is a good point to take stock of some of the language that is being used. In the preceding chapter we discussed the design of the abstract syntax *tree*. Now, suddenly we are talking about *graphs* of types. What has happened here? The truth is that the *AST* is only a tree so long as we are looking only at the *structural* attributes. Consider the fragment of *Pascal* declarations that occurred earlier in this section. The *AST* fragment corresponding to this is shown in Figure 6.1. In this figure type descriptors are shown shaded, while identifier descriptors are unshaded. In this diagram we are taking an extreme position, in which no identifiers have been resolved during tree building. All used occurrences of type names have been denoted by an opaque type descriptor in the tree. A less extreme, and more commonly chosen, position would be to attempt to bind each name during tree building and to create opaque type descriptors only if the name was unbound in the local scope.

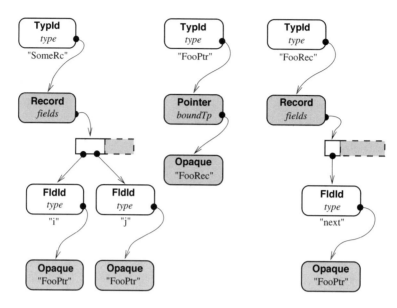

Figure 6.1: Fragment of type tree with unbound types

After binding the type names and replacing references to the opaque descriptors by the types that they denote, we are left with Figure 6.2. Notice that the tree has now become a thoroughly interconnected, directed graph of type descriptors.

The process of type resolution consists of replacing references to named types by references to the types that are named. In order to facilitate this, the (virtual) method

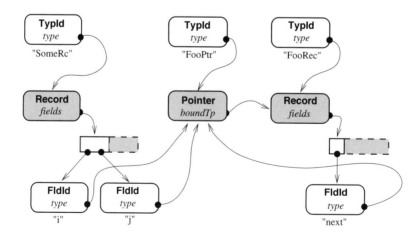

Figure 6.2: Fragment of type graph after binding

Resolve is a value returning function. The function returns a fully resolved replacement reference for its own receiver.

Because of the possibly cyclic structure of the graph, we need to mark nodes as they are visited, so as to prevent runaway recursion. For most descriptors, type resolution is quite simple. For example, in order to resolve a *Pointer* descriptor we take the pointer descriptor reference, *this* (say), and call —

```
this.boundTp := this.boundTp.Resolve();
return this;
```

The situation with *Record* descriptors is the only significantly complex case. For records we must first resolve the base type that the record extends. Since this necessarily involves recursing up the inheritance hierarchy, this is a good time to perform all of the consistency checks. To choose just one example, if this record has been declared abstract, then the type that it extends must be abstract also. We then resolve the type of each field of the record, by iterating over all the identifiers on the field sequence.

Some OO languages allow for inherited fields of records or classes to be hidden by the declaration of another, equally named field. *C#* and *Java* both have this property, while in *Component Pascal* all visible field names must be distinct. Of course, in all of these languages method names may be redefined; indeed, this is the essence of method overriding. Since *Component Pascal* does not allow redefinition of field names, we need to enforce this rule. This is done in *gpcp* by inserting the field names of the current record into a symbol table attached to the record descriptor. An attempt is then made to insert all the inherited field names into the same table. This has two consequences. Firstly if insertion fails for some field, then an error may be reported. Secondly, once the namespace for fields has been flattened in this way future binding of field names is more rapid. This is so because the lookup does not have to recurse up the inheritance tree, as is necessary for method names.

Evaluating Expression Type

Computation of the datatype of every expression is the fundamental building block of attribution in all statically typed languages. This information is used to determine whether or not the expressions are well formed and as a preliminary to the semantic checking of statements. In the case of object-oriented languages, rather than find *the* type of an expression, we may be computing a *bound* on the type.

Although we refer to what is happening as "attribution," typically there is more going on than just the decoration of the *AST* with type information. It is usually convenient to perform certain kinds of *tree rewriting* during the same traversal. The point is that we wish to go on to code generation with a tree that as closely as possible represents the code that

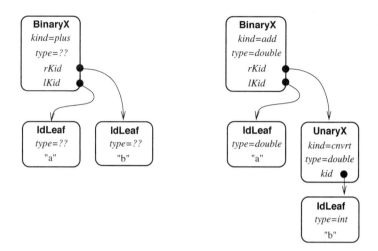

Figure 6.3: Rewriting the tree to make type coercion explicit

we are about to emit. One example will suffice to make the point. Suppose that we have a binary tree of the form represented on the left in Figure 6.3. This tree corresponds to the expression $a + b$.

In this diagram the information from the identifier and type descriptors has been placed in line in the nodes, in the interests of readability. Suppose now that the identifier a binds to a variable of floating point double datatype, while b binds to a variable of integer datatype. We may conclude several things.

First of all, we may conclude that the meaning of the "+" is arithmetic addition, rather than any of the overloadings of the operator that denote set union, string concatenation, and so on. We may therefore edit the *BinaryX* node to set *kind=add*. This particular process is known as *operator identification*. We shall cover this in more detail in the next subsection.

Next, we may conclude that since the two subtrees of the binary node are not of equal type, we must coerce the narrower type to be equal to the wider type, *double* in this case. We may thus rewrite the tree as shown on the right of the figure, with the type fields filled in and the type conversion node made explicit.

Thus, although we speak of attributing the tree, we may also think in terms of rewriting the tree from an *abstract syntax tree* to an attributed *code tree*.

Operator Identification

The example in Figure 6.3 is an almost trivial example of operator identification. In general we have a certain repertoire of operators that are meaningful in the code tree, and we wish to map the node kind designated by the source file into a designation of the applicable runtime operation.

The implicit type conversion rules of the language often allow operator identification to be simple and unambiguous. The previous example was of this kind. However there are more difficult cases in many languages. A typical difficulty occurs in the matching of actual parameter lists to method signatures in the presence of overloaded method names. In such cases the language definition must spell out exactly how the choice is to be made. Extreme care needs to be taken in the implementation of this matching, as it is easy to get it wrong and difficult to perform complete test case coverage.[1]

A famous case arose in language *Ada*. In this language operators may be overloaded, and the compiler must try to resolve the overloading by considering all consistent meanings for the expression. If there is exactly one consistent meaning, the operators are thereby identified. If there is either no consistent meaning or several, then the expression is erroneous.

In this case it turns out that operator identification may be completed in just two passes over the tree. In the first pass, the bottom-up pass, the set of possible types of every node is computed. We call these sets the *offered type* sets. If the language permits implicit type conversions, then at each step we must find the *closure* of the set, by adding every type that may be obtained by applying a permitted implicit conversion to a member of the set. At every operator node, the set of possible meanings of the operator symbol is considered against the sets of types offered by the subtrees. In general, only certain identifications of the operator will correspond to types that are "on offer" from the subtrees, and so only certain result types from the operator are possible.

When this computation reaches the root of the expression tree, the set of offered types must have exactly one element. If there are no elements, there is no consistent operator identification for the expression. If there is more than one element, then the expression is ambiguous.

Finally, having produced a singleton *offered type* set at the root of the expression, we must then propagate this information down the tree as a *demanded type* value. Note that the offered types are sets, while the demanded type is a single, definite value. Going back down the tree, the demanded type unambiguously selects one meaning for the operator. This in turn selects a single demanded type for each of its subexpressions.

It may be noted that this process only works if there is some restriction of the signatures of overloaded operators. In particular, for any given result type, there cannot be two signatures that have corresponding input types that are related by an implicit conversion.

Attributing Expressions in gpcp

In *gpcp* expression attribution is performed by a set of methods that extend an abstract method with signature —

---

[1] Although compiler writers should avoid abusive messages to users, it might not hurt to consider a warning message. The message could ask, "If the compiler finds it so hard to know which method you want to call, how is a human being reading the code going to understand this?"

```
PROCEDURE (this : Expr)exprAttr() : Expr,ABSTRACT;
```

These procedures return their own replacement trees, so that the general pattern of recursion with the *BinaryX* node, as an example, is —

```
PROCEDURE (node : BinaryX)exprAttr() : Expr;  (* final *)
BEGIN
  node.lKid := node.lKid.exprAttr();
  node.rKid := node.rKid.exprAttr();
  <now process this node>
  RETURN node;
END exprAttr;
```

This particular pattern of recursion relies on the fact that the datatype attribute of expressions in *Component Pascal* may be computed in a single pass over the trees. In this language expression type is a synthesized attribute, so that the type depends only on the datatypes of the subexpressions and the operator kind. This is true of most languages of the *C* family, in which even user-defined overloading may be resolved locally.

The processing for each node-type incorporates operator identification, constant folding, and tree rewriting. Constant folding is just a special case of tree rewriting, in which *exprAttr*() is dispatched on some expression tree and returns a new tree consisting of a single *LeafX* node.

There is a helpful convention, used for all of these attribution calls, that tries to keep spurious error reporting under control. Any call of *exprAttr*() that detects an error makes an error notification and returns **nil**. This allows nodes higher up the tree to detect the return of a **nil** subexpression and themselves return **nil** with no further notification needed.

```
IF (node.lKid = NIL) OR
   (node.rKid = NIL) THEN RETURN NIL END;
```

Binary nodes.   The code for the *BinaryX* nodes is straightforward. There is a considerable volume of code in the helper procedures that performs the constant folding, of which we shall look at just one example.

Directly after the method calls that attribute the two child subexpressions, and following the error skipping idiom, there is a choice construct that peels off various cases. Here is the fragment that deals with all of the processing of numerical expressions —

```
rslt := NIL;
IF ... THEN ...
ELSIF node.rKid.isNumericExpr() THEN
  rslt := numOp(node)  (* process numerics *)
ELSIF ... THEN ...
END;  (* if then else *)
RETURN rslt;
```

Of course, all of the real work is done in the *numOp* procedure. This procedure is typical of the eight or so helper procedures that are embedded in the *BinaryX::exprAttr* method. There are two control branches. One performs constant folding, in the event that both of the subexpressions are literal constants. The other branch performs operator identification for the nonliteral cases.

The procedure starts by computing the return type from the subtree types and the operator, as shown in Figure 6.4. The function *coverType* is a helper that returns the least covering type for two unequal datatypes. This function implements *Component Pascal*'s binary type conversion rules. The next two statements rewrite the subtrees as necessary, to incorporate any type coercion nodes as was shown in Figure 6.3. The function *coerceUp* returns a rewritten version of its first argument, coerced to the type of its second argument. Notice that it may happen that both of the trees need to be coerced.

```
procedure numOp(n : Expr) : Expr;
  <local variable declarations>
begin  (* numOp body *)
  ...
  if n.kind = slash then
    rsTp := Builtin.realTp;  (* result of '/' is REAL *)
  else
    rsTp := coverType(n.lKid.type, n.rKid,type);
  end;
  if n.lKid.type # rsTp then (* # is ≠ operator *)
          n.lKid := coerceUp(n.lKid, rsTp) end;
  if n.rKid.type # rsTp then (* # is ≠ operator *)
          n.rKid := coerceUp(n.rKid, rsTp) end;
  ...
```

Figure 6.4: Skeleton of the *numOp* function

Having dealt with these preliminaries, the result type is known and the subtrees have been rewritten with widening type coercions as necessary. We now perform constant folding and return the rebuilt tree —

```
    . . .
IF (n.lKid.kind = numLt) & (n.rKid.kind = numLt) THEN
  <return a newly created leaf node with the folded value>
ELSE
  n.type := rsTp; RETURN n;
END;
END numOp;
```

There is an important category of binary nodes that we wish to fold the results of. These are the binary operators of Boolean type. We need to fold these so that if some conditional control flow depends on a statically known expression, we may simplify the flow. In this case we depend on a Boolean analog of the *numOp* function just described.

This function needs to be able to fold the results of equality and inequality tests, returning an appropriate **true** or **false** leaf expression if the result is statically computable. We must also perform Boolean simplification according to axiomatic relations such as —

$$\textbf{true } OR \ rKid = \textbf{true}$$
$$lKid \ OR \ \textbf{true} = lKid$$

Rather than increasing the height of the trees, as *coerceUp* does, these transformations delete nodes from the trees, reducing the height. Consider the expression —

```
(target = "net") & expr
```

where "&" is logical **and**, and *expr* is some arbitrary Boolean expression. The compiler will know from its arguments whether the first term is true or false. If it is true, the whole expression is replaced by its own right child, decreasing the expression tree depth by one. Alternatively, if the first term is known to be false, the whole expression is replaced by the literal leaf node denoting **false**.

Unary nodes.

Unary nodes. Recall from Figure 5.4 that there are two specializations of unary expression nodes in *gpcp*. The parent node-type *UnaryX* is processed in a way that closely follows the pattern discussed for binary nodes. The specializations are rather different, and it is these differences that suggest the use of different descriptors in the first place.

Unary nodes with an identifier descriptor as a structural attribute are represented by the *IdentX* specialization. These nodes occur in just three contexts.

First, there is field selection on a designator. The *kid* attribute of the node, inherited from *UnaryX*, denotes the expression from which we shall select a member. Tree rewriting occurs in a couple of special cases. If the *kid* field has pointer type, then we insert a *UnaryX* node to denote dereference of the pointer to obtain the bound record type. We then perform field selection on that record type. The second case in which an *IdentX* node is rewritten occurs when the designator denoted by *kid* is an *IdLeaf* denoting a typename, and the *ident* field selects a static constant field. This happens, for example, whenever we reference an enumeration literal from the *CLS*. In this case, we must fold the node into a new constant *LeafX* node.

The second context that uses an *IdentX* node is type assertion. This operation is equivalent to a checked type-cast in *C#*. In this usage, the *kid* field holds the designator on which we wish to perform the type test at runtime. The inherited *ident* field will be a *TypId* type identifier descriptor. The *TypId* denotes the type that we assert the *kid* expression will have at runtime. A number of semantic checks need to be performed. To choose just one example, the test type must be a subtype of the static type of the *kid* expression. If the test type is a supertype, the test cannot fail, so the tree may be rewritten without the test. On the other hand, if the types are unrelated the test will always fail and the program is in error.[2]

The final context that uses an *IdentX* node is type conversion. In this case the inherited *ident* attribute holds the type identifier of the destination type. In fact this is a bit of an oddity. An ordinary *UnaryX* node would have been sufficient, with the *type* attribute denoting the destination type and *kid.type* denoting the source type. It seems that the type identifier field is only used for compiler diagnostics.

The *CallX* specialization of the *UnaryX* node is used for all procedure call statements and for function evaluation expressions. Most of the attribution that needs to be done is semantic checking of various kinds. There is just one special case that involves tree rewriting.

The built-in functions of *Component Pascal*, with one exception, are implemented by inline code rather than a function call. The exception is the call *LEN*(s$), where s$ is a character array treated as a string. In this special case we must call a runtime helper that scans the array to find the position of the first **nul** character. All other uses of *LEN* are inlined, as are all other built-in functions. Once a *CallX* node is known to bind to a standard function, we check the arguments and replace the tree with a new tree denoting an appropriate inline expression. Figure 6.5 gives an example of the inlining of a "call" to the binary *MAX* function. Possible encodings of this expression in *IL* are given in Figures 7.14 and 7.15.

The checking of actual parameters in the case of the built-in functions needs to be done by special code in *gpcp*, as several of these functions are overloaded. Since *Component Pascal* does not support user-defined overloading, there is no general-purpose infrastructure for binding calls to sets of overloaded procedures. Thus for the few built-in cases, each case must be treated separately by special code. Just to belabor the point, Figure 6.6 shows the rewriting that occurs for the *unary* usage of the *MAX* function. The unary form

---

[2]Well, actually here is an interesting point. Some language standards insist that code must be generated for tests, even if the tests are known to generate a runtime exception. *Ada* has such a rule. In any case the compiler should probably issue a friendly warning, if not an error.

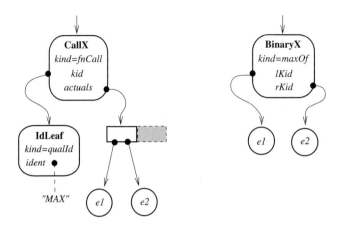

Figure 6.5: Rewriting of built-in "function call" *MAX(e1,e2)*

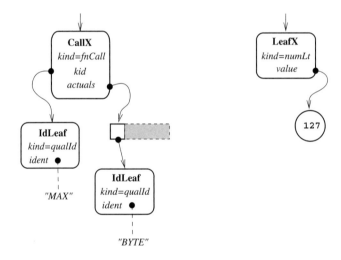

Figure 6.6: Rewriting of built-in "function call" *MAX(BYTE)*

selects the (constant) maximum value of the built-in type that its argument names.[3]   In
contrast, Figure 6.5 showed the rewriting of the *binary* form of the function.

In the general case *CallX* nodes denote the designator of the procedure to be called
as the value of the *kid* attribute. This subexpression is attributed first and will have a *type*
attribute of *Procedure* type. The list of actual parameters to the call is held in the *actuals*
attribute of the *CallX* and is a sequence of expressions.

---

[3]Recall that the *BYTE* type in *Component Pascal* is a signed type with range [−128 . . . 127].

We proceed by attributing each of the actual parameter expressions in order, iterating over the indexed, expansible array —

```
FOR ix := 0 TO node.actuals.tide-1 DO
  node.actuals.a[ix] := node.actuals.a[ix].exprAttr();
END;
```

This iteration pattern is almost a cliché of *gpcp*.

The final step is to check the conformance of actual parameter expressions against the formal types demanded by the procedure signature. We do a parallel iteration over the *actuals* sequence of the *CallX* node and the *formals* sequence of *kid.type*. This check needs to implement the precise semantics demanded by the language definition. This means not only conformance as to type, but also such constraints as not allowing a reference to a read-only datum to be passed to an **out**-mode formal. At the end of the iteration, if the lengths of the two sequences were not the same, we emit either a "not enough args" or a "too many args" error message.

Leaf nodes.   Recall from Figure 5.4 that there are two specializations of leaf expression nodes in *gpcp*. The parent node-type *LeafX* has no computed attributes. The *type* attribute of a plain leaf is an intrinsic attribute set by the parser.

The *IdLeaf* node is used to denote identifiers. Attribution of this node-type consists of binding the name of the *ident* field. If the identifier denotes a variable, then the *type* of the expression is the declared datatype of the variable. If the identifier denotes the name of a manifest constant, then the tree is rewritten as a plain *LeafX* node containing the appropriate constant value. Finally, if the identifier denotes a type name, then the *type* of the expression is a special built-in type denoting a metatype.

The *SetExp* case is a little more involved, since this structure contains a list of scalar and range expressions. Computing the attributes for this expression type consists of computing the attributes for every expression and range in the list. We wish to separate out all of the constant parts of the set into a statically known set, leaving all the nonconstant parts in a rebuilt *varSeq* list.

The constant part is accumulated in a variable *cPart*. We iterate over the *varSeq* list, attributing each expression in turn. If a list item reduces to a literal scalar, then the value is included in *cPart*, and the expression is not placed on the new *varSeq* list. Similarly, if a list item reduces to a literal range, then each value of the range is included in *cPart*, and once again the expression is not placed on the new *varSeq* list. Finally, if the item does not reduce to a constant, the attributed expression is placed on the new *varSeq* list.

Figure 6.7 shows the *AST* fragment resulting from the partial folding of the same set expression seen in Figure 5.5. In this example the set is {*i*, *j..k*, 0..3}. The original *SetExp* node had three items on the *varSeq* list, as seen in Figure 5.5. We assume that the first two

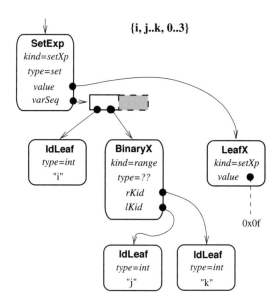

Figure 6.7: Set expression with constant part folded

of these are not statically known and remain on the rebuilt list. The last item is a literal range 0..3, which folds into the literal bit pattern 0x0f.[4]

The reason for performing this transformation should be clear. At runtime, evaluation of a set expression starts with the statically known part of the set or with an empty set. Each element expression must then be evaluated, and corresponding bits inserted into the set. There will be one insertion at runtime for every element on the *varSeq* list at compile time. By moving as many elements as possible to the statically known part of the set, we minimize the number of insertions that are required at runtime.

How Much Attribution Should Be Done During Parsing?

Some of the attributes that have been discussed in this chapter may be computed during parsing rather than in a separate traversal of the completed tree. There are some advantages in doing at least some computation of attributes earlier rather than later. The advantages come down to the possibility of finding some semantic errors during tree building, and the reduction in the number of tree nodes that are constructed and then later rewritten away. For languages that have some syntactic ambiguities, it is also possible to use semantic information to direct the tree-building control flow.

---

[4]The set {0..3} is denoted by a machine word with bits 0, 1, 2, and 3 set, and all others zero. In hexadecimal terms this is the number 0x0f.

On the negative side, the separation of semantic analysis from tree building leads to a conceptually clean design. The mixing up of attribution and parsing makes the design less pure and arguably harder to understand.

In practice, all compilers perform some attribution during parsing. In some cases this may be no more than the insertion of lexical attributes into the tree nodes. However, it is also quite common to perform some name binding during parsing. Figure 6.1 is an example of the additional node creation that arises from the failure to bind names on the fly.

If it is decided to try to bind names during parsing, then some caution is required if correctness is to be maintained. The following case study illustrates the difficulties.

Early *Pascal* compilers were invariably incremental compilers and computed attributes as early as possible. As identifiers were declared, they were inserted into the name-scope, and used occurrences were bound as soon as they were met. Now consider the following program fragment —

```
type Foo = record ... end;          (* first Foo *)
  ...
procedure LocalProc();
  var i :   Foo;            (* which Foo is this? *)
  type Foo = array ...;            (* second Foo *)
begin
  ...
end; (* of LocalProc *)
```

When the used occurrence of typename *Foo* appears in the local variable declaration inside the procedure, a direct attempt to bind the name will find the declaration of the first *Foo* type. The underlying question is, "Where are the limits of the textual region throughout which the second declaration of *Foo* should be effective?" One possibility is that a declaration is only effective from the point of its completion. If this is the case then binding to the outer *Foo* is correct. A second possibility is that the declaration takes effect throughout the scope in which it appears. In this case, the identifier should bind to the second *Foo*, and binding during parsing may give the wrong answer. A third possibility is that a declaration takes effect throughout the scope in which it appears, but it is illegal to refer to an identifier before its point of declaration. In this case, which is the rule for *Modula-2*, the program should be declared to be illegal.

The third of these scope rules may be implemented by performing name binding during parsing but remembering all of the names that have been bound to nonlocal identifiers. Whenever a new identifier is declared, we simply check that the name is not on the list of names that have already been bound nonlocally. If such a case occurs, we flag an "illegal forward reference to this object."

The second possibility, declarations being effective throughout their scope, has particular relevance to our running example, since this is the rule for type declarations in *Component Pascal*. In this case we may still bind names immediately, provided we use a little trick. The trick is to only look up typenames in the local scope and not use the full hierarchical name binding algorithm. If a name is unbound, then it might be a forward reference, and we create a new opaque type descriptor for it. At the end of all type declarations, the type resolution algorithm replaces all opaques by their correct bindings. If the reference was a forward reference to a local type, then this is the binding that the type resolver will find. If, on the other hand, the binding really is to a nonlocal type, then that is discovered and the correct substitution is made.

In *gpcp* names are bound by the parser. Although it would be possible to compute the static type of every expression during parsing, *gpcp* settles for a lesser goal. As a compromise, *designators* and constant expressions have their types evaluated during tree building. Since it is the designator syntax that is ambiguous, this compromise still guarantees that there is enough type information available when the parser needs it. Note, however, that since designators may have embedded function calls, function names and types must be bound during parsing also.

We end up with a curious mixture. The conformance of actual and formal argument types is validated during parsing in the case of value-returning functions, but is validated for proper procedures during the separate *AST* traversal. Similarly, expressions that semantically have to be constant have a call of *exprAttr*() dispatched on them immediately, while other expressions wait for the later traversal. This choice allows declarations of the form —

```
CONST twopi = 2 * Mathlib.pi;
```

to be reduced to literals immediately or a suitable error indication to be given. Of course, the same attribution code is used by both the parser and the semantic analyzer, so the chosen structure is really a matter of convenience.

It may be noted that this particular division of labor might not work for other languages. Constant expressions in *Component Pascal* have restricted types, and type names cannot occur in constant expressions. In *ISO Modula-2*, by constrast, constant expressions can contain constructors for constant instances of structured types. In that language constant expression attribution cannot be done until all type declarations in the current scope have been seen.

Despite its arbitrary appearance there are some hidden advantages in dividing up the work. If an error is discovered during tree building, we may decide to not bother proceeding with detailed statement checking. This means that a number of simplifying assumptions may be made in statement-checking code, since it is known that all designators are well-formed and have a non-**nil** *type* attribute.

Statement Attribution

The attribution and checking of statements is relatively straightforward. This simplicity follows from two sources. First of all, most of the real work is done in the attribution of the component expressions of the statements. For many statement types, once we have the attributes of the expressions, we need only to check that the types are correct. Furthermore, in general we do not rewrite the nodes during this process.

In *gpcp* semantic checking of statements is performed by a set of dispatched methods that extend an abstract method —

```
PROCEDURE (stmt : Stmt)StmtAttr(scope : Scope),ABSTRACT;
```

Note that this is a proper procedure, rather than a value-returning function. For statements we will seldom expect to wish to replace a descriptor with a rewritten one, as we did with expression attribution. We need to pass the current scope to the method, because some statements will need to check their attributes against attributes declared in the surrounding scope.

We deal quickly with those simple statement types for which we discussed the abstract syntax in the section on designing the abstract syntax (page 140).

Simple Statements

Firstly, the checking of our compound statement type *Block* is a simple iteration over the sequence of statements, recursively calling *StmtAttr* on each —

```
PROCEDURE (stmt : Block)StmtAttr(scope : Scope);
  VAR index : INTEGER;
BEGIN
  FOR index := 0 TO stmt.body.tide-1 DO
    stmt.body.a[index].StmtAttr(scope); (* recurse! *)
  END;
END StmtAttr;
```

Assignment statements illustrate the interrelationship between statement and expression attribute computation. As a simplifying point we note that the designator expression on the left-hand side of the assignment has been attributed during parsing and has a non-**nil** type attribute. Thus we need only compute the attributes for the expression tree on the right-hand side and perform some semantic checks.

The checks include making sure that the designator on the left denotes a datum that is mutable. (Remember that *Component Pascal* is able to declare read-only modifiers for many features.) We need to rewrite the tree on the right with added nodes for any dereference or type coercion that is implied and semantically permitted. Finally, we need to check that the two types conform to the definition of "assignment compatibility" in this language.

Return statements need the *scope* attribute that is passed to calls of *StmtAttr*. Return statements inside proper procedures must not attempt to return a value. Return statements inside value-returning functions *must* return a value, the type of which must be assignment-compatible with the declared return type of the procedure type descriptor.

Finally, in the case of *ProcCall* statements, we simply perform expression attribution on the embedded *CallX* expression. There is some additional checking for "super" calls that we ignore here.

Various Loop Statements

Most loop statement forms in *Component Pascal* share the same *TestLoop* descriptor type. This has a *test* attribute that denotes the termination test expression, and a *body* attribute that denotes the loop body statement. This structure is used for both **repeat** and **while** loops. It is even used for the endless **loop** construct, with the *test* attribute in that case conventionally set to **nil**.

The processing of this statement descriptor consists of evaluating the attributes of the test expression, if there is one, using *exprAttr*. It is an error, of course, if the expression type is not Boolean. We then recursively dispatch *StmtAttr* on the *body* statement.

Notice that this is one instance where semantic checking might usefully change the statement type. Since attribution of the test expression might reduce the test to a Boolean constant, the following transformations might be considered —

$$
\begin{array}{rcl}
\textbf{while true do } \text{body } \textbf{end} & \rightarrow & \textbf{loop } \text{body } \textbf{end} \\
\textbf{repeat } \text{body } \textbf{until } \text{false} & \rightarrow & \textbf{loop } \text{body } \textbf{end} \\
\textbf{while false do } \text{body } \textbf{end} & \rightarrow & (*\ skip\ *) \\
\textbf{repeat } \text{body } \textbf{until } \text{true} & \rightarrow & \text{body}
\end{array}
$$

Against this must be weighed the fact that we may achieve the same effect during code emission, once the expression has been folded. In addition, there are other kinds of control flow rewriting that we would like to consider at the same time, such as irregular exits from the loop using return, halt, or throw statements.

Choice Statements

For the *Choice* descriptor that is used for **if**, **then**, **else**, and **with** statements, we need to iterate over the predicates and block-lists. We rewrite the elements of the predicates list with the fully attributed, possibly rewritten, expressions. We check that all such expressions are of Boolean type, as predicates must be. Then, we recursively call *StmtAttr* on each statement on the *blocks* sequence.

Although it was not mentioned in the discussion of expression attribution in the previous section, there are a number of semantic checks that are important for the **is** tests that the predicates of the **with** statement are represented by. In the test —

$$\textit{designator } \textbf{is } \textit{typename}$$

the type of the designator must be an extensible type; otherwise, there is nothing to test. Furthermore, if the type denoted by the typename is not a subtype of the designator type, the test is in error.

Case Statements

The statement type that requires the most complex processing is the *Case* statement. The processing is complicated by two factors. Firstly, there are subtle conditions that the lists of case selector lists must fulfill. Secondly, the most favored method of encoding such statements requires considerable processing of the lists to discover dense groups of ranges of selector values.

We begin by dispatching a call of *exprAttr* on the selection expression of the statement. In *Component Pascal* this expression must have either integer or character type. The next step in semantic checking of the *Case* statement is to iterate over the *blocks* sequence, recursively calling *StmtAttr* on each statement. We do the same for the statements in the default branch, if there is one. The hard work starts when the *labels* sequence must be processed.

It is a typical condition of syntactic constructs, such as **case** or **switch** statements, that no label value be repeated. Logically, it would be more minimal to insist that no label value can select more than one statement, but the more stringent test is easier to implement.

In the case of *gpcp* the statement descriptors contain a list of *Triple* elements, where each element has three fields: *minR*; *maxR*; and *index*. The first two denote the minimum and maximum values of the selected range, while the third denotes the index in the *blocks* sequence that this range selects.

Sorting and merging the ranges.   As a first step we need to do two things. We wish to merge contiguous ranges that select the same statement sequence, and we need to check for overlaps in the ranges. We achieve both by sorting the triples on the first field, *minR* —

```
PROCEDURE QuickSort(VAR arr : TripleSeq;
                        lo,hi : INTEGER);
BEGIN
  ... (* sort on minR field *)
END QuickSort;


  ...

QuickSort(stmt.labels, 0, stmt.labels.tide-1);
  ...
```

The first parameter of *QuickSort* is of **inout** mode, and it sorts and overwrites its actual parameter sequence. The other two parameters are the low and high bounds of the array.

After sorting, we perform a single pass over the array, merging ranges that are contiguous and select the same block. We rebuild the triple list, from the merged triples of the old list. The algorithm is described in Figure 6.8. A small issue is that the abstract syntax for **case** statements is very abbreviated and has no lexical attributes associated with the triples list. When we come to report an overlap error, we shall have to use the position information from the selected statement. Thus the error message may end up with a format such as —

```
        CASE ch OF
        | '0'..'9', 'A'..'F' :
            ProcessHexDigit();
****            ^-- selector overlap error for this case
        | 'a'..'z', 'A'..'Z' :
            ProcessAlpha();
****            ^-- selector overlap error for this case
```

```
if old list not empty do
    move first element of old list to new list;
    while triples left in old list do
        select next element and compare to top of new list;
        if ranges contiguous and have same index then
            merge range with top of new list
        elsif ranges overlap then
            report an overlap error
        else
            append selected element to new list
        end (* inner if *)
    end (* while loop *)
end (* outer if *)
```

Figure 6.8: Range-merging algorithm

We cannot point directly to the offending constant expression, but in instances like this, where two statements are involved, we may point to both selected statements.

Figure 6.9 shows the relevant portion of the sorted triples list for the erroneous statement. We merge the ranges, starting from the bottom of the table. When we compare the second- and third-from-the-bottom ranges, we immediately spot the error.

minR	maxR	index
...	...	...
97	122	1
65	70	0
65	90	1
48	57	0

Figure 6.9: Fragment of triples list with overlap

Dealing with density.

The usual way in which **case** or **switch** are encoded is to create a *jump table*. This table is a static data structure with a list of code addresses, one for each selector value. The first address in the table would be for the destination selected by the lowest nondefault selector value, and the last address is selected by the highest nondefault selector value. The case code is selected by indexing into the table and executing an indirect jump. The *CLR* provides direct support for this encoding through the "switch" instruction.

It may be noted that, ignoring cache effects, statement selection using a jump table does not depend on the size of the table. That is, branching takes constant time.

One of the classic problems for encoding such statements is dealing with low density tables. Traditionally, density has been defined as the quotient *number of nondefault selector values* divided by *total number of selector values*. The usual jump table implementation of this construct becomes very inefficient when the density is low. For example, a jump table implementation of the code —

```
switch (val) {
    case SHRT_MIN  :  s0; break;
    case 0         :  s1; break;
    case SHRT_MAX  :  s2; break;
    default        :  s3;
}
```

would use 256 *kilobytes* of memory. The density of this statement is —

$$\rho = 3/65536 = 5 \times 10^{-5}$$

Of the 64k entries in the table, all but three point to the default case.

Many compilers tackle this problem either by rejecting large, low-density **switch** statements, or by re-encoding low-density statements using a *pair table*. A pair table consists of a list of nondefault pairs of the form (*selector value*, *code address*). Such a structure is used by searching for a match on the selector value field and jumping indirectly to the corresponding code address. Note that for the example above the pair table would occupy only 24 *bytes* of memory. Unfortunately, the *CLR* does not provide direct support for this implementation method, but the effect could be obtained using lower-level instructions.

If the pair table is sorted in selector value order, the search of the table may be implemented by a "binary chop" algorithm. In this case at most $\log_2 N$ comparisons will be required to find the value, where N is the number of pairs.

In practice many **switch** tables have regions of high density, even if the overall average density is low. In such cases both of the methods described are inefficient. Jump tables waste space, and pair tables waste time. Fortunately there is a tunable compromise that combines the best of both methods, due to Fraser and Hanson. This algorithm has $\log N$ behavior in the low-density case and constant time behavior in the high-density case.

The essence of the algorithm is to split the selector range into regions of some minimum acceptable density. We perform conditional branches in a branching tree to select the dense region in which the value lies. Then we finally do a constant time selection within that region using a jump table. Suppose, for simplicity, that we have a switch statement that has two dense regions, say, from $0\ldots9$ and from $90\ldots99$. A jump table for this example would use 400 *bytes*, and would take constant time to select a destination. A pair table would occupy 160 *bytes* and would take a maximum of five comparisons to make a choice. The Fraser and Hanson algorithm would have two jump tables of 40 *bytes* each and would make one more comparison than the jump table case. In effect, the single **switch** statement —

```
switch (val) {
    case  0 : s0;  break;
    case  1 : s1;  break;
    . . .
    case  9 : s9;  break;
    case 90 : s90; break;
    case 91 : s91; break;
    . . .
    case 99 : s99; break;
    default  : sDef;
}
```

is automatically recoded as if it had been written —

```
if (val < 90) {
    switch (val) {
        case 0 : s0;  break;
        case 1 : s1;  break;

          . . .

        case 9 : s9;  break;
        default : sDef;
    }
} else {
    switch (val-90) {
        case 0 : s90; break;
        case 1 : s91; break;

          . . .

        case 9 : s99; break;
        default : sDef;
    }
}
```

In general, the rewriting will do the equivalent of nested **if** statements if there are many dense regions. In the extreme case if every dense region consists of just one single selector value, then the algorithm will construct a binary decision tree with the promised logarithmic time complexity.

The original algorithm deals exclusively with single selector values, which leads to curious behavior in cases where the dense regions are *ranges* that all select the same statement. If we apply the original algorithm to the modified problem —

```
switch (val) {
    case  0 : case  1 :  ... case  9 : s0;  break;
    case 90 : case 91 :  ... case 99 : s90; break;
    default  : sDef;
}
```

then we will end up with two degenerate **switch** statements with jump tables, in which every index selects the same destination. Since *gpcp* has a data structure that deals with *selector ranges* rather than *selector values*, we may use this information to improve the algorithm. In the modified algorithm we effectively recode the statement as if it had been written as the obvious —

```
if (val < 90)
    if (val < 9) s0; else sDef;
else
    if (val-90 < 9) s90; else sDef;
```

No matter whether the original or the modified algorithm is going to be used to generate code, we must find regions of the selector space in which nondefault values are locally dense.

Finding dense regions.   We wish to partition all of the ranges in our data structure into groups of adjacent ranges such that the group achieves some minimal acceptable density. We suppose that our ranges are sorted, merged, and indexed, and that range i, say, extends from $i.minR$ to $i.maxR$. Now consider a *group* of ranges starting at range n and ending at range m. The density of the group is given by —

$$\rho_{nm} = \frac{\sum_{i=n}^{m}(i.maxR - i.minR + 1)}{m.maxR - n.minR + 1} = \frac{nondefault\ values}{m.maxR - n.minR + 1}$$

Note that the density of a singleton group, that is, a group consisting of just one range, is always exactly 1.

Each group is denoted by a triple, with fields that are the range index of the first range in the group, *mnRg*; the last index in the group, *mxRg*; and the number of nondefault selector values, *elNm*. We begin by making a list of groups that consist of a single range only and try to coalesce adjacent groups. We require two passes over the array of groups, one upward and one downward. Groups are merged if the merger results in a new group with density greater than the minimum. Choosing a minimum density in the range 0.5 to 0.8 is usual.

Suppose R is the array of range triples, and G is the array of group triples. If we consider two adjacent groups $G[n]$ and $G[n + 1]$, we may merge these two groups if —

$$\frac{G[n].elNm + G[n + 1].elNm}{R[G[n + 1].mxRg].maxR - R[G[n].mnRg].minR + 1} > \rho_{min}$$

It is necessary to perform two passes over the group list, to ensure that outlying ranges at the edge of a dense region get merged no matter which side of the region that they lay on. Figure 6.10 shows the data structure for a **case** statement with six ranges and three groups.

This figure shows the groups that would result from choosing a minimum density, ρ_{min}, between 0.6 and 0.8. It is left as an exercise to show that just two groups would result if the density limit were chosen at 0.5, and only one group if the density limit was less than 0.47.

The code generation chapter will show how these data structures are used in the emission of switch statement code.

Using the Visitor Pattern

During semantic checking we have several kinds of traversal patterns that occur. The most obvious examples are those traversals that walk over the *AST* structures. Almost all of this chapter has been concerned with such attributions, so no more need be said.

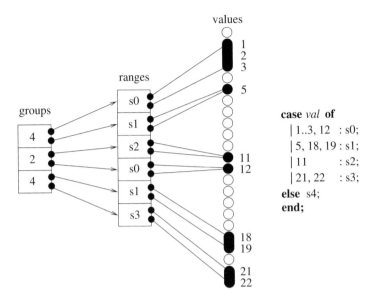

values

case *val* **of**
  | 1..3, 12   : s0;
  | 5, 18, 19 : s1;
  | 11   : s2;
  | 21, 22   : s3;
else s4;
end;

Figure 6.10: Groups, ranges, and values for a **case** statement

There are also traversals that iterate over *AST* attributes that are of sequence type. We have seen some examples of these here and shall meet several more in the code generation chapters.

There is one further kind of traversal that is used fairly widely in *gpcp*, which iterates over all entries in a symbol table. This particular *visitor pattern* is the subject of the rest of this section.

It should be admitted that all of the purposes for which the visitor pattern is employed could have been achieved by other means. For example, when we wish to perform some processing on every type identifier in a symbol table, we might have planned for this by having an appropriate sequence defined in the abstract syntax. Nevertheless, the visitor pattern is important as it achieves its effect without having to add spurious attributes to the *AST*. Once the use of the pattern is understood, it becomes a powerful technique in the compiler writer's bag of tricks.

Defining the Visitor

The idea behind the visitor pattern is to get functionality which might be described by the pseudocode —

forall *Idnt in SymTab* **do** *something* **end**

In general, we do not care about the order in which the entries are processed. Of course, the something that we want to do to the identifier descriptors may be different for each identifier kind.

We begin by defining an abstract class, *SymForAll*, which will form the base class of all visitor classes. *SymForAll* has a single abstract method, the concrete replacements for which will specify the "*something*" that the particular visit wishes to perform. Here is the definition —

```
TYPE SymForAll* = POINTER TO ABSTRACT RECORD END;
(* base class has no fields *)
...
PROCEDURE (v : SymForAll)Op*(id : Idnt),NEW,ABSTRACT;
(* the something method applied to each identifier *)
```

Concrete extensions of this class simply specify the operation to be performed as the body of the overriding *Op* method. For example, *gpcp* has some diagnostic code that was used during development. We wish to invoke the *Diagnose* method on each identifier descriptor. We achieve this by extending the *SymForAll* class with a new *SymTabDump* class with an appropriate operation. The complete code is just three lines —

```
TYPE SymTabDump*= POINTER TO RECORD (SymForAll) END;

PROCEDURE (v : SymTabDump)Op*(id : Idnt); (* final *)
BEGIN id.Diagnose(0) END Op;
```

In this instance, the extended type requires no additional fields, and the *Op* operation body is a simple method application.

The key to the flexibility of the technique is the fact that we may define a shared navigation method that knows how to iterate over symbol tables. The exact design depends on the particular data structure that the symbol table uses. In the case of *gpcp* the tables are binary trees with a hash table entry as key, as described in "Symbol Tables and Scope Representation" (see page 161). In this case we define an instance (nonvirtual) method *Apply* that performs a preorder traversal of the symbol table structure. The code is straight-forward —

```
PROCEDURE (tab : SymbolTable)Apply*(sfa : SymForAll),NEW;
BEGIN (* new and not extensible ⇒ instance method *)
  IF tab.root # NIL THEN tab.root.Visit(sfa);
END Apply
```

The *Apply* method launches a recursive preorder traversal on the binary tree.

```
PROCEDURE (node : SymInfo)Visit(sfa : SymForAll),NEW;
BEGIN (* call Op on this node's ident, then recurse *)
  sfa.Op(node.val);
  IF node.lOp # NIL THEN node.lOp.Visit(sfa) END;
  IF node.rOp # NIL THEN node.rOp.Visit(sfa) END;
END Visit;
```

Notice that these methods take any instance of an extension of the *SymForAll* class as their argument. The *Apply* method is public, while the *Visit* method has module visibility.

In order to invoke a visitor pattern for a *SymTabDump*, for example, we need to create a visitor object and pass it to the *Apply* method invoked on the symbol table of interest —

```
NEW(stDump); mySymTab.Apply(stDump);
```

The flexibility of the pattern arises from the fact that the iteration code is fixed and applied to all possible visitors. To use the pattern, an extension of *SymForAll* is defined, adding instance fields if necessary, and the *Op* method is overridden. We consider just one further example.

The NameDump Visitor

The *NameDump* method is used to construct a comma-separated list of the names of all the identifiers in a symbol table. This pattern is used, among others, by diagnostic code that lists identifiers that violate some condition.

For example, consider a nonabstract type that extends an abstract type. The concrete type has a contractual obligation to implement every single abstract method that it inherits from its supertypes, all the way up to *Object*. During semantic analysis, when we get to the end of declarations for the type, we must check if all such obligations have been discharged. We do this by some kind of traversal up the inheritance path of the type graph. We want to give a helpful diagnostic that says, "Error: abstract methods <*the-list*> have not been implemented" or something similar.

A possible design traverses the inheritance path in the type graph, looking for abstract methods and testing to see if a lookup in the current scope resolves the names to a concrete method.[5] If the test fails, we insert the identifier of the abstract method into a symbol table. We do it this way, rather than just placing the descriptor on a list, since we do not wish to duplicate names. At the end we turn the symbol table into the string of names that the diagnostic message needs.

---

[5] We might use another visitor pattern for that traversal also.

The *NameDump* type is an extension of *SymForAll* —

```
TYPE NameDump* =
        POINTER TO RECORD (SymForAll)
          str : CharOpen; (* pointer to array of char *)
        END
```

The *Op* method takes each identifier, and concatenates it to the string that is already stored in the *str* instance field of the visitor object.

```
PROCEDURE (t : NameDump)Op*(id : Idnt); (* final *)
  VAR name : CharOpen;
BEGIN
  name := NameHash.charOpenOfHash(id.hash);
  IF t.str = NIL THEN t.str := name;
  ELSE (* append a comma, then the name *)
    t.str := LitValue.strToCharOpen(t.str^ + ", " + name^);
  END
END Op;
```

We may wrap this whole mechanism inside a static procedure, so that generating the name string appears as a simple function call applied to a symbol table. Here is the idea —

```
PROCEDURE dumpList(tab : SymbolTable) : CharOpen;
  VAR nDmp : NameDump;
BEGIN (* create NameDump; launch visitor; return string *)
  NEW(nDmp); tab.Apply(nDmp); RETURN nDmp.str;
END dumpList;
```

There are a number of different ways to use the visitor pattern in *gpcp*. As noted at the beginning, it is always possible to achieve the same effect by defining additional attributes in the abstract syntax. This is even necessary whenever the order of iteration over the elements is important. However, for all the other cases the visitor pattern is a simple, lightweight, and flexible mechanism to use. This should be in every compiler writer's toolkit.

Notes on Chapter 6

The material on initialization analysis described in Appendix A logically belongs with this chapter. It has been moved to the appendix because it is rather lengthy and may be safely skipped on a first reading. Nevertheless, when the material is tackled, it should be read in conjunction with this chapter.

The switch statement algorithm described here and in Chapter 9 is a refinement of the algorithm of Fraser and Hanson. That algorithm was first published in the journal *Software Practice and Experience*, but is more accessible in their book *A Retargetable C Compiler: Design and Implementation*, Benjamin Cummings, 1995.

The visitor pattern, as a general organizing principle for program design, is one of the classic patterns of the famous "pattern book." The details are: Gamma, Helm, Johnson, and Vlissides, *Design Patterns: Elements of Reusable Object-Oriented Software*, Addison-Wesley, 1995.

In this chapter, the issues involved in strong names for assemblies, and metadata generally, have been only mentioned in passing. The system documentation may be consulted for further information about the tools "`sn`", which creates strong names, and "`gacutil`", which manages the global assembly cache. Partition II of the draft *ECMA* standard deals with the metadata in as much detail as one might wish. Finally, the extraction of metadata from compiled assemblies is the task of the *System.Reflection* classes. If this particular metadata path is chosen, then some study of the facilities of that namespace will be necessary.

Overview of Code Generation

7

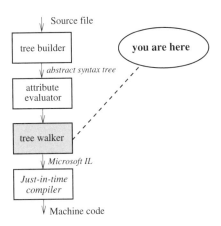

This chapter is a general introduction to code generation for *.NET*. The next two chapters deal specifically with code generation for expressions and for generating flow-of-control.

At this stage we focus specifically on an architecture corresponding to the left-hand side of Figure 1.2. That is, we assume that code is to be emitted to a textual *CIL* file. In Chapter 11 we shall look at the differences that using *Reflection.Emit* might make.

The major structuring unit of the *CIL* is the class. Although there may be enclosing structures, such as namespaces and modules, all of the code lives inside methods that are inside classes. Although the emission of code for any particular expression or statement may be quite intricate, the *traversal* of the *AST* that leads to the emission is relatively predictable. The situation is not so clear in the case of the classes, particularly for languages in which some other language construct is mapped into the class structure of the *CTS*. In *Component Pascal*, as an example, the need for class declarations in *IL* arises as a side effect of type declarations in the source. The emission of class declarations thus arises from some kind of traversal of the web of type descriptors.

In *gpcp* the emission of all code is controlled by a worklist algorithm. Although some of the structure is a result of the particular mapping of *Component Pascal* syntax onto the structures of the *CTS*, the pattern is typical. An *Emitter* object is created, with fields to hold the module descriptor, a worklist of type identifier descriptors, and an output file data structure. This object has an *Emit* method called on it, which indirectly emits all of the code of the compilation unit.

Each item on the worklist of the *Emitter* structure becomes a class definition in the *IL*. Items are put on the list as they are discovered during code emission. In languages in which classes are explicitly declared, the classes would already be on a list constructed by the parser.

The *Emit* method opens up an output file, emits suitable prolog declarations, and processes its worklist. After exhausting the worklist, it then emits some epilog text. The epilog text for `ilasm` does no more than emit a closing brace, matching the opening brace that followed the declaration of the namespace. The real work is all performed in the worklist processing. Identifier descriptor elements are taken from the list one by one. If the element is a module descriptor, then a synthetic static class is emitted for this module, with detailed semantics that we shall decribe later. Type identifier descriptors become either value or reference class definitions in the *IL*, depending on the values of specific semantic attributes. Again the detail will be discussed later.

All of the emission of code depends on infrastructure for such things as the generation of *IL* names, tables of identifier names, and so on. This infrastructure is the topic of the next section.

Emitter Infrastructure

There is a need to provide a number of utility functions for the emission of code in *.NET*. The way in which this is done is not a critical design feature, but a good choice makes all of what follows more simple.

In *gpcp* code emission is encapsulated in two modules. *MsilMaker* has the code that traverses the overall *AST* structure, and knows how to walk over statement and expression descriptors. The module *IlasmUtil* contains all of the emitter utilities that are the subject of this section.

Emitter Utilities

IL-Name construction. All named objects in the source language must have a sufficiently qualified name in *CIL*. These names need to be assembled from the simple name of the object, together with qualifying strings that depend on the context in which the name was declared. This means that we usually need to take into account the defining scope, the binding class, and so on.

As a result of semantic analysis, the compilation unit *AST* will have bound identifier descriptors as leaves of the trees. These identifiers will usually have multiple used occurrences, so it makes sense to assemble the name of the object once, as a code attribute of the descriptor, and access the assembled name as needed.

gpcp adopts a lazy approach to name construction, in which every descriptor has fields that are **nil** in the case of the *CIL* name not having been constructed. If a **nil** name is discovered, one of a set of procedures is called that constructs the namestrings. One procedure is called *MkTypeName*, which maps type descriptors to the corresponding *CIL* class name, and another is *MkIdName*, which maps identifier descriptors to the corresponding *CIL* name. These two procedures call specialized procedures that, for example, generate the names for the record, pointer, and enumeration types. In cases where the kind of the descriptor is already known, the specialized descriptors are called directly.

The name mapping that is used in *gpcp* is probably best explained by first giving an example. Figure 7.1 shows a typical module structure, with *CIL* class names added to

```
module Foo;
   type Rec1*  = record ... end;        (* class name is Foo.Rec1 *)
   var anon*  :  record ... end;        (* class name is Foo.$T12 *)

   procedure Bar ( ... );
      type Rec2  = record ... end;      (* class name is Foo.Rec2@Bar *)
      var anon  :  record ... end;      (* class name is Foo.$T15 *)
      procedure Bzz ( ... );
         type Rec3  = record ... end;   (* class name is Foo.Rec2@Bzz@Bar *)
         var anon  :  record ... end;   (* class name is Foo.$T17 *)
      begin ...
      end Bzz;

   begin ...
   end Bar;

begin ...
end Foo.
```

Figure 7.1: Generating *CIL* class names for *Component Pascal*

records as comments. The names shown in the figure are the *IL* names by which the types will be known within their respective scopes inside the defining module. In this design, the type namespace is flattened, so that all types appear in *CIL* defined at the level of the module namespace. The names of types that are declared as local to a procedure have unique synthetic names constructed by "*name mangling*." In the case of named types local to procedures, the name of the procedure is appended to the type name. For anonymous types prepending the procedure name is not necessary, as anonymous types are given a unique serial number as part of the type name.

The global-level exported identifier *Rec1* will be referred to in the defining module as *Foo.Rec1*. The corresponding class will be a value class, which in the *IL* of any importing module will be known as *[Foo]Foo.Rec1*. In *Component Pascal*, the anonymous type of the variable *anon* can never be exported even if, as in this example, the variable itself is exported.

In the case of class-based languages, such as *C#*, classes may be declared local to other classes, rather than being declared local to procedures. Such nested classes are directly supported by the *CLR*, using a built-in name-mangling scheme in which the slash character '/' is used as a separator between name components.

Array types have names in *IL* that are derived from the name of the array element type. Thus for languages that have named array types, the type identity is lost in the *IL*. As discussed in Chapter 4, pointer types may be mapped to object references or perhaps references to boxed value types. In unverified contexts the names of function pointer types (procedure types in *Component Pascal*) may be generated by the same machinery that generates method signatures.

Procedures and functions in the source map into method names in the *IL* with the pattern *ClassName::MethodName*. In the case of languages with global procedures the corresponding methods belong to a synthetic static class.

For languages with nested procedures the names of methods in the *IL* are also subject to name mangling. In the case of *gpcp* the synthetic static class has the same name as the module name, and nested procedures have their *IL* names formed by using the enclosing simple procedure name as a suffix. Figure 7.2 shows some simple examples. In this figure, *Mth* is an instance method of the record type *Rec*. The name within the defining module will be *Foo.Rec::Mth*. If the method were exported, then the *IL* name used within an importing module would be *[Foo]Foo.Rec::Mth*. As in the case of type names, the name mangling places the simple name first, so that if two procedures, *Proc1* and *Proc2*, each have a nested procedure named *Helper*, then the simple mangled names will be *Helper@Proc1* and *Helper@Proc2* respectively. For deeply nested procedures the surrounding procedure names are appended from the inside out.

Along with the procedure names we must generate the procedure signatures as well. An abbreviated form of the signature is used for occurrences at call sites, with additional

```
module Foo;
  type Rec = record ... end;                        (* class name is Foo.Rec *)

  procedure Bar (...);              (* procedure name is Foo.Foo::'Bar' *)
    procedure Bzz (...);            (* proc name is Foo.Foo::'Bzz@Bar' *)
    begin ...
    end Bzz;
  begin ...
  end Bar;

  procedure (in t :   Rec) Mth ();      (* IL name is Foo.Rec::'Mth' *)
    procedure Bzz (...);            (* proc name is Foo.Foo::'Bzz@Mth' *)
    begin ...
    end Bzz;
  begin ...
  end Bar;

  begin ...                    (* entrypoint name is Foo.Foo::'.CPmain' *)
  end Foo.
```

Figure 7.2: Generating *CIL* procedure names for *Component Pascal*

attributes used in the method declaration. The form used at call sites is the one we want
to generate and store, since it is only this form that may be used multiple times. In *gpcp* a
method called *IlasmUtil.NumberParams* iterates over the formal argument list of the procedure, generating an array of strings.[1] Each formal argument adds at least one string, and
every one after the first adds a comma as well. Figure 7.3 spells out the details. In this figure, the last two columns give the suffixes that are required for **in** or reference (**var** or **out**)
modes. Normally **in**-mode parameters are passed by reference, but for built-in scalar types,
enumerations, and pointers *gpcp* uses value mode. Since **in**-mode formal parameters are
read-only, this is a safe optimization. For arrays and for records that are implemented by
reference classes—that is, for reference surrogate types—the data object is only accessible
through the object reference. For these two cases, it is not necessary to do anything extra
for reference mode, since the argument is a reference already.

As a final step, the strings of the array are concatenated to form the method signature.
This signature is stored as the type name of the procedure type descriptor, so that it may be
reused at call sites with no additional computation required.

Having constructed the names of types and identifiers, we may now see how the
various parts fit together in utilities that do things such as emit method calls in the *IL*.

---

[1] The method actually creates these strings as a side effect of numbering the formal parameters of the procedure
being processed. Hence the name of the method.

Formal type	Implementation	String to append	in	ref
Base type	built-in scalar	built-in special name		+'&'
Array type	array object	recurse on elType + '[ ]'		
Record type	value class	**value class** *ClassName*	+'&'	+'&'
	reference class	**class** *ClassName*		
Pointer type	ptr to array	recurse on elType + '[ ]'		+'&'
	ptr to value class	**class** *BoxedClassName*		+'&'
	ptr to ref class	**class** *ClassName*		+'&'
Enum type	value class	**value class** *EnumName*		+'&'

Figure 7.3: Signature element generation for *gpcp*

The utility that emits method call instructions in *gpcp* takes three parameters. These are the integer instruction selector, which must select either "call" or "callvirt", the procedure id-descriptor, and the procedure type descriptor.

```
procedure
    (os : IlasmFile)CallIT*(opc : INTEGER;       (* the op-code *)
                            pId : Procs;          (* proc ident-desc. *)
                            pTy : Procedure); (* proc type-desc. *)
```

The elements of the instruction syntax in the *IL* are emitted in order. We begin by emitting the string corresponding to the op-code. If *pId* is a method descriptor, as opposed to an ordinary procedure descriptor, we emit the string "instance". The return type is emitted by the *RetType* utility, based on the type name of the return type field of *pTy*, or "void" as the case may be. A call to utility *PIdnt* emits the procedure name, based on *pId*. Finally, the signature of the method is emitted. The signature is held in the type name attribute of the procedure type descriptor *pTy*.

In the example in Figure 2.21 on page 44, the string "void" is emitted by *RetType*, everything from the left bracket through to "WriteLine" is emitted by *PIdnt*, and the the rest of the signature, including the enclosing parentheses, is part of the type name string of the procedure type descriptor.

String constant pool. In *gpcp* a module *IlasmCodes* holds all of the constant strings that are used in the textual *IL*. In particular, there are integer constants declared that define the name strings associated with each instruction, directive, and attribute value. This allows integer arguments to be passed to the low-level procedures that emit individual instructions.

For mnemonic purposes the name of the constant corresponding to each instruction derives from the instruction name, but with the dot character replaced by a lowline '_' character. Thus the instruction "ldc.i4.8" is selected by the constant with name "opc_ldc_i4_8".

For attributes the module defines a number of integer constants that may be used together in a bitset. When attributes for a declaration need to be emitted, the attribute set is passed to a utility, and the attribute names are emitted for each of the bits in the set that are "on."

Instruction helpers.   The emitter utilities module is also the location to place the various instruction helper procedures. There are a number of these, the most obvious of which is the helper that emits a possibly specialized "ldloc" instruction to push onto the stack the value of the local variable with ordinal *ord*. Figure 7.4 is the code of the *PushLocal* method in *gpcp*.

```
procedure (iFil : IlasmFile) PushLocal* (ord: INTEGER) , new;
begin
  if ord <= 255 then
    case ord of
    |  0 : iFil.Code(Asm.opc_ldloc_0);          (* ldloc.0 *)
    |  1 : iFil.Code(Asm.opc_ldloc_1);          (* ldloc.1 *)
    |  2 : iFil.Code(Asm.opc_ldloc_2);          (* ldloc.2 *)
    |  3 : iFil.Code(Asm.opc_ldloc_3);          (* ldloc.3 *)
    else iFil.CodeI(Asm.opc_ldloc_s, ord);      (* ldloc.s ord *)
    end; (* case *)
  else iFil.CodeI(Asm.opc_ldloc, ord);          (* ldloc ord *)
  end;
end PushLocal;
```

Figure 7.4: Utility to push a local variable value

The emission of the actual code to the *IL* file is performed by a set of methods named "Code*". There are versions for each of the instruction formats. The two versions that appear in the figure are a plain method, which simply takes the opcode as argument, and another, which takes an opcode and an integer argument. In an implementation language that supports overloaded procedures, these could all have the same name.

Similar procedures are used for all of the instructions that have specialized versions for small arguments. The most intricate of these is the procedure that pushes a four-byte integer constant. There are 10 specialized versions of the "ldc.i4" instruction, as well as the short version. Figure 7.5 shows the code for this utility.

The emission of code to load the value of a variable is also a primitive operation that is usefully delegated to a utility. A possible structure for such a utility is a set of dispatched methods that emit different code for each subclass of the identifier descriptor class. Thus one method emits code to load the value of a static field, using the "ldsfld" instruction, while other methods emit "ldloc" and "ldarg" instructions to push local variables and formal parameters. The body of procedure *PushLocal* in Figure 7.4 is essentially the local identifier specialization of this method.

```
procedure (iFil : IlasmFile) PushInt * (num:  INTEGER) , new;
begin
  if (-128 <= num) & (num <= 127) then
    case num of
    | -1 : iFil.Code(Asm.opc_ldc_i4_M1);        (* ldc.i4.M1 *)
    |  0 : iFil.Code(Asm.opc_ldc_i4_0);         (* ldc.i4.0 *)
    |  1 : iFil.Code(Asm.opc_ldc_i4_1);         (* ldc.i4.1 *)
    |  2 : iFil.Code(Asm.opc_ldc_i4_2);         (* ldc.i4.2 *)
    |  3 : iFil.Code(Asm.opc_ldc_i4_3);         (* ldc.i4.3 *)
    |  4 : iFil.Code(Asm.opc_ldc_i4_4);         (* ldc.i4.4 *)
    |  5 : iFil.Code(Asm.opc_ldc_i4_5);         (* ldc.i4.5 *)
    |  6 : iFil.Code(Asm.opc_ldc_i4_6);         (* ldc.i4.6 *)
    |  7 : iFil.Code(Asm.opc_ldc_i4_7);         (* ldc.i4.7 *)
    |  8 : iFil.Code(Asm.opc_ldc_i4_8);         (* ldc.i4.8 *)
    else iFil.CodeI(Asm.opc_ldc_i4_s,  num);    (* ldc.i4.s num *)
    end; (* case *)
  else iFil.CodeI(Asm.opc_ldc_i4,  num);        (* ldc.i4 num *)
  end;
end PushInt;
```

Figure 7.5: Utility to push an integer constant

The case of formal parameters is further specialized, since parameters may be either passed by value or by reference. In the case of reference mode, the value of the formal is pushed, and an appropriate "ldind.*" instruction follows.

The idea of using a dispatched set of emission methods for common tasks, such as pushing variable values, has the consequence of mixing up the methods for *IL* emission with all the other methods dispatched on identifier type. For an architecture such as that used by *gpcp*, this structure is not really attractive. The problem is that the design has been factored so that different output languages may be added in a modular fashion. Code emission is encapsulated in the methods of various classes, one for each output language. Each of these classes extends an abstract class called *ClassMaker*. In principle, the kind of structure that supports this design would use *multimethods* that were dispatched on both identifier type *and* output target language.

In the event, the utility that emits code to push variables in *gpcp* has multiple layers. The higher-level procedures select lower-level methods on the basis of type tests on the identifier type, rather than direct dispatch. Figure 7.6 has the signatures of the various methods. The reason that the code of the lower levels is exposed as named methods, rather than just being inline code in *GetVar*, say, is that we often call the *Push** methods directly. For example, temporary local variables are only known by their ordinal number and their type. We do not have an identifier descriptor to pass to *GetVar* to push such values. And even if we did have one, it is faster to call the final method directly.

```
procedure (iFil : IlasmFile) GetVar (id :   Idnt);
(* call either GetStatField(), or GetLocal() *)

procedure (iFil : IlasmFile) GetStatField (id :   VarId);
(* emit — ldsfld fType fName *)

procedure (iFil : IlasmFile) GetLocal (id :   LocId);
(* call PushLocal(), PushArg(), or PushArg() then LoadIndirect() *)

procedure (iFil : IlasmFile) PushLocal (ord :   INTEGER);
(* emit equivalent of — ldloc ord *)

procedure (iFil : IlasmFile) PushArg (ord :   INTEGER);
(* emit equivalent of — ldarg ord *)

procedure (iFil : IlasmFile) LoadIndirect (typ :   Type);
(* emit — ldind.*, ldind.ref or ldobj *)
```

Figure 7.6: Utilities to push a variable value

The *LoadIndirect* method selects its output instruction on the basis of the bound type of the reference parameter that has just been pushed. For the various built-in scalar types the appropriate load indirect instruction to emit is selected by indexing into an array of instruction ordinals. If the bound type is a value record, then the value is loaded by the "ldobj" instruction. Finally, if the bound type is a reference then "ldind.ref" is emitted.

As well as the cases that have been detailed here, we require analogous utilities for pushing the various other kinds of expression leaf nodes. There are also similar methods— *PutVar*, *StoreIndirect*, and the corresponding lower-level procedures—for popping and storing top-of-stack values into the various kinds of locations.

Emitting the Structure

The preamble. The structure of a module in textual *CIL* begins with a preamble that contains various directives. The module may define an assembly and will in any case declare the other assembly names that are known to the current source. These correspond, in *C#* terms, to the assemblies that are referenced on the command line of the compiler with the "/R:*filename*" flag. There may also be a definition of a module name for this module and import declarations for other modules that this module accesses.

In the case that a module defines an assembly, it will declare various data, which end up in the assembly manifest. The module defines an assembly if it contains an assembly directive. The directive has the following *EBNF* syntax —

AssemblyDecl   →   **.assembly** { AsmAttr } DottedName "{" { AsmDecl } "}" .
    AsmAttr   →   *<Various assembly attributes>* .
    AsmDecl   →   *<Various assembly declarations>* .

The *DottedName* is the name of the assembly that is being defined. Most of the various as-sembly attributes are not implemented in version *V1* of the *CLR* and may be safely ignored for the moment.

It is possible to leave the assembly declarations entirely empty, which is what the first release of *gpcp* does. In such cases the assembler will fill in default values for any mandatory attributes. Some of the most likely attributes to be added manually are given by the syntax —

        AsmDecl   →   **.ver** *int32* ":" *int32* ":" *int32* ":" *int32* .
             | **.originator** = "(" Bytes ")" .
             | **.custom** CustomDecl .

The four constants in the version number declaration are the major version, minor version, revision, and build numbers respectively. The default data inserted in the absence of such a declaration is "`0:0:0:0`".

The **.originator** argument specifies the public key of the originator. This may be used to look for integrity checks on the assembly that are based on public key cryptography. The use and declaration of custom attributes is dealt with in "Custom Attributes" (see page 299).

Other declarations in the preamble that form part of the assembly manifest are the **.corflags**, **.file**, **.manifestres**, and **.subsystem** directives. The details of these directives are found in the `ilasm` reference manual. For example, the **.file** directive declares that a particular file is a resource of the assembly. Such a declaration specifies the filename, and optionally the hash value of the file, to ensure integrity. Normally, the hash value will be generated automatically by the linker `al` when the assembly is linked.

Whether or not the module includes an assembly directive, it will usually include one or more references to external assemblies. Such references have the form —

     AssemblyRef   →   **.assembly extern** { AsmAttr }
                            DottedName "{" { AsmRefDecl } "}" .
     AsmRefDecl   →   *<Various assembly declarations>* .

The *DottedName* is the name of the assembly that is being referenced. This name must exactly match the name in the **.assembly** directive in the defining assembly manifest. Thus, although on many platforms the names of the files in which assemblies reside are not case sensitive, the **.assembly** names must match character case.

There are various assembly reference declarations, the most important of which is the version declaration. This has the form —

$$AsmRefDecl \quad \rightarrow \quad \textbf{.ver}\ int32\ \text{``:''}\ int32\ \text{``:''}\ int32\ \text{``:''}\ int32\ .$$

If no version declaration is given, the runtime will attempt to run the code with any old assembly that it can find, irrespective of version number.

All programs will need to import the *mscorlib* assembly, which contains the whole system namespace. This import may be either implicit or explicit. An explicit import is not required, if no particular version number of *mscorlib* is requested.

Modules. Every file that is assembled by `ilasm` constitutes one module in an assembly. By default `ilasm` places every module in an assembly on its own, but many separate modules may be linked into a single assembly using the linker `al`. The name of the module may be specified by means of a module directive. In the case that no such directive is given in the *IL*, the assembler will give the module a default name equal to the full file name. Thus if we assemble the *IL* file "`hello.il`", and the file has an entry point, then the resulting module will be given the default name "`hello.EXE`".

In case there are several modules within a single assembly, it is necessary to able to reference specific module names, as well as being able to define modules. The format of the directive that defines the name of a module is —

$$ModDecl \quad \rightarrow \quad \textbf{.module}\ filename\ .$$

The file name should match the name of the file into which the module will be assembled, including extension and character case.

Access to an external module of the same assembly is gained by using a directive to import a module by name. The format is —

$$ModRef \quad \rightarrow \quad \textbf{.module extern}\ filename\ .$$

The file name should match the name of the file in the corresponding module definition directive.

Whenever a feature of an imported module needs to be accessed, the syntax that is used is a variation of the pattern shown in Figure 2.21 for referencing a type. The syntax, for non-nested types, is —

$$
\begin{aligned}
TypeRef \quad &\rightarrow \quad [\ \text{ResolutionScope}\ ]\ \text{DottedName}. \\
ResolutionScope \quad &\rightarrow \quad \text{``['' } \textit{AssemblyName} \text{ ``]''} \\
&\quad | \quad \text{``['' } \textbf{.module}\ \textit{filename} \text{ ``]'' .}
\end{aligned}
$$

As expected, types within the same module require no resolution scope to be specified. Types from other assemblies will use an explicit assembly name, while types from other modules in the same assembly will use the second form.

Namespaces.   Namespaces are used in the *CLR* simply as a syntactic mechanism for qualifying used occurrences of names. The definition of a namespace does not have any semantic significance for the runtime, but simply declares that all identifiers defined within that namespace will have dotted names that use the namespace identifier as a prefix. Namespaces may be nested and are declared using the format —

> NamespaceDecl   →   **.namespace** DottedName "{" { Declarations } "}".

Of course, within the namespace we would expect to find class definitions at the next level of syntactic nesting. In turn, we expect to see method and field definitions inside the classes.

Chaining to the assembler.   In the event that a compiler produces textual *IL*, it is desirable to have the compiler, or its driver program, automatically invoke the assembler. It appears that `ilasm` is not a loadable assembly, so it is necessary to create a new operating system process to run the assembler.

It is entirely possible that there are more elegant ways of achieving this outcome than the one that *gpcp* uses. The only virtue of the method outlined here is that it actually does work.

Figure 7.7 shows a somewhat simplified version of the *C#* code of the module *MsilAsm* that invokes the assembler. This module supplies the implementation of a dummy *Component Pascal* module of the same name. The module has two public static methods. One initializes a process descriptor object, if necessary. The other method is the one that actually calls `ilasm`. This method takes two strings and a Boolean as input arguments. The strings are the file name and the possibly empty option string. The Boolean indicates whether the module to be assembled contains an entry point.

The class of the process descriptor object is *System.Diagnostics.Process*. Associated with the object is an object of *StartInfo* class that specifies the command name, option strings, and window-style markers. The call of the *Start* method on the *Process* object causes a command window to be created and the specified command to be executed. In order to be less annoying to the user, the command window remains in the minimized state throughout. The method waits for the command process to end and retrieves the exit code for any necessary diagnostic messages.

Class Definitions

Class definitions are used to define the various kinds of class types in the *CTS*. The syntax of the definitions is given by —

```
using System;
using System.Diagnostics;
  public class MsilAsm {
    private static Process asm = null;

    public static void Init() {
      if (asm == null) {
        asm = new Process();
        asm.StartInfo.FileName = "ilasm";
        asm.StartInfo.WindowStyle =
                              ProcessWindowStyle.Minimized;
      }
    }

    public static void
              Assemble(string fil, string opt, bool main) {
      int retCode;
      string optNm = opt + " /debug ";
      if (main)
        optNm = optNm + " /exe ";          // create file fil.EXE
      else
        optNm = optNm + " /dll ";          // create file fil.DLL
      asm.StartInfo.Arguments = optNm + fil + ".il";
      asm.Start();                         // fork the process
      asm.WaitForExit();                   // wait for completion
      retCode = asm.ExitCode;              // save the return value
      ...                                  // test the return value
    }
```

Figure 7.7: Chaining to the ilasm assembler

ClassDecl   →   .class ClassHeader "{" { MemberDecl } "}" .
ClassHeader →   { ClassAttr } *ident* [**extends** TypeRef]
                      [**implements** TypeRef { ',' TypeRef }] .
MemberDecl   →   *<Member Declaration>* .

A class definition consists of a class header declaration and a number of member declarations enclosed in braces. We shall expand on the member declarations in the next section.

The class header has a sequence of class attributes, an identifier that names the class, and optional type references that declare the relationship of this class to any other classes. The dotted name of the class will be constructed from any enclosing namespace name followed by the simple identifier name in the class header.

Type references are simply dotted names with optional resolution assembly or module scope markers. The type reference following the **extends** keyword declares the supertype of this class. The comma-separated list of type references following the **implements** keyword declares the interface types that this class contracts to implement. If there is no **extends** clause, the class implicitly extends *System.Object*.

The most common class attributes were given in Figure 3.7. From the *Beta-2* release, value classes are signalled by their inheritance from *System.ValueType*.

In *gpcp* the infrastructure for defining classes and methods defines constants corresponding to each attribute. Bitsets of such values are created from the semantic attributes of the *AST* and are passed to the methods that emit the headers. The code of the emission methods iterate over the elements of the bitset, emitting the corresponding keyword for each bit that is "on" in the set.

As noted earlier, classes are emitted by a worklist algorithm. Each descriptor corresponding to a class is passed to a method that emits the syntactic markers as shown in the grammar given above. In the body of the method, code traverses the descriptor structure, calling other methods for the emission of class members, including fields, methods, and constructors.

Class Members

As noted in the virtual object system section (see page 55), class members consist of *fields*, *methods*, *properties*, and *events*. Here is the syntax of the member declarations —

MemberDecl	→	**.field** FieldDecl
	|	**.method** MethodHead "{" { MethodBodyItem } "}"
	|	**.event** EventHead "{" { EventMember } "}"
	|	**.property** PropertyHead "{" { PropertyMember } "}"
	|	**.data** DataDecl | **.pack** *int32* | **.size** *int32* .

There are also certain other declarations within classes that appear at the same syntactic level as members. These are used for declaring static data and properties of the explicit layout.

We need infrastructure to emit the syntactic markers for each of these member kinds. In *gpcp* there are specialized methods for emitting fields, and emitting static and instance methods. These are named *EmitField*, *EmitProc*, and *EmitMethod*. However, there are other runtime structures that need to be emitted, which do not have explicit representation in the *AST* of a *Component Pascal* program. These include the constructors, which we deal with presently, and the elementwise copy method.

Remember that in *Component Pascal* we encapsulate all module-level procedures and data into a synthetic static class that has no instance data. Conversely, record types have instance fields and methods, but no static members. We emit these two different kinds of classes using two different methods. *EmitModBody* emits the class definition for the synthetic static class, while *EmitRecBody* emits the class corresponding to a record type.

The skeleton of *EmitModBody* is shown in Figure 7.8. The code begins by emitting the class header, then the static fields. The static fields are retrieved by iterating over an extensible list attached to the module descriptor in the *AST*.

```
begin (* EmitModBody *)
    <Emit the class header>;
    for index := 0 to locals.tide-1 do (* iterate over var-decl list *)
        iFil.EmitField(locals.a[index], att_static);
    end;
    if <module has entrypoint> then
        <Emit static initializations to ".cctor">;
        <Emit module body as Main method ".CPmain">;
    else
        <Emit static initializations and module body to ".cctor">;
    end; (* if *)
    for index := 0 to procs.tide-1 do (* iterate over proc-decl list *)
        iFil.EmitProc(procs.a[index], att_static);
    end;
    <Emit the class trailer>;
end; (* EmitModBody *)
```

Figure 7.8: Procedure *EmitModBody* to emit synthetic static class

If the module has an entry point, the module body is "*.CPmain*"; otherwise the module body is initialization code that is placed in the class constructor. In either case any initializations of static data structures are placed in the class constructor. This is required for data that is semantically static in the *Component Pascal* program but will be implemented at runtime by a dynamically allocated object.

Finally, after this preamble the static procedures of the module are emitted. Once again, the procedures are retrieved from the *AST* by iterating over an extensible list attached to the module descriptor. A small curiosity is the fact that the list only holds the file-level procedures of the module. Any nested procedures are emitted by a depth-first traversal of the local procedure lists in the procedure descriptors within the code of *EmitProc*.

The skeleton of *EmitRecBody* is shown in Figure 7.9. As in the static case, the code begins by emitting the class header. In this particular case, the class header requires more computation. Record types may be implemented either as value or reference classes, and reference classes may declare that they implement an arbitrary number of interfaces.

Following the header, the instance fields are emitted by iteration over an extensible array in the type descriptor. These are followed by the default constructor and the copy

```
begin (* EmitRecBody *)
    <Emit the class header>;
    for index := 0 to fields.tide-1 do (* iterate over field-decl list *)
        iFil.EmitField(fields.a[index], att_empty);
    end;
    if <class is a reference class> then
        <Emit no-arg constructor ".ctor">;
        <Emit copy method "_copy_">;
    end; (* if *)
    for index := 0 to methods.tide-1 do (* iterate over method-decl list *)
        method := method.a[index];
        if <method is bound to boxed type> then
            <append method to boxed method list>;
        else
            iFil.EmitMethod(method);
        end; (* if *)
    end; (* for *)
    <Emit the class trailer>;
    if <class is a value class> then (* emit the boxed class *)
        <Emit the boxed class header>;
        <Emit no-arg constructor ".ctor">;
        for index := 0 to boxLst.tide-1 do (* iterate over boxed list *)
            iFil.EmitMethod(boxLst.a[index]);
        end; (* for *)
        <Emit the boxed class trailer>;
    end; (* if *)
end; (* EmitRecBody *)
```

Figure 7.9: Procedure *EmitRecBody* to emit record implementation code

method. If the record type is implemented by a value class, then we need neither a constructor nor a copy method. In the value case the "initobj" and "cpobj" instructions provide for initialization and entire assignment respectively.

Methods are emitted by iterating over the *methods* list in the record descriptor. A slight complication is that for value classes we may have instance methods that are bound to the record type and other methods that are bound to pointers to the record type. The first group of methods is emitted directly, while the second group is emitted as methods of the boxed class corresponding to the value class.

In the case of value classes, after emitting the class definition trailer, we emit the definition of the boxed class. The boxed class has a constructor but requires no copy method. We emit the methods that have been queued up during the emission of the corresponding value class.

Constructors

Instance constructors come in two flavors. There are the default, no-arg constructors that the compiler is able to generate without help from the programmer, and the constructors that are explicitly defined in the program source. Constructors cannot be **static** or **virtual**, and must be named ".ctor" and have the **specialname** and **rtsspecialname** attributes. They may not return a value.

In languages such as *C#* the generation of a no-arg constructor is extremely simple. The *IL* of Figure 7.10 could be the code of almost any instance constructor. All of the fields of the new object will be set to their default "zero-like" values, and the only responsibility of the constructor is to call the constructor of the supertype. In this case we have assumed that the supertype is *System.Object*.

```
.method public rtsspecialname specialname instance void .ctor() il managed
{
    .maxstack 1
    ldarg.0                                  // pointer to new object, from CLR
    call instance void object::.ctor()
    // nothing more to do
    ret
}
```

Figure 7.10: Generic no-arg constructor for *C#*

For other languages things may not be quite so simple. For example, in languages that implement value arrays by *CTS* array objects, the initializations that are implicit in the source code will need to be explicit in the *IL*. The same principle applies to every language that has types that have value semantics but are mapped into *CTS* reference types. That is, the principle applies to any language that uses *reference surrogates*. Any such additional initialization will go into the constructor at the postion in Figure 7.10 where the comment proclaims that there is nothing more to do.

An example might make this clear. Assume that we have a *Component Pascal* record type that embeds two fields of different record types. We shall further assume that one of the nested records will meet the criteria for implementation as a value type, while the other must be implemented as a reference type. The type might be —

```
type Rec =    record
                  fld1 : ValT; (* ValT is implemented as a value class *)
                  fld2 : RefT; (* RefT is implemented as a reference class *)
              end
```

The point is that at runtime *fld2* will be a reference to a dynamically allocated instance of the *RefT* type. Therefore, whenever we allocate an object of the outer type, we must

allocate and initialize the embedded object. The code of the constructor for the *Rec* type
will be precisely the same as Figure 7.10, with the comment "nothing more to do" replaced
by the code —

```
    . . .
// create and initialize embedded object
    ldarg.0                              // pointer to containing object
    newobj instance void NmSpc.RefT::.ctor()
    stfld class NmSpc.RefT NmSpc.Rec::'fld2'
    . . .
```

Here we have assumed that the types are defined in some namespace *NmSpc*. If the embedded type was an array type, rather than a reference class type, then the code would have
been slightly different. In that case, we would have had a "newarr" instruction, rather
than a "newobj". In the case of an array of arrays, we would have needed to include code
similar to Figure 3.22 to initialize the inner dimensions.

It may also be noted that structures like the last example, which are "flat" in the
source semantics but are implemented by multiple objects at runtime, require special code
for entire assignment. When performing an entire assignment on an object of the *Rec* type,
the value fields may be copied by a "ldobj / stobj" instruction pair. The reference
fields need to be copied by a recursive call to the copy method of the embedded class, or
an inline loop in the case of an embedded array.

Constructors with arguments have the same structure as Figure 7.10, except that the
constructor signature shows the formal parameter types. The code that arises from the
user-defined body of the constructor goes in place of the "nothing more to do" comment
in the figure. The code for the constructor body may be emitted by the same infrastructure
that emits other method bodies. However, special rules apply to the code, since constructors have permission to assign to **initonly** fields of their bound type. In most cases this
difference is one for semantic checking rather than for code emission time.

Finally, we must consider type initializers, otherwise known as *class constructors*.
These initializers are executed when the class in loaded and are responsible for setting any
initial values into the static fields of the class. Type initializers must be **static** and cannot
take any arguments. The skeleton of a typical initializer is shown in Figure 7.11.   In

```
.method static public rtsspecialname specialname void .cctor() il managed
{
    // do any initialization work here
    ret
}
```

Figure 7.11: Skeleton of generic class constructor

languages such as *C#* there is no method in the source code that corresponds to the type initializer. Instead, the compiler collects together all of the initialization code for all of the static features of a class and emits these as the class constructor. As noted earlier, in *Component Pascal* the class constructor initializes static value structures and also contains the body of a module if the module does not have an entry point.

Method Definitions

Methods contain the instructions that define the behavior of classes. In textual *IL* the format of method definitions is as follows —

> MethodDecl   →   **.method** MethodHead "{" { MethodBodyItem } "}"
> MethodHead   →   { MethodAttr } [CallConv] TypeRef *DottedName*
>   '('[Parameter { ',' Parameter }] ')' { ImplAttr } .

The method heading consists of, in order, method attributes, an optional call convention marker, the return type reference, the name of the method, the parameter list, and finally the implementation attributes. The various values that the attributes may take were described in "Defining Methods" (see page 88).

The body of the method is a sequence of method body items. As well as the instructions and labels that we shall study in the next two chapters, the following kinds of items may appear —

> MethodBodyItem   →   **.locals** '(' [VarList] ')'
> | **.entrypoint** | **.zeroinit**
> | **.maxstack** *int32* | **.line** *int32*

Method Emission Infrastructure

In order to emit method definitions to the file, we need to be able to transform the attributes of the *AST* into the syntax given above. In *gpcp* this is done by means of two procedures, *EmitMeth* and *EmitProc*, for instance and static methods respectively. The code that traverses the *AST* to emit instructions can be shared between the two cases. This is done by making *EmitMeth* chain to *EmitProc* after it has computed the method attributes from the method descriptor.

The skeleton of *EmitProc* is given in Figure 7.12. It takes a procedure descriptor as the formal parameter *proc*. The real code in module *MsilMaker* is slightly more complex than this, since it has to deal with the possibility of exception handling. The procedure begins by recursively emitting any nested procedures that are declared within this procedure. It then emits the method header and the opening curly bracket. The closing curly bracket is emitted after all of the instructions and directives have been emitted.

```
        var index :   INTEGER; live :   BOOLEAN;
begin (* EmitProc *)
    for index := 0 to nestPs.tide-1 do (* iterate over nested-proclist *)
        iFil.EmitProc(nestPs.a[index], att_static);
    end;
    <Compute the method attribute set>;
    iFil.MethodDecl(attrSet, thisProc); (* emit header *)
    iFil.LeftBrace(); (* emit '{' *)
    if <mth is not abstract> then
        <Emit initialization of locals, if needed>;
        this.EmitStat(proc.body, live; (* Finally, the code! *)
        if live & <void method> then iFil.DoReturn() end;
        iFil.MethodTail(proc); (* emit .locals, etc. *)
    end; (* if not abstract *)
    iFil.RightBrace(); (* emit '}' *)
end; (* EmitProc *)
```

Figure 7.12: Procedure *EmitProc* to emit method body

If the method is abstract, there is nothing between the opening and closing braces. Otherwise, the statement descriptor *proc.body* is passed to the method *EmitStat*.

The method that emits statements, *EmitStat*, returns an out parameter of Boolean type. The return value is **true** if it is possible that control flow might return after execution of the statement in the call. For example, the emission of a **return** or **throw** statement will return **false** as the Boolean parameter. The purpose of this flag is to avoid the emission of dead code. We shall see many examples of the use of this flag in Chapter 9. At the level of *EmitProc* we use the flag to suppress the emission of a redundant return instruction at the end of a proper procedure, if control flow cannot reach the end.

The ProcInfo type.   During the emission of *IL* for a method, there is a certain amount of state data that needs to be computed and updated. As we shall see in the next few sections, it is necessary to keep track of the current evaluation stack depth, as well as the maximum stack depth, the "high tide mark." We also need to keep track of any temporary local variables that have been allocated, together with their types and allocation status.

It would be possible, but unattractive, to keep this information as local variables of the emission procedure, because these variables would be passed to almost all of the methods that are called. Instead, as a design pattern we advocate the definition of a procedure information descriptor, *ProcInfo*. A reference to this object is a field of the emitter object, which is the **this** of the emission methods. In this way, all methods that need access to the state are able to get it through their receiver reference.

In *gpcp* the *ProcInfo* type has fields that hold the procedure descriptor of the current method, some data associated with the current exception handling context, the stack depth information, and the temporary local variable handler data structures.

Numbering the Locals

In general, local variables are referred to by ordinal numbers, as are formal parameters. The formal parameters have their numbers determined by their positions in the signature, numbering either from zero or from one. For instance methods, whether virtual or not, the receiver is always argument zero, and the other parameters count from one. For static methods the parameters count from zero.

Local variables have space allocated to them on entry to a method, and the space is reclaimed automatically when the activation record is released at method return. This allocation is generally faster than is object creation.

Locals are declared explicitly in textual *IL* and are numbered sequentially by default. A method may contain several local variable declaration sections. The syntax is —

LocalDecl	$\rightarrow$	**.locals** [**init**] '(' [VarList] ')' .
VarList	$\rightarrow$	VarDecl { ',' VarDecl } .
VarDecl	$\rightarrow$	['[' number ']'] TypeSignature [VarName] .

The optional marker **init** determines that all locals in this method will be given the default initialization.

Each local variable declaration has an optional ordinal number, enclosed in square brackets. If this is absent, then the variable being declared will take the next available unused ordinal number. The type signature of the variable declaration must be a sufficiently qualified name, together with markers such as **class** or **method**, as required. No other attributes are allowed. The use of explicit names for the variables is optional but is helpful to the debugger. This information is persisted into the debug metainformation file. It is legal to use variable names rather than ordinals for used occurrences of local variables in textual *IL*. In this case ilasm will map the names to the ordinal positions that appear in the *PEM*.

Using the option to explicitly assign ordinal numbers to declared variables, it is possible to force variables to share the same location in the activation record. However, it is only possible to do such overlapping of variables if all variables sharing the same ordinal have precisely the same type. Unless the default numbering of local variables is overidden, every local has a unique ordinal within that method. It is helpful to remember that local variables in *CIL* are an abstraction. The *JIT* will certainly try to map local variables to machine registers on the underlying hardware platform. In doing so, it will reuse registers for live ranges of local variables without regard to type. The reservation of particular local variable ordinal values for one particular type does not have any influence on the register pressure on the final hardware.

In *gpcp* the formal parameters and local variables are given interim numbers from a single sequence during dataflow analysis. The two sets of variables must be renumbered in separate sequences prior to code generation. This is done at the same time that the procedure name string is generated. Since there are no variables declared in nested blocks in *Component Pascal*, it is possible to list all local variables in a single declarative block at the end of the code of the method.

Locals on demand.   During code generation it is often necessary to define temporary local variables. This need usually arises because values on the stack are in the wrong order, or a value needs to be saved and reused later.

In any case, it is necessary to be able to create new local variables as the need arises. It is probably also wise to try to limit the total number of temporaries in any method, by recycling temporaries once they are no longer required. A typical mechanism is used in *gpcp*. The temporary local variable handler has procedures for allocating and freeing locals. These are called *newLocal* and *ReleaseLocal*. The functionality is implemented by an array of local variable type descriptors, together with an indication of whether the variable at that index is currently free or allocated. In order to allow for demand allocation during code emission, the array is extensible.

If a request is made for a temporary local variable of a particular type, the allocator scans the type array, looking for a free variable of the matching type. The algorithm looks for a match on exact type, rather than seeking assignment compatible types. If no suitable free variable is found, a new variable is appended to the type list.

The list of local variables may therefore grow during code emission. Fortunately, ilasm is happy to accept the local variable declarations at the end of the method. We therefore emit the list after all code has been emitted, and the extent of temporary variable creation is known.

Block locals.   For languages that allow local variables to be defined inside scope blocks within procedures, we may use multiple local declarations. At the point of entry to each block we simply emit another group of local declarations.

It is most simple to use the default allocation scheme, which will lead to no overlapping of values in the activation record of the *abstract* machine. As pointed out above, this does not prevent the *JIT* from overlapping the values in real storage, although it may make it more difficult to do so.

As an alternative strategy, it is possible to explicitly overlap the variables for nonoverlapping scope blocks using the same mechanism as described for demand local variables. At the entry to each block, calls to *newLocal* will return either a new local slot or a recycled location from a previous block. At the end of each block, the locals of that block must be marked as free in the local allocator data structure. In this case explicit numbering of local variables must be used. Figure 7.13 shows the skeleton of a typical case, in *C* and in *IL*.

```
//    void Foo() {
//        int i,j;
//        ...
//        { double x; ... }
//        { double y; ... }
//    }

.method public static void Foo() {
{ .locals([0] int32 'i', [1] int32 'j')
        ...
   { .locals([2] float64 'x')            // nested variable in slot 2
        ...
   }
   { .locals([2] float64 'y')            // nested variable in same slot
        ...
   }
}
```

Figure 7.13: Translation of local scope blocks

Computing Stack Height

Each method definition in *IL* has an optional declaration of stack height. This directive has the format —

$$\text{StackHeight} \quad \rightarrow \quad \textbf{.maxstack } \textit{int32} \text{ .}$$

If this declaration is missing, then `ilasm` allocates a default stack size of eight. One of the checks that the verifier performs is that the evaluation stack does not exceed the maximum stack height declared by the program. This means that compilers that produce verifiable code must compute the maximum stack height for each method.

At the most simple-minded level, the computation of stack height is not difficult. Essentially, we need machinery that computes the stack height after the execution of each instruction. As part of the *ProcInfo* structure, we need just two integer data. One is the current stack height, and the other is the maximum stack height for the method. After each instruction we apply the known *stack-*Δ to the current stack height to compute the new height. If the new value is greater than the current maximum, we must update the maximum. For all but a few instructions the *stack-*Δ is a known constant that may be stored in an array indexed on instruction opcode. The exceptions are the call instructions "call", "callvirt", "calli" and the constructor call instruction "newobj". For all of these we must compute the *stack-*Δ from the signature, taking into account the number of arguments, the absence or presence of a return value, and a receiver object reference. The "ret" instruction is the other exception, since this instruction has a *stack-*Δ of either zero or one, depending on whether the return is from a method returning **void** or not. As it turns out, ilasm is happy to accept the stack height directive at the end of the method. Thus we may compute the height as we emit the code to the *IL* file and emit the directive when we get to the end.

If all of our methods consisted of straight-line code, that would be all that there was to the computation. We could simply set both the current height and the maximum height to zero at the entry point of the method and perform our stereotyped adjustment after emitting each instruction.

Unfortunately it is not always so simple. The problem arises if the evaluation stack is not always empty at branches and labels. If we could design our code generator so that it *did* guarantee that the stack was always empty at labels, then once again we might adopt the simple approach. It is not possible to do so, however. Consider the following design issue. We want to implement the *Component Pascal* function that computes the maximum of two arguments. We want to produce code that leaves one or the other of the two arguments on the stack, where we can assign the value or do whatever is required with it. As discussed on page 179, the function "call" will have been transformed into a binary expression in the *AST* with a *maxOf* operator. One strategy for evaluation is to compute each of the operands onto the evaluation stack, saving a copy of each in suitable local variables, such as "tmp1" and "tmp2". We then compare the two values on the stack and push one or other of the two temporaries, as appropriate. Figure 7.14 has the code for this case. In the figure, the stack height *after* each instruction is shown at the start of the comment.

```
        <push e1>         // height =1
        dup               // height =2
        stloc 'tmp1'      // height =1, save the left operand
        <push e2>         // height =2
        dup               // height =3
        stloc 'tmp2'      // height =2, save the right operand
        bgt    lb1        // height =0, compare the two values
        ldloc 'tmp2'      // height =1, push the saved rhs value
        br     lb2        // height =1
lb1:                      // height =0
        ldloc 'tmp1'      // height =1, push the saved lhs value
lb2:                      // height =1, result is on the stack
```

Figure 7.14: Inline code for the function $MAX(e_1, e_2)$ with stack anomaly

Notice the anomaly at the first label, "lb1". The height coming into the label is not the height from the previous instruction, but rather the height at the jumping off point from which the label is reached, zero in this case.

We have essentially two possible approaches to deal with this problem. Firstly, we may perform a special correction for all of the code generating constructs that cause this effect.[2] In the case of *Component Pascal* there are only two cases. These are the *MAX* and *MIN* functions, as seen in the example, and the computation of Boolean values by means of "jumping code." In each case the jumps are forward, so that we may reset the height to its jumping off value when the branch target label is encountered.

The other possibility is to recognize that it is always possible to emit code that does not produce this anomaly. It is not possible to ensure that the stack is always *empty* at branches, since, for example, we may be in the middle of pushing a list of method arguments when we have to emit branching code. What we may guarantee is that the stack height never changes at a label. This may require a little cleverness in cases where values need to be merged along several paths. Figure 7.15 shows one way to do this for the same maximum function. In this case, instead of pushing the result onto the stack along the two control flow paths, we write the values to a shared local variable. After the label at which the control flows merge, we simply push the value in the local variable.

```
        <push e1>           // height =1
        dup                 // height =2
        stloc 'tmp1'        // height =1, save the left operand
        <push e2>           // height =2
        dup                 // height =3
        stloc 'tmp2'        // height =2, save the right operand
        bgt    lb2          // height =0, compare the two values
        ldloc 'tmp2'        // height =1, push the saved rhs value
        stloc 'tmp1'        // height =0, overwrite the lhs value
lb2:                        // height =0, result is in local tmp1
        ldloc 'tmp1'        // height =1, result is on the stack
```

Figure 7.15: Inline code for the function $MAX(e_1, e_2)$ without stack anomaly

The design principle is very simple. We must *never* try to merge values along converging control flow paths. Instead, we move any such values into local variables and push the value on the stack downstream of the merge-point label.

A more general context in which this problem arises is the conditional expressions of *C*-family languages. According to our design principle, we should implement such expressions by allocating a temporary local variable of an appropriate type. We then compute the Boolean value and conditionally branch on it. Along each branch we compute the expression into the temporary variable, and below the merge-point label we push the temporary onto the stack.

---

[2]This is the method that *gpcp* uses. I actually now have a preference for the other method.

Finally, it is important to note that for languages that allow arbitrary control flow, stronger measures are required. In the most general case, it may be necessary to perform computations on an explicit control flow graph. Essentially, we must compute the *stack-Δ* for each basic block in the *CFG*, rather than for each instruction. We must then solve for stack height by propagating stack height values along the forward edges of the graph. Of course, it is an error if the stack height is not the same along all edges incident to a particular label. The verifier has to do a very similar computation on each method without the benefit of an *AST* to guide it. In that case, it is not just the stack *height* that must be consistent along merging edges, but also the types of all corresponding elements of the stack.

Emitting Short Branches

As will be recalled from Chapter 2, branching instructions have both a short and a long form. The short branches use a single offset byte in the binary format and may jump only about 127 bytes. The long branches take up four bytes for the offset but may jump any distance. Clearly it would be advantageous to use the short form whenever possible. As it turns out, it is difficult to do this in the case of textual *IL*.

The difficulty is that the textual form of *IL* deals with code locations in terms of *labels* rather than byte offsets in the binary file. It is relatively simple to compute the offset of each instruction as it is emitted, by carefully computing the length of any argument values that follow each instruction. Most instructions take up only one byte, with a small number using two bytes. The problem is that knowing the byte offsets of every instruction once it has been emitted does not completely solve the problem. Certainly, for *backward* branches we might look up the mapping of labels to offsets and emit short branches whenever possible. A substantial majority of branches are forward, however, and it is not possible to work out if they are short or long until the offset of the label has been computed. We have two choices. We may emit instructions to a buffer rather than directly to the *IL* file. In this case it is simple to modify the branch instructions in the buffer and then dump the buffer to the file when the code for the method is complete. Alternatively, we may emit the *IL* into a random access text file, and *backpatch* the instruction in the file when forward branches are found to be short after all.

This is actually a classic problem of assembler design. We need to compute the offsets so as to know whether to emit long or short literals to the code stream. Unfortunately changing the literal width changes the very offsets that we are trying to compute. A sensible compromise is to compute interim offsets on the basis of the long literal form. In this case the branch offsets can only get shorter, and a single iteration gets near optimal results.

Notes on Chapter 7

The design of the infrastructure for code emission is almost certain to require several iterations. The code can become rather verbose, but it is hard to judge the possibilities for factoring until a prototype has been constructed. Another consideration is the possibility of sharing code between the infrastructure that emits textual *IL* and the infrastructure that uses *Reflection.Emit*, if both are to be supported. If both code generation methods *are* supported, the design of suitable abstractions should allow the tree-walking code to be shared, along with much of the instruction selection code.

There is at least one alternative to Figure 7.7 for invoking `ilasm` from within a compiler, based on invoking the *ANSI C* functions *fork* and *exec*. Provided it can be guaranteed that these libraries will be present at compiler runtime, this is a good solution. The details may be discovered by disassembly of a short test program compiled by the managed *C* compiler.

Emitting Code for Expression Evaluation

In this chapter we look at the evaluation of expressions in *CIL*. In the next we shall consider flow of control and the emission of *IL* for structured statements. Expression evaluation is the basic building block of all that follows.

We shall also consider the emission of *IL* for assignment statements and procedure calls. Neither of these involve flow on control, and both give a natural setting for the consideration of expression evaluation.

In all of the concrete examples, for the sake of uniformity, the program fragments assume the following code structure. Methods that deal with expressions and statements are dispatched on an object of *MsilEmitter* type, usually called "emtr". This object holds state information of the module emission, and also has a field "outF" that is a reference to the *IlasmFile* object. In the examples, the local variable holding the *IlasmFile* reference is named "iFil".

The utility methods that were discussed in the previous chapter are dispatched on the *IlasmFile* object. This object holds state information for the output file and for label allocation, and holds the current *ProcInfo* state. As discussed in the last chapter, the *ProcInfo* object holds state for local variable management, stack depth, and so on.

For the most part we shall consider the evaluation of expressions using verifiable code. In some cases we shall consider the unverifiable alternative also.

Pushing Primitive Values

The most basic operation of expression evaluation is the pushing of values onto the evaluation stack. All manipulation of values in .*NET* takes place on the stack, so loading values is a first step of every evaluation. Our first task therefore is to determine how to push arbitrary data values.

The key procedure of expression evaluation is *PushValue*. This is the main recursive procedure that performs the post-order traversal of expression trees. It takes a single argument of *Expr* type. The main features of the code follow from the structure of the expression nodes in the abstract syntax. The pushing of values is therefore specialized according the various expression descriptor node types. For the sake of concreteness, we shall assume the *AST* structure described in Chapter 5.

In this first outline of a design we consider the most common cases. The details of the exceptional cases will be described in a later section. For binary tree nodes, the pushing of expression values is completely straightforward. The emission procedure recursively pushes the values of the two subtrees, and then emits whatever code is necessary to operate on the two top-of-stack values. Similarly, the pushing of values defined by unary nodes involves pushing the value corresponding to a child subtree followed by emission of *IL* to operate and transform the top-of-stack value. The outline of these two cases is shown in Figure 8.1. The figure also shows how simple *IdLeaf* variable designators utilize the

```
procedure (emtr  :   MsilEmitter)PushBinary(exp  :   BinaryX);
begin
  emtr.PushValue(exp.lKid);              (* push the left expression *)
  emtr.PushValue(exp.rKid);              (* push the right expression *)
  <operate on two TOS values>;
end PushBinary;


procedure (emtr  :   MsilEmitter)PushUnary(exp  :   UnaryX);
begin
  emtr.PushValue(exp.child);             (* push the child expression *)
  <operate on TOS value>;
end PushUnary;


procedure (emtr  :   MsilEmitter)PushIdLeaf(exp  :   IdLeaf);
begin
  emtr.outF.GetVar(exp.ident);           (* recall Figure 7.6 *)
end PushIdLeaf;
```

Figure 8.1: Pushing binary, unary, and simple identifier expressions

infrastructure described in the previous chapter. In the third of the procedure skeletons shown in the figure, the code takes the identifier attribute of the *IdLeaf* and passes that on to the *GetVar* method of the *IlasmFile* object.

The figure does not show the ordinary leaf node case that corresponds to constant values in the *AST*. The pushing of individual *constant* values has already been covered in some detail. The "`ldc.*`" instruction is used for string, integer, and floating point constants. As described in the previous chapter, the emission of constants is conveniently hidden behind a utility that encapsulates the special cases. The pushing of the values of completely general variable designators is much more challenging.

Pushing Variable Values

We start with an expression tree that denotes a *variable designator* in the *AST*. This expression may be a single leaf node, or more complicated if it denotes a selected component of some aggregate data structure. In order to motivate the discussion, we shall consider the emission of *IL* for an assignment statement. We consider the unverified case first, since this follows a code emission pattern that is conventional for an abstract stack machine.

Assignments in unverified code.   We suppose that the assignment statement descriptor has the abstract syntax shown on page 158. The descriptor has two structural attributes, both of expression type. *lhsX* is the designator of the destination location, while *rhsX* is the value to be assigned.

The pattern for emission of *IL* for such a statement is —

```
<push address of designator exp.lhsX>        (* push 'lValue' *)
emtr.PushValue(exp.rhsX);                     (* push 'rValue' *)
emtr.ValueAssign(exp.lhsX);                   (* do assignment *)
```

The code begins by computing the address of the location denoted by the left-hand side expression of the statement descriptor. This is what would be called the *lValue* in language *C*. The value of the right-hand side expression is pushed on the stack, and a value assignment invoked. The *ValueAssign* procedure is passed the left-hand side expression so that the datatype of the destination location is known. The procedure will emit a suitable store indirect instruction, "`stind.*`", for scalar values, or a "`stobj`" instruction with a suitable *typeRef* as operation argument for value classes. In an unverified context object locations that are assigned using a "`stobj`" instruction are likely to be memory blobs with explicit layout.

Clearly, the computation of the address of a location denoted by a designator expression is a key operation of our code generation infrastructure, at least in the unverified case. We note that such a primitive also provides a general solution to the problem of loading the contents of a location specified by an arbitrary designator. We simply push the location address—that is, the designator *lValue*—and then perform an address "dereference."

The dereference operation is performed by an appropriately typed "ldind.*" load-indirect instruction or by a "ldobj" instruction, whichever is appropriate for the location datatype.

The details of the *IL* that pushes the address of a designator may be understood by exhaustive case analysis of the node types that occur in unverified designator expressions. The four cases are *field selection, array indexing, pointer dereference*, and primitive *leaf variable* nodes. Field selection is denoted by an *IdentX* node. The *IL* to push the address of a selected field is emitted by the code —

```
<push address of designator "node.child">;
emtr.PushLit (<offset of field "node.ident">);
emtr.outF.Code(opc_add);              (* add field offset *)
```

For the case of array indexing, the node is a *BinaryX* descriptor. The emitted *IL* must push the left-hand side designator, and then add the element offset in order to compute the address of the array element —

```
<push address of designator "node.lKid">;
emtr.PushValue(node.rKid);            (* push index value *)
<scale index by element-size, then add>;
```

The case of pointer dereference is similarly straighforward. The node-type will be a *UnaryX* descriptor of some pointer datatype. We wish to form the address of the datum that the pointer dereference denotes. In this case the *value* of the pointer expression *is* the address that we wish to load —

```
emtr.PushValue(node.child);           (* push pointer value *)
```

So far we have been traversing the tree by recursively calling *PushAddress* on the child subtrees. Here we switch by calling *PushValue* instead, since it is the pointer value that we want rather than the address of the pointer. The child subexpression here is not even guaranteed to be a designator expression, at least for languages that permit explicit address arithmetic.

Finally, we must consider the basis case from which our recursions construct other addresses. If the node is a descriptor of *IdLeaf* type, then the node denotes some named location. In order to push the address of that location we must use one of the following instructions: "ldsflda" to load a static field address; "ldloca" to load the address of a local variable; "ldarga" to load the address of a value parameter; or finally "ldarg" to load the address contained in a reference parameter.

As an example of assignment in an unverified context, we shall consider the *ANSI C* assignment —

```
a[3]->y  =  null;                     /* assign null to struct field */
```

where *a* is an array of six elements. Each element of the array is a pointer to a **struct**, where the structure has three fields, *x*, *y*, and *z*, each of the same pointer type. Implementing the value array as a memory blob of 24 bytes, and the **struct** as a value class with explicit layout, gives us the *IL* declarations in Figure 8.2. The *AST* fragment of the designator ex-

```
.class public value explicit sealed Blob24        // value array memory blob
        extends [mscorlib]System.ValueType {
    .pack 4
    .size 24
}
.class public value explicit sealed StructX       // explicit layout struct
        extends [mscorlib]System.ValueType {
    .field [0] public StructX* 'x'
    .field [4] public StructX* 'y'
    .field [8] public StructX* 'z'
}

    . . .
    .field public static Blob24 'a'                // the value array 'a'
    . . .
```

Figure 8.2: *IL* declarations for *ANSI C* assignment

pression on the left-hand side of the example assignment statement is shown in Figure 8.3, on the left of the diagram. The figure also shows the layout of the structures in memory, on the right.

One possible encoding of the assignment statement in *IL* is shown in Figure 8.4. The emission of *IL* for the assignment statement begins by pushing the address of the destination designator. The code will recurse down to the leftmost leaf of the *AST* and call *GetVarAdr* to push the address of the array memory blob. In this example the object is a static instance of a value class, so we emit the "load static field address" instruction. As the recursion unwinds from the tree leaf, the offset of the selected array element is added. (The multiplication of the constant three by the element size four has been folded, of course.) The dereference node is implemented by a load-indirect instruction. In this case it is the "ldind.ref" variant, since it is a pointer value that is being loaded. The final step in evaluation of the *lValue* is encoding the field-selection by adding the field offset to the address on the top of the stack. Since we have explicit object layout, we know that the offset of the '*y*' field is four.

The assignment statement is completed by pushing the value on the right-hand side, **null** in this example, and an indirect store to the selected location. Since this is assignment of a pointer value, the "stind.ref" instruction is used.

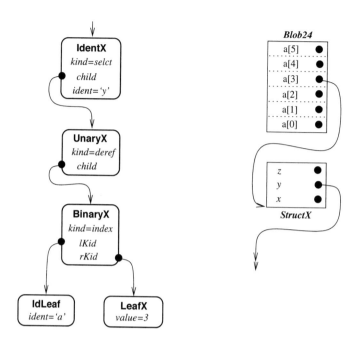

Figure 8.3: Designator *AST* for (a[3]->y), and layout in memory

```
// begin push of designator address
ldsflda Blob24 ThisMod::'a'      // TOS is now address of 'a'
ldc.i4 12                        // offset of index=3 element
add                              // TOS is now address of a[3]
ldind.ref                        // get element pointer value
ldc.i4.4                         // offset of field 'y'
add                              // TOS is now address of field 'y'
// end push of designator address
ldnull                           // push null value on stack
stind.ref                        // store null to field 'y'
```

Figure 8.4: Encoding of *ANSI C* assignment — "a[3]->y = **null**"

Verified assignment code. When producing verified code for .*NET*, we cannot perform arbitrary address computations of the kind just discussed. Apart from the fact that this would be unverifiable, there is also the small matter that the offsets of fields within an object are abstracted away. We do not know the offsets of particular fields of classes at compile time, since for automatic layout of classes, the runtime decides the offsets for itself when the class is loaded on any particular machine.

What we would like to achieve is an abstraction similar to the *PushAddress* abstraction that we use for unverified code. The task is complicated by the fact that there are about 14 different cases to consider. Figure 8.5 shows all of them. The figure shows the code outline for assignment to seven different kinds of location. For each of these seven location kinds, the figure shows the code for assignment of a value of some *scalar* type, and also for assignment of a value of some *value class* type. The scalar types include object references, as well as the usual numerical, character, and Boolean kinds.

	Assign scalar value	Assign value object
Local variable	`<push rValue>` `stloc` *N*	`ldloca` *N* `<push rValue>` `stobj` *TRef*
Value parameter	`<push rValue>` `starg` *N*	`ldarga` *N* `<push rValue>` `stobj` *TRef*
Static field	`<push rValue>` `stsfld` *TRef CRef::fNam*	`ldsflda` *TRef CRef::fNam* `<push rValue>` `stobj` *TRef*
Ref. parameter	`ldarg` *N* `<push rValue>` `stind.`*TT*	`ldarg` *N* `<push rValue>` `stobj` *TRef*

Field of ref. class	`<push object ref>`
	 `<push rValue>`
	 `stfld` *TRef CRef::fNam*
		`<push object ref>`
		 `ldflda` *TRef CRef::fNam*
		 `<push rValue>`
		 `stobj` *TRef*

Field of val. class	`<push object address>`
	 `<push rValue>`
	 `stfld` *TRef CRef::fNam*
		`<push object address>`
		 `ldflda` *TRef CRef::fNam*
		 `<push rValue>`
		 `stobj` *TRef*

Element of array	`<push array ref>`
	 `<push array index>`
	 `<push rValue>`
	 `stelem.`*TT*
		`<push array ref>`
		 `<push array index>`
		 `ldelema` *TRef*
		 `<push rValue>`
		 `stobj` *TRef*

Figure 8.5: All possible assignments in *.NET*

In Figure 8.5 *TRef* denotes a type reference, *CRef* denotes a class reference, *fNam* denotes a field name, and *N* is the ordinal number of a local variable or parameter. In the instructions of the form "∗.*TT*", the notation *TT* denotes the two- or three-character type suffix. We have abstracted away all details of the construction of the value that is to be assigned, using the notation "`<push rValue>`".

In at least one of these cases there is an alternative code sequence that achieves the same result[1] and is still verifiable. For the assignment of a scalar value to an array element (the bottom left entry in Figure 8.5), we may choose either of the code sequences in Figure 8.6. The left-hand variant is the precisely the *IL* sequence used in the final entry in Figure 8.5.

//**Assign element #1**	//**Assign element #2**
<push array ref>	*<push array ref>*
<push array index>	*<push array index>*
<push rValue>	`ldelema` *TRef*
`stelem.`*TT*	*<push rValue>*
	`stind.`*TT*

Figure 8.6: Alternative *IL* for array element assignment

In the left-hand variant, the array element is accessed using two data on the stack. The first is the array reference, the second is the array index. The value may then be accessed by a "`ldelem.*`" or a "`stelem.*`" instruction. In the second, right-hand variant in Figure 8.6, the two data are reduced to a single transient pointer on the stack using a "`ldelema`" instruction. The array element may then be accessed using the "`stind.*`" and the "`ldind.*`" instructions. It is difficult to see an advantage for the second form, except in some rather special circumstances that are discussed later.

The abstraction that is suggested here for loading and storing is called the "*data handle*". For an assignment the handle is the contents of the stack just prior to the "*<push rValue>*" in Figure 8.5. From that figure, it may be seen that the handle consists of zero, one, or two data on the stack for various different cases.

The same handle abstraction may be used for both loading and storing values. Thus, the abstraction may be used for both purposes in much the same way as pushing the location address is used both for loading and storing data in the unverified case.

In the verifiable case the overall structure of the code that emits assignment statements has the form —

```
emtr.PushHandle(exp.lhsX);        (* push 'lValue' *)
emtr.PushValue(exp.rhsX);         (* push 'rValue' *)
emtr.ValueAssign(exp.lhsX);       (* do assignment *)
```

The code begins by pushing the handle. As noted, this may be zero, one, or two stack elements. The value of the right-hand side expression is pushed on the stack and a value assignment invoked.

---

[1] Well, if you want to be picky, *almost* the same result. If the array index is out of bounds, for one code style the error is notified before the evaluation of the *rValue*, while in the other style the error would be notified after the evaluation.

Pushing the handle. The handle of a designator expression may be thought of as the preliminary information about the expression that is loaded onto the stack, so as to make the final loading or storing of the value a single simple load or store instruction. In order to see how to generate code to push the handle value, we need to make some sense of the set of cases in Figure 8.5. As a first observation, we may notice that for all the value class cases, the handle consists of a transient pointer to the value object. In all the scalar cases the handle is loaded by executing all of the instructions to push the *value* of the designator expression *up to but not including the final selection instruction.*

If we peel off all of the value object cases with a test on the datatype at the root of the designator expression, then we may deal with the two columns of Figure 8.5 separately. All of the value object cases may be dealt with using another abstraction, *PushRef*, that pushes a transient pointer to the value object instance. As we shall see, such an abstraction is required anyway, in more general form, for passing transient pointers as actual parameters to reference-mode formals. The details of that more general case will be discussed later.

Turning now to the scalar case, we compare what is needed for *PushHandle* to the skeleton code of the various *PushValue* actions shown in Figure 8.1 at the start of this chapter. The *PushValue* procedures traverse the tree recursively calling *PushValue*, to emit postfix stack code. For *PushHandle* we want to emit precisely the same code that *Push-Value* would have, except for the emission of the final instruction. The trick is to traverse the tree recursively calling *PushValue*, but treating the root node differently. Figure 8.7 has the outline.

As noted for the unverified case, there are only four different node-types that perform selection in designator expression trees. These are *field selection*, *array indexing*, *pointer dereference*, and primitive *leaf variable* nodes. Each of these appears as a different type in our model abstract syntax, so we may guide the control flow using a **typecase** choice structure. The code for the binary node case is typical. We push the reference to the array object by calling *PushValue* on the left child, then push the index expression by calling *PushValue* on the right child. Then, just when we were about to emit the "ldelem.*" instruction, we stop short.

It is assumed in Figure 8.7 that used occurrences of reference parameter identifiers in the source code have been expanded in the *AST* to directly represent pointer dereferences. In effect, we are assuming that such occurrences, either at tree construction time or during a subsequent tree rewriting stage, are finally denoted by a *UnaryX* node, where *kind = deref*. The child of the dereference node is an *IdLeaf* bound to the reference parameter descriptor.

This design choice is not the one that *gpcp* uses. In *gpcp* the same *AST* has to do for both *.NET* and *JVM*, and the *JVM* version has to implement reference parameters without the benefit of dereference instructions. Therefore, *gpcp* for *.NET* has to recognize the special reference parameter case "on the fly," during code emission.

If used occurrences of reference parameters are not rewritten in the *AST*, then the final branch of the typecase statement of Figure 8.7 has the expanded form shown in Figure 8.8.

```
procedure (emtr :   MsilEmitter) PushHandle (exp :   ExprDesc) ;
begin
  if <exp.type is value class> then
    emtr.PushRef (exp) ;                        (* push address of val. object *)
  elsif <exp.type is ref. surrogate> then
    emtr.PushValue (exp) ;                      (* push reference surrogate *)
  else (* the scalar case *)
    with exp :   BinaryX do                     (* assert: exp is array index *)
        emtr.PushValue (exp.lKid) ;                 (* push the array ref. *)
        emtr.PushValue (exp.rKid) ;                 (* push the array index *)
    | exp :   IdentX do                         (* assert: exp is field select *)
        if <exp.child.type is value class> then
          emtr.PushRef (exp.child) ;            (* push the object address *)
        else
          emtr.PushValue (exp.child) ;            (* push the object ref. *)
        end (* if *)
    | exp :   UnaryX do                         (* assert: exp is ptr dereference *)
        emtr.PushValue (exp.child) ;                (* push the object ref. *)
    | exp :   IdLeaf do (* skip leaf node *)
  (* else this is an error, so trap *)
    end (* with *)
  end (* if *)
end PushHandle;
```

Figure 8.7: Pushing a variable designator handle

```
    . . .
    | exp :   IdLeaf do                         (* check if ref. param *)
        if <exp.ident is a ref. param> then
          emtr.outF.PushArg (exp.ident.varOrd) ;      (* else skip *)
        end (* if *)
  (* else this is an error, so trap *)
    end (* with *)
  end (* if *)
end PushHandle;
```

Figure 8.8: Pushing a *IdLeaf* handle with implicit dereference

If the *IdLeaf* is bound to a reference parameter, we push the argument value. Otherwise we do nothing, as before. The *PushArg* procedure will emit a "ldarg" instruction. In this case the handle consists of just the argument value, as shown in the fourth row of Figure 8.5.

In view of what was said in the previous chapter about distinguishing between source semantics and implementation representation, it is wise to be clear about what the predicates in Figure 8.7 mean. In particular, the test "**if** $<T\ is\ value\ class>$ **then** ..." is a question about the *representation type* and not the source language semantics. For example, suppose that we have two "record" types in our source language, and in the mapping to the *CLR*, one has been mapped to a value class V and the other to a reference class R. Suppose further that both types have an *int32* instance field named 'i'. The assignment of a zero value to that field in one case leads to the following *IL* —

```
ldloc N                          (* push reference class handle *)
ldc.i4.0
stfld int32 MyMod.R::'i'
```

In the case of the type with the value class implementation, the same source statement will lead to the following *IL* —

```
ldloca N                         (* push value class handle *)
ldc.i4.0
stfld int32 MyMod.V::'i'
```

In both cases we have assumed that the object is in local variable N. In the first example the local variable has a *reference* to the object, and in the second example the local variable has the *value*.

Value assignment.   Earlier, we glossed over the details of the *ValueAssign* procedure. Now that we have seen what the various handle structures are, we may use the same selection structure to emit the appropriate value assignment code. Mirroring the structure of Figure 8.7, we have the code of the procedure in Figure 8.9. Once again, we have assumed that dereferences associated with reference-mode formal parameters have been made explicit in the *AST*. The changes to Figure 8.9 corresponding to the implicit dereference case of Figure 8.8 are left as an exercise for the reader.

Pushing references.   In order to pass arguments to formals of reference mode, we must be able to create transient pointers on the evaluation stack. Previously we saw one use for a *PushRef* abstraction, generating the transient pointer that is the handle for an object of some value class. This was the first conditional branch of Figure 8.7. We must be able to generate such transient pointers for arbitrary designator expressions if they occur as actual parameters. We must therefore consider the case of arbitrary designator datatypes.

Figure 8.10 traverses a designator expression, emitting code to load the location address. The code follows the same **typecase** structure as *PushHandle* and *ValueAssign*. The *IdentX* branch of the code is interesting, as it recursively calls *PushHandle* to load a reference to the child object. Mutual recursion between these two procedures can occur in the unusual circumstance of value class objects encapsulating fields of value class type. In such a case a sequence of adjacent "ldflda" instructions will be emitted, equal in length to the nesting depth of the value types.

```
procedure (emtr :   MsilEmitter)ValueAssign(exp :   ExprDesc);
  var iFil :   IlasmFile;
begin
  iFil := emtr.outF;
  if <exp.type is value class> then
    iFil.CodeT(opc_stobj, exp.type);
  elsif <exp.type is ref. surrogate> then
    <emit manual copy code>
  else (* the scalar case *)
    with exp :   BinaryX do                  (* assert: exp is array index *)
        iFil.PutElem(exp.type);                   (* emit "stelem.*" *)
    | exp :   IdentX do                    (* assert: exp is field select *)
        iFil.PutField(exp.ident);                   (* emit "stfld" *)
    | exp :   UnaryX do                (* assert: exp is ptr dereference *)
        iFil.StoreIndirect(exp.type);            (* emit "stind.*" *)
    | exp :   IdLeaf do               (* assert: exp is simple variable *)
        iFil.PutVar(exp.ident);         (* emit some store instruction *)
  (* else this is an error, so trap *)
    end (* with *)
  end (* if *)
end ValueAssign;
```

Figure 8.9: Assigning a value to a pushed handle

```
procedure (emtr :   MsilEmitter)PushRef(exp :   ExprDesc);
  var iFil :   IlasmFile;
begin
  iFil := emtr.outF;
  with exp :   BinaryX do                   (* assert: exp is array index *)
      emtr.PushValue(exp.lKid);                 (* push the array ref. *)
      emtr.PushValue(exp.rKid);                 (* push the array index *)
      iFil.CodeT(opc_ldelema, exp.type);
  | exp :   IdentX do                     (* assert: exp is field select *)
      emtr.PushHandle(exp.child);             (* push the object handle *)
      iFil.GetFieldAdr(exp.ident);               (* emit "ldflda" *)
  | exp :   UnaryX do                  (* assert: exp is ptr dereference *)
      emtr.PushValue(exp.child);               (* push the object ref. *)
  | exp :   IdLeaf do
      iFil.GetVarAdr(exp.ident);            (* push the object address *)
  (* else this is an error, so trap *)
  end (* with *)
end PushRef;
```

Figure 8.10: Pushing a variable designator reference

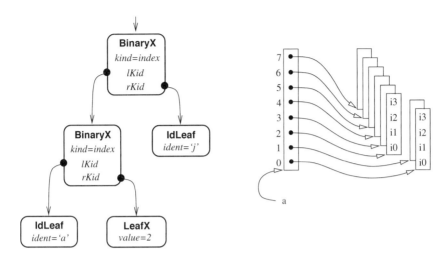

Figure 8.11: Designator *AST* for (a[2][j]), and layout in memory

As an example of a verifiable assignment statement, we consider the emission of *IL* for the *C#* assignment statement —

```
a[2][j] = 0;                          // assign 0 to array of array element
```

In this example we assign a zero value to an element of an array of array of **int**. The data structure is the same as the one that was discussed in connection with Figure 3.6.

The *AST* expression for the designator, and a possible memory layout of the data structure are shown in Figure 8.11. We shall consider the emission of *IL* to implement this assignment statement. In the first instance *PushHandle* is called on the tree root node. This procedure calls *PushValue* on its left child. The binary node version of *PushValue* will recursively call *PushValue* on its two child nodes and then call *GetElem*. The lower *BinaryX* node in the *AST* has the type attribute value int32[], so the *GetElem* will emit the "ldelem.ref" version of the load element instruction.

As the recursion unwinds into the *PushHandle* call, the code to load the second array index is emitted. *PushHandle* then returns, leaving an object handle consisting of two stack elements. At runtime the stack will contain a reference of datatype int32[] and the value of the variable *j*. To complete the encoding of the assignment statement, code to push a zero value is emitted and *ValueAssign* is called. This final call will emit a "stelem.i4" instruction. The complete *IL* code sequence is shown in Figure 8.12.

```
// begin push of designator handle
ldsfld int32[][] ThisMod::'a'      // TOS is now array ref
ldc.i4.2                           // push first array index
ldelem.ref                         // TOS is now a[2]
ldsfld int32 ThisMod::'j'          // push second array index
// end push of designator handle
ldc.i4.0                           // push zero value on stack
stelem.i4                          // store zero to array element
```

Figure 8.12: Encoding of *C#* assignment — a[2][j]=0;

Value assignment with reference surrogates.

In Figure 8.5 we tabulated all possible assignments of scalar and value object types. The procedures to emit code for pushing handles and references take into account the representation type, testing where necessary whether or not a particular type has a value class representation. However, so far we have ignored the possibility that the types that we wish to assign are represented by *reference surrogates*. In this case the source type has value semantics, but the runtime representation is by a reference type.

The first thing that needs to be said is that the *CLR* supports assignment of so-called *entire variables* only for the scalar and value class cases. If we want to assign an entire array, or any other structure that is implemented by a reference surrogate, then we must do it ourselves, manually. It is important to note that these strictures do not apply to unverified contexts. In the unverified case we may declare arbitrary fixed-size memory blob types as explicit value classes, and the "ldobj" and "stobj" instructions will do the rest. Even in the case of memory blobs of dynamic size, we just push the destination and source pointers, then the dynamically determined size, and finally invoke "cpblk".

The issue of value types implemented by reference surrogates is resolved in *gpcp* by using separate mechanisms for value arrays and value records. In the case of source-language record types, the declaration of the reference surrogate class in *IL* defines an instance method that performs a field-by-field copy of the structure. This method is called "__copy__". Since some of the fields of the source record type may themselves be represented by reference surrogates, the code of the copy method may recursively invoke copy methods of embedded members. The declaration of the copy method for a typical surrogate class starts as shown in Figure 8.13. This method begins by recursively calling the copy method of the supertype, if there is one. Note that this makes for an interesting semantic limitation. Types that extend foreign reference types cannot have entire assignments. We cannot recursively call the copy method of the supertype, because the foreign supertype will not have such a method defined. This means that we could copy the fields of the extended part of the type but not the inherited fields.

```
.class public MyClass extends SpClass {
  .method public void __copy__(class MyClass) il managed{
  // call __copy__ on super-type
  ldarg.0                    // push destination reference
  ldarg.1                    // push source reference
  call instance void SpClass::__copy__(class SpClass)
  // now copy fields of this type
  <do field by field copy>
  }
}
```

Figure 8.13: Typical copy method declaration in context

Every language that has value arrays and produces verifiable code must necessarily represent value arrays by reference surrogates. For *Component Pascal*, *gpcp* emits inline code to perform an element-by-element copy of any such arrays. The copy is usually performed by a loop, but the current version unrolls the loop if the number of elements is four or less. Note carefully that the elements of the loop may be of types that are themselves represented by reference surrogates. Thus the copy loop may contain calls to copy methods or, if the arrays are nested, nested loops. In the next chapter we shall look specifically at the efficient encoding of multidimensional array copies.

Figure 8.14 shows the code that is emitted to perform all possible value assignments on types that are represented by reference surrogates. The column on the left of the figure is a repeat of the right-hand column of Figure 8.5. This allows a comparison of the code required for value class objects and reference surrogates.

It should come as no surprise that the code is very similar. In the value class object case we begin by generating a transient pointer to the destination object. We then push the new value and perform a "stobj" instruction. In the reference surrogate case we need to push the destination reference, as before. However, in this case instead of pushing the *rValue*, we must push a reference to the source object. This is simply done by a call of *PushValue*, since the source object is only accessible via a reference anyway. Finally, we complete the assignment by emitting code either to call the copy method or to perform the element-by-element copy.

Operating on the Stack

In this section we consider the emission of *IL* for expression evaluation in a little more detail. The previous section considered the loading and storing of variables but did not consider the operations that we might need to perform on values once they are successfully loaded. Figure 8.1 has given just a hint as to how expressions more general than variable designators might be emitted.

	Assign value object	*Assign ref. surrogate*
Local variable	`ldloca` *N*	`ldloca` *N*
	<push rValue>	*<push ref. to rValue>*
	`stobj` *TRef*	*<manual copy code>*
Value parameter	`ldarga` *N*	`ldarga` *N*
	<push rValue>	*<push ref. to rValue>*
	`stobj` *TRef*	*<manual copy code>*
Static field	`ldsflda` *TRef CRef::fNam*	`ldsflda` *TRef CRef::fNam*
	<push rValue>	*<push ref. to rValue>*
	`stobj` *TRef*	*<manual copy code>*
Ref. parameter	`ldarg` *N*	`ldarg` *N*
	<push rValue>	*<push ref. to rValue>*
	`stobj` *TRef*	*<manual copy code>*
Field of ref. class	*<push object ref>*	*<push object ref>*
	`ldflda` *TRef CRef::fNam*	`ldflda` *TRef CRef::fNam*
	<push rValue>	*<push ref. to rValue>*
	`stobj` *TRef*	*<manual copy code>*
Field of val. class	*<push object address>*	*<push object address>*
	`ldflda` *TRef CRef::fNam*	`ldflda` *TRef CRef::fNam*
	<push rValue>	*<push ref. to rValue>*
	`stobj` *TRef*	*<manual copy code>*
Element of array	*<push array ref>*	*<push array ref>*
	<push array index>	*<push array index>*
	`ldelema` *TRef*	`ldelema` *TRef*
	<push rValue>	*<push ref. to rValue>*
	`stobj` *TRef*	*<manual copy code>*

Figure 8.14: Reference surrogate assignments in *.NET*

The structure of the code emission procedure for pushing values of each expression descriptor node-type will often become a large **case** or **switch** statement. It makes sense to separate out the cases for nodes of different arity, whether or not the implementation uses method dispatch or a typecase structure. We shall look at each of the node-types in turn, for those operations that map directly onto the instruction set of *CIL*. For any given language there are likely to be operations of the source language that are not directly supported by the instruction set, which therefore require some ingenuity to implement. A discussion of some examples is given later, in "Tailoring the Semantics" (see page 256). We shall take the abstract syntax of Chapter 5 as a working basis for the discussion. Most other procedural languages will be very similar.

Binary expression nodes.   Figure 8.1 suggested that the code to emit *IL* for a binary expression node should look like this —

```
procedure (emtr :  MsilEmitter) PushBinary (exp :  BinaryX);
begin
  emtr.PushValue (exp.lKid);              (* push the left expression *)
  emtr.PushValue (exp.rKid);              (* push the right expression *)
  <operate on two TOS values>;
end PushBinary;
```

This is not a bad start. We cover almost all the possible binary node-types with this pattern, with an expansion of the final line into a **case** statement selected on the expression descriptor *kind* tag. The nodes for most of the arithmetic operations, and the bitwise logical operations such as *XOR*, *AND*, and *OR*, require the emission of a single *IL* instruction.

```
procedure (emtr :  MsilEmitter) PushBinary (exp :  BinaryX);
begin
  ...                                      (* operands are pushed *)
  case exp.kind of
  | bitXor : emtr.outF.Code (opc_xor);
  | bitAnd : emtr.outF.Code (opc_and);
  | ...                                    (* other cases *)
```

Some of the arithmetic operations will require special treatment for languages that specify overflow checking. *gpcp* computes a Boolean flag *ovfl* at the top of the *PushBinary* procedure. The flag is true if the expression type is an integer type and the current procedure descriptor has the *ovfChk* attribute. The addition case is typical —

```
case exp.kind of                           (* operands are pushed *)
| ...                                      (* other cases *)
| plus : if ~ovfl then emtr.outF.Code (opc_add);
         else emtr.outF.Code (opc_add_ovf);
         end;
| ...                                      (* other cases *)
```

There are some binary expressions that require more than a single instruction to implement or do not start by pushing the two subexpressions. For example, for array indexing we need an extra instruction if the element type is implemented by a value class —

```
case exp.kind of                           (* operands are pushed *)
| ...                                      (* other cases *)
| index : if isValCls (exp.type) then
            emtr.outF.CodeT (opc_ldelema,  exp.type);
          end;
          emtr.outF.GetElem (exp.type)
| ...                                      (* other cases *)
```

Of course, if the subexpression values were not already pushed, we could have achieved the same stack state by simply calling *PushHandle* and then *GetElem*.

String concatenation is an interesting case in *Component Pascal*, since we can freely mix character arrays and literal strings. In a native code context we would probably represent literal strings by character arrays in some read-only memory area. String concatenation would then always reduce to a call to a runtime support method that took two-character array arguments. In the *CLR* it probably makes sense to use *System.String* for string literals and to emit different calls for the different concatenation cases. In *gpcp* concatenation is implemented by calls to static methods in the runtime system. There are four methods, one for each possible combination of array and literal string operands.

As a final, "normal" example consider the implementation of type tests. In our model abstract syntax, the test "*expression* **is** *typeIdent*" is represented by a binary expression node. The left-hand subexpression is the expression, and the right-hand subexpression is an *IdLeaf* expression node. We must use the "isinst" instruction to test the type, and then check if the top of stack is **null**. The *IL* that we wish to generate is —

```
<push LHS expression>
isinst  typeRef
ldnull                      // compare with null
cgt.un                      // Boolean is on stack
```

Note that the right-hand subexpression does not get pushed, but just contributes the *typeRef* operation argument for the "isinst" instruction.

We defer discussion of the evaluation of Boolean expressions that require *jumping code* until the following chapter.

Unary expression nodes.
The unary expression nodes follow a similar pattern to the binary nodes just considered. In the unary case we have two descriptor subtypes. For function calls we have the *CallX* node-type, and for identifier expressions the *IdentX* node-type. Procedure and function calls are considered in a later section.

The simple cases of unary expressions are shown in Figure 8.15, which includes a number of interesting tricks. Arithmetic negation is a simple, single instruction from the *IL*, and the *capCh* node that arises from the *Component Pascal* built-in *CAP* function is a simple call to the *toUpper* character library function.

The bitwise complement operation is not directly supported by the *CLR*, but can be synthesized by a pair of instruction. We first push the literal value −1, which has a bit-pattern of all bits set. We then execute the "xor" instruction to flip all the bits in the datum.

Similar tricks are used to synthesize Boolean negation and the *ODD* test. For Boolean negation we push a literal value 1 and again execute "xor". Since true and false have representation of 1 and 0 respectively, this *IL* sequence complements the logical value. This is *much* better than the painful idea of "**if** <*TOS is true*> **then** <*push zero*> **else**

```
procedure (emtr :   MsilEmitter)PushUnary(exp :   UnaryX);
  var iFil :   IlasmFile;
begin
  emtr.PushValue(exp.child);           (* push child expression *)
  iFil := emtr.outF;
  case exp.kind of
  | neg     : iFil.Code(opc_neg);      (* arithmetic negation *)
  | capCh   : iFil.StaticCall(toUpper);(* call 'toUpper' *)
  | compl   : iFil.PushLit(-1);        (* bitwise complement *)
              iFil.Code(opc_xor);
  | blNot   : iFil.PushLit(1);         (* Boolean negation *)
              iFil.Code(opc_xor);
  | oddTst  : iFil.PushLit(1);         (* the 'is-odd' predicate *)
              iFil.Code(opc_and);
  | ...                                (* other cases *)
  end;
end PushUnary;
```

Figure 8.15: *PushValue* for the simple unary cases

<*push one*> **end**". The *oddTst* node kind arises from the *Component Pascal* built-in *ODD* predicate. The function returns true if its integer argument is an odd value. We implement this by simply masking off the least significant bit of the top-of-stack datum. If the bit is one, we have our Boolean result for free!

There is one unary node-kind that requires some extra consideration. The absolute value node requires different treatment for the trapping and nontrapping cases. Overflow-checking semantics are probably best obtained by calling the appropriate member of the overloaded *System.Math::Abs* method collection. We would like to avoid the overhead of the function call in the nontrapping case, but we do not seem to be able to do any better than a test-and-branch *IL* sequence. The concept is to conditionally negate the top-of-stack value —

```
        dup                  // duplicate TOS value
        <push properly typed zero>
        bge   lb1            // skip if ≥ 0
        neg                  // polymorphic negate
  lb01:                      // absolute value is TOS
```

We must begin by duplicating the value, since the test uses up one copy.

The *IdentX* node-type in our model abstract syntax is used for expressions that have a single child expression but have another attribute that is an identifier descriptor. We have already discussed the use of this node for field-selection in designator expressions. In that case the identifier descriptor is a *FldId* denoting the selecting field. Inside *PushValue* we will call *PushHandle* on the child expression, and then *GetField* with the identifier descriptor as parameter.

IdentX nodes are also used for type conversions and type assertions. In both of these cases, the *child* field of the node will denote the expression to be converted, and the identifier field will hold a reference to the *TypId* of the destination type. Conversion expressions only occur in *Component Pascal* for built-in types. We may distinguish between narrowing and widening conversions. The narrowing conversions may overflow, while the widening ones cannot. In *gpcp* a utility chooses the instruction to emit on the basis of the incoming and destination types, and the *ovfChk* flag of the current procedure. Different combinations may choose any one of 15 different "conv.*" instructions.

Finally, for type assertions we use the "castclass" instruction. This instruction returns either a top-of-stack reference cast to the nominated type or raises an exception. We first push the child expression of the node. The *TypeRef* corresponding to the type-identifier attribute of the node is used as operation argument for the emission of the "castclass" instruction.

Expression leaf nodes.   In our model abstract syntax, there are two subtypes of the expression leaf type *LeafX*. One is the *SetExp* node, which is used for set constructor expressions and is discussed later. The other subtype is the *IdLeaf* node-type, which is used for leaf nodes that have an identifier attribute. In rough terms the parent *LeafX* type is used for literal constants, and the *IdLeaf* type is used for variables. In *gpcp* any trees that denote static constant values are transformed into *LeafX* nodes during a tree-rewriting step. Figure 8.1 suggested that the specialization of *PushValue* for the *IdLeaf* type should look like this —

```
procedure (emtr :   MsilEmitter)PushIdLeaf(exp :   IdLeaf);
begin
  emtr.outF.GetVar(exp.ident);                (* recall Figure 7.6 *)
end PushIdLeaf;
```

Unlike the binary and unary cases, there is nothing more to add.

For the literal constant nodes denoted by the parent *LeafX* node type, we need to select on constant type and then call a suitable utility. Figure 8.16 shows the code. Note that many cases here end up as calls to the *PushInt* utility procedure that was described in Figure 7.5. The only slightly unusual case is the last one. *Component Pascal* and *Modula-2* do not distinguish lexically between string quotes and character quotes. A character literal is just a string of length one. During semantic analysis the "meaning" of any particular used occurrence is deduced, and an appropriate type assigned to the *LeafX* expression descriptor. In *gpcp* the literal value itself is left untransformed,[2] and the code in Figure 8.16 extracts and emits the character value or the string value as directed by the expression datatype.

---

[2]Indeed, in the case of a manifest constant the same constant descriptor might be used as a string literal in one used occurrence and a character literal in another.

```
procedure (emtr : MsilEmitter) PushLeaf (exp : LeafX);
  var iFil :   IlasmFile;
begin
  iFil := emtr.outF;
  case exp.kind of
  | Xp.nilLt  : iFil.Code (opc_ldnull);            (* NIL *)
  | Xp.tBool  : iFil.PushLit (1);                  (* TRUE *)
  | Xp.fBool  : iFil.PushLit (0);                  (* FALSE *)
  | Xp.charLt : iFil.PushLit (exp.value.char ());
  | Xp.numLt  : iFil.PushInt (exp.value.int ());
  | Xp.realLt : iFil.PushReal (exp.value.real ());
  | Xp.strLt  : if exp.type = charTp then
                    iFil.PushInt (exp.value.chrVal ());
                else
                    iFil.PushStr (exp.value.strVal ());
                end
  end (* case *)
end PushLeaf;
```

Figure 8.16: Pushing various literal values

Incrementing Variables, Allocating Objects

In this section we consider the emission of *IL* for various "built-in procedures" of *Component Pascal*. These are constructs of the language that have special semantics and are usually implemented as inline code, but appear in the source syntax as procedure calls. There are many such functions and procedures, but we shall discuss only *INC*, which increments variables; *LEN*, which returns the length of the *N*th dimension of an array; and *NEW*, which allocates objects. All of these appear, perhaps in different syntactic form, in many other languages.

The *INC* built-in corresponds to the familiar postincrement operations of *ANSI C*. There are two forms. "INC (*var*)" adds one to the variable denoted by the designator expression *var*. The second form, "INC (*var,exp*)", evaluates the integer expression *exp* and adds the value to the variable denoted by the designator *var*. These correspond to the C expressions "(*var*) ++" and "*var*+= *exp*" respectively.

The implementation of these operations is interesting, since it is a requirement that the *lValue* be evaluated only once. This is important if the evaluation has side effects, or if the expression is so complicated that re-evaluation would be inefficient. Because of this requirement, it is not possible to replace the "(*var*) ++" by the *usually* equivalent "*var=var+1*". In this case, "usually" is not good enough.

There are at least two different ways in which we might correctly implement the increment operation. The first method is based on the following pattern —

```
<push var handle>
<duplicate handle>
<load value from handle>
ldc.i4.1                    // in general case, push exp
add                         // add increment to the value
<assign to handle>
```

Note that other instances of this pattern may need to use an overflow-checked addition or may operate on *int64* values.

This particular pattern works out very well for most cases. The only tricky case is that of array elements, where the handle occupies two slots on the evaluation stack. Since we have no way of duplicating a *pair* of stack elements, we must save them in two temporary local variables. In the case of variable designators that are simple leaf nodes, the handle is empty and the *<load value from handle>* becomes a simple load of the variable. The source code to do all this has the skeleton shown in Figure 8.17. Two temporary local variables, *tmp1* and *tmp2*, are needed to duplicate the two-element handle. The types of these temporaries will be *int32* and the array element type respectively. The code pattern involved in duplicating an array handle is an idiom that occurs in other places as well. In some other abstract stack machines a two-element duplicate is a primitive instruction. When translating languages with many *assignment operator* access patterns, it would probably make sense to create a special emitter method that pushes a preduplicated handle.

```
emtr.PushHandle(arg0);              (* destination handle *)
with exp  :   IdLeaf do             (* simple var *)
    emtr.PushValue(arg0);           (* TOS is current value *)
|  exp  : IdentX do                 (* field select *)
    iFil.Code(opc_dup);             (* duplicate handle *)
    iFil.GetField(exp.ident);       (* TOS is current value *)
|  exp  : BinaryX do                (* array index *)
    <duplicate handle>              (* using temporary locals *)
    iFil.GetElem(exp.type);         (* TOS is current value *)
end; (* with *)
emtr.PushValue(arg1);               (* push increment amount *)
iFil.Code(opc_add);                 (* add ... or add_ovf *)
emtr.ValueAssign(exp.type);         (* result is stored! *)
```

Figure 8.17: Emitting an increment, version #1

The second method of generating code for an increment operation uses a transient pointer, rather than a handle, to hold the destination address. The code pattern is —

```
<push var reference>
dup                    // duplicate reference
ldind.i4               // load current var value
ldc.i4.1               // in general case, push exp
add                    // add increment to the value
stind.i4               // store new var value
```

Once again other instances of this pattern may need to use an overflow-checked addition or may need to load and store *int64* values.

On the face of it, this second code pattern looks simpler to generate, and it is still verifiable. However, in some simple cases the code generated by the first code pattern is rather nicer. Figure 8.18 is a comparison of the code generated by the two patterns for incrementing a simple local variable and an element of a local reference array. On the left of the figure, we have the code produced by the first method. In the array element case, we assume that a utility has pushed a duplicated handle, using two temporary local variables, *P* and *I*. This consumes eight *IL* instructions. Notice, for a simple variable denoted by an *IdLeaf* node, there is no handle to duplicate, and no explicit *lValue* is created. In this leaf node case there can never be any side effect of evaluation of the *lValue* so method #1 is correct as shown.

IL to increment local variable	
Method #1	**Method #2**
`ldloc N`	`ldloca N`
`ldc.i4.1`	`dup`
`add.ovf`	`ldind.i4`
`stloc N`	`ldc.i4.1`
	`add.ovf`
	`stind.i4`
IL to increment local array element	
Method #1	**Method #2**
`ldloc N`	`ldloc N`
`stloc P`	`<push index>`
`<push index>`	`ldelema int32`
`stloc I`	`dup`
`ldloc P`	`ldind.i4`
`ldloc I`	`ldc.i4.1`
`ldloc P`	`add.ovf`
`ldloc I`	`stind.i4`
`ldelem.i4`	
`ldc.i4.1`	
`add.ovf`	
`stelem.i4`	

Figure 8.18: Comparing *IL* for increment instances

For simple leaf nodes the first method is best, while the second method is better for the array case, even with the best possible method of duplicating the handle. This suggests that the optimal strategy may be a hybrid method that uses the first method except for array elements.

The *LEN* function in *Component Pascal* has two forms and is used in two different contexts. The function may be applied to character strings, where it returns the length of the string. When applied to arrays, the function returns the number of elements in the array. For multidimensional arrays (which are arrays of arrays in *Component Pascal*) the form "*LEN(var,N)*", where N is a integer literal, returns the length of the $(N+1)$-st dimension. "*LEN(var)*" has the same meaning as "*LEN(var,0)*". In *gpcp* the two contexts in which the function occurs are mapped into separate binary expression nodes.

Many occurrences of the length function may be statically evaluated. For example we may apply the function to literal strings and to arrays of fixed length. However, the function is also used for character strings hosted in character arrays and also for open arrays. In both of these cases the value is evaluated by *IL* code at runtime.

The expression node that computes string length is encoded as a simple call to the static *strLen* method in the runtime support. The runtime computation of array length is more interesting. The binary tree node has a left child that is the variable designator and a literal right child that is the index of the required array dimension. *CIL* has a single instruction, "`ldlen`", that returns array length and hence implements the function for one-dimensional arrays. In order to get the length of the Nth dimension the code must step through the reference arrays for the lower-ordered dimensions. Figure 3.6 will remind you of the memory layout in the two-dimensional case. As an example, to find the length of the first dimension of a three-dimensional open array, the source expression "*LEN(var,0)*" would translate into the *IL* —

```
<push array reference>
ldlen                          // TOS is length of var
```

In order to find the length of the *third* dimension of the same three-dimensional open array, the source expression "*LEN(var,2)*" would translate into the *IL* —

```
<push array reference>
ldc.i4.0
ldelem.ref                     // TOS is reference to var[0]
ldc.i4.0
ldelem.ref                     // TOS is reference to var[0][0]
ldlen                          // TOS is length of var[0][0]
```

The correctness of this code relies on the fact that in *Component Pascal* open arrays are either **nil** or are *completely* allocated. This is in contrast to some other languages in which a variable declared to be an array of arrays may have only *some* of the dimensions allocated.

In general, the *IL* emission code for the binary *lenOf* node is just another branch in the *PushBinary* procedure. Since the left-hand side is necessarily an array reference, the *PushValue* call on the left child of the expression will load the reference. The literal right operand is not pushed. The code goes like this —

```
if exp.kind = lenOf then
  emtr.PushValue(exp.lKid);
  for ix := 0 to intVal(exp.rKid)-1 do
    iFil.PushLit(0); iFil.Code(opc_ldelem_ref);
  end
  iFil.Code(opc_ldlen);
elsif ...                           (* other expression kinds *)
```

The inline code emitted by the loop steps its way through the dimensions, if there are more than one, by successively loading a reference to the zeroth array element. The final call of "ldlen" loads the length that we seek.

It might be noted that in an unverified context, arrays of any dimensionality are passed as single memory blobs. In such cases, all such length functions would simply access the appropriate hidden parameter.

For languages that have true multidimensional arrays, as distinct from the *Pascal*-family arrays of arrays, all of this functionality is provided by methods of the *System.Array* class.

Object allocation in *Component Pascal* is performed by the *NEW* procedure. This procedure has two forms. One is used for pointers to records or fixed length arrays. The variant form is used for allocating pointers to arrays of dynamic length, so the call must specify the array length or lengths. In the abstract syntax of *Component Pascal*, calls to *NEW* have an argument sequence with at least one element. Calls to *NEW* on pointers-to-record and fixed array types take only one argument, a designator expression that denotes the pointer variable. For open arrays there are as many additional integer-valued "length" arguments as there are open array dimensions. The actual emission of the allocation *IL* is performed by three utilities that allocate records, fixed length arrays of any dimensionality, and open arrays of any dimensionality. In all cases, because of the possibility that array element or field types are reference surrogates, these utilities may need to recursively emit code to allocate subobjects. The top-level code chooses between the three cases, as shown in Figure 8.19. For the open array case the lengths are pushed on the stack, and the *MkOpenArray* utility emits the allocation *IL*. In the fixed array case the utility *MkFixedArray* finds the array lengths from the array type descriptor and emits the required *IL*. In both cases the detail may include the emission of nested loops for element initialization. This detail is spelled out in the next chapter.

The *IL* for the allocation of dynamic record objects may require nested allocations but does not require emission of any flow of control. The *MkNewRecord* utility always emits a single instruction —

```
dstT  :=  <bound type of arg0.type>;
if <only one arg> then
  with dstT  :  Record do
      iFil.MkNewRecord(dstT);
  |  dstT  :  Array do
      iFil.MkFixedArray(dstT);
  end
else (* open array *)
  for <all length arguments> do <push the length value> end ;
  iFil.MkOpenArray(arg0.type);
end (* if *)
```

Figure 8.19: Top-level code to emit calls to *NEW*

newobj **instance void** *ModName.ClassName*::.ctor()

Any allocation and initialization of nested objects is hidden away inside the no-arg constructor of the object.

Procedure and Function Calls

Procedure and function calls in our model abstract syntax are always *CallX* expression nodes. In the case of value-returning functions these nodes occur during ordinary expression evaluation. *CallX* nodes also occur as attributes of procedure call *statement* descriptors. *CallX* nodes are subtypes of the *Unary* expression type. As well as a child node that denotes the expression to call, they have an expression sequence attribute, *actuals*, that specifies the actual parameter expressions, as shown in Figure 8.20. On the left is a call to a static function returning an **int** and taking three arguments. On the right is a call to a method that takes a **this** reference and three arguments. The method also returns an **int**.

The *IL* corresponding to a *CallX* node follows a simple pattern. The receiver object, if any, is pushed on the stack. The arguments are then pushed, in order, and an appropriate "call" or "callvirt" instruction emitted.

We need to distinguish a number of special cases that are signalled by the child expression type, and properties of the procedure identifier. In our model abstract syntax, the child designator must be either an *IdLeaf* or an *IdentX*. Leaf designators correspond to calls to static procedures, the names of which are denoted by the identifier descriptor field of the *IdLeaf*. *IdentX* nodes correspond to member selection and hence to dispatched calls with the child node of the *IdentX* specifying the receiver object.

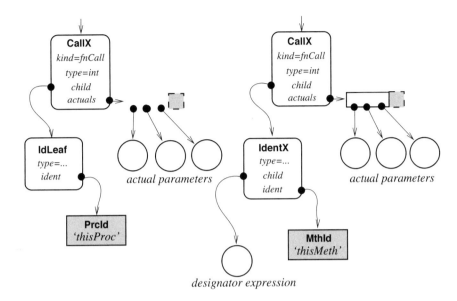

Figure 8.20: *CallX* nodes for static and dispatched calls

Static calls.   If the child node of the *CallX* is an *IdLeaf*, then we know that we have a static call. We still need to check the attributes of the procedure identifier, to determine whether or not the identifier corresponds to a constructor or to an ordinary static procedure. For an ordinary static procedure we must emit the instruction —

> `call` *TypeRef ClsRef* : : *MthNam(signature)*

where *TypeRef* is the return type reference, *ClsRef* is the class reference, *MthNam* is the simple method name, and *signature* is the method signature.

For constructors, the corresponding instruction will be —

> `call` **instance void** *ClsRef* : : . ctor*(signature)*

where in this case *signature* is the constructor signature.

Dispatched calls.   If the child node of the *CallX* is an *IdentX*, then we know that this is a dispatched call and that the method receiver will have already been pushed as the first "argument." We still need to examine the method identifier descriptor to know whether or not to emit a virtual or a static call. We have the following special cases —

- If the bound type of the method is an interface, we emit a virtual call.

- If the method is a nonvirtual instance method, then we must emit a static call.

- If the method is a "supercall" to a virtual method, then we must emit a static call.

- If the receiver class is **sealed** then the more efficient static call may be used.

- If the method is marked **final** then the more efficient static call may be used.

- Otherwise a virtual call must be used.

If the selected method is an interface method then we have no choice but to use a virtual call. Similarly, if the method is a nonvirtual method then we must use a static call instruction. However, ordinary virtual methods may be invoked statically whenever it is correct to do so. In effect, we must be able to guarantee that the method that we specify statically is exactly the method that would be dispatched by a virtual call. The two cases in the list use simple static properties to ensure correctness. There are more complex computations based on *type-flow analysis* that can find more such cases.

Pushing the actual parameters.

Pushing the actual parameters of a call involves iterating over the *actuals* sequence of the *CallX* node, pushing either the value or a reference. For value parameters we push the expression value, while for reference parameters we push a transient pointer to the value.

In native code compilers it is necessary to decide on a call convention for passing structures by value. There are three different methods that are used. The *calling* procedure may provide space in its own activation record, copy the value into that space, and then pass a reference to the copy. Alternatively, the *called* procedure may provide the space for the copy in its own activation record, accept a reference to the original value, and make the copy in its prolog. Finally, the copy may be made in the argument area that is common to the called and calling activation records.

In the *CLR* we deal with this issue at a more abstract level. *IL* does not deal directly with the activation records of the called and calling procedures. Instead, values are pushed onto the evaluation stack in order, prior to the call, and appear "automagically" as numbered arguments in the activation record of the called procedure. In principle the *JIT* could map this abstraction into any one of the three traditional methods. The choice might well be different for different machine architectures, depending on the number of available machine registers, for example. In any case, it is probably simplest to imagine that the abstract mechanism maps onto the third method.

The code to push an actual parameter, in the simplest case, is just a call to either *Push-Value*, for a value mode formal, or *PushRef*, for a reference mode formal. This formulation is sufficient for languages that do not require the use of reference surrogates.

Pushing reference surrogate arguments.

If a language maps some aggregate value types onto reference surrogates, then the passing of parameters needs a little more care. Figure 8.21 sets out the four possible cases.

Expression type	Value-mode formal	Reference-mode formal
Value arrays with memory blob impl.	<push expr. value>	<push variable address>
Value arrays with ref. surrogate impl.	<push expr. value> <make array clone>	<push variable value>
Value structs with value impl.	<push expr. value>	<push variable address>
Value structs with ref. surrogate impl.	<push expr. value> <make object clone>	<push variable value>

Figure 8.21: Various cases of pushing aggregate type arguments on the stack

If value arrays are implemented as value classes by means of a suitably defined memory blob class, then the encoding is straightforward. For a value mode formal parameter we simply push the value onto the evaluation stack with an instruction sequence finishing with a "ldobj". For reference mode formals we will just push the memory blob address. Of course, such an implementation will use array indexing operations that are unverifiable.

If value arrays are implemented by reference arrays, then the *value* of the location selected by the actual parameter will be a reference to the actual array. For a value mode formal parameter we must copy the array value to obtain correct semantics. Since the *CLR* does not support array copies directly, we must clone the array manually. We first get the length of the array, then allocate a new array of the same length. Finally, we perform an element-by-element copy. The length of the array might either be statically known or obtained by using the "ldlen" instruction. *gpcp* performs any such array copies by using an inline loop. The issues that arise for copying multidimensional arrays are discussed in the next chapter. In contrast the reference mode case is simple. When passing a reference array to a reference parameter, we simply push the actual expression value.

The case of value structures implemented as value classes is simple. The *CLR* directly supports such datatypes. We push the expression value or the variable address, for value and reference mode formals respectively.

The other case of reference surrogates arises when value records are implemented as reference classes. In this case, as with array reference surrogates, the *value* of the expression is a reference to the actual data. When we wish to pass such a value to a value mode formal parameter, we must manually clone the value. We do this by allocating a new object of the same type and calling the same "__copy__" method that is used for assignment of entire values of this type. It may be noted that the use of the *Object.clone* method does not give the correct semantics in all cases. If a reference surrogate type has fields that are themselves reference surrogates, then the *clone* method will only perform a shallow copy, rather than the deep copy that is required for correctness. As with array surrogates, the reference mode case is simple. When passing a reference class object to a reference mode formal parameter, we simply push the actual expression value.

Tailoring the Semantics

There are a number of expression operators that occur in programming languages that are not directly supported by the instruction set of *CIL*. Since the instruction set is computationally complete, we can be sure that we may realize such operations, but we may need to synthesize them from sequences of primitive instructions. We have already seen some examples of this for operations such as absolute value.

In this section, we consider a number of indicative cases of synthesizing other operations out of *IL*. The examples have been chosen to give some flavor of the possibilities.

MAX and MIN

The emission of *IL* for the maximum and minimum functions was previously described, in connection with the discussion of computing the maximum stack height. Figure 7.14 on page 222 and Figure 7.15 give two possible variants.

The underlying idea is to push the two values onto the stack, and then compare the two values. Whichever of the values is the needed value is then pushed onto the stack as the result. The only real issue here is that, except in trivial cases, the expressions should only be evaluated once and must be saved in temporary local variables. In the case of expressions with side effects it would be both inefficient and incorrect to evaluate $MAX(e_1, e_2)$ by the C-style conditional expression $(e_1 > e_2 \,?\, e_1 : e_2)$.

Range and Index Checking

For languages that have subrange types and bounded enumeration types the checking of values against the bounds of the type are a common occurrence. In unverified contexts, as well as range checks, programs must perform their own array index bounds checks, since the bounds checking of the *CLR* will not be invoked. We thus consider the synthesis of an *IL* sequence that checks the top-of-stack value against known literal bounds. We wish to throw an exception if the test fails and leave the top-of-stack value unchanged otherwise. We may think of this operation as being a generalization of the bounds checks that are applied by the "cvt.*.ovf" instructions.

Suppose that we wish to assert that the top-of-stack value is in the closed range $[n, m]$, for some literal integers n and m. This appears to require *two* comparisons, but an old compiler writer's trick comes to the rescue. We begin by subtracting n from the value under test. This *translates* the valid values into the range $[0, (m - n)]$. We now perform an *unsigned* comparison of the translated value against $(m - n)$. All values outside the range will return false for an "unsigned less than or equal to" comparison. Possible *IL* is shown in Figure 8.22. Of course, in practice the creation of the exception object would be done so as to ensure that the object carried useful information regarding the origin and nature of the error.

```
    . . .                   // test TOS value is in N..M
    dup                     // duplicate the test value
    ldc.i4  $N$             // N is lower bound of range
    sub                     // subtract lower bound
    ldc.i4  $R$             // R is literal (M–N)
    ble.un   lb001          // skip for valid case
    <create informative exception object>
    throw
lb001:                      // value is validated
```

Figure 8.22: *IL* for range assertion

Although this example is based on literal limits, the same principle works for variable bounds as well. This way of replacing a double-ended test by an unsigned single-ended test is a useful idiom. We shall use the same idea in implementing **switch** statements, to trim the default cases before recursing down the decision tree.

Shift Expressions

The shift instructions of the *CLR* have undefined results if the shift amount exceeds the word length. It follows that if the semantics of the source language require that such operations be well-defined, then a new operation must be synthesized.

Let us assume that a language defines the semantics of the shift operation so that left shifts by amounts larger than the word length return zero. We might express the semantics by defining a function that behaves in the right way. Here is one possibility —

```
public static int Lsh0 (int lVal, unsigned int rVal) {
    if (rVal > 31) {
        return 0;
    else
        return lVal << rVal;
}
```

Having this template to work from, let us see how we might perform the same operations using inline code. We shall assume that the two operands have been pushed in the normal order. We need to emit *IL* like Figure 8.23. In the exceptional case the left operand that is sitting on the stack needs to be thrown away and replaced by a literal zero. In the usual case the shift proceeds normally. The local variable N is a temporary that holds the right operand value. Note that this code does not have a stack height anomaly.

The equivalent well-behaved semantics for an arithmetic right shift would ensure that shifts after the first (word length – 1) places should leave the result unchanged. In effect a

```
         <push left operand>
         <push right operand>
         dup                          // duplicate and save rOp
         stloc N
         ldc.i4 31                    // word length minus one
         blt  lb001                   // skip for < 31 case
         pop                          // discard left operand
         ldc.i4.0                     // push zero instead
         br lb002                     // go to exit
lb001:
         ldloc N
         lsh                          // do the left shift
lb002:
```

Figure 8.23: *IL* for well-defined left shift operation

very long right shift should leave the result word full of bits that all duplicate the sign bit of the original operand. Here is the definition of a plausible try —

public static int Rsh0(**int** lVal, **unsigned int** rVal) {
    return lVal >> MIN(rVal,31)
}

where *MIN* returns the lesser of its two operands.

    The *IL* that we need is as shown in Figure 8.24. In this example we do not need a temporary local variable, since we simply replace the top of stack by the literal 31 if the right operand is larger. In that case we fall through into the common code that performs the shift.

```
         <push left operand>
         <push right operand>
         dup                          // duplicate rOp
         ldc.i4 31                    // word length minus one
         blt  lb001                   // skip for < 31 case
         pop                          // discard right operand
         ldc.i4.s 31                  // push explicit shift
lb001:
         rsh                          // do the right shift
```

Figure 8.24: *IL* for well-defined arithmetic right shift operation

It may be noted that the code that emits this *IL* should not miss the opportunity to make simplifications if the right operand is a literal. For the literal case the "branching" is done at compile time, and the runtime code needs no test-and-branch behavior.

Component Pascal has another variation in the "tricky shifts" department. The *ASH* function performs an arithmetic shift either to the right or to the left depending on the sign of the right operand. For the common case where the right operand is a literal, this poses no problem. If the right operand is a variable, then it is necessary to perform a test and branch at runtime. The source of *gpcp* shows how.

Pesky Divisions

The division and remainder operations that are supplied in *CIL* have the common "round to zero" semantics. These are certainly the operations that most contemporary hardware supports. These operations are not the ones favored in many numerical contexts, where the preference is often for the alternative "round to minus infinity" semantics.

In any case, it is necessary to synthesize whatever operations the source language specifies. In the case of *Pascal*-family languages the operators *MOD* and *DIV* are defined so that —

$$a \text{ 'DIV' } b = \lfloor a/b \rfloor$$
$$a \text{ 'MOD' } b = a - (a \text{ 'DIV' } b) \times b$$
$$a \text{ 'DIV0' } b = \mathcal{R}_0(a/b)$$
$$a \text{ 'REM' } b = a - (a \text{ 'DIV0' } b) \times b$$

where the "/" operators on the right denote exact division, and where $\mathcal{R}_0 : \mathcal{R} \rightarrow \mathcal{I}$ is the *round toward zero* function. The "$\lfloor . \rfloor$" symbols denote the *floor* function, with signature $\mathcal{R} \rightarrow \mathcal{I}$, that rounds towards minus infinity. The alternative operators *DIV0* and *REM* are extensions to *Component Pascal* that access the more efficient default division and remainder operators of *IL*.

Here is a table that gives an example of the results of applying the various division and remainder operations to some typical operands on the stack. In each case the top of stack is the right operand for the operation, while the left operand is below that.

stack top	10	−10	10	−10
next elem.	31	31	−31	−31
DIV0	3	−3	−3	3
REM	1	1	−1	−1
DIV	3	−4	−4	3
MOD	1	−9	9	−1

The synthesis of *MOD* and *DIV* relies on using the "div" and "rem" instructions and performing a correction when required. As a first attempt, we might allow the code generator to "wimp out" and call a runtime support function. The method for *DIV* has the following code in *C#* —

```
public static int cpDivI (int lVal, int rVal) {
    int rslt = lVal / rVal;          // default division
    int rmdr = lVal % rVal;          // default remainder
    if ((lVal < 0 != rVal < 0) && (rmdr != 0))
        rslt--;                      // correction step
    return rslt;
}
```

The need for correction is signalled by the signs of the two operands being different and the remainder being nonzero. The correction step is to decrement the quotient by one, so as to obtain the correct rounding behavior. The same test is applied to detect the need for correction for the *MOD* function, which has the *C#* code —

```
public static int cpModI (int lVal, int rVal) {
    int rmdr = lVal % rVal;          // default remainder
    if ((lVal < 0 != rVal < 0) && (rmdr != 0))
        rmdr += rVal;                // correction step
    return rmdr;
}
```

In this case the correction consists of incrementing the default remainder by the value of the right operand.

Implementing these schemes by inline code is challenging. Once the operands have been loaded into local variables, each of the functions requires about 10 to 12 *IL* instructions. As we shall see later, the common case of literal right operands can be achieved much more simply. First however we shall consider the inline expansion of the *MOD* operation. Disassembly into *IL* of method *cpModI* shows that anything under 22 instructions would be a win. There are many ways to implement the function. One reasonable idea is —

```
int rmdr = lVal % rVal;
if (rmdr != 0)
    if ((lVal xor rVal) < 0)
        rmdr += rVal;                       // correction step
```

As it turns out, the not-zero test can use the "brfalse" instruction, and the "xor" provides a nice trick for testing for unequal signs of the two operands. We may even avoid allocating a local variable for *rmdr* by keeping the value on the stack. Figure 8.25 has the *IL* that we need. This encoding uses just 12 *IL* instructions. The comments at the right of the figure denote the stack contents after each instruction. During the development of *IL* sequences of this kind such annotations are an invaluable aid to the design.

```
            ldloc 'lVal'            // stack: ... lVal
            ldloc 'rVal'            // stack: ... lVal, rVal
            rem                     // stack: ... rmdr
            dup                     // stack: ... rmdr, rmdr
            brfalse lb001           // stack: ... rmdr
            ldloc 'lVal'            // stack: ... rmdr, lVal
            ldloc 'rVal'            // stack: ... rmdr, lVal, rVal
            xor                     // stack: ... rmdr, xval
            ldc.i4.0                // stack: ... rmdr, xval, 0
            bge lb001               // stack: ... rmdr
            ldloc 'rVal'            // stack: ... rmdr, rVal
            add                     // stack: ... rmdr'
lb001:                              // stack: ... result
```

Figure 8.25: *IL* for inline expansion of *MOD* operation

Statistically a high proportion of occurrences of *MOD* and *DIV* have literal, positive right operands. It turns out that significant simplifications can be made in this case. In particular, since we statically know the sign of the right operand, we only need to test the left sign. For the *DIV* operation if the left operand is also positive, no correction is ever needed. If the left operand is negative, then presubtracting $(rVal - 1)$ ensures that the "div" instruction will always give the right answer.

For the *MOD* operation we may perform a single test that gives the same result as the compound test on sign and remainder. If the raw remainder is negative, then a correction is necessary, since such a value can only arise if the left operand was negative and was not exactly divisible by the right operand.

Each of these simplified cases may be encoded in seven instructions of *IL*. Figure 8.26 shows the *IL* for the case of a *DIV* by a literal right operand of ten. Figure 8.27 shows the *IL* for the case of a *MOD* by a literal right operand of ten.

Set Constructor Expressions

As a final example of synthesis of compound operations, we consider the construction of bitset values. This will be the most complicated example of "bit-twiddling" that we shall consider. Set constructors in our model abstract syntax consist of a literal set and a sequence of variable elements. The static part is computed during expression attribution, as discussed in connection with Figures 5.5 and 6.7. The variable elements may be single values from the set base type or may be ranges with given upper and lower bounds.

```
// Compute "lVal div 10" to top of stack
        <push left operand>
        dup                     // duplicate lVal
        ldc.i4.0                // compare with zero
        bge lb001               // skip if positive
        ldc.i4.s 9              // load rVal-1
        sub                     // subtract
lb001:
        ldc.i4.s 10             // load rVal
        div                     // result is on TOS
```

Figure 8.26: *IL* for *DIV* by literal 10

```
// Compute "lVal mod 10" to top of stack
        <push left operand>
        ldc.i4.s 10             // load rVal
        rem                     // get trial remainder
        dup                     // duplicate remainder
        ldc.i4.0                // compare with zero
        bge lb001               // skip if non-negative
        ldc.i4.s 10             // load rVal
        add                     // do correction
lb001:                          // result is on TOS
```

Figure 8.27: *IL* for *MOD* by literal 10

The algorithm for constructing the set consists of pushing a literal value on the stack, equal to the static part of the set. We then iterate over the *varSeq* sequence of the descriptor, inserting elements. Figure 8.28 has the outline of the code. The magic is all in the line of code that is abstracted away. There are two cases to consider. If the element is a singleton, n say, we want to construct an *int32* value with the nth bit on. We may do this in a number of ways, but the simplest is to push a literal one and shift it by the element value —

```
ldc.i4.1                    // push a literal one
<push the element value>
shl                         // shift bit into correct position
```

If the element expression is a range, $[n..m]$ say, then we wish to construct an *int32* value that has all bits set from bit n to bit m, where bits number from zero at the least significant end. The word that we want to construct will have a bit pattern like this —

```
procedure (emtr : MsilEmitter) PushSetExp (exp : SetExp);
begin
  emtr.PushValue (exp.value.int ());
  for i := 0 to exp.varSeq.tide-1 do
    <push the i-th element value>;
    emtr.outF.Code (opc_or);              (* add to running total *)
  end;
end PushSetExp;
```

Figure 8.28: Constructing a set value

```
                          ......m.....n.....0
Most significant bit     0...0011...1100...0     Least significant bit
```

where the bit indices are as shown. There are two possible methods that deserve consideration.

The first method works as follows. We push a one value and shift it into position $(m + 1)$. The top-of-stack word now has the form —

```
     ......m..........0
     0...0100...0000...0
```

We now arithmetically negate the value. This leaves the least significant "1" bit on and flips all bits to the left of this position. The word is now —

```
     ......m..........0
     1...1100...0000...0
```

All of the bits from $(m + 1)$ up are now set. We now construct another word by shifting another one bit up to the nth position and negating. This word will have bit pattern —

```
     ............n.....0
     1...1111...1100...0
```

This word has all the bits from n upward set. We may now compute our desired word using the "xor" instruction —

```
                    ......m.....n.....0
        word1       1...1100...0000...0
        word2       1...1111...1100...0
  word1 xor word2   0...0011...1100...0
```

```
ldc.i4.1                          // push a literal one
<push high of range + 1>
shl                               // shift bit into correct position
neg                               // arithmetic negatation of word
ldc.i4.1                          // push a literal one
<push low of range>
shl                               // shift bit into correct position
neg                               // arithmetic negation of word
xor                               // result is on top of stack
```

Figure 8.29: Constructing a bit-range, version #1

The *IL* to construct the bit-range word by this method is shown in Figure 8.29.

The second method of constructing a bit-range starts with a word that has all bits set. It then chops the unneeded bits off the two ends to achieve the desired result. The algorithm starts by pushing a value of -1, which has all bits set.

```
1...1111...1111...1
```

We *logically* shift the word to the right by $(31-m)$ places. We must use a logical (unsigned) right shift, because we want to shift zero bits into the most significant end of the word. The resulting word is —

```
      ......m..........0
0...0011...1111...1
```

We now shift a further n bits to the right, and then immediately shift to the left by the same amount. This clears out the rightmost n bits of the word, leaving us with the required result.

```
                    ......m.....n.....0
         -1    1...1111...1111...1
TOS >>> (31 - m)   0...0011...1111...1
    TOS >>> n   0...0000...0011...1
     TOS << n   0...0011...1100...0
```

In order to implement this idea, we may combine the first two shifts. We compute the total shift amount of $(31 - m + n)$ and then perform a single unsigned right shift. We then perform the left shift to complete the computation. Figure 8.30 shows typical *IL*.

There does not seem to be much to choose between these two methods of computing range words. *gpcp* happens to use the second method. There are a number of special cases, occurring when one of the limits of the range is statically known, that might usefully be recognized when implementing this algorithm.

```
ldc.i4.M1                        // push a literal -1
ldc.i4.s 31                      // push a literal 31
<push high of range>
sub                              // compute: 31–high
<push low of range>
dup
stloc 'tmp'                      // save low of range in temp
add                              // compute: 31–high+low
shr.un                           // logical right shift
ldloc 'tmp'                      // push low of range from temp
shl                              // shift all bits to final position
```

Figure 8.30: Constructing a bit-range, version #2

It is useful to note that the second of these schemes uses an idiom that is also used for *bit-field extraction* in *ANSI C*. Suppose, in *C*, we wish to extract a bit-field that extends from bit n to bit m. If the bit-field is unsigned, then we could shift the field into the least significant position by a right shift of n places. We could then mask off the required bits using an "and" instruction with an appropriate mask word. In the case of a *signed* bit-field, the plan just described does not perform the needed sign extension of the field. In this case we must begin by shifting the sign bit of the field into the sign bit of the word. We then *arithmetically* right shift the result to move the field into the least significant position of the word, with the sign bit propagated all the way down. Figure 8.31 has the *IL* that is required. Finally, we may note that this same *IL* would work for unsigned fields, if the "shr" instruction was replaced by a "shr.un".

```
// Extract signed bit-field n..m
<push value>
ldc.i4 X                         // X is "31–m"
shl                              // bit-field sign now in bit 31
ldc.i4 Y                         // Y is "31–m+n"
shr                              // result is on top of stack
```

Figure 8.31: Extracting a signed bit-field

Notes on Chapter 8

Producing unverified *IL* for variable designators in *.NET* is relatively simple because of the elegant abstraction of *l-value* formation. Producing verified *IL* does seem to necessitate the kind of case analysis that occupied the first part of this chapter. There is a certain amount of code bloat here, but the *handle* abstraction keeps the structure relatively clean. At least the handle abstraction prevents the appearance of multiple occurrences of switch statements predicated on selector kind. There may be other possible abstractions that structure the code in other ways.

For those readers who enjoy puzzles, the challenge of producing new primitive operations out of *IL* will be an endless source of pleasure. Here are a couple of suggestions, with approximate *IL* instruction counts. The *JIT* should distill most of these down to a much smaller number of native machine instructions.

A rotate instruction may be synthesized out of shifts and bitwise *OR*. This should take about seven instructions—nine for a variable distance rotate—to rotate by some literal number of bit positions.

Swapping the bytes of the value in a local variable should take about 19 instructions for an **int32**, and 31 instructions for an **int64**. The best algorithm uses a nice recursive decomposition.

Counting the '1' bits in a word also yields to a recursive decomposition. In this case 49 instructions should do for an **int32** and 59 instructions for an **int64**. Compare this to the instruction count for a "one bit at a time" loop algorithm.

Finally, on the same recursive theme, a complete bit reversal of an **int32** seems to be possible in 59 instructions, with just a further 12 instructions required for the **int64** case.

Emitting Code for Flow of Control 9

In this chapter we consider the emission of *IL* for statements that require labels and branching. This includes all of the choice statements and the loops. We also consider the very special case of short-circuit evaluation of Boolean expressions that was deferred from the previous chapter.

Boolean Expressions

Boolean expressions occur in two distinct contexts in programming languages. The most common case is that of expressions which are evaluated in order to affect flow-of-control. All of the Boolean expressions that occur in conditional statements fall into this category. The other possibility is that of evaluation of an expression, so as to store the value or pass it as a parameter to a subprogram. Most contemporary languages specify *short circuit* (lazy) evaluation of Boolean expressions,[1] so that correct semantics are always obtained by evaluating Boolean expressions using what we shall call *jumping code*.

---

[1] *Ada* is an exception, as it allows the programmer to specify either full evaluation (the default) or short circuit evaluation using the special operators 'or else' and 'and then'.

Jumping code evaluates expressions incrementally and exits from the code just as soon as a result is known. The main advantage of this feature is not so much efficiency (it is not always the most efficient) but the possiblity of writing guarded code such as —

> **if** (ptr # **nil**) & (ptr.size <= 8) **then** . . .

In the case of a language with full evaluation this would have to be written as the alternative —

> **if** ptr # **nil then**
>   **if** ptr.size <= 8) **then** . . .

Jumping Code

Jumping code is produced by a recursive traversal of expression trees in the abstract syntax. There are two fundamental operations for which we must allow. We need to be able to produce code that evaluates Boolean expressions and conditionally passes control to one of two specified labels. We must also be able to evaluate expressions with correct semantics, where the result is a Boolean value on the top of the stack. We may achieve both of these objectives within the same framework, with just two recursive procedures that we call *FallTrue* and *FallFalse*.

Branching and falling through.   As we emit instructions to the *IL* stream, we need to emit conditional branches in two different circumstances. First, we have situations where we want the control flow to branch to some known target label if some Boolean expression evaluates to **true**. For example, suppose we have a *post-tested* loop structure of the form "**do ... while** (*BoolExp*)". When we come to emit the code for the end of this loop, we will know the label at the top of the loop to which control must return if the condition evaluates true. Thus we want to emit instructions that jump to the loop header label if the expression is true. If the expression evaluates to false, we want control to fall through to the next sequential instruction.

Equally, we have situations where we want the control flow to branch to some known target label if some Boolean expression evaluates to **false**. For example, suppose that once again we have a *post-tested* loop structure, but this time instead of a **do ... while** loop we have a loop of the form "**repeat ... until** (*BoolExp*)". When we come to emit the code for the end of this loop, we wish the control flow to fall through to the next instruction if the condition evaluates true, but to branch to the loop header label if the expression is false.

We shall see that all conditional branching may be reduced to instances of just these two cases. In order to emit the code for these two circumstances, we create two code-emission procedures named *FallFalse* and *FallTrue*. The other infrastructure components that are needed are a label allocator, to allocate unique labels on demand, and a utility that emits label-definitions to the *IL* stream. In *gpcp* these are supplied by two methods of the *IlasmFile* class, with signatures —

```
procedure (iFil :   IlasmFile)newLabel()  :   INTEGER;
(* return unique index of new label *)
procedure (iFil :   IlasmFile)DefLabel(labl :   INTEGER);
(* emit definition of label in IL *)
```

In this case *newLabel* returns an integer datum. When this integer is passed to *DefLabel*, the emitted label will be constructed from the value. In *gpcp* the label will be "lb*NNNN*" where *NNNN* is the number.

FallTrue and FallFalse.

We wish to define two methods of the *MsilEmitter* class that take a Boolean-valued expression and emit branching code. The first of these is the method *FallFalse*, with the *Component Pascal* definition —

```
procedure   (emtr : MsilEmitter)FallFalse(exp : Expr;
                                          lbl : INTEGER);
```

The first parameter, *exp*, is the expression tree that we wish to evaluate. The second parameter, *lbl*, is the label to which we wish to branch if the expression evaluates true.

The second method is *FallTrue*, with the similar *Component Pascal* definition —

```
procedure   (emtr : MsilEmitter)FallTrue(exp : Expr;
                                         lbl : INTEGER);
```

The first parameter, *exp*, is the expression tree that we wish to evaluate. The second parameter, *lbl*, is the label to which we wish to branch if the expression evaluates false. The method receiver, named *emtr* in both cases, provides access to the current procedure state, in case additional labels need to be allocated inside the emitted code.

These two methods recursively call themselves and each other in the course of Boolean evaluation. As an aid to understanding how the pattern of self-recursion works in any particular case, we shall use the graphical notation shown in Figure 9.1. In this notation, the sequential control flow proceeds straight down the page, just as it would in a code listing. The out-of-line arrows represent branching control flow targeted on some specified label.

The graphical construct on the left of the figure represents the code emitted by *Fall-False*. The open circle on the bottom of the figure is a reminder that this fall-through path is the exit that we use for a Boolean zero. The construct on the right represents the code emitted by *FallTrue*. The filled circle on the bottom of the figure is a reminder that this fall-through path is the exit that we use for a Boolean one.

As a first example of the use of these primitives, we consider generating *IL* for program assertions. In *Component Pascal* the *ASSERT* method takes a first argument of some

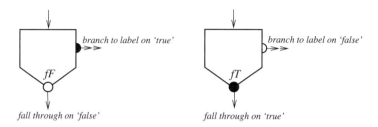

Figure 9.1: Boolean control-flow primitives

Boolean expression and is a simple application of the *FallTrue* and *FallFalse* procedures. At runtime the argument expression is evaluated, and an exception is thrown if the result is false. This simple mechanism is the key to inserting tests that enforce pre- and post-conditions of the source code.

Firstly, it should be noted that under some circumstances the assertion may be able to be statically evaluated by the compiler. If this is the case then the evaluation may either be removed as redundant or translated into an unconditional exception generation. In general however the predicate really does need to be evaluated at runtime. The idea behind the translation is to generate code as if the statement *ASSERT(expr)* had been written, in *C#*, as —

```
if (!expr) {
    throw new System.Exception(<message>);
}
```

Since we are going to create an exception object, we use a constructor that takes a string argument, so as to pass some useful information to the catcher. Many languages have assert facilities that allow the programmer to specify some failure code or message. A good default is to automatically generate a string that incorporates the statically known source line number of the statement. The string may appear as either a literal in the *IL* or a parameterised call to a locale-specific runtime string-creation method.

The emission of *IL* for an assertion is straightforward, once we have the *FallTrue* and *FallFalse* primitives. We allocate a new label and call *FallFalse* on the predicate expression —

```
okLb := iFil.newLabel();
emtr.FallFalse(arg0, okLb);          (* jump to okLb if true *)
iFil.EmitTrap(<message string>);
iFil.DefLabel(okLb);                 (* emit the label okLb *)
```

The message string in *gpcp* is "Assert error at <*module name : line number*>". The control flow for the emitted code, using our graphical notation, is as shown in Figure 9.2.

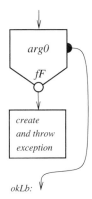

Figure 9.2: Control flow for program assertion

Conditional expressions.   Explicit conditional expressions occur in many *Algol*-family languages. Language *C*'s conditional expressions are a familiar instance. Figure 9.3 is an example which shows how to push the value of the expression —

$$(exp_1 ? exp_2 : exp_3)$$

We must allocate two labels. Since we wish to fall through into the true-case evaluation code, we need a label to branch to in the false-case. The second label is used to define the point where the control flow merges once again. This code, as shown, emits *IL* with the structure seen in Figure 9.4. This particular method of generating *IL* produces an example of the kind of stack height anomaly that was discussed on page 222. If the code generator design does not allow for this, then the values of the two expressions should be moved to a temporary local variable along each branch and loaded downstream of the merge label.

```
fLab := iFil.newLabel();           (* label for exp1 false *)
mLab := iFil.newLabel();           (* merge point label *)
emtr.FallTrue(exp1, fLab);
emtr.PushValue(exp2);              (* true branch, push exp2 *)
iFil.CodeLb(opc_br, mLab);         (* jump to the merge point *)
iFil.DefLabel(fLab);               (* emit the false label *)
emtr.PushValue(exp3);              (* false branch, push exp3 *)
iFil.DefLabel(mLab);               (* emit the merge label *)
```

Figure 9.3: Code to emit *IL* to push the value $(exp_1 ? exp_2 : exp_3)$

```
            <IL from "FallTrue(exp1, fLab)">
            <push value of exp2>
            br mLab
    fLab:
            <push value of exp3>
    mLab:
```

Figure 9.4: Emitted *IL* to push the value $(exp_1? \ exp_2: \ exp_3)$

Constructing Boolean values. Even in languages without conditional expressions, we still have at least one case of conditional expression evaluation. This case occurs whenever a Boolean value has to be constructed by an expression that is implemented by jumping code. When we have to push the value of a Boolean expression on the stack, we have two cases. If the expression is a function call or any other variable designator, we simply push the value as for any other scalar type. If the expression needs to be evaluated by jumping code, we simply evaluate the conditional expression — "$(BoolExp? \ 1: \ 0)$" — according to the outline given in Figure 9.3.

Recursing inside FallFalse and FallTrue. The actual emission of jumping code relies on the self-recursion of the *FallTrue* and *FallFalse* methods. Critical to this self-recursion is the pattern by which the **or** and **and** operators are implemented. Figure 9.5 shows how the two methods decompose expressions of the form *A* **or** *B*. The left of the figure shows how *FallFalse* would decompose the expression. If the expression *A* evaluates to true, we may immediately branch to the alternate label, *labelX* in the figure. If the expression *A* evaluates false, then control falls through to the second evaluation. When the subexpression *B* is evaluated, if the result is true then once again we branch to the alternate label. Otherwise the whole expression *A* **or** *B* has evaluated false, and we must fall through, as required. The code inside *FallFalse* to emit the *IL* for the **or** operator will look like this —

```
procedure (emtr  :  MsilEmitter)FallFalse(exp  :  Expr;
                                          lbl  :  INTEGER);
    ...                         (* case exp.kind of *)
  | orOp  :  emtr.FallFalse(exp.lKid, lbl);
            emtr.FallFalse(exp.rKid, lbl);
  |  ...       (* other cases *)
```

This is particularly simple. The code just calls itself on the two subtrees, passing the same alternate label to each invocation.

The right of Figure 9.5 shows how *FallTrue* would decompose the expression. In this case, as before, we begin by evaluating *A*. Only if this first evaluation returns false do we evaluate the second term. We must thus begin with a *FallFalse* on *A*. If the second

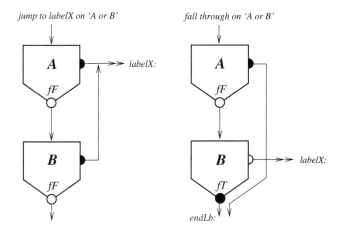

Figure 9.5: Control flow of *FallFalse* and *FallTrue* for "*A* **or** *B*"

term returns true then we fall through as required. Only if both of the evaluations return false will we branch to the alternate label, *labelX* in the diagram. If the first evaluation returns true then we immediately branch to the "fall-through" location in the *IL*. Because the control flow *branches* to the "fall-through" location as well as *falling through* to the location, we must allocate a label to the location. The code inside *FallTrue* to emit the *IL* for the **or** operator will look like this —

```
procedure (emtr : MsilEmitter)FallTrue(exp : Expr;
                                       lbl : INTEGER);
   ...                            (* case exp.kind of *)
 | orOp : ftLb := iFil.newLabel();
           emtr.FallFalse(exp.lKid, ftLb);
           emtr.FallTrue(exp.rKid, lbl);
           iFil.DefLabel(ftLb);      (* emit the label ftLb *)
 | ...      (* other cases *)
```

This case is more complicated since we must get a new label to use for the short-circuit branch to the fall-through location. We must also emit that label, when we reach the end. Otherwise, the pattern of recursion is as shown on the right of Figure 9.5.

The decomposition of the **and** operator is dual to that for the **or**. Figure 9.6 shows how the expression *A* **and** *B* would be decomposed. The left of the figure shows how *FallTrue* would decompose the expression. If the expression *A* evaluates to false, we may immediately branch to the alternate label, *labelX* in the figure. If the expression *A* evaluates true, then control falls through to the second evaluation. When the subexpression *B* is evaluated, if the result is false then once again we branch to the alternate label. Otherwise the whole expression *A* **and** *B* has evaluated true and we must fall through, as required. The code inside *FallTrue* to emit the *IL* for the **and** operator will look like this —

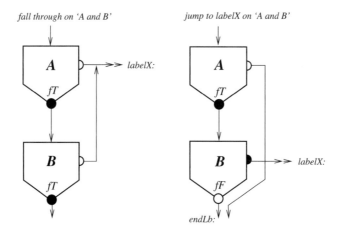

Figure 9.6: Control flow of *FallTrue* and *FallFalse* for "*A* **and** *B*"

```
procedure (emtr : MsilEmitter) FallTrue (exp  : Expr;
                                         lbl  : INTEGER);
   ...                               (* case exp.kind of *)
 | andOp  : emtr.FallTrue (exp.lKid, lbl);
            emtr.FallTrue (exp.rKid, lbl);
 | ...          (* other cases *)
```

This is particularly simple. The code just calls itself on the two subtrees, passing the same alternate label to each invocation.

The right of the figure shows how *FallFalse* would decompose the same expression. In this case, as before, we begin by evaluating *A*. Only if this first evaluation returns true do we evaluate the second term. We must thus begin with a *FallTrue* on *A*. If the second term returns false, then we fall through as required. Only if both of the evaluations return true will we branch to the alternate label, *labelX* in the diagram. If the first evaluation returns false, then we immediately branch to the "fall-through" location in the *IL*. Because the control flow *branches* to the "fall-through" location as well as *falling through* to the location, we must allocate a label to the location. The code inside *FallFalse* to emit the *IL* for the **and** operator will look like this —

```
procedure (emtr : MsilEmitter) FallFalse (exp  : Expr;
                                          lbl  : INTEGER);
   ...                                (* case exp.kind of *)
 | andOp  : ftLb := iFil.newLabel ();
            emtr.FallTrue (exp.lKid,  ftLb);
            emtr.FallFalse (exp.rKid, lbl);
            iFil.DefLabel (ftLb);  (* emit the label ftLb *)
 | ...          (* other cases *)
```

Finally, we should consider what to do inside these methods for other expression descriptor node-kinds. The case for the "notOp" operator is rather cute. No code is emitted, but the code recurses by calling the dual method on the subtree. Consider the case of *FallTrue*. We have —

```
procedure (emtr : MsilEmitter) FallTrue (exp : Expr;
                                         lbl : INTEGER);
   ...                            (* case exp.kind of *)
  | notOp : emtr.FallFalse (exp.child, lbl);
  | ...                           (* other cases *)
```

If the expression (**not** A) is supposed to fall through on a true result, then we get the same effect by falling through if A evaluates false! You may be able to verify that this code implements the identity $\forall A \in \mathcal{B} : \neg(\neg A) = A$ at zero runtime cost.

If the expression is a variable designator, or a function returning a Boolean result, then we drop out of the branching code by calling *PushValue* on the designator. We follow this by the *IL* instruction "brfalse" or "brtrue" for *FallTrue* and *FallFalse* respectively. If the expression is a Boolean literal (possibly as a result of constant folding during semantic analysis) then we may emit an unconditional branch, or nothing at all, as required.

Finally, as a basis case, we must consider the blocks from which all jumping code is built. These are the comparisons that will translate into the various compare-and-branch instructions. Let us for the moment concentrate just on the whole-number comparisons; the added complication of other types can wait until later. For the whole-number types, we usually have six binary node-kinds, $\{=, \neq, <, \leq, \geq, >\}$, and the unary zero/nonzero tests. The binary comparisons all follow the same pattern. We push the values of the two subtrees and perform a compare-and-branch instruction. Since the names of the branch instructions are taken from the condition for which the branch is *taken*, the mapping is immediate for the *FallFalse* method. Figure 9.7 shows the detail. The corresponding code for *FallTrue* needs the sense of the comparisons reversed, since we wish to branch if the test fails. The pattern is the same as Figure 9.7, but the emitted instructions are all different, as seen in Figure 9.8.

Of course, as well as these whole-number comparisons, we also have comparisons on other types. The *IL* for the floating point types requires little further work, since the compare-and-branch instructions in *.NET* are polymorphic.[2] However string comparisons require some additional work. The strategy that *gpcp* uses for string comparisons is to call a runtime support function that returns -1, 0, or $+1$, according to whether the left string is less than, equal to, or greater than the right string. If we are encoding an equality or inequality test, we may emit a "brfalse" or "brtrue" instruction. Otherwise we push a literal zero and perform the same compare instructions as in the two previous figures.

---

[2]Well, if precise behavior for floating point values is required, the branch instructions in Figures 9.7 and 9.8 should only be used for whole-number types, and the instructions in Figure 2.18 substituted in the floating point case.

```
procedure (emtr : MsilEmitter) FallFalse (exp : Expr;
                                          lbl : INTEGER);
  ... (* other node kinds *)
  emtr.PushValue(exp.lKid);
  emtr.PushValue(exp.rKid);
  case exp.kind of
  | eqOp : iFil.CodeLb(opc_beq, lbl);      (* branch if = *)
  | neOp : iFil.CodeLb(opc_bne_un, lbl);   (* branch if ≠ *)
  | ltOp : iFil.CodeLb(opc_blt, lbl);      (* branch if < *)
  | leOp : iFil.CodeLb(opc_ble, lbl);      (* branch if ≤ *)
  | geOp : iFil.CodeLb(opc_bge, lbl);      (* branch if ≥ *)
  | gtOp : iFil.CodeLb(opc_bgt, lbl);      (* branch if > *)
  end; (* case *)
end FallFalse;
```

Figure 9.7: Comparison code inside *FallFalse*

```
procedure (emtr : MsilEmitter) FallTrue (exp : Expr;
                                         lbl : INTEGER);
  ... (* other node kinds *)
  emtr.PushValue(exp.lKid);
  emtr.PushValue(exp.rKid);
  case exp.kind of
  | eqOp : iFil.CodeLb(opc_bne_un, lbl);   (* fall if = *)
  | neOp : iFil.CodeLb(opc_beq, lbl);      (* fall if ≠ *)
  | ltOp : iFil.CodeLb(opc_bge, lbl);      (* fall if < *)
  | leOp : iFil.CodeLb(opc_bgt, lbl);      (* fall if ≤ *)
  | geOp : iFil.CodeLb(opc_blt, lbl);      (* fall if ≥ *)
  | gtOp : iFil.CodeLb(opc_ble, lbl);      (* fall if > *)
  end; (* case *)
end FallTrue;
```

Figure 9.8: Comparison code inside *FallTrue*

It is also usually the case that there are other comparisons as well as those discussed so far. *Component Pascal* has an *instance of* test for extensible types and a bitset membership test. The first uses the "isinst" instruction in a straighforward manner. Set membership involves some bit-twiddling to shift and mask out the bit of interest.

Putting it all together: pushing Booleans.

The methods that emit branching code do so in two different contexts. First, there are the places where the purpose of evaluating the Boolean expression is to affect flow of control. In such cases it is clear that the code emitter will call for the emission of jumping code. The second context is one in which the purpose of evaluating the expression is the pushing of a Boolean value on the stack. In such cases, the emission of jumping code is required only if the language semantics demand it. In short, sometimes we call *FallFalse* or *FallTrue* because we want control to branch. Other times we really do want *PushValue* but are forced to resort to jumping code anyway.

In general, for languages that specify short-circuit evaluation, jumping code is specified whenever a Boolean **and** or **or** operator is encountered. Whenever that is the case, we must, in effect, compute the Boolean as a conditional expression. Figure 9.9 shows how these cases are handled inside *PushBinary*. We must begin by allocating two new labels, one for branching within the expression and the other for the exit label at the end. This is no more than a special case of code that evaluated a conditional expression in Figure 9.3. The emitted *IL* will have the form —

```
              <IL from "FallTrue(exp, fLab)">
              ldc.i4.1                       // push a true value
              br mLab
      fLab:
              ldc.i4.0                       // push a false value
      mLab:
```

```
procedure (emtr  :   MsilEmitter)PushBinary(exp  :   BinaryX);
    ...                                    (* case exp.kind of *)
 | boolOr, BoolAnd :
      fLab := iFil.newLabel();             (* false label *)
      xLab := iFil.newLabel();             (* exit label *)
      emtr.FallTrue(exp, fLab);            (* branch to fLab if false *)
      iFil.PushLit(1);                     (* push the "true" value *)
      iFil.CodeLb(opc_br, xLab);           (* branch to exit label *)
      iFil.DefLabel(fLab);
      iFil.PushLit(0);                     (* push the "false" value *)
      iFil.DefLabel(xLab);
 | ...                                     (* other cases *)
```

Figure 9.9: Pushing a Boolean expression, using jumping code

The runtime cost of jumping code is quite high for most architectures. It is always best to avoid branching of any kind, so as to keep the processor pipeline full. Therefore jumping code should be avoided unless the semantics demand it. Consider the pushing of Boolean values arising from the comparison operators. We *could* use the same case statement branch that is shown in Figure 9.9, but this is almost certainly not best. Instead, we should use the nonbranching code shown in Figure 2.14.[3] Figure 9.10 shows how to emit the code for the integer cases. The floating point and string comparisons require a little extra code but do not require the emission of jumping code either.

```
procedure (emtr  :   MsilEmitter) PushBinary (exp  :   BinaryX);
   ...                                      (* case exp.kind of *)
   | eqOp, neOp, ltOp, leOp, geOp, gtOp :
        emtr.PushValue (exp.lKid);
        emtr.PushValue (exp.rKid);
        iFil.Code (<instruction from Figure 2.14>);
        if <exp.kind ∈ {neOp, geOp, leOp}> then
          iFil.PushLit (1);
          iFil.Code (opc_xor)
        end
   | ...                                        (* other cases *)
```

Figure 9.10: Pushing an *integer* Boolean comparison, avoiding jumping code

The underlying principle is very simple. Branching control flow carries a penalty, and the transition *back* from jumping to value code adds another cost. Therefore, if we are pushing a value, we should try to avoid switching to jumping code. However, once we have been forced to make the switch, it is best not to convert back to Boolean values on the stack until forced.

The simple strategy that has been discussed here generates good code in a majority of situations. Nevertheless, the switch between jumping code and stack evaluation is based on local information. Truly optimal results require dynamic programming on entire trees. This may be done elegantly, using *bottom-up tree rewriting*, but requires specialized tools.

A typical but rare pathological case is the comparing of Boolean expressions, when at least one of the values must be evaluated by jumping code. Consider the task of generating *IL* to take a conditional branch on the expression $(A = B)$, where A and B are Boolean expressions that must be evaluated using jumping code. The problem is that our code generator will want to perform the equality test after *pushing* the two Boolean values. These Boolean values will be computed by the ugly transition from jumping to value code emitted by Figure 9.9. In effect we switch from jumping to value code, and then back to jumping code, accumulating multiple runtime penalties.

It is easy to show by exhaustive case analysis that the control flow of Figure 9.11 correctly implements branching on the expression $(A = B)$. Figure 9.12 compares the *IL* sequences that would be produced by the two strategies. On the left is *IL* that constructs the two Boolean values on the top of the stack and then compares them. On the right is

---

[3] In the *JVM* there are no equivalent instructions, and the creation of Boolean values from comparisons cannot avoid the emission of jumping code.

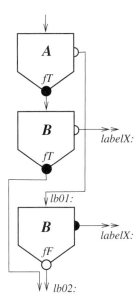

Figure 9.11: Control flow for $(A = B)$, where A and B are Boolean expressions

the *IL* that implements the control flow of Figure 9.11. The *IL* on the right is not necessarily shorter, since the jumping code for B is repeated. However, the number of branch instructions executed along every path on the right is less.

<IL from FallTrue(A,lb01)> ldc.i1.1 br lb02 lb01: ldc.i1.0 lb02: <IL from FallTrue(B,lb03)> ldc.i1.1 br lb04 lb03: ldc.i1.0 lb04: bne.un labelX	<IL from FallTrue(A,lb01)> <IL from FallTrue(B,labelX)> br lb02 lb01: <IL from FallFalse(B,labelX)> lb02:

Figure 9.12: Comparing *IL* for $(A = B)$, where A and B are Boolean expressions

Of the six possible comparisons of Boolean values, four are able to be transformed away during tree rewriting. We may transform the Boolean comparisons by means of the following identities —

$$
\begin{array}{rcl}
A \leq B & = & \textbf{not } A \textbf{ or } B \\
A < B & = & \textbf{not } A \textbf{ and } B \\
A \geq B & = & A \textbf{ or not } B \\
A > B & = & A \textbf{ and not } B
\end{array}
$$

If that is done, then the existing infrastructure of the *Fall** methods will produce the spectacularly more efficient *IL* for these four cases.

For the remaining two cases, equality and its opposite, the situation is much more difficult to handle. There does not appear to be any standard way to express the control flow shown in Figure 9.11 as an expression. Apparently the best we can do is —

```
if A then
    if not B then goto labelX end
else
    if B then goto labelX end
end
<fall through code here>
```

Because expressions of these kinds are so rare, even *gpcp* does not attempt to optimize these cases.

Choices and Loops

Encoding Choices

The control flow statements comprise the *choice* constructs and the *loop* constructs. In *Component Pascal* there are three choice statements. The **if ... then ... else ... end** construct and the typecase **with** statement share the same abstract syntax. The multiway **case** statement branch is unique, and is described in a separate section.

Folding Boolean constants.   In our model architecture constant expressions were folded aggressively, and the trees in the *AST* rewritten accordingly. However, statements were not rewritten, so that on occasions the code emitter may have to emit *IL* for a branch that is predicated on a Boolean *literal*. This possibility suggests that some of the statements of the *AST* may be statically known to be unreachable.

There is another source of dead code in *IL* that should also be avoided. Suppose we have a structure —

```
if <condition1> then
    return                          (* exit from procedure *)
elsif <condition-2> then
    . . .
```

The normal encoding of a **then** clause is to emit the *IL* for the controlled statements of the clause, and then emit an unconditional branch to the end of the entire **if** statement.

```
                <IL for "if" test>
                bXX nxtTst                 // if false branch to next test
                <IL for "then" statements>  // controlled statements here
                br   exitLb                // branch to end of if statement
        nxtTst: ...                        // start next elsif test here
```

In our example with the *return* statement the unconditional branch instruction "`br`" will be unreachable, as the control flow finds the "`ret`" instruction in the "then statements" first. Return, throw, and halt statements all have analogous consequences.

One way of handling both of these reachability concerns is to use a utility that emits the *IL* for statements and returns a Boolean indicating whether control might possibly return from the emitted *IL*. Whenever it is known that it is impossible for control to return, the utility returns a false value. A first example of the use of this "liveness" flag is the encoding of the compound statement. Figure 9.13 has the details. In this code we iterate over the statements of the statement sequence. If for some reason the *IL* emitted for one of the statements will not return at runtime, then *EmitBlock* returns, emitting no *IL* for later statements of the sequence. Furthermore, we return a false result as the out value of the invocation of *EmitBlock*.

```
procedure (emtr : MsilEmitter) EmitBlock (stat : Block;
                                          out live :  BOOLEAN);
  var index :  INTEGER;
begin
  live  := TRUE;                          (* flag initially set live *)
  for index := 0 to stat.sequ.tide-1 do
    emtr.EmitStat (stat.sequ.a[index], live);
    if ~live then return end;
  end; (* for *)
end EmitBlock;
```

Figure 9.13: Emitting code for compound statement, showing live flag

If-then-else structures.

If statements, in our model abstract syntax, have a structure with two equal length sequences. One is a sequence of statements, while the other is a sequence of predicates. Each predicate is the condition for the corresponding statement. The last predicate in the sequence may be **nil**, denoting that the last statement is the unconditional **else** part.

The overall structure of the emitted *IL* is a sequence of predicate evaluations and their corresponding *controlled statement*. A true evaluation of the predicate causes the code to fall through into the controlled statement. A false evaluation causes control to branch to the next predicate evaluation, if there is one. At the end of each controlled statement except the last we insert an unconditional branch to the end of the exit label. Figure 9.14 has the skeleton of an implementation for an *IL* emission algorithm. This simple algorithm does not show the computation of the output liveness parameter *rslt*. This value should be set to true if any of the calls to emit the controlled statement *IL* returns true. Similarly, if the statement does not have an **else** part, then the result liveness parameter should be set to true, since control can reach the exit by falling through from the final predicate evaluation.

```
procedure (emtr : MsilEmitter)EmitIf(stat : Choice;
                                 out rslt :   BOOLEAN);
  var indx :  INTEGER;        (* sequence index *)
      exLb :  INTEGER;        (* exit label *)
      nxtP :  INTEGER;        (* next predicate label *)
begin
  exLb := emtr.outF.newLabel();          (* allocate exit label *)
  for indx := 0 to stat.blocks.tide-1 do
    nxtP := emtr.outF.newLabel();        (* next predicate label *)
    if stat.preds.a[indx] # nil then      (* not the else branch, so... *)
       emtr.FallTrue(stat.preds.a[indx], nxtP);
    end;
    emtr.EmitStat(stat.blocks.a[indx], live);
    <if live and not last branch, emit "br exLb">
    emtr.outF.DefLabel(nxtP);
  end; (* for *)
  emtr.outF.DefLabel(exLb);
  <set rslt flag>
end EmitIf;
```

Figure 9.14: Emitting code for **if ... then ... else**

There are a number of improvements that may be made to the code of this emission algorithm, if optimal accuracy is a goal. Firstly, we note that if any of the predicates has been folded to a Boolean literal, then this should be taken into account. If the predicate is true, then any further branches are dead code and should be suppressed. Similarly, if the predicate is false, neither the predicate nor the controlled statement should be emitted.

In view of what was discussed in the previous section, we should check the *live* flag after emitting *IL* for each controlled statement. If the flag is false, we do not emit the unconditional branch. Similarly, we also do not wish to emit a senseless unconditional branch following the final controlled statement.

In this example, we accumulate the liveness result in the output parameter. Each of the calls to emit *IL* for a single branch of the statement returns a liveness result. If any one of these returns true, then we know that the exit label *exLb* is reachable. If the statement has no unconditional **else** part, then behavior is the same as if the statement had an empty else part, and the exit is always reachable.

Encoding typecase structures.
Typecase statements have the same abstract syntax as sequential **if** statements in our model and share the same decision structure in the *IL*. The nature of the tests is somewhat different, however.

Each test in a typecase structure has a predicate that is an "`isinst`" instruction. This instruction returns **null** if the test fails, so that we may follow the instance test with an unsigned test against **null**. With the right choice of encoding of the *AST*, we may almost use the code of Figure 9.14 unchanged. An important semantic difference between the two forms in *Component Pascal* is that **with** (typecase) statements that do not have an explicit **else** part trap at runtime if no predicate evaluates to true. We need to add code similar to the following to the end of the equivalent of Figure 9.14 —

```
procedure (emtr : MsilEmitter) EmitWith(...);
    ... (* similar to if statement *)
  end; (* of per-branch for loop *)
  if <no else-part> then emtr.EmitTrap() end;
  emtr.outF.DefLabel(exLb);
  <set rslt flag>
end EmitWith;
```

In the *IL* for a typecase statement, in order to ensure verifiability, it is necessary to copy the selected value to a local variable. After the "`isinst`" instruction, if the top of stack is **null**, control branches to the next test or the else part perhaps. If the value is non-**null**, we copy it to a temporary local variable that is declared to be of the selected type. Of course, within the guarded region used occurrences of the selected variable must be bound to the temporary. If a language allowed mutation of the selected variable, the temporary would need to be copied back to its original location at the end of the guarded region.

Encoding Loops

Leaving to one side the specialized loops, such as the **for** loops in many procedural languages, we have two varieties of loop. We have loops that test for continuation at the top of the loop, the so-called *pretested* loops, and those that test for continuation at the bottom of the loop, the so-called *post-tested* loops.

Pre- and post-tested loops.
The pretested loops are the **while ... do** loops of many languages, while the post-tested loops variously include **repeat ... until** and **do ... while** loops. The essential semantic difference between these two types is that in the latter case we are guaranteed that the loop body will be entered at least once. In the former case it is possible that the loop body will be executed zero times.

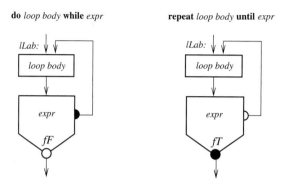

Figure 9.15: Post-tested loop layout

The post-tested loops are simple. The structure of the *IL* is as shown in Figure 9.15. In both cases, control flow falls into the loop body. Any control flow that emerges from the loop body falls into *IL* that evaluates the predicate. In the case of a **do ... while** we want control to exit if the predicate evaluates false, so we emit the *IL* with *FallFalse*, with the top-of-loop label *lLab* as the alternative. In the case of a **repeat ... until** we want control to exit if the predicate evaluates true, so we emit the *IL* with *FallTrue*, with the top-of-loop label *lLab* as the alternative.

The layout of **while** loops is a little more involved, since there are multiple possibilities to consider. Figure 9.16 shows three of these possibilities. On the left of the figure is the layout that is most intuitive from the source language syntax. Control flow falls into the test, which is a *FallTrue* evaluation. If the evaluation is true, control falls into the loop body. The loop body is followed by an unconditional branch that takes control back to the top of the predicate test. In this case we must allocate an explicit exit label, *xLab* in the figure, to which control branches to exit (or bypass) the loop.

The middle diagram of Figure 9.16 is the layout used for **while** loops by a majority of compilers. The control flow *begins* with an unconditional branch to the top of the test, label *eLab* in the diagram. The test branches on true to the loop label at the top of the loop body. If the test evaluates false, control falls out of the test and into the next sequential statement.

The final layout considered here is the one used by *gpcp*. In this case, shown on the right of Figure 9.16, there are two tests in the *IL*. A test at the top, emitted by *FallTrue*, checks if the loop should be skipped over altogether. This test is always performed exactly once. If the first test evaluates true, control falls into the loop body. Any control flow emerging from the loop body falls into the second test. This second test is emitted by *FallFalse* and will be performed as many times as the loop is executed. If the second test evaluates to false, control falls out of the loop and on to the next sequential statement. If the evaluation returns true, the loop continues by branching to the loop header label, *lLab*. This particular loop layout uses a little more code space because of the repetition of the two tests,

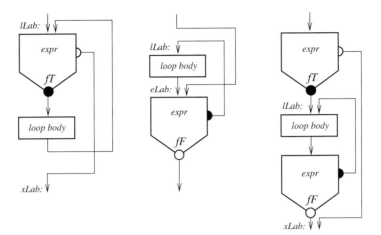

Figure 9.16: Pretested **while** loop layout

but it achieves a much nicer control flow. For many simple benchmarks the performance is better for this layout.

No matter which layout is adopted for pretested loops, there is always the possibility that semantic analysis will determine that the loop will always execute at least once. Most usually this would be determined by constant propagation. Where this is the case, the **while** loop may usefully be transformed into a **do ... while** and laid out as on the left of Figure 9.15.

Harder cases: the for loop. The encoding of **for** loops provides further opportunities for specialization, since we have more semantic information about the intended behavior than is the case for other loops. The precise semantics of these loops is quite variable from language to language. In *ANSI C* the statement —

> **for** (*<expr1>*; *<expr2>*; *<expr3>*)
> 　*<loop body>*

is equivalent to the expanded form —

>   {
>   *<expr1>*;
>   **while** (*<expr2>*) {
>   *<loop body>*;
>   *<expr3>*;
>   }
>   }

Of course, the expressions *expr1* and *expr3* are usually evaluated only for their side effects. In *C* the expressions are unrestricted in their form.

The *Pascal*-family languages have a more constrained **for** loop structure, in which a control variable is incremented or decremented on each iteration. Nevertheless, there are significant differences between the detailed semantics of the statement in different family members. In both *ISO-Modula-2* and *Component Pascal* the form of the statements is —

```
for cvar := <expr1> to <expr2> by <step> do
    <loop body>
end
```

The variable *cvar* is called the *control variable* of the loop. In this syntax the "**by** *step*" part is optional, and *step* must be a compile-time constant expression. Nevertheless, given this shared syntax, the semantics are different in the two languages. In *Component Pascal*, as in *Oberon-2*, the semantics of this statement are *defined* as being equivalent to the following sequence —

```
temp := <expr2>; cvar := <expr1>;
while cvar <= temp do
    <loop body>;
    INC(cvar, step);
end
```

This is the expansion for the case where *step* is greater than zero. For the negative, "counting down" case, the test and increment operations have the obvious changes.

In *ISO-Modula-2* the expansion of the code is the same, but the semantic conditions for correctness make the implementation of the statement dramatically different. In *Modula-2* the control variable must be an entire variable that is local to the scope. It may not be a component of a structure, may not be imported, and may not have its value *threatened* within the body of the loop. The language standard spells out in gruesome detail exactly what is meant for a variable to be threatened. The idea is that there should be no way that the control variable may be mutated within the loop except by the ordered increment or decrement of the definition. Therefore, within the loop body, a control variable may not be on the left of an assignment statement, may not be passed as an actual parameter to a reference-mode formal parameter, and may not have its address taken. The precise definition of threatening requires about 15 pages of formal semantics in *VDM-SL* notation.[4] It might have just been easier to say that legal programs treat the control variable as read-only inside the loop. In any case, the consequence of the intended *Modula-2* semantics is to ensure that the control variable is an *induction variable* and may be transformed or optimized away under many circumstances. It also means, for native code compilers, that the control variable can reside in a register throughout the loop body. In the case of *IL* the read-only guarantee means that within the loop the control variable value may always

---

[4]And turns out to be ineffective anyhow. There is a sneak path in which the control variable is passed to a reference formal *outside* the loop but has its address taken by the called procedure. This allows arbitrary mutation of the control variable in secret ways within the loop body.

reside in a temporary local variable, even if the control variable is (say) a static variable *outside* the loop.

It should also be noted that in practice a large proportion of all **for** loops have limits that are literal constants. When this is the case, the **while** loops of the definitions may be able to be expanded into the more efficient **do ... while** form. If your language has sufficiently strong guarantees of control variable immutability, or the static analysis of your compiler front-end is sufficiently smart, you may be able to determine the exact number of iterations at compile time. This may allow loop unrolling to be considered.

In *gpcp*, as a matter of convenience, emission of **for** loops is performed by four separate methods. There are separate cases for the up-counting and down-counting versions and separate code for integer and long-integer control variables. All of this could have been done in one big method, but the separate cases are easier to understand.

Generating Inline Loops

There are a number of circumstances in which copying of value arrays occurs. Languages that allow entire assignments of array values provide one example, but any language that allows value arrays to be passed by value requires array copies also. In such cases the mechanism by which the copy is realized is left to the the compiler to determine. In contrast, for languages that do not have value arrays it is necessary to explicitly specify an element-by-element copying loop in the source code if an array has to be duplicated.

It would be possible to perform such array copies by means of a call to a static procedure, but it is probably a better choice to emit an inline loop. Multidimensional arrays of arrays and arrays of dynamic length pose interesting problems for the generation of *IL*. In this section we explore some of the possibilities.

There are two scenarios in which array copying takes place. In the first, the destination array is already allocated and is known to have the same shape as the source array. The second scenario requires a *clone* of the array to be created. The first case is much simpler.

If multidimensional arrays are realized by means of the facilities of the *System.Array* class, then all of these operations are provided by library methods. Therefore we consider the single dimensional array case, where the array elements may themselves be reference arrays.

Copying array contents. Suppose that we wish to perform a "*deep copy*" of the contents of one array to another, when the destination array already exists. This is what is needed to achieve the entire value assignment in the presence of reference surrogates. We shall assume that it is statically known that the two arrays have the same dimensionality and the same length in each dimension. The convention that we shall adopt is the same as for any other assignment. The source array reference is on the top of the evaluation stack, with the destination array reference immediately below that. At completion, the stack should be empty.

The per-element copy loop will make use of three temporary local variables. These are the source and destination references, and the element index. The *IL* in the case of scalar element types could be as shown in Figure 9.17. In this particular case the array index counts down from highest index to zero. This allows a cheap test for loop termination, by checking whether the zeroth element has just been copied. Just above the loop label, we copy the source and destination references to the temporary local variables and initialize the temporary *elIx* to the length of the array. This may take the value from either the compile time array descriptor, if the array is of a known, fixed length, or the "ldlen" instruction, to fetch the array length at runtime. As was noted earlier, array element assignments may also be performed by taking the addresses of both source and destination elements, then copying the element with a "ldind, stind" instruction pair.

```
        <initialize temporary locals>
lLab:                                   // the loop label
    ldloc 'elIx'                        // get array index
    ldc.i4.1
    sub
    stloc 'elIx'                        // ... and decrement
    ldloc 'dstRef'                      // stack: ... dst
    ldloc 'elIx'                        // stack: ... dst,ix
    ldloc 'srcRef'                      // stack: ... dst,ix,src
    ldloc 'elIx'                        // stack: ... dst,ix,src,ix
    ldelem.NN                           // stack: ... dst,ix,elem
    stelem.NN                           // stack: ...
    ldloc 'elIx'                        // get array index
    brtrue lLab                         // loop if not zero
```

Figure 9.17: Per-element array copying loop, scalar element case

There are three other element kinds to consider. As well as the scalars in the example, the array elements could be value class objects, reference class objects, or reference arrays. The *IL* required for these three cases shares a common structure with the scalar case. This suggests that it is a simple matter to emit all four cases with the same emitter method, conditionally emitting any unique instructions as required for each particular element kind. Figure 9.18 compares the three cases. The middle column, for the value class element kind, almost exactly mirrors the alternative version of the scalar case in which the element addresses are computed.

When the array elements are themselves reference surrogates, the copying must be performed explicitly. For reference class elements, a call to the copy method of the class is required. For nested arrays, a recursive call to the same emitter procedure will generate a nested loop. Note that the evaluation stack at the point of the copy is exactly as required, with the source reference on top and the destination reference underneath.

scalar element	value class element	object ref. element
lLab:	lLab:	lLab:
\<decrement elIx\>	*\<decrement elIx\>*	*\<decrement elIx\>*
ldloc 'dstRef'	ldloc 'dstRef'	ldloc 'dstRef'
ldloc 'elIx'	ldloc 'elIx'	ldloc 'elIx'
	ldelema *TpRef*	ldelem.ref
ldloc 'srcRef'	ldloc 'srcRef'	ldloc 'srcRef'
ldloc 'elIx'	ldloc 'elIx'	ldloc 'elIx'
	ldelema *TpRef*	ldelem.ref
ldelem.*NN*	ldobj *TpRef*	*\<recursive copy\>*
stelem.*NN*	stobj *TpRef*	
\<test and branch\>	*\<test and branch\>*	*\<test and branch\>*

Figure 9.18: Per-element array copying loop, various element kinds

Cloning an array. When a new array must be created, and the contents of the source array copied into the new array, we say that the source array has been *cloned*. Array cloning occurs in languages with value arrays, whenever such an array is passed by value to a formal array argument. We may achieve this result by creating a new array of the same shape as our source array, then applying the same inline copying *IL* discussed above. The overall outline of the *IL* in the general case has this form —

> *\<allocate temporaries l_1 to l_n\>*
> *\<compute lengths into temporaries\>*
> ldloc l_1
> newarr *TRef$_1$*   // *allocate outer array*
> *\<initialize elements with loop if necessary\>*
> *\<release temporaries l_1 to l_n\>*

where *TRef$_1$* is a type reference to the array element type. The elements of the array need an initialization loop whenever the element type is a reference surrogate. In the case of an explicit reference type the elements will be initialized to **null** by the "newarr" instruction.

If the elements are reference class objects then the initialization may be performed as shown in Figure 9.19. In this figure, the element objects are allocated and initialized inside the loop, and assigned by the "stelem.ref" instruction.

In the case of arrays of arrays, the "newobj" instruction is replaced by another initialization loop. Figure 9.20 is the skeleton of the entire inline code required to create an array in which to copy an array of arrays of some class *T*. In this case we need two nested loops. One allocates the second dimension of the array of arrays, while the inner loop invokes the constructor that allocates the element objects of type *T*. At entry to the code, the stack holds a reference to the array that is to be cloned. At completion the new array is on the top of the stack. It follows that to duplicate and copy the array, we would need to save

```
        ldloc lᵢ                              // push i-th length
        newarr TRefᵢ                          // allocate i-th dimension
        stloc 'aRef'                          // save array reference
    lLab:                                     // loop label
        <decrement lᵢ>
        ldloc 'aRef'                          // push array reference
        ldloc lᵢ                              // push array index
        newobj instance void TRefᵢ::.ctor()   // allocate element object
        stelem.ref                            // store new element ref.
        <branch to lLab if lᵢ not zero>
```

Figure 9.19: Initializing an array of reference objects

```
    ...                                       // source array is on stack
    dup
    ldlen
    stloc.0                                   // local 0 is l₁
    ldc.i4.0
    ldelem.ref                                // get src[0] array
    ldlen
    stloc.1                                   // local 1 is l₂
    ldloc.0
    newarr T[]                                // allocate first dimension
    stloc.2                                   // save array reference
    lLab1:                                    // outer loop label
        <decrement local 0>
        ldloc.2                               // push array reference
        ldloc.0                               // push outer index
        newarr T                              // allocate inner array
        stloc.3                               // save element reference
        lLab2:                                // inner loop label
            <decrement local 1>
            ldloc.3                           // push array reference
            ldloc.1                           // push inner index
            newobj instance void T::.ctor()   // allocate element object
            stelem.ref                        // store new element ref.
        <branch to lLab2 if local 1 not zero>
        stelem.ref                            // store new element ref.
    <branch to lLab1 if local 0 not zero>
    ldloc.2                                   // push array reference
```

Figure 9.20: Initializing an array of array of object, prior to copying

the source array, so as to push it again after the allocation, before falling into the array copy *IL* on the right-hand column of Figure 9.18.

Of course, if the array to duplicate is an array of known length in each dimension, we may skip the code at the beginning of Figure 9.20. This is the more common case in *Pascal*-family programs, with the exceptional case occurring when an incoming conformant (open) array is passed out as a conformant actual parameter.

Switch Statement Encoding

In the statement attribution section (see page 184) the semantic analysis of **case** or **switch** statements was discussed. In this section we shall look at the implementation of such statements. In the first instance we shall treat the raw facilities provided by *CIL*, based on *jump tables*. In following sections we shall look at the improved methods based on the recognition of groups of dense ranges.

Jump Tables

The *CLR* provides for the implementation of multiway branches using a jump table. This facility allows for a straightforward implementation of multiway branches. A typical use of the "switch" instruction looks like this —

```
        <push selector value on stack>
    switch (           // start label table
            lb01,      // first label
            ...,
            lb07)      // last label
    br      lb08       // branch to default label
```

The action of the instruction is to check the top-of-stack value. If it lies between zero and the length of the label list, then control transfers to the destination location found by indexing into the list. If the selector value is outside the range of the list, then control transfers to the next *IL* instruction following the list. In the example this would be an unconditional branch to the default statement sequence. Of course, we might have arranged for the default code to immediately follow the list.

In a native-code setting, the emitted code would have had explicit instructions to detect values outside the table range and to branch to the default label in such cases. In *.NET* this checking is encapsulated into the operational semantics of the "switch" instruction. This is a necessary design choice, because the verifier must be satisfied that it is impossible to index outside the table bounds. In general it would be difficult for the verifier to ensure that the code explicitly guaranteed the boundedness, so building the semantics into the instruction resolves the difficulty.

In order to emit this *IL*, we need to allocate labels to the entry points of the various cases, the default case, and an exit label. We assume that we have computed the minimum and maximum selector values and have a list of the values, in order, with a map to the ordinal of the selected case statement sequence. The code that emits this *IL* would have the form of Figure 9.21. Not shown in the figure is the code that accumulates the liveness result for the emission method. This flag should be true if any one of the cases returns a true live result. In languages such as *Component Pascal*, in the event that there is no default branch to the statement, a trap should be emitted in the default statement position.

```
for <all cases in switch> do
    iFil.DefLabel(<this case label>);
    emtr.EmitStat(<this case statement>, live);
    if live then iFil.CodeLb(opc_br, xLab) end;
end; (* for *)
emtr.PushValue(<selector expression>);
<emit code to subtract lowest case selector>;
<emit start of switch instruction>;
iFil.EmitLabelList(stmt);              (* emit case label list *)
<emit end of switch instruction>;
iFil.DefLabel(defL);                   (* emit the default label *)
emtr.EmitStat(<default statement>, live);
iFil.DefLabel(xLab);                   (* emit the exit label *)
```

Figure 9.21: Code to emit *IL* for simple switch statement

In this example, we are assuming that the range of case selectors does not necessarily start at zero. Since the first entry in the table is for index zero, we need to construct the value *<selector expression – minimum value>* on the top of the stack. In the example we have emitted the default case directly after the switch statement, so as to avoid a branch to a branch at runtime. The emission of the label list iterates over the case selector value list. We must remember to fill in any gaps in the list with references to the default label. For the data structure based on a triples list, as shown in Figure 6.9, we have one triple per selector range, in the form (*minR*, *maxR*, *index*), where *minR* is the low element of the range, *maxR* is the high element of the range, and *index* is the index of the selected case. Since the triples are sorted in ascending order of *minR* value, we may emit the label lists by iterating over the complete selector range from the minimum value, *min*, to the maximum value, *max*. For each selector value if the value is less than the minimum of the current range, we emit a default label. If the value is within the current range we emit the label of the selected case. Finally, when we have emitted the selector value corresponding to the maximum of the current range, we increment the triples index to select the next range.

```
j := 0;                          (* j is index into triples array *)
for i := min to max do
  if i < triple[j].minR then <emit default label>
  else
     <emit label of case triple[j].index>;
     if i = triple[j].maxR then INC(j) end
  end (* if *)
end (* for *)
```

In the next section we consider the special algorithms that take advantage of the collection of ranges into groups of dense ranges. The emission of switch instructions for individual jump tables is a necessary part of that algorithm.

Dense Ranges

In this section we shall assume that the statement has been analysed and the case selector values have been collected into dense groups. An example of the data structure was shown in Figure 6.10. We have a list of triples, each of which denotes a dense group of ranges. Each triple in the group list contains the starting and ending index of that group in the range list and the total number of selector values contained in the group. The *range list* is also an array of triples. In this case the triples contain the smallest and largest value of the range and the index of the statement that is selected by the values in that range. Of course, if a range is a singleton value, then the smallest and largest values of the range will be the same.

The idea behind the algorithm is to emit the *IL* of a binary decision tree to select the appropriate dense group. At runtime we then use a jump table to select within the values of the group in the usual way. It is a standard result that the maximum number of test and branch steps required to select one from N groups is $\lceil \log_2 N \rceil$. The "$\lceil \ . \ \rceil$" symbols denote the *ceiling* function, with signature $\mathcal{R} \rightarrow \mathcal{I}$, that rounds towards positive infinity. Of course, once we have selected the appropriate group, we still have to perform further tests to find out which element of the group has been selected.

Bisecting the group list. In order to select the group of interest we must perform tests that at each step eliminate half of the groups. We may do this by recursively peforming a *less-than* test to compare the selector value with the lower bound of the group element one past the middle of the current sublist. An example may make this clearer. Suppose that we have a list of eight groups, which we denote $A, B, \ldots H$. We assume that the minimum selector values of each group are denoted $a, b, \ldots h$, respectively. The control flow and the tests to achieve selection are as shown in Figure 9.22, where s is the selector variable value. It may be noted that, as promised, no selection requires more than three tests.

In order to emit such *IL*, we require a simple recursion that emits a test as shown, bifurcates the group list, and recurses on the two sublists. When the sublist is of length

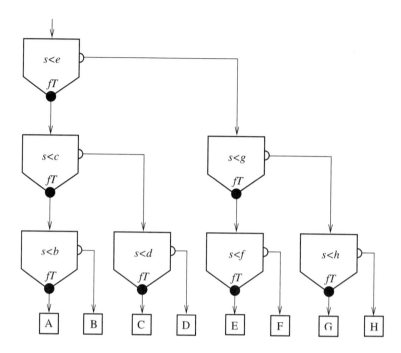

Figure 9.22: Selecting one from eight dense groups

one, except for some special cases discussed below, we call the procedure that contains the code in Figure 9.21 to emit the "`switch`" instruction.

Of course, Figure 9.22 does not really show how the *IL* is laid out in sequence, even though that is the intent of the graphical notation. Each straight-line sequence of blocks in the diagram is set out in order, falling through as shown. The sequences across the figure are always connected by branches and never fall through from one to another. Therefore the sequences may be emitted in any order. In *gpcp* they appear in *IL* in an order corresponding to left to right across the figure.

For reasons that become clear later, we wish to know the range of possible selector values that may reach a particular location in the control flow. This information may be simply computed during the recursive emission of *IL* for the decision tree. We may assume that at the root of the recursion the range of possible selector values will be the entire range of the selector datatype. After we have emitted a "less-than" test and branch on some literal, v say, then our emitter method will be called recursively on the left and right group sublists. If the incoming selector interval passed to the method that emitted the test was $[\min S, \max S]$, then the interval passed to the recursion on the left sublist will be $[\min S, (v-1)]$. The interval passed to the recursion on the right sublist will be $[v, \max S]$. For example, in Figure 9.22 when control enters the block denoted C, it is known that the selector value s has the constraints $c \leq s < d$. When control enters the block denoted

H, on the other hand, it is only known that $s \geq h$. In the event that there was only one dense group to start with, the range of the possible selector values is the entire range of the selector datatype.

Peeling the elements. Finally, when the *IL* for selection between groups has been emitted, we must emit the code that chooses between the cases of a single group. Of course, for a reasonable proportion of source programs, **switch** statements are dense, and we start off with only one group. It was suggested above that in that case we should simply invoke the code of Figure 9.21 to emit a "`switch`" instruction. This is the most probable outcome, but there are a number of special cases that benefit from being treated separately. These special cases occur when there is a very small number of ranges in the remaining group, and a jump table may be inefficient.

The code that emits the *IL* for selection within a single group has the following information available. The upper and lower bounds of the possible selector values are known, as are the minimum and maximum nondefault selector values. The number of separate ranges in the group is also known.

If the number of ranges in the group is very small, then we might consider some kind of sequential test for the various values. Testing the values one by one will have $O(N)$ complexity, where N is the number of ranges. A jump table, in theory, will have constant time complexity although in practice caching effects often make larger tables slightly slower. In any event, the question is, "How many sequential tests can be performed in the time taken to dispatch through a jump table?" This is an empirical question, which depends on the machine architecture and the properties of the *JIT* compiler. However it appears for a variety of machines if the number of ranges is three or less, then sequential tests may be faster.

It seems that a good compromise is to check the number of ranges in the group. If the number is greater than or equal to four, a jump table is emitted, as discussed in the previous section. If the number is three or less, then the ranges are "peeled off" from lowest to highest. As usual, recursion does the job for us.

At each stage in the recursion we wish to emit *IL* that removes one range from the group, recomputes the possible selector value range, and recurses on the reduced group. If we do not have the selector interval information we will end up emitting additional or redundant tests. This will attract a speed penalty at runtime and risk the scorn of other compiler writers. The general case is as shown in Figure 9.23. In this figure *minS* is the known minimum of the possible selector value range, *maxS* is the known maximum of the possible selector value range, *minG* is the minimum nondefault selector of the group, and *maxG* is the maximum nondefault selector of the group. The selector values that select nondefault actions are shown shaded, and the values that select the default action are unshaded. The steps involved in peeling a range from the group are sufficiently complex, with sufficient special cases, that it is worth working through the detail.

Since we are recursively removing ranges from the group, we should first consider what is required to end the recursion. We have a basis case when there is only one range

Figure 9.23: General case of single dense group

remaining in the group. If this is a singleton value, then we emit an equality test for this value, conditionally branching to the selected statement. We then emit an unconditional jump to the default label.

If the one remaining range is not a singleton value, then we may have to perform more than one test. There are three cases, involving zero, one, or two tests. If $minS = minG$ **and** $maxS = maxG$ then no test is required,[5] and control branches unconditionally to the selected statement label. If only one of the equalities holds, then we need only a single test against the other range boundary, with control falling into an unconditional branch to the default label if the test fails. Finally, if neither of the two equalities hold, then we might use two tests against the upper and lower bounds of the range. A better alternative, however, is to use the same old trick that was described in Figure 8.22 on page 257. Here, we perform a double ended test using a single, unsigned test and branch. Suppose that we wish to test if the selector value is between $minG$ and $maxG$. We emit the *IL* sequence —

```
. . .                      // selector is on top of stack
ldc.i4 L                   // L is literal minG
sub                        // subtract lower bound
ldc.i4 D                   // D is literal (maxG – minG)
ble.un  targetLabel        // unsigned branch
br      defaultLabel
```

Having dealt with the basis, we must now deal with the recursive cases that peel a single range. Once again there are a number of special cases to consider.

If the first range in the group is a singleton value, then we emit an equality test for that value and remove the range from the group. If the singleton was hard up against the end of the possible range—that is, if $minS = minG$—then we adjust $minS$ up by one; otherwise we leave $minS$ unchanged in the recursion.

If the first range is not a singleton value, then we have two cases to consider. If the range is hard up against the possible selector range, as shown in Figure 9.24, then we emit a "less-than-or-equal" test against the maximum value of the lowest range, peeling off that range and adjusting $minS$ upward, so as to be one greater than the literal in the test. We then recurse onward with the reduced group.

In the general case, the lowest range in the group will be as shown in Figure 9.23. We could trim the range of possible selector values by testing against $minG$, branching to the

---

[5] Note that since, by assumption, we have only one range left in the group, the bounds of the group $minG$ and $maxG$ are necessarily also the bounds of the range.

Figure 9.24: Lowest range hard against the possible value minimum

default label if true, but this is inefficient. Instead we should emit *IL* to subtract *minG* from the selector value, performing an unsigned less-than-or-equal test against the length of the range *maxR – minR*, where *minR* and *maxR* are the minimum and maximum values of the range. If the test result is true, control branches to the selected statement. When this *shifted* test is used, the value of *minS* that is passed to the recursion is left unmodified, since no branch will have taken place for selector values between the incoming *minS* and *minG*.

Notes on Chapter 9

To Optimize or Not to Optimize

The question of whether or not *IL* generators for *.NET* should attempt to perform classical code optimizations is an interesting one. The problem is that after the *IL* generator has done its thing, the *JIT* must do *its* thing. It is not yet clear to what extent fiddling with the *IL* becomes merely making changes that the *JIT* can do better anyway.

There are probably at least two exceptions to this principle. Firstly, constant propagation is always a good idea, particularly if it leads to the static evaluation of Boolean expressions that may allow the control flow to be restructured. In almost all optimization scenarios, repeated rounds of constant propagation and constant folding are either helpful or at least harmless. It is also almost certainly a good idea to perform some kind of type inference on the control flow, since that may lead to opportunities to turn virtual method dispatches into static calls.

Over the next few years it will become apparent which optimizations are best left to the *JIT* and which are better done in the front-end. Certainly, given the tight time-budget of the typical *JIT*, it is clear that really costly optimizations will need to be done in the front-end. This will be a fascinating development to watch. Stay tuned.

Switch Statement Encoding

Earlier, it was suggested that the crossover point between sequential selection and a jump table occurs when the number of ranges N is in the vicinity of three to four. With one or two ranges, sequential selection is faster, and above four or five the jump table is faster. These are figures empirically found by measuring test programs on the early *.NET* releases. It is perhaps surprising that this crossover value is comparable with the numbers found when comparing native-code implementations of the same algorithms on a variety of machine architectures.

Comparing sequential selection against a jump table compares a linear time algorithm against a constant time algorithm, at least in theory. What if one compares a logarithmic time algorithm, such as binary chop, against the constant time jump table method? Alas, measurements suggest that although for a sufficiently high N binary chop is faster than sequential search, by that time both methods are significantly slower than the jump table method.

Calling the Wider World 10

This chapter deals with the issues involved in interfacing to the code that originates outside your own compiler. As a priority, this involves accessing the frameworks that conform to the *CLS*. In this case we may share the object model as well as the ability to invoke static procedures. In particular, we shall consider the issues involved in creating *CLS full consumers*.

The other theme of the chapter is the mechanisms that are used to call unmanaged code. These mechanisms access not just the world outside your own compiler, but the world outside of the *.NET* runtime.

The chapter begins by exploring an aspect of *.NET* that has only been briefly mentioned so far, custom attributes.

Custom Attributes

The facilities of *.NET* allow for *custom attributes* to be attached to any item of metadata, except to other custom attributes. A custom attribute is an instance of a specially marked class. The object may be retrieved at runtime or from *PEM* files by tools that process assembly metadata.

There are a number of custom attributes that are already defined for various purposes in the *CLR*. However, the great strength of the design is that tools and even individual programs may define their own custom attribute types and attach them to program components.

Defining Custom Attribute Types

Custom attributes are defined by class definitions, as might be expected. They should always inherit from the class *System.Attribute*. These classes may contain arbitrary methods and data in the usual way. A key design consideration for the types is the constructor semantics, since it is by calling the constructors that the custom attribute instances are created. It is a convention that the names of attribute classes should always end in *-Attribute*.

It is common for attribute classes to themselves have a system attribute of type *System.AttributeUsageAttribute*. This marker attribute indicates some useful information about the intended usage of the attribute to which it is attached—that is, the intended usage of the *target attribute*. The properties of this usage attribute include a Boolean value, *Allow-Multiple*, that indicates whether multiple instances of the target attribute may be attached to a single metadata element. Another Boolean property, *Inherited*, indicates whether the target attribute is inherited by subclasses. Finally, a property of enumeration type, *ValidOn*, indicates the kinds of metadata elements to which the target attribute may be attached. Values of the *AttributeTargets* include *All*, *Assembly*, *Class*, *Method*, *Module*, *Event*, *Field*, and many others. The *ValidOn* value may be set to a bitwise *OR* of any of these values. The default is *All*.

At the start of the section it was stated that custom attributes can be attached to any item of metadata except other custom attributes. The use of the *System.AttributeUsage-Attribute* type does not violate the exception, since these attributes are attached to the definition of the custom attribute *class* and not to the instances of the class that are the custom attributes in the metadata.

Attaching Custom Attributes

Custom attributes are declared in *CIL* according to the following grammar and attach to the declarative entity that they immediately follow —

$$\begin{array}{lll} \text{AsmDecl} & \rightarrow & \ldots \qquad\qquad\qquad \textit{// other AsmDecl clauses} \\ & | & \textbf{.custom } \text{CustomDecl .} \\ \text{CustomDecl} & \rightarrow & \textit{constructor } [\text{ ``='' ``('' BinaryBlob ``)'' }]. \end{array}$$

In this syntax *constructor* is the usual constructor format as it would follow a "newobj" instruction. The optional binary blob contains the values of the mandatory and any optional arguments that are passed to the constructor. This information may be left out, if the constructor takes no arguments.

For example, we might attach a custom attribute to a class definition as shown in Figure 10.1. In this case the attribute constructor takes a single argument of string type. The binary blob format contains a *UTF8*[1] string literal, in this case the string "*KJG*". The ilasm tool does not convert symbolic values for the constructor arguments to the binary blob format, so it is necessary for the compiler to construct the byte sequence for the blob.

```
.class public sealed Hello {
  .custom instance void
    [ProgInfo] ProgInfo.AuthorAttribute::.ctor(string)
                = ( 01 00 03 4B 4A 47 00 00 ) // ...KJG..
  . . .                                        // rest of class definition
```

Figure 10.1: Attaching an attribute to a class

The calling convention for constructors of custom attributes uses a feature that we have not discussed so far. As well as the mandatory arguments of the constructor, it is possible to add optional arguments that set other fields or properties of the attribute object. These optional arguments appear as named associations in the binary blob. In *C#* the syntax for creating attribute instances is as follows —

$$
\begin{aligned}
AttributeCtor &\rightarrow \text{"["} \; AttrClassName \; \text{"("} \; [\text{Arguments}] \; \text{")"} \; \text{"]"} \; . \\
Arguments &\rightarrow args \mid \text{OptionalArgs} \mid args \; \text{","} \; \text{OptionalArgs} \; . \\
OptionalArgs &\rightarrow \text{NamedAssociation} \; \{ \; \text{","} \; \text{NamedAssociation} \; \} \; . \\
NamedAssociation &\rightarrow identifier \; \text{"="} \; value \; .
\end{aligned}
$$

The mandatory arguments, if there are any, must appear first. These are specified as a comma-separated list of values, as usual. They must be listed in the same order as the formal parameters in the constructor definition and hence are sometimes called *positional arguments*.

The optional arguments are *named associations* and may appear in any order. The *C#* source syntax is directly reflected in the memory blob format. Notice that although the use of the attribute class name mimics the syntax for other constructor calls, there is no **new** marker here. Another special feature of the *C#* syntax is that the name of the attribute class may be shortened by the removal of the "Attribute" suffix. For example if we have defined a custom attribute named *AuthorAttribute* that takes a single string argument in its constructor, we may attach this attribute to a program element with the call —

```
[Author("KJG", year = 2001)]
```

---

[1] *UTF8* is one of the standard encodings for strings of unicode characters.

In this example the named association with the identifier *year* is an optional argument that initializes a field of this name in the *AuthorAttribute* object. The binary blob corresponding to this definition is shown in Figure 10.3.

The SerString format.

The SerString format.   Strings in memory blobs use a special compressed format. In the common case of strings that are shorter than 128 characters and that use only the 7-bit *ASCII* subset, the format uses only a single byte for the byte count and a single extra byte for each character of the string. This is called the *SerString* format.

These strings begin with a packed length byte-count, which may be one, two, or four bytes wide, followed by the *UTF8* string of wide characters. The packed byte-count uses a single byte for numbers in the range 1 to 127. That byte has the binary form —

> 0xxxxxxx

where the 'x' characters are the bits of the original number. For counts between 128 and 16,383 the number is packed into two bytes. These two bytes have the binary form —

> 10xxxxxx, xxxxxxxx

where the most significant six bits are in the first byte, and the least significant eight are in the second byte. Finally, for counts that are greater than or equal to 2^{14}, a four-byte format is used —

> 110xxxxx, xxxxxxxx, xxxxxxxx, xxxxxxxx

In this case the count may be as high as 2^{29}, corresponding to *UTF8* strings of about 500Mb in size. Unlike other data in memory blobs, the most significant part of the packed length datum *must* come first, so that we may know how many other bytes will follow.

The *UTF8* string has a representation that encodes each wide character into one, two, or three bytes. If the character ordinal is less than 128, we use a single character, with the seven significant bits encoded thus —

> 0xxxxxxx

For character ordinals between 128 and 2,047 a two-byte format is used, with the most significant five bits in the first byte and the lower six in the second byte —

> 110xxxxx, 10xxxxxx

Finally, for characters with an ordinal of 2,048 or more a three-byte format is used. In this final case the most significant four bits are placed in the first byte, with six bits in each of the next two bytes —

> 1110xxxx, 10xxxxxx, 10xxxxxx

Notice that the byte count for a *SerString* is the number of bytes that are needed for the *UTF8* string. This is not the same as the length of the original character string. It follows that the conversion must be computed before the byte count is known.

Custom attribute memory blob format.   The memory blob format for custom attributes has the following syntax —

$$
\begin{array}{rcl}
\text{BinaryBlob} & \rightarrow & prolog \; \{\; \text{FixedArg} \;\} \; count \; \{\; \text{NamedArg} \;\} \; . \\
\text{FixedArg} & \rightarrow & value \; . \\
\text{NamedArg} & \rightarrow & mark \; name \; value .
\end{array}
$$

Except for the packed length counts that precede *UTF8* character strings, all numbers in the binary format are emitted in *little-endian* order. That is, the least significant byte comes first, followed by the more significant bytes. The *prolog* and *count* elements are both unsigned **int16** values. The prolog is the constant 1, while the count is the number of named arguments to follow. If there are no named arguments, a count of zero must be specified.

Argument values are literal constants, in little-endian order for numeric quantities, while string literals and type names are represented as *SerStrings*.

The fixed arguments do not have any kind of datatype information associated with them, as the exact signature of the constructor method is known. The named arguments each begin with a marker. This marker begins with a single byte that denotes whether the argument is a field (byte 0x53) or a property (byte 0x54). There is also a one-byte type marker. The most common byte values for the marker are shown in Figure 10.2. The name in a named argument is a *SerString*, and the value is in the same format as for the fixed arguments.

Type	*Value*
bool	0x02
wchar	0x03
int32	0x08
int64	0x0A
float32	0x0C
float64	0x0D
string	0x0E

Figure 10.2: Type marker values for named arguments in custom attributes

An example may make this more clear. Suppose we return to the *C#* example in which we had one fixed argument of **string** type and a single **int32** named association. Figure 10.3 shows how the memory blob would be decomposed in this case.

```
// [Author("KJG", year = 2001]
.custom instance void
    [ProgInfo] ProgInfo.AuthorAttribute::.ctor(string)
        = ( 01 00                    // prolog
            03 4B 4A 47              // "KJG"
            01 00                    // count = 1
            53 08                    // field, int32
            04 79 65 61 72           // "year"
            D1 07 00 00 )            // 0x7D1 = 2001
```

Figure 10.3: Decomposition of attribute example

Accessing custom attributes.   Custom attributes may be accessed at runtime, using the facilities of the system libraries. In particular, the *GetCustomAttributes* method of the *System.Reflection.MemberInfo* class retrieves an array of custom attribute objects from its receiver. The return value is an array of *System.Object*, which may be cast to the known attribute type or at least to the base class *System.Attribute* from which all custom attributes are derived.

Typically, such a call would be dispatched on a *System.Type* object, or on any member of the type, such as a method or a field. The *System.Type* class is a subtype of *System.Reflection.MemberInfo* class as is the *System.Reflection.MethodInfo* class.[2]

An example usage in *C#* might be the code in Figure 10.4, which shows how the custom attributes might be fetched for a particular named type. The code fragment also shows how the custom attributes of the methods associated with the type might be fetched. Once we have the attributes, we may then access the data of the attribute or call any method that we may have defined on the type.

There are a large number of library methods defined on the *System.Reflection.MemberInfo* type. *System.Type* is a subtype of this type and, as pointed out earlier, is the portal into the whole world of program introspection.

It may be useful to know that custom attribute values are constructed lazily. That is to say, the constructors for the attribute objects are not called unless the values are requested by the *System.Reflection* methods.

---

[2]The main features of the class hierarchy of these reflection types are shown in Figure 11.1 in the following chapter.

```
using System; using System.Reflection;
...
Type tDsc = typeof(MyClass);
Object[] aArr = tDsc.GetCustomAttributes();
// we may now operate on these attributes ...
...
MethodInfo[] mArr = tDsc.GetMethods();
for (int i = 0; i < mArr.Length; i++) {
    Object[] mAt = mArr[i].GetCustomAttributes();
    // we may now operate on these attributes ...
```

Figure 10.4: Fetching attributes for types and methods

Mapping Names

Names in the *CLR* have a very general structure. In particular, simple class names may be qualified by the names of hierarchically structured namespaces. In order to interact with the *CLS*, or even with the facilities of the *System* framework, it is necessary to be able to access such hierarchically named entities. The design of the *CLR* is sufficiently general to provide facilities for a majority of languages. The problem of the compiler writer is quite a different one: How may programs refer to methods in possibly nested namespaces using languages that do not have such a rich naming structure?

The problem is the inverse of one of the issues in Chapter 4. In that chapter the issue was to map the naming structure of the target language onto the rich naming structure of the *CLR*. Here the issue is how to allow the target language to reach the full range of possible *CLR* names.

Perhaps the problem posed for *Component Pascal* is typical. In this language imported types are referred to by their qualified names, in the form *ModuleName.TypeName*. Module names are drawn from a "flat" global naming scope and are simple identifiers. If module names map onto namespaces in the *CLR*, then module names will map onto simple namespace names only. This simple, two-level naming is insufficiently general to specify the arbitrary dotted names of imported namespaces.

There are various ways to attack this problem. However, for all of them it is helpful to remember that namespaces are simply syntactic sugar within source programs. In the *CLR*, at runtime, namespaces have no representation. Namespaces are simply customary prefixes for the dotted names that are the real type names. For our most general type name, we have the fully qualified representation —

[assemblyName] namespaceName.className

where *namespaceName.className* is the full type name. The prefix, *namespaceName*, is the possibly dotted name that we think of as the name of the namespace. In *C#* the full type name is constructed from the simple name of the type together with the name of the namespace in the **using** clause that was used to bind the name. Since there is no necessary relationship between the full type name and the name of the assembly in which it is found, it is necessary to specify the assemblies that should be searched by means of compiler options. In summary, for *C#* the full type name is statically specified in the source of the module referencing the type, and the assembly name is specified by a "/r:*name*" option on the command line.

In the world of *Component Pascal* it is the convention that the names of imported modules are expected to specify *both* the assembly name and the namespace name. This works well with *PEM* producers that use the same convention but fails when the types are not packaged in this way. It is therefore necessary to have some kind of escape mechanism for the more general case. There are two issues. First, it must be possible to access types with completely general names. Second, it must be possible for the compiler to locate the assemblies in which the types are defined.

If the naming structure of the source language is not to be changed, then there must be some way of specifying a mapping from the restricted names to the full *CLR* names. There are two possible locations to specify this mapping. If the compiler reads metadata by reflection on the compiled assemblies, then the producer of the metadata can know nothing of the needs of the client compiler. In this case the mapping must be specified in the source code of the client module. If, on the other hand, the compiler relies on some customized metadata format of its own choosing, then the mapping may be specified as part of the transformation from the generic metadata to the language specific header or symbol file.

Hiding the mapping in the metadata.   If a compiler uses custom metadata, then the mapping may be hidden away in the metadata format itself. Thus in *Component Pascal* an import statement such as

```
import mscorlib_System_Reflection;
```

would cause a symbol file with the corresponding name to be sought on the path defined by the appropriate environment variable. Inside that symbol file, the metadata would have information specifying that the symbol file actually contained the metadata for the namespace with the *CLR* name "*[mscorlib]System.Reflection*".

The scheme relies on a rather obvious name-mangling transformation. This very obviousness allows programmers to predict what the name of the dummy definition module will be for any given namespace. However, since *Component Pascal* uses fully qualified names everywhere, the very long names that result are potentially awkward. As it turns out, another language feature lessens the impact. It is possible to define a *local module-name alias* for an imported module, so that it may be referred throughout the text of the module by the (shorter) alias name. Thus it would be usual to have something of the form —

```
import Rflct := mscorlib_System_Reflection;
```

and thereafter refer to the features of the namespace using the alias name *Rflct* as the qualifying module name.

Declaring the mapping in the source code.

In the event that the metadata is read directly from the compiled assemblies, the mapping must be made explicit in the client code. In this case it is necessary to introduce some kind of fairly innocuous syntactic extension. For *Component Pascal* a likely extension would be to enhance the existing syntax for defining module-name aliases. In the existing syntax the right-hand side of the alias definition is the name of the module to be imported. The additional production would allow the right-hand side to be some arbitrary literal string that identified the assembly to be accessed and the namespace to be imported from that assembly. For our previous example we might have —

```
import Rflct := "[mscorlib]System.Reflection";
```

With this mechanism in place we do not need to rely on a language-specific metadata format item to specify the mapping from the simple identifier in the client module to the full *CLR* name.

Handling Overloading in Languages that Don't

The *CLR* identifies methods using an "identifier" that includes the method name, the whole method signature, and any modifiers. Technically, the *CLR* knows and cares nothing about overloaded names. Nevertheless, the simple names that are obtained by stripping the signatures from methods in the class libraries can be and are "overloaded." This poses an immediate problem for languages that do not permit name overloading. If an implementation of such a language wishes to consume such class libraries, then there must be some way for the methods of the library to be accessed in the native syntax of the implementation.

There are at least two separate approaches to this problem. One is easy to implement, requiring almost no cooperation from the compiler, but is ungainly, fragile, and error-prone in use. The other is harder to implement but exposes the overloading to the library users.

The scenario that we consider is the following. The compiler for a language that does not support overloading needs to allow its programs access to *CLS* class libraries. In particular, the programs must be able to access and distinguish between individual members of a set of methods with the same simple name. We may think of this process as *disambiguation*, since the overloaded names would be ambiguous in a language that does not allow overloading.

Before considering these two approaches, we must touch on an even simpler approach that works for static methods and requires no cooperation at all from the compiler. This method can he helpful in the early stages of bootstrapping a compiler but is too limited for general use. The idea is very simple. We define a *wrapper module* in our desired source language that exports the static methods that we require, but with the names of our own choosing. We do not actually compile this module but instead implement the wrapper in, for example, *C#*. The wrapper methods each contain a single line. They take their incoming parameters and pass them straight to a call of the *CLR* method with the overloaded name.

The limitations of this strategy should be clear. Users have to rely on the supplied wrappers. If they wish to interface to a *CLR* library to which they do not have a wrapper, then they must be able to write programs in the two languages involved and also understand the name mapping between *CLR* names in the two languages. This strategy does not extend to dispatched methods, since object identity would be lost in the wrapping process.

Name-Mangling Approaches

The name-mangling approach to disambiguation consists of giving each member of an overloaded set of names a unique *local name*. This is a kind of consistent renaming scheme. The idea is that in the *AST* the descriptors to which method calls are bound each have *two* names. One name is the local name to which any used occurrence in the source is bound in the symbol table of the local scope. The other is the name that is used when emitting the *IL*—that is, the name known to the *CLR*. For example, we might have two methods that are known in the *CLR* as —

> **.method public void** Foo (**int32,int32**)
> **.method public void** Foo (**int64,int64**)

These are the names that will be used in *IL*, but within the source these two might be referenced as "FooII" and "FooLL" respectively.

The characteristics that are desirable for any such name-mangling scheme are —

- The name mapping should be automatically generated, collision free, and repeatable.
- The mangled names should be predictable.
- The mangled name should be memorable.

The mapping must be automatically generated, since different modules compiled at different times should give the same disambiguated name to a given *CLS* method. Furthermore, tools such as class browsers must also be able to inform the programmer how to access any given method.

The advantages of predictability of names should be clear also. Particularly in the case where a programmer has access to documentation of a library in some "language independent" form, the name in the source language to be used should be predictable, at least most of the time. Some kind of *mnemonic content* in the name is obviously helpful. That is why in the example the two *Foo* method names were mangled with suffixes that indicated the signature.

A very simple approach to mapping was adopted for early *gpcp* prototypes. In effect, if two or more methods of a particular class had the same simple name, then the subsequent methods had a sequence number appended to the name. In this way a set of overloaded methods called *Foo* would appear with mangled names *Foo*, *Foo1*, *Foo2*, and so on. Almost everything about this strategy is bad. In the first place, the names are not predictable; the programmer has no way of knowing that it is actually *Foo42* that is the method that is needed. It clearly fails the memorability test as well. However, the most dangerous property of all is a lack of robustness against version changes. Suppose that an additional *Foo* method is added to a new release of the class library and appears in the declarations between the two methods that were previously second and third (say). In the mangled namespace the names *Foo* and *Foo1* will refer to the same methods as before, but all later methods will have changed their names. This will break user code in very serious and significant ways. Usually we would expect the adding of another method to a class in a minor revision to be a nonbreaking change, so this is a very serious failing.

A better approach is to try to build in some signature information into the name-mangling algorithm. This seems simple enough in the case of base types. The mappings int32 → "I", int64 → "L", and so on are compact, predictable, and memorable. However, the whole scheme breaks down in the case of object types. The compromise adopted by the first release version of *gpcp* is to use such a one-character mapping for base types, with a lowercase 'o' for object types. Whenever one or more object types appear in the signature part of a mangled name, a hash code is appended to the name. The hash code is computed from the complete signature as it appears in the *IL*. This looks ugly, and violates the predictability and memorability criteria. However, it is very unlikely to be broken by a class library revision, since the same signature will always transform into the same hash code suffix.

With any name-mangling approach, there are certain issues that require some care. It is obvious that calls to overloaded methods will bind to name descriptors with the paired name structure (local name, external name) described above. What, however, of type extension and method *overriding?* Of course, we would expect to specify the new methods using the same names that are used to refer to the original methods in the same program. That is, the new methods will be defined with mangled names. This means that the method descriptors in the *AST* must copy the explicit external name from the method that is being overridden, so that the new method will appear consistently named in the *IL* and will be placed in the correct slot of the *v-table*.

Just Do It Anyway

The previous discussion may give the impression that name mangling does not offer an elegant solution to the overloading problem. An alternative is to simply "bite the bullet" and implement overloaded names. This requires some extra semantics in the compiler but does provide an elegant solution to the problem.

What is being suggested here is not a wholesale adoption of fundamental change in the language being implemented, but a recognition that access to foreign language resources may require different rules. The minimal approach would be to insist that methods that have overloaded names cannot be *defined*, but foreign classes imported from the *CLS* may be *accessed* using their simple but overloaded names.

This minimal formulation sounds innocuous enough, since programs only deal with overloaded names when they are forced to. However, the overloading creeps further into the program than might be expected. Consider the case where a program extends a foreign class with overloaded method names. When the methods of the class are overridden in the program, the new methods must be consistently named. Hence the program may have to define new methods using existing overloaded names, even if the introduction of new overloadings is not permitted.

Binding overloaded names.   The possibility of overloaded method names requires some changes to the abstract syntax of program representation and significant changes to the name-binding mechanisms. At the least, symbol table structures need to be enhanced, so that one of the identifier kinds that is retrieved by a lookup is a descriptor for a *set* of method descriptors that share the same simple name.

When a name binds to a set of equally named methods, the completion of the name binding will require the actual parameter types to be evaluated. Once the number and apparent type of the actual parameters are known, then the name binding may proceed. Such a process would typically contain multiple steps, as follows. First, discard all methods with the wrong number of parameters. Next, check if any remaining method has a matching signature, in the absence of type coercions. Finally, if a match has not been found, then matching in the presence of coercions must be considered. The final step is not as simple as might be thought. On the face of it, it appears that the existing *formals vs. actuals* type-checking predicate will answer the question for us. This is only *usually* the case. Consider the following two static methods —

> **.method public void** Foo (**int32, class** Mod.Parent)
> **.method public void** Foo (**float64, class** Mod.Child)

where class *Child* is a subtype of class *Parent*. What are we to make of a call that has a first argument that is an integer expression and a second that is a static expression of *Child* type? The call might be —

```
Foo(42, thisChild);
```

The problem is just this: It is permissible to pass an object of the subtype to the value parameter in the second parameter position. Similarly, for many languages (including *Component Pascal*) integer expressions may be implicitly promoted from **int** to **double**. A call to our existing *formals vs. actuals* type-checker will correctly decide that the call matches *both* of the methods. This is an unpleasant but possible situation.

If we were implementing a language that specified method name overloading, the next step in the process would be clear. We would look at the fine print of the language specification and find out which of the alternatives was the "correct" one. But that is not the situation! We are discussing the *invention* of semantics for an interoperability extension to a language that doesn't otherwise accept overloading. Under the circumstances, the most prudent course of action seems to be to report an error and make the programmer indicate explicitly which method is intended. That is, the programmer must use one of the two forms —

```
Foo(42.0, thisChild);
Foo(42, (Parent) thisChild);
```

so as to put the issue beyond doubt. This strict approach is very strongly recommended in this context. This is particularly so because the programmers using this facilty are outside the familiar semantic context of the rest of the program.

Properties, Events, and Other Exotica

The *CLR* allows members of classes to be declared as properties, delegates, and events. These kinds also appear in the public interfaces of *CLS*-conformant libraries. However, languages that do not have such things may still wish to access the functionality of these libraries. This is almost always possible to arrange. The question is just one of finding a way to map some legal syntactic construct of the source language onto the *CLR* facility.

Accessing Properties

Accessing properties of classes from languages that do not have properties is straightforward. The syntax for access to properties in languages such as *C#* is the same as the syntax for access to fields of classes. In this case, the property name is used exactly as if it were a field name. However, the functionality is actually provided by *get_<propName>* and *set_<propName>* methods defined on the class. In many cases these methods merely encapsulate and regulate access to an underlying, private *backing field* of the same name, but other possibilities exist.

If the library source language makes the *get* and *set* methods directly visible, then these methods may be called using the same syntax as any other procedure call. In other words, the fact that the methods are treated by *other* languages as properties does not prevent a language dealing with the procedural interface.

As well as the ordinary properties that were discussed on page 65 there are also *indexers*, sometimes also known as *indexed properties*. In *C#* such properties are accessed as though the object with the indexer was an array. For example, suppose that some class *ClsWithIdx* is defined in *C#* with a one-dimensional indexer. This class may also have fields that will be accessed in the usual way. Within a *C#* program we may use the indexer as though it were an index on the object itself. Here is an example —

```
ClsWithIdx arr = new ClsWithIdx();
...
arr[25] = arr[24] + 1;
```

When such a class is defined, the indexer is defined with similar syntax to that used for defining a property, except in this case there is no name for the property. The definition uses instead the keyword **this**. Figure 10.5 shows a class definition that has both an indexer *and* a property of array type. Notice that the property is read-only and is of an array type. The indexer has a "signature" that declares that it is indexed by a single integer value. In the set method the identifier "value" refers to an implicit argument of the property datatype, in this case **int**.

```
public class public IdxAndProp {
  private int[] idx = new int[100];
  private int[] jdx = new int[100];

  public int[] Idx {                        // property declaration
    get { return idx; }                     // property is read-only
  }

  public int this[int index] {              // indexer declaration
    get { return jdx[index]; }
    set { jdx[index] = value; }             // "value" is implicit arg
  }
}
```

Figure 10.5: Class with indexer *and* array property

The *C#* syntax for access to the two properties defined in this class is quite different. For example if we wish to retrieve the index-3 element of each array, we would use the two expressions —

```
IdxAndProp obj = new IdxAndProp();
...
int i = obj[3];              // access the indexer
int j = obj.idx[3];         // access the property
```

All of this is a standard part of the *C#* language. However, what if we wish to access the properties of this class from another language?

To access the *idx* property of a *IdxAndProp* object within *IL* we simply call the accessor method, which in this case will have the signature —

.method public rtsspecialname instance int32[] `get_Idx()`

The indexer is a little more perplexing, since it does not have an explicit name. In this case, the access methods are given default names as though the indexer was a property field with the name "`Item`". The two access methods in this case will be —

.method public rtsspecialname instance int32
`get_Item(`**int32**`index)`
.method public rtsspecialname instance int32
`set_Item(`**int32** `index,` **int32** `value)`

The indexer may be accessed through these method declarations in the same way as any other property. This fact may be viewed in two different ways. One might think of indexers simply as the *C#* way of applying syntactic sugar to a particular way of using the underlying property facilities of the *CLR*. Alternatively, one might think of the semantics of indexers being *mapped* to the property facilities by the sort of considerations that were discussed in Chapter 4. View it as you will, Figure 10.6 shows the property declarations in the *IL* arising from the *C#* code in Figure 10.5.

```
.property instance int32 [] Idx() {
    .get instance int32 [] IdxAndProp::get_Idx()
} // end of property IdxAndProp::Idx

.property instance int32 [] Item() {
    .get instance int32 IdxAndProp::get_Item(int32)
    .set instance int32 IdxAndProp::set_Item(int32, int32)
} // end of property IdxAndProp::Item
```

Figure 10.6: Property declarations in *IL*, from Figure 10.5

As a final point on indexers, note that it is possible for a *C#* program to use a standard custom attribute to override the default name of the indexer as it is seen by other languages. For example, the indexer in the example in Figure 10.5 would have been named *Jdx* if the definition had begun —

```
[name("Jdx")]                    // attribute overrides default name
public int this [int index] { ...
```

In that case, the access methods would have been named *get_Jdx* and *set_Jdx* rather than the default names *get_Item* and *set_Item*.

Accessing Events

Participation in the event-handling system is an important goal for programs that wish to access the full functionality of the framework classes. For example, the writing of *GUI* programs requires some kind of participation in the *.NET* event-handling model.

There are several aspects to this participation. Programs must be able to access the facilities of the system, for example, by being able to call methods on the standard *System.EventArgs* class and the classes, such as *System.MouseEventArgs*, that derive from it. Along with this access, it is necessary to be able to declare locations of event types, and to register and deregister methods on particular multicast delegates.

Understanding the *C#* facilities for event handling gives a hint as to the necessary facilities. In the first place, the *C#* compiler understands that if a public field *Fld* of some event type is defined, then it is necessary to automatically construct two methods named *add_Fld* and *remove Fld*. *C#* also has special syntax for registering and deregistering call-back delegates, overloading the "+=" and "-=" assignment operators. As described earlier, these operators translate into calls to the automatically constructed *add_** and *remove_** methods associated with the target multicast delegate. It is also possible to call directly the underlying *Combine* and *Remove* methods of the *System.Delegate* class. The delegate objects themselves are created in *C#* by the normal mechanisms of object creation using the **new** keyword.

Creating delegate values.   In order to be able to *declare* new event types, it is necessary for a language to be able to define extensions to the *System.Delegate* type. However, the ability to do so is not a necessary condition for participation in the event model. In most cases the event types are already defined in some library, and the ability to create instances of delegate types is a sufficient capability.

Delegates may be created by direct calls to the constructor or indirectly, by calls to various methods that return new delegate values. In order to call the delegate constructor, it is necessary to generate *IL* that loads a function pointer on the stack. For languages such as *ANSI C*, *Component Pascal*, or *Modula-2* that have some notion of values of procedure (function pointer) type, there is little problem. In such languages there will be existing syntactic constructs that translate into "ldftn" instructions. It follows that the compiler should be able to call a delegate constructor without any further help. Languages that have operations for taking addresses, but do not have the function pointer construct, may need to be a little more creative. For example, in *Visual Basic 7* it is not permitted to take the address of a method directly. However it *is* possible to take the address of an object member that happens to be a method, using the syntax "**AddressOf** *obj.meth*", where *meth* is some method of the class of the object reference. Presumably, in such cases the compiler needs to be able to work out what is happening in order to correctly emit the "ldftn" instruction.

As a last resort for languages that do not have procedure types or the ability to take arbitrary addresses, there is a nice workaround that builds on the reflection capabilities of the *.NET* framework. In short, the idea is to use one of the static *CreateDelegate* methods of the *System.Delegate* class. The particular method takes two parameters. The first is the *System.Type* object of the delegate type that is to be created. The second is the *System.Reflection.MethodInfo* object corresponding to the static method that is to be encapsulated in the delegate. Both of these parameters may be obtained starting from the names of the type and method respectively.

It is not suggested that the code for calling the reflection methods be emitted inline in the *IL*. Instead, what is suggested is that the functionality be hidden in a runtime support routine. This routine would take the names of the delegate class and the method as literal strings and perform the various lookups. The skeleton of the code in *C#* is shown in Figure 10.7. The routine takes three strings. One is the name of the delegate class, the second is the name of the class that contains the target method, and the third is the name of the method. Slightly more complicated code is required if the method name is overloaded. It should also be pointed out that in practice the code should have some exception handling added, so as to cope with erroneous argument values.

```
using System;
using System.Relection;
...
  Type  dTyp  =  GetType(<delegate type name>);
  Type  tDsc  =  GetType(<name of class with method>);
  MethodInfo info  =  tDsc.GetMethod(<method name>);
  return CreateDelegate(dTyp, info);
```

Figure 10.7: A delegate created by reflection

It is fair to comment that this technique has some runtime cost at the time of delegate creation, due to resorting to runtime reflection. However, delegates are not created very often. Typically they are created once and called many times. The delegates that are created this way are just as efficient as those that would be created in a language that was directly able to call the delegate constructor. The advantage of this technique is that it requires no cooperation from the compiler at all. The compiler simply generates an innocuous call to the support routine specified in the user program. The compiler may be unaware of the existence or semantics of delegate types and need not even know about the "ldftn" instruction. However, it is a limitation of the technique that the *GetMethod* method that fetches the *MethodInfo* object will only find public methods. By contrast, a direct call of a delegate constructor may be passed the address of even a private method.

This discussion has been focused on the creation of delegates that encapsulate static methods. There is a corresponding *CreateDelegate* method that will perform the same task for an instance method, taking an additional parameter.

The material in this section has been motivated by the need to obtain a function pointer value in languages that do not directly permit this. It is also possible to look at the two alternatives that have been considered in terms of *binding time*. For all those cases that end up with the emission of a "ldftn" instruction, the binding of the method name to a unique token is done by the compiler. For those cases where a library resolves strings to a unique *MethodInfo* object, the binding takes place at delegate instantiation time. Apart from issues of efficiency, there are also issues of error detection that distinguish these two approaches. If we process a source file that calls a constructor with the name of a nonexistent method, the compiler will detect the error. Alternatively, if we call our runtime support delegate routine with a literal string that does not correspond to any accessible method, we will get an error at runtime.

Registering and deregistering.

Registering and deregistering.   We have discussed the creation of delegate objects. The other capability for participation in the event handling model is the ability to register and deregister delegates for events. The way in which this has to be done depends on the degree to which the compiler understands the special semantics of events. In order to see the range of possibilities, we discuss two extreme cases and one compromise.

As noted earlier *C#* has several features that depend on the special semantics of events. When a field of event type is declared, the compiler automatically emits definitions of the add and remove methods, as well as a private backing field of the declared datatype. There is also special syntax for registering and deregistering for such events.

At the other extreme, let us consider a language that understands nothing at all of the semantics of events. The issues here are orthogonal to the question of how delegate instances are created. Imported event locations will have associated *add_** and *remove_** methods that may be explicitly called. Making these calls requires no semantic understanding, and indeed there will be no other way of registering or deregistering for the multicast delegate, since the backing field will almost certainly be private. Registration for imported multicast delegates is thus not a difficult problem. Consider, however, the problem of *declaring* locations of event type. Since the compiler does not understand the semantics, it cannot know to automatically create the *add_** and *remove_** methods. There are two solutions, neither of which is attractive. The programmer may explicitly define the methods, using the facilities of the underlying *System.Delegate* methods. Alternatively, the program could use the *add_** method when registering for an imported multicast, but use the *System.Delegate::Combine* method when registering for a local multicast.

In between these two extremes is the solution adopted in *gpcp*. In this case the syntax of the language is extended by the addition of event type declaration syntax, modelled on the procedure type declaration syntax. Whenever a static or instance field of event type is declared, the compiler automatically defines associated *add_** and *remove_** methods, just as *C#* would do. There is no overloading of existing syntax to denote registration and deregistration; instead two nonstandard built-in procedures *REGISTER* and *DEREGISTER* capture the required functionality. In the case of static or instance fields of event type the procedures translate into *IL* calls to the corresponding *add_** and *remove_** methods. In the unusual case of local variables of event type no such methods can exist, so the compiler knows that it must instead emit inline calls to the underlying *Combine* and *Remove* methods of the *System.Delegate* class.

Calling Unmanaged Code

The simplest approach to adopt, when programming for the *.NET* framework, is to use the facilities of the base classes of the framework. In this case the managed code produced by your compiler calls the managed code of the base classes. These classes provide a comprehensive foundation for most applications.

Nevertheless, there are times when it is necessary to directly call methods that are implemented by unmanaged code. As well, many methods of the base classes depend on facilities of the underlying operating system. Base class methods must thus call unmanaged code, at least in the deeper layers of the software architecture.

Under most circumstances when a call is made from managed to unmanaged code, the arguments of the call must be marshalled. This may involve very little work in the case of the standard arithmetic types, but may involve quite complicated processing in cases where the format of objects needs to be transformed. Under such circumstances the runtime supplies a *runtime stub* that is called by the managed code. The stub marshalls the arguments as required and makes the transition between the managed code and whatever call conventions are required by the unmanaged callee. In order to do this, the runtime must know the signature and call conventions on *both* sides of the call stub.

Interoperation with COM

The requirement for interoperation with existing components from previous versions of Microsoft's *Common Object Model* (*COM*) is so common that there are special mechanisms to support this. Interoperation with *COM* is supported by a number of special tools.

In the *COM* world, components have their interfaces defined in *type libraries*, rather than the metadata in the assemblies of the *.NET* framework. The `tlbimp` tool takes a type library and creates a managed code assembly that contains the necessary stubs. This assembly, as usual, contains the metadata that describes the interface to the facilities of the assembly.

The formula for interoperation with *COM* components is thus almost routine. The `tlbimp` tool creates an assembly containing metadata and stubs. In the case of compilers that expect metadata in some language-specific format there may also be an "assembly metadata to symbol file" transformation step. In any case, once the metadata is in the required form, the usual class browsers and other tools may be used to explore the interfaces and call the methods just as for ordinary managed code.

There is a matching tool that exports managed code, so that components defined in managed code may be accessed from the *COM* world. In that case the managed code component must be restricted so as to only export features that are able to be represented in *COM*. It is also usual to register the managed component in the registry.

Platform Invoke

Native-code methods that are exported from an unmanaged *DLL* may be called using the platform invoke (*PInvoke*) functionality of the *CLR*. *PInvoke* may only be used for static methods, but it automatically provides all of the functionality that is required for marshalling of arguments and making the transition from managed to unmanaged code.

Methods that are to be invoked using the *PInvoke* functionality must be declared in the *IL* and must be marked with the "`pinvokeimpl`" method attribute. This attribute is an addition to the attributes that were listed in Figures 3.28 and 3.29. The relevant syntax fragment is —

> MethodAttr   →   *<other attributes>*
> | **pinvokeimpl** "(" *DLLname* [**as** *Alias*] { PinvAttr } ")" .

DLLname is a literal string, enclosed in the usual quote characters ' " ', that specifies the *DLL* in which the method implementation will be found. The optional "**as** *Alias*" phrase declares an alias for the method name. *Alias* is an identifier, enclosed in quotes. The alias facility is sometimes useful, since the method name in the declaration must exactly match the name in the *DLL*, no matter how cryptic that might be. The *PinvAttr* attributes specify the calling conventions of the native-code method and the character set to which the method name must be mapped.

The rest of the method declaration for a *PInvoke* method follows the syntax given for method declarations on page 88. The method declaration must have the implementation attributes **native** and **unmanaged**, and must have an empty body. Here is an example of a *PInvoke* declaration for a native-code method *Foo* exported from the *DLL* "`Native-Stuff.dll`" —

> **.method public static pinvokeimpl** (`"NativeStuff.dll"` **cdecl**)
> **void** `Foo`(**int32**) **native unmanaged** { }

In some environments the names by which native-code methods are known within their *DLL* are mangled and bear little relationship to the simple name of the method in the source. The `dumpbin` tool is useful for finding the internal names, so that the *IL* declarations may specify precisely the right name for each method.

Having declared a native-code method with the "`pinvokeimpl`" attribute, the method is called from within *IL* exactly as any managed method would be. The *CLR* does the rest.

Notes on Chapter 10

This chapter has glossed over some details. In particular, the treatment of custom attributes and *PInvoke* have not spelled out all of the possibilities. If knowing the whole truth becomes important, the *ECMA* documents are the authoritative source.

It is often helpful to use the *C#* compiler, together with `ildasm`, to explore some of these features. A compact but comprehensive introduction to the full *C#* language is the book *C# Essentials* by Albahari, Drayton, and Merrill, published by O'Reilly, 2001.

Skipping the Assembler: Using Reflection.Emit

11

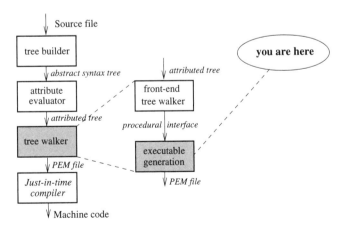

The facilities of the *System.Reflection.Emit* namespace allow for the construction of dynamic assemblies. Within these assemblies we may programmatically define modules, classes, methods, and so on. There are at least two separate uses for these facilities. At the end of the construction phase it is possible to save the assembly to the file system, where it becomes an ordinary loadable *PEM* assembly. In this case we call the dynamic assembly a *persistent assembly*. It is also possible to apply the *Reflection* facilities to the dynamic assembly so as to instantiate objects of the newly defined classes without ever saving the assembly to the file system. In this case we refer to the dynamic assembly as a *transient assembly*.

In this chapter we shall be mostly interested in the first use—that is, the use of *Reflection.Emit* to write out *PEM* files. However, we shall also consider the possibilities inherent in the runtime generation of program code.

Reflection and Reflection.Emit

The *System.Reflection* namespace in the *mscorlib* assembly defines a number of classes corresponding to the main program-structuring units. There is an *Assembly* class, and classes for *Type*, *Module*, and so on. Some of the more important of these types are shown in the class hierarchy diagram in Figure 11.1. These classes are used to represent the structure of program entities at runtime in order to allow *program introspection*, or synonymously, *reflection*. Thus if we have an object of *System.Type*, we may ask for a list of its members, or more narrowly of its methods or constructors, or so on. All of the classes in Figure 11.1 except for *System.Type* and *System.Object* belong to the *System.Reflection* namespace.

Corresponding to each of these descriptor classes in *System.Reflection*, we have a derived class in *System.Reflection.Emit*. These classes have corresponding names with the -*Builder* suffix. Thus we have *AssemblyBuilder*, *TypeBuilder*, *FieldBuilder*, *MethodBuilder*, and so on. Because these types derive from the *Reflection* types, we inherit all of the introspection methods of the parent type. What is added in the derivation is a set of new methods that allow new substructures to be added to the construction. The relationship between some of these builder types and their parents is shown in the class hierarchy in Figure 11.2. In this diagram the *AssemblyBuilder*, *TypeBuilder*, and *FieldBuilder* classes are sealed. This figure shows only a few of the many different -*Builder* classes.

The overall structure of our enterprise is thus clear. We create an *AssemblyBuilder* object. Within that we create and add one or more *ModuleBuilder* objects. Within each of these we add *TypeBuilder* objects as required.

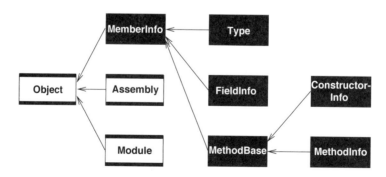

Figure 11.1: Hierarchy of reflection types

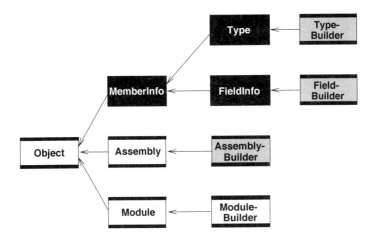

Figure 11.2: Reflection hierarchy and the corresponding builder types

For each *TypeBuilder* object we create members as required using *FieldBuilder*, *MethodBuilder*, and *ConstructorBuilder* objects. In order to insert *IL* into the methods and constructors, we use *ILGenerator* objects to append new codes to the bodies.

Finally, when we have done with adding ingredients to the *AssemblyBuilder*, we "bake" the result by a call to *CreateType* on each *TypeBuilder* object. We then save the assembly to a file.

It is possible to view what is happening here in a number of different ways. From the compiler writer's perspective it is probably most helpful to think of the data structure that is being created as some kind of abstract syntax representation of the final executable module. One may think of the saving of the file or files at the end as being some kind of traversal of this syntax representation. Alternatively, it is possible to think of the *PEM* as being some kind of serialization of the *AssemblyBuilder* structure.

Persistent Assemblies

Creating Dynamic Assemblies

All dynamic code creation is performed in the context of a *dynamic assembly*. This assembly is created by instantiating an assembly builder object in the current application domain. In the usual case where we plan to emit a single *PEM* file from the compilation unit, we immediately define a dynamic module on the assembly builder.

Perhaps the easiest way to understand the process is to work through fragments of typical code. In order to aid discussion of these fragments, we shall assume the definition of an emitter object that holds some useful state. Figure 11.3 gives an outline of the object state for the *PE-emitter* class.

```
using System;
using System.Reflection;
using System.Reflection.Emit;

public class PEemitter {
  String          modNam;        // stem name, set by .ctor
  AppDomain       appDom;        // the application domain
  AssemblyName    asmNam;        // the assembly name object
  AssemblyBuilder asmBld;        // the assembly builder object
  ModuleBuilder   modBld;        // the module builder object
  <more fields and methods later ...>
}
```

Figure 11.3: Framework for dynamic assembly creation

Later we shall add some other fields to this class to do such things as hold a reference to the current type builder object and to hold other necessary states. Many of the code examples have also been simplified by removing some detail of the error recovery actions. All of the examples are shown in *C#*, since they rely very heavily on the methods from *mscorlib* that typically have overloaded names.

When *Reflection.Emit* defines a dynamic assembly, it may contain one or more dynamic modules. If the dynamic assembly is persistent, each of the dynamic modules will be saved to a different *PE* file. We may choose one of the modules to be saved to the same file as the main assembly file that contains the assembly manifest. We need to make that choice at the time that we define the dynamic module. In any case we shall assume in what follows that we will create only one module in the assembly and save that module to the assembly *PE* file.

Code generation with *Reflection.Emit* begins and ends with rather stereotyped code. Figure 11.4 shows how the context is created by creating an *AssemblyBuilder* object and creating a single *ModuleBuilder* object attached to that. The code begins by fetching the application domain and creating the builder objects. A helper method creates the *Assembly-Name* structure. This object has a number of information fields that might be usefully set at this time. When *DefineDynamicAssembly* is called, the second argument to the call must be one of three values from the *AssemblyBuilderAccess* enumeration. These are *Save*, *Run*, or *RunAndSave*. This choice determines whether we shall have a persistent or transient assembly. Since we want to write the assembly to the file system, rather than wanting to reflect on the completed product, we need a persistent assembly, so we specify *Save* in this case.

There are several overloadings of the *DefineDynamicModule* method. If we were creating a transient assembly, we would call a version of the method that takes a single string argument. In our present example we want to create a persistent assembly, so we

```
public void BeginModule(string extn) {         // method of PEemitter
    appDom = Threading.Thread.GetDomain();
    asmNam = MkAsmName(extn);
    asmBld = appDom.DefineDynamicAssembly(
                     asmNam, AssemblyBuilderAccess.Save);
    modBld = asmBld.DefineDynamicModule(
                     modNam + "_mod", asmNam.DefaultAlias);
}

private AssemblyName MkAsmName(string extn) { // method of PEemitter
    AssemblyName an = new AssemblyName();
    an.DefaultAlias = modNam + extn;       // .dll or .exe extension
    an.Name  = modNam + "_asm";
    an.Title = "Title " + modNam;          // maybe other string fields
    return a;
}
```

Figure 11.4: Boilerplate code for beginning a module

supply a second string argument to specify the name of the default file in which the module will be saved. Since we want the module to be emitted into the same file as the assembly manifest, we give the module the same default filename as the assembly. Later we may choose to override the default name. If we do, the fact that the *ModuleBuilder* and the *AssemblyName* were defined with the same default name will ensure that both will share the same file, no matter what the name of that file turns out to be. There are also versions of the *DefineDynamicModule* method that take a Boolean argument to specify whether or not debug information will be produced.

Completion of the assembly creation process is also straightforward. Figure 11.5 shows the *EndModule* method corresponding to the *BeginModule* method shown in Figure 11.4. In this fragment, unlike most of the code examples here, the exception handling is shown explicitly.

```
public void EndModule() {                  // instance method of PEemitter
    try {
        String str = asmNam.DefaultAlias;
        asmBld.Save(str);                  // save assembly as a PE module
    } catch (Exception e) {
        <can't create outfile – emit error message>
    }
}
```

Figure 11.5: Boilerplate code for saving a module

Creating Types

When we come to emit code into the methods of a dynamic assembly, we frequently require arguments that are *System.Type* references. These may either be *type references*, which refer to types imported from other assemblies, or *type definitions*, which refer to types defined in the assembly that is under construction.

Class types are defined inside modules by creating *TypeBuilder* objects. Enumeration types are defined using a separate *EnumBuilder* object, but all other types use *TypeBuilder* objects. Typically we shall define one class at a time, using a new field in our *PEemitter* structure to denote the current builder —

```
public class PEemitter {
  <previous fields>
  TypeBuilder currTp;                  // the current type builder
  . . .
```

In order to be able to refer to previously constructed types, we must save a reference to the *System.Type* object resulting from each *TypeBuilder*. The reference should be saved in the corresponding type descriptor of our *AST*. In the case that the metadata for imported types was derived by reflecting on *PEM* assemblies, type references to imported objects should have been saved in the *AST* at the time. In all other cases we shall have to construct type objects for type *references* as well as for type *definitions*.

We create a new type builder by a calling the method *DefineType* on the module builder object. We must supply the class name for the new type and a bitset of type attributes. The type attributes are an enumeration that specifies all of the attributes of classes that were listed in Figure 3.7 and all of the attributes that were left out of the figure. These values may be logically **or**-ed together to create the attribute bitset.

There are a number of methods that create *TypeBuilder* objects. These are all instance methods in the *ModuleBuilder* class, and all are named *DefineType*. The simplest of these takes a string that names the class and the attribute bitset —

```
public TypeBuilder DefineType(string name,
                                   TypeAttributes attr);
```

There are more specialized versions that allow declaration of the type that the new class extends, taking one extra argument of *System.Type* type. The argument *parent* declares the supertype of the new class —

```
public TypeBuilder DefineType(string name,
                        TypeAttributes attr, Type parent);
```

In the case that a class is to be defined that implements one or more interfaces, another version of *DefineType* is required. This version takes one extra argument, of type **array**

of *System.Type*. The argument *implSeq* declares the list of interface types that this class implements —

```
public TypeBuilder DefineType(string name,
    TypeAttributes attr, Type parent, Type[] implSeq);
```

It is also possible to declare a type with a parent type but no interface implementations and add the interfaces later. There are other specialized versions of *DefineType* that declare value classes with explicit layout and an explicit memory size.

The string that is sent as first argument to the call of *DefineType* is the fully qualified name of the class. This will usually be a dotted name. Recall that the runtime has no concrete representation of namespaces, and classes are known at runtime by their full names. Namespaces are simply a bit of syntactic sugar for the source language. Tools such as class browsers and `ildasm` infer the presence of namespaces by finding common prefixes of the classnames. So far as the tools are concerned, a namespace is all of the characters of a dotted classname up to the last "." character.

Once the type builder has been created, and stored in the *AST* if necessary, the members of the type are defined using *FieldBuilder* and *MethodBuilder* objects. We shall look at the details later.

"Baking" the type.

"Baking" the type.   Types are defined by *DefineType*. The type members are then defined and added to the type builder. When the definition is complete, the construction is completed by calling the *CreateType* method. Based of the imagery of adding ingredients to a cake according to a recipe, the call of *CreateType* is colloquially referred to as "baking" the class. The method takes no arguments —

```
public Type CreateType();                     // Bake the class
```

The returned object is the newly completed *System.Type* object. This is the object reference that needs to be saved in the *AST* and referenced for used occurrences of the type.

Adding Members

Classes may define members that are fields, methods, properties, and events. We shall concentrate on the first two of these. Properties usually involve the definition of a private field and one or two methods, as do event definitions.

Defining fields.

Defining fields.   Fields of classes are defined by creating a *FieldBuilder* object attached to a *TypeBuilder* object. The *DefineField* method of *TypeBuilder* takes arguments to specify the name of the field, the *Type*, and the method attributes. The attributes are taken from an enumeration that declares the semantics of the field.

Defining methods.   Methods of classes are defined by creating a *MethodBuilder* object attached to a *TypeBuilder* object. This is done by dispatching a call to the *Define-Method* function on the *TypeBuilder* object. Constructors are defined by a separate method discussed later. The definition of *PInvoke* methods also uses a separate method call.

The define method function takes four parameters. These are the *name* of the method, of **string** type; the *attributes* of the method, from the *MethodAttribute* enumeration; the *return type* of the method, of *System.Type* type; and the *formal argument types* of the method, of **array of** *System.Type* type.

The attributes values are from an enumeration which is partly exclusive and partly set-valued. Thus although the various enumeration constants may be logically **or**-ed together to create the final value, only one member specifying accessibility may be chosen.

The result type for a pure procedure may be **null**, but it is probably more correctly specified by the value denoted in *C#* by **typeof**(*System.Void*). The types of the formal parameters are specified by an array of *System.Type*. In the case of a no-arg method the actual parameter may be set to **null**.

If a method is the entry point for the assembly, then it must be declared to both the assembly and to the module. The call might look as seen in Figure 11.6.

```
AssemblyBuilder asm;
ModuleBuilder mod;
...
MethodBuilder meth;                    // the main method
...
asm.SetEntryPoint(meth);               // set main in assembly
mod.SetEntryPoint(meth);               // set main in module
```

Figure 11.6: Setting the program entry point

Constructors are defined using a separate method *DefineConstructor* that is comparable to *DefineMethod*. The method takes three arguments and returns a *ConstructorBuilder* object. The arguments are the method attributes, the calling convention enumeration value, and the argument *Type* array. Note that there is no need to specify a name (it will be ".ctor" anyway) nor a return type. In the usual case the calling conventions will be the enumeration value *CallingConventions.Standard*. The body of the constructor is defined in exactly the same was as for any other procedure.

If all that is required is a default no-arg constructor, the whole task can be achieved with a single call. The method *DefineDefaultConstructor* creates a *ConstructorBuilder* that simply calls the parent type constructor. The define method needs only to specify the method attributes.

In the case of *PInvoke* methods it is necessary to construct a *MethodBuilder* object that defines the incoming and outgoing signatures as well as any call convention information. The *DefinePInvokeMethod* method allows all of this information to be supplied. Of course, in this case the body will be left empty.

Inserting IL Code

Once we have created the *MethodBuilder* objects we finally get to specify the *IL* in the bodies of the methods. This step is performed by creating an object of *ILGenerator* type —

```
MethodBuilder meth;                          // the current method
...
ILGenerator iGen = meth.GetILGenerator();
```

We insert code by calling various *Emit* methods on this generator object.

The signature of the method is defined by the array of types that is sent to the call of *DefineMethod* that creates a *MethodBuilder* object. However, it is necessary to explicitly define any local variables of the method.

Local variables are declared by dispatching method *DeclareLocal* on the current *ILGenerator* object. The method returns an object of *LocalBuilder* type. A single argument declares the type of the variable that the object denotes. The local builder objects are used as arguments to the some of the calls of *Emit*.

Calling Emit. The *Emit* methods of the *ILGenerator* type are overloaded, with one variant for each of the *IL* instruction formats, as seen in Appendix B. All of these methods take a first argument of the *OpCode* type. There are special methods for emitting call instructions for "var-arg" methods, and for the "`throw`" instruction.

The *OpCode* type is a structure that contains information about the instruction that it represents. The value corresponding to each named instruction may be retrieved as a static field of the *OpCodes* class. Thus in order to emit an add instruction, we will take the *ILGenerator* object (named *iGen*, say) and dispatch –

```
iGen.Emit(OpCodes.Add);                      // emit add instruction
```

The names of the static fields of the *OpCodes* class correspond to the `ilasm` instruction names, except that the first letter is capitalized and dots are replaced by lowline characters "_".

The various *Emit* instructions have signatures shown in the overload list in Figure 11.7.

```
void Emit(OpCode)                        // plain instruction
void Emit(OpCode, Label[])               // used for "switch"
void Emit(OpCode, string)                // used for "ldc"
void Emit(OpCode, FieldInfo)             // takes field descriptor
void Emit(OpCode, MethodInfo)            // takes method descriptor
void Emit(OpCode, SignatureHelper)
void Emit(OpCode, wchar)                 // character argument
void Emit(OpCode, uint8)                 // unsigned byte argument
void Emit(OpCode, int16)                 // short int argument
void Emit(OpCode, int32)                 // int argument
void Emit(OpCode, int64)                 // long int argument
void Emit(OpCode, float32)               // float argument
void Emit(OpCode, float64)               // double argument
void Emit(OpCode, Label)                 // label argument
void Emit(OpCode, ConstructorInfo)       // used for "newobj"
void Emit(OpCode, Type)                  // used for casts etc.
void Emit(OpCode, LocalBuilder)          // local variable argument
```

Figure 11.7: Signatures of various *Emit* methods

Declaring and marking labels.

Declaring and marking labels.   Label objects are used as arguments whenever branching instructions are emitted into the *IL*. Labels are opaque structures and may be *defined* at any time. Labels are defined by a call to the *DefineLabel* method. The call is dispatched on the current *ILGenerator* object. Defining a label does not place it at any particular position within the instruction stream. A label is positioned by being passed as an argument to the *MarkLabel* method of *ILGenerator*. Roughly speaking, *DefineLabel* and *MarkLabel* correspond to our *newLabel* and *DefLabel* utilities for textual *IL*. The first allocates a label value, and the second places it in a particular position in the instruction stream.

As an example, the code to emit *IL* for a conditional expression might be as shown in Figure 11.8. Compare this to Figure 9.3.

Declaring structured exception handling blocks.

Declaring structured exception handling blocks.   The *ILGenerator* class has various methods for beginning and ending structured assembly blocks. We shall look at just the **try** and **catch** block cases. The methods —

```
public virtual Label BeginExceptionBlock()
public virtual void EndExceptionBlock()
```

begin and end a structured assembly handling region. The label returned by the begin method is the label that will be automatically placed at the end of the region. Within the

```
fLab = iGen.DefineLabel();          // label for exp1 false
mLab = iGen.DefineLabel();          // merge point label
emtr.FallTrue(exp1, fLab);
emtr.PushValue(exp2);               // true branch, push exp2
iGen.Emit(OpCodes.Br, mLab);        // jump to the merge point
iGen.MarkLabel(fLab);               // emit the false label
emtr.PushValue(exp3);               // false branch, push exp3
iGen.MarkLabel(mLab);               // emit the merge label
```

Figure 11.8: Code to emit *IL* to push the value $(exp_1\,?\,exp_2 : exp_3)$

exception-handling region the end of the **try** block is marked by the start of the first **catch** block. This is emitted by the method —

public virtual void BeginCatchBlock(Type exType)

The condition for entry into the catch is that the exception object is of the type given in the method argument. If the condition is not met, control passes to the next catch block. The end of the catch block is marked by the start of another catch or by the end of the region.

Reflection.Emit automatically ends the try and catch blocks with an appropriate "leave" instruction. It is an error to explicitly emit a "leave" instruction at the end of the block. If control needs to exit from a block from anywhere except the end, an explicit call to "leave" should be emitted, with the target label being the label returned by the initial call of *BeginExceptionBlock*. Figure 11.9 shows the skeleton of some test code and the resulting *IL*. In this example the use of the *BeginFinallyBlock* is illustrated also. Note the use of the nested **.try** blocks arising from the repeated call of *BeginExceptionBlock*.

Revisiting Hello World

The canonical "Hello World" program as emitted by *gpcp* was shown in Figure 2.23. The *IL* of the module body calls some console methods and a runtime system helper that transforms *.NET* native strings into character arrays. A short *C#* program that emits the assembly "REhello.exe" is shown in Figure 11.10. Since there is no *AST* to traverse in this case, the emission of *IL* is performed by inline code in the figure. The fetching of the *MethodInfo* objects has been abstracted from the code, since there are several options to consider. In order to save some clutter in the text, we have assumed that we have defined suitable constants, such as *psAtt*, to stand in place of "MethodAttributes.Public | MethodAttributes.Static".

In an environment in which metadata is derived from *System.Reflection*, the required object references will have been stored in the *AST*. For a stand-alone program, as in Fig-

```
Label exLab = iGen.BeginExceptionBlock(); // exit label
Label fiLab = iGen.BeginExceptionBlock(); // end-try label
<emit try block IL>;
iGen.BeginCatchBlock(typeof(Ex1));
<emit IL for exception-type = Ex1>;
iGen.BeginCatchBlock(typeof(Ex2));
<emit IL for exception-type = Ex2>;
iGen.EndExceptionBlock();  // "fiLab" goes here!
iGen.BeginFinallyBlock();
<emit finally block IL >;
iGen.EndExceptionBlock();  // "exLab" goes here!


.try {
    .try {
        <try block IL>
        leave fiLab
    } catch Ex1 {
        <catch block IL>                 // don't forget to pop exception
        leave fiLab
    } catch Ex2 {
        <catch block IL>                 // don't forget to pop exception
        leave fiLab
    } // end handler
    fiLab:  leave exLab
} finally {
    <finally block IL>
    endfinally
} // end handler
exLab:
```

Figure 11.9: Test code to emit exception blocks, and resulting *IL*

ure 11.10, we may simulate that situation by invoking the reflection methods directly. In order to fetch the *MethodInfo* object for "[RTS]CP_rts::strToChO" we would call the function —

```
private static MethodInfo RTSstrToChO() {
    Type cprts = typeof(CP_rts);           // get [RTS]CP_rts
    return cprts.GetMethod("strToChO");
}
```

This simple structure of this example depends on the fact that there are no overloaded method names in the *gpcp* runtime system. If method names were overloaded, the call to *GetMethod* would take a second argument with an array of *System.Type* objects specifying the formal parameter types.

```
using System;
using System.Threading;
using System.Reflection;
using System.Reflection.Emit;

public class MkHello {
    public static void Main(string[] args) {
        CreateAsm(new PEemitter("REhello"));  // see Figure 11.3
    }
    private static void CreateAsm(PEemitter emtr) {
        MethodInfo ccws = <MethodInfo for Console::WriteString>;
        MethodInfo ccwl = <MethodInfo for Console::WriteLn>;
        MethodInfo schO = <MethodInfo for CP_rts::strToChO>;
        emtr.BeginModule(".exe");                 // see Figure 11.4
        emtr.currTp = emtr.modBld.DefineType(
                                   "Hello.Hello", pubAtt);
        MethodBuilder main = emtr.currTp.DefineMethod(
                   ".CPmain", psAtt, typeof(System.Void), null);
        emtr.asmBld.SetEntryPoint(main);   // asm-bld entry point
        emtr.modBld.SetEntryPoint(main);   // mod-bld entry point
        ILGenerator iGen = main.GetILGenerator();
        iGen.Emit(OpCodes.Ldstr, "Hello World");
        iGen.Emit(OpCodes.Call, schO);    // call CP_rts::strToChO
        iGen.Emit(OpCodes.Call, ccws);    // call Console::WriteString
        iGen.Emit(OpCodes.Call, ccwl);    // call Console::WriteLn
        iGen.Emit(OpCodes.Ret);           // emit return
        emtr.currTp.CreateType();         // bake the class
        emtr.EndModule();                 // see Figure 11.5
    }
} // end class MkHello
```

Figure 11.10: Module that emits "Hello World" program

In order for the *C#* compiler to be able to generate type tokens using the **typeof** construct, the program needs to be compiled with a reference to the *RTS* runtime assembly. The command "csc /r:RTS.dll MkHello.cs" is typical. An alternative is to perform the binding at *MkHello* runtime using the *GetType* method —

```
Type cprts = Type.GetType("CP_rts");  // get [RTS]CP_rts
```

In either case, when programs like *MkHello* perform reflection, the relevant assemblies must be loaded. If the program performing the reflection does not otherwise reference an assembly, then it must be explicitly loaded with a statement such as —

```
System.Reflection.Assembly.Load("RTS.dll");
```

In an environment in which metatdata is derived from some other source, such as a header file for example, different considerations apply. In such a case it is possible to construct the various reflection objects without reference to any assembly. The idea is to create dummy definitions for the types and methods that are required. These definitions will not be persisted, and the signatures will match the real types and methods that are encountered at runtime. A sensible way to achieve this is to define a factory module that creates dummy reflection objects on demand.

For the purposes of *Reflection.Emit* we want objects of the "real" reflection types *Type*, *MethodInfo*, and so on. What our factory will produce is the derived types *Type-Builder*, *MethodBuilder*, and so on. This still works. We need to create an *AssemblyBuilder* object corresponding to each imported assembly as a context in which to create the various types as required. One small but important point is that the dummy assembly objects must be created with the *RunAndSave* flag. The persistent assembly that is being created will have references to the various dummy assemblies, and persistent assemblies cannot reference transient assemblies. Of course we do not ever save the dummy assemblies, but we need to declare them as *potentially* persistent. Typically we would define a *AsmFactory* class that encapsulates references to the dummy assembly, the dynamic module, and the current type builder. The class would define methods to add new types and methods on demand by creating the appropriate *-Builder* objects.

In the example in Figure 11.10 all of the external methods come from the same *RTS* assembly. We therefore need to construct a single factory object —

```
AsmFactory rtsAsm = new AsmFactory("RTS");
rtsAsm.AddType("Console", pubAtt);       // create [RTS]Console
```

We may then use this assembly factory to produce the *MethodBuilder* objects that we shall use as surrogates for the *MethodInfo* objects that the emitter methods expect. For example, in order to get the method information for *Console.WriteLn* in Figure 11.10, we would replace the pseudocode on the right-hand side of the definition by the function call —

```
MethodInfo ccwl = rtsAsm.AddMethod(
                    "WriteLn", psAtt, typeof(System.Void), null);
```

The *AddMethod* function will create a *MethodBuilder* object. There is one quirky aspect of this misuse of the method definition machinery for method references. Although the bodies of the dummy *MethodBuilder* objects will never be used, the objects are invalid if they do not have a body defined. Because of this it is necessary for the *AddMethod* code to insert at least a return instruction in the body.

The more usual context for *Reflection.Emit* is one in which a compiler emits output during the traversal of an *AST*. In this case the descriptors of imported modules, types, and members would be decorated with the dummy reflection objects. It is sensible to perform this decoration lazily. In general only a subset of the objects from an imported assembly will be used as references in the persistent assembly, so it makes sense to create the dummy reflection objects on demand.

Transient Assemblies

If we define a dynamic module with the *Run* flag, we create a *transient assembly*. Transient assemblies may be used to define types and to create instances of those types, but the assemblies cannot be saved to the file system. The mechanism thus provides a facility for creating new code at runtime.

There are a number of scenarios in which runtime code generation might be considered. Runtime code generation can find a place in some query-driven environments in which a query might be compiled into *IL* and then executed. In order to justify this, the speed advantage of a *IL* solution over a table-driven or interpreted solution would have to be large enough to offset the time taken to emit the *IL* in the first place.

Perhaps a more interesting example is one in which code is generated at runtime to instantiate some generic code. Generics (or equivalently *parametric polymorphism*) allows code to be defined that takes one or more *type parameters*. Uses of the code specify the actual type that will be substituted for the formal type in the definition. There are two possible approaches to implementing such facilities. Firstly, the "template" code may be expanded at every occurrence of use. Alternatively, the code may be instantiated by runtime code generation, on demand, at runtime.

The issues involved in checking the semantic correctness of code that uses generics would take the discussion too far from our topic, so we shall consider a simple example that explores the *IL* generation issues. But first, we consider the machinery of transient assembly generation.

Runtime Code Generation

Declaring transient assemblies.   The creation of a transient assembly closely follows the pattern that was seen in Figure 11.4 for a persistent assembly. In this case we use the "*Run*" value for the assembly builder access flag and do not define a default alias for the dynamic module. Figure 11.11 has code that is comparable to the previous figure. As before the code begins by fetching the application domain and creating the builder objects. A helper method creates the *AssemblyName* structure. In this case we call the version of the *DefineDynamicModule* method that takes a single string arugment. The creation of class and method builder objects for transient assemblies is exactly the same as for the persistent case.

Using transient assemblies.   The whole point in creating transient assemblies is the possibility of creating new types and instantiating instances of those types at runtime. It

```
public void BeginModule(string extn) {          // method of PEemitter
    appDom = Threading.Thread.GetDomain();
    asmNam = MkAsmName(extn);
    asmBld = appDom.DefineDynamicAssembly(
                          asmNam, AssemblyBuilderAccess.Run);
    modBld = asmBld.DefineDynamicModule(modName + "_mod");
}

private AssemblyName MkAsmName(string extn) { // method of PEemitter
    AssemblyName an = new AssemblyName();
    an.Name  = modNam + "_asm";
    an.Title = "Title " + modNam;              // maybe other string fields
    return a;
}
```

Figure 11.11: Boilerplate code for declaring a transient assembly

is not possible to instantiate a type that has not been "baked," but once that has been done, we may create objects of the type at will.

Code wishing to create an object of a type defined in a transient assembly must either have a handle on the transient assembly or a handle on the *Type* object of the newly created class definition. Starting from the *AssemblyBuilder* object, the *C#* code to fetch the *Type* object goes like this —

```
AssemblyBuilder asm;
...
Module mod = asm.GetModule(string modName);
Type   typ = mod.GetType(string typName);
```

Once the type object has been found, the methods of the *System.Activator* class may be used to create instances. Two of the most likely methods are —

```
public static object CreateInstance(Type typ);
public static object CreateInstance(Type typ, object[] args);
```

The first of these invokes the standard no-arg constructor, and the second invokes the constructor with arguments that match the possibly boxed values in the object array. Creating an object of the given type using the first method would look as follows —

```
System.Activator.CreateInstance(typ);  // no-arg constructor
```

Generic expansible arrays.   The concept and implementation of arrays that are expanded by amortized doubling was described in the sidebar on page 134. Under normal circumstances if a user wants to use arrays of several different element types, then it is necessary to write the code that declares the type and supplies the append method.

Now consider a programming language in which such arrays are a primitive type constructor. Thus one may declare (say) —

> **var** seq : **vector of** SomeType;   (* *for any type SomeType* *)

just as one may declare an ordinary array of any named type. The implementation issue is this: Whenever an append operation is performed on such a datum, the compiler must specify how to do it. Since the compiler knows what the actual element type is, it could expand the append inline. However, if the append is to be implemented by a method call, some module somewhere must define that method.

If we restrict the possible types of vector elements to the reference types, then it would be possible to implement the append method for a vector of *System.Object* types and use "castclass" on element fetches. This strategy corresponds to the implementations of generics based on *type erasure*. If we want to be able to create vectors of any type, including primitive types and arbitrary user-defined value types, then this approach simply will not do.

An alternative strategy would be for the compiler to generate a private append method for every vector type that was met in any particular compilation unit. This strategy has the disadvantage of duplicating code.

There are elegant solutions based on runtime code generation. For example, the compiler could "know" that the type "**vector of** *T*" for any *T* will be represented at runtime by a type with some agreed name. In each case the type would have an instance method named *Append*. The name could be formed from the name of the element type, in the same way as the type "**array of** *T*" for any *T* is represented by "*T* [ ] " at runtime. The only remaining problem is, "Which module is responsible for producing the *IL* that defines the type and the method?" The "demand-driven" answer to this question would be that the first module that needed an instance of the type would arrange for the *IL* to be produced. Thereafter, every module of the same program that required an instance of the type would find it in the usual way.

Well, that is the general idea. One of the complicating factors is that unless the assembly is written to disk and then loaded in the normal way, the other modules of the program will not be able to see the assembly. At least, that is a limitation of the current release of *.NET*.

There is a way around the problem, which involves the compiler just accepting that objects of vector types cannot be instantiated using the usual mechanism. Instead we set up a *vector factory* that produces instances of the required classes as needed. The factory would generate a new class whenever it received the first request for some new vector type.

A more minimal alternative approach involves implementing all vector types as a single value class type with three fields. One is the read-only "hi-tide" value of **int32** type. The second is a reference to the varying length array, delared to be of **object** type. The final field is a function pointer to the *Append* method for the actual vector type. Whenever such an array is initialized, a request is made to the *method factory* in the runtime system, passing the *System.Type* object of the element type as an argument. The factory creates a new append method if required and returns the function pointer. Subsequent append operations may then be invoked with minimal overhead.

Of course, the verifier will not like this approach. However, the verifier will be unable to verify the earlier approach either, since the statically created *IL* refers to a type that the verifier cannot even find, let alone check.

Notes on Chapter 11

Preliminary measurements indicate that the use of *Reflection.Emit* as the compiler output-writer does not lead to reductions in overall compile time in current releases of *.NET*. This is a bitter disappointment.

In principle the architecture has the potential to give useful speed gains. For example, the *JVM* emitting backend for *gpcp* has two versions. One writes out textual assembly language for the "jasmin" byte code assembler, while the other uses an architecture very comparable to the "*Builder" types to write binary class files directly. In this *JVM* example, the compiler can construct and write out a class file in the same time that it takes to write the corresponding textual assembly file. Even if the jasmin assembler was infinitely fast, the direct-writing alternative would still win the race. Of course, the *PEM* and *JVM* class file formats are very different. However, the intrinsic complexity of the two formats is comparable. This fact gives some hope that some future replacement for *Reflection.Emit* might have better performance.

So far as is known, all of Microsoft's own compilers for *.NET* write their *PEM* output files directly, without using *Reflection.Emit*.

For those who have downloaded the source of *gpcp*, the code for the *JVM* emitters is in the files "JavaUtil.cp", "ClassUtil.cp", and "JsmnUtil.cp". The first of these contains the common code, while the others contain the code for emitting the class and the jasmin files respectively.

There are several examples of the *MkHello* module of Figure 11.10 available on the *SoftwareAutomata* website. These illustrate various strategies for obtaining the metadata objects for the imported methods. The reflection sample programs that are released with the *.NET SDK* may prove helpful also.

There is a further approach to the implementation of "**vector of** *SomeType*" objects. This involves type erasure, but avoids the restriction to elements of reference types by boxing and unboxing element instances as needed. This approach works but was not mentioned in the body of the chapter, since it does not involve runtime code generation.

Further Explorations

In this chapter we explore some of the challenges of compiling language features that don't quite fit the facilities of the *CLR*. In particular, we shall consider how to work around the absence of some of the features that some languages require. In some cases there is more than one way of bypassing the problem. The first two issues are ones that arise from *Component Pascal* but are typical of the issues that arise with many other languages.

Covariant Return Types

Some languages allow the return type of overriding methods to be narrowed, compared to the return type of the method that they override. Suppose that we have two classes, *BaseRcvT* and *SubRcvT*, where *SubRcvT* extends *BaseRcvT*. If the superclass defines a function *Foo* returning some type *BaseRetT*, the subclass overrides this with a method returning *SubRetT*, and *SubRetT* is a subtype of *BaseRetT*, then we say that the method has a *covariant* return type. The name indicates that the return type varies in the same direction as the receiver type—that is, the method dispatched on the subtype receiver returns a subtype object. Here is an example —

339

```
procedure (rcv :   BaseRcvT)Foo()  :   BaseRetT, new,extensible;
procedure (rcv :   SubRcvT)Foo()   :   SubRetT, extensible;
```

Very frequently the contexts in which it makes sense to use return type covariance are ones in which the return type and the receiver type are the same.

Methods with covariant return types are innocuous in their effect on the usual type safety guarantees. Consider a situation where we have a variable, statically known to be of type *BaseRcvT*. The contract that we have from the type is that if we dispatch *Foo* on this reference, we will get back a return value of at least type *BaseRetT*.[1] This guarantee is obviously fulfilled even if the exact type of the object that is referenced is the subtype. However, if we have a reference that is statically of type *SubRcvT*, then we have a guarantee that the return value of the function will be at least *SubRetT*. Of course further extensions of the type may return even narrower subtypes, but these will always be compatible with the guarantee.

The *CLR* does not allow return types to vary in this way. Indeed, if we define the two example methods exactly as shown in *IL*, then `ilasm` and the runtime will silently accept them. The two headings might begin as shown in Figure 12.1. All this is accepted without protest. Unfortunately the two methods do not go into the corresponding slots of the two *v-table*s. Thus the intended overriding semantics of the methods will not be achieved.

```
.class public BaseRcvT {
    .method public virtual class BaseRetT 'Foo'() il managed
    { <body of BaseRcvT::Foo> }
}

.class public SubRcvT extends BaseRcvT {
    .method public virtual class SubRetT 'Foo'() il managed
    { <body of SubRcvT::Foo> }
}
```

Figure 12.1: Unsuccessful attempt to define methods with covariant return types

Implementing Covariance

Suppose that we have the definitions in Figure 12.2 in some hypothetical language with *C#*-like syntax, but allowing return type covariance. Now we presume that following these definitions we declare two variables, one each of the two receiver types. The declarations might be —

---

[1] By *at least type T* we mean type *T* or some subtype of *T*.

```
BaseRcvT bRcv;                  // the base type
SubRcvT  sRcv;                  // the subtype
```

Now we consider two method calls, where each function return value is assigned to a variable of the corresponding return type —

```
BaseRetT bRet = bRcv.Foo();     // Foo returns a BaseRetT
SubRetT  sRet = sRcv.Foo();     // Foo returns a SubRetT
```

You should check the type-correctness of these two assignments. The second is valid, because the object on which *Foo* is called is known to be of at least *SubRcvT* type and hence returns at least a *SubRetT* object.

```
public class SubRetT : BaseRetT { ... }            // return types

public class BaseRcvT {                            // base receiver type
    public virtual BaseRetT Foo() { ... }
    ...
}

public class SubRcvT : BaseRcvT {                  // sub receiver type
    public virtual SubRetT Foo() { ... }
    ...
}
```

Figure 12.2: Definition of methods with covariant return types

If the two methods are encoded in *IL* in the way shown in Figure 12.1, the semantic failure occurs in the execution of the first assignment. If the object referenced by the variable *bRcv* is actually of the subtype *SubRcvT*, then correct semantics would have the method "SubRcvT::Foo" being invoked. Instead, because the two methods do not share the same slot index in the *v-table*, the method "BaseRcvT::Foo" will be called.

Our task is thus clear. We must find a way of tricking the *CLR* into invoking the correct method in the circumstance described. There are at least two ways to achieve this. One involves the definition of wrapper methods, and the other requires adjustments at each call site.

Defining covariant wrappers. A first solution to the problem arises from the observation that the *IL* in Figure 12.1 would work correctly if the return type was not covariant. Now the second of our model assignments would be in trouble with the verifier, because we would appear to be trying to assign a return value of type *BaseRetT* to a variable of type *SubRetT*. The compiler may know that the return value is actually of the subtype, but the verifier cannot deduce this from the declarations.

The solution is to emit *two* methods to the *IL* for the class with the subtype. One of these declares that it returns the noncovariant type, so that it will be allocated to the correct slot in the *v-table*. The other declares that it returns the subtype but in its body simply chains to its noncovariant partner. It also performs a cast on the return value, so as to satisfy the verifier. If we want the code to be *CLS* conformant, we cannot name the overriding method and the wrapper with the same simple name, since the signatures of the two methods differ only in return type. However, we can call the overriding method by a *different* name, and force it to occupy the overriding slot in the *v-table*, by means of a *MethodImpl* delaration. Figure 12.3 shows the skeleton of the *IL*. In this skeleton, the **.override** directive forces the *Foo_Impl* method to occupy the same *v-table* slot as the inherited *Foo* method.

```
.class public BaseRcvT {
  .method public virtual class BaseRetT 'Foo'()  il managed
  { <body of BaseRcvT::Foo> }
}

.class public SubRcvT extends BaseRcvT {
  .method public virtual class BaseRetT 'Foo_Impl'()  il managed
  { <body of SubRcvT::Foo> }

  .override BaseRcvT::Foo with instance class BaseRetT 'Foo_Impl'()

  .method public virtual class SubRetT 'Foo'()  il managed {
    ldarg.0                            // push this
    callvirt instance class BaseRetT BaseRcvT::Foo()
    castclass SubRetT                  // guaranteed ok!
    ret
  }
}
```

Figure 12.3: Implementing covariant return types with a wrapper method

Notice that the call instruction inside the wrapper method is "`callvirt`" rather than a static call. This recognizes the fact that this method may itself have covariant overrides that need to be properly dispatched.

Casting the function result. The second technique for implementing covariant return types works in the same way as the wrapper method but does not require the definition of a wrapper. In this case all of the methods are declared without a covariant return type, and the return object is typecast at the call site, rather than inside the body of the wrapper. This is the method used in *gpcp*.

You may think of this particular approach as doing no more than inlining the wrapper method at the call site. For the second of our test case assignments, we would have called the wrapper method with the following *IL* —

```
// SubRetT sRet = sRcv.Foo()
ldsfld class SubRcvT StatCls::'sRcv'          // push this
callvirt instance class SubRetT SubRcvT::Foo()// call wrapper
stsfld class SubRetT StatCls::'sRet'          // assign result
```

Here we have assumed that all of the declared variables are static fields of some class named *StatCls*.

In this second approach to implementation, instead of the above *IL*, we call the apparently *non*covariant method, and then cast the return result —

```
// SubRetT sRet = sRcv.Foo()
ldsfld class SubRcvT StatCls::'sRcv'          // push this
callvirt instance class BaseRetT SubRcvT::Foo()// call noncovar.
castclass class SubRetT                        // cast result
stsfld class SubRetT StatCls::'sRet'           // assign result
```

The definitions to allow this approach are shown in Figure 12.4. In the case of deeply nested hierarchies of classes with methods that declare covariant return types, it is necessary to reference the most general return type in the call. This means that the compiler may need to traverse the method descriptors in the *AST* to find that most general return type.

```
.class public BaseRcvT {
    .method public virtual class BaseRetT 'Foo'() il managed
    { <body of BaseRcvT::Foo> }
}

.class public SubRcvT extends BaseRcvT {
    .method public virtual class BaseRetT 'Foo'() il managed
    <custom marker "actual return-type = SubRetT">
    { <body of SubRcvT::Foo> }
}
```

Figure 12.4: Implementing covariant return types with a call-site cast

What are the relative merits of the two approaches? The main advantage of the approach using wrappers is that the compiler emitting *IL* for the call need not be aware that the method has a covariant return type. The compiler simply generates a virtual call to the method with the signature as shown in the metadata. By contrast, the second approach requires the compiler to generate a call to the method with the generic return type, and then cast the result. The compiler cannot take advantage of the narrower return type unless it understands the convention for this particular approach. On the other side, it is clear that the second method is more efficient, since it saves an additional method invocation.

Finally, a word on safe language interworking. We would like to be able to declare covariant return type methods in such a way that clients written in other languages can at least correctly call the methods. As just noted, the wrapper approach does not require the compiler to understand the covariance. Thus the metadata automatically derived from the definitions in Figure 12.3 will allow a client to call either the direct or the wrapper method. For the second approach, the metadata automatically derived from the definitions in Figure 12.4 will also allow an unaware compiler to generate calls correctly to the generic method. Of course, in order to take advantage of the narrower return type, the compiler would need to understand the custom metadata.

We may conclude that compilers for languages that do not understand return type covariance are able to safely *call* covariant methods, no matter which implementation approach is taken. Unfortunately, the same conclusion cannot be taken in the case of the *extension* of types with such methods. Suppose that a *Component Pascal* compiler exports public types with methods with covariant return types. A *C#* compiler, for example, might innocently extend such a type and override one of the methods. Now, because the compiler does not understand the custom metadata, the new method will believe that it is entitled to return the wider type. If it does so, the contract of the supertype will be violated. It follows that types with such methods are useful within a particular language framework but should be avoided when working across language boundaries. Such methods are in any case not *CLS* conformant.

Structural Compatibility of Types

Some languages allow for *structural compatiblility* of types. In contrast, in the *CTS* two types are compatible if they have the same name. The idea of structural compatibility is that two types are equivalent if they have the same structure and their corresponding substructures are equivalent. The advantage of such a rule is that independently defined types that happen to have the same structure can be used interchangeably. This kind of equivalence is seldom required for object types. The chances of two object types being interchangeable seem slight. Not only would the two types be required to have the same structure but also the same behavior. However, structural compatability is a real issue for procedure types or, equivalently, for delegate and event types.

Suppose that two independently created components have each declared a delegate type for methods with some particular signature. Each of the components will have declared a *name* for this type, but the names will not (and acutally *cannot*) be the same. Of course, the set of methods that may be encapsulated by the two types are exactly the same. This is so because when a delegate value is created, the *signature* of the concrete method must match the signature of the *Invoke* method of the delegate. However, if we have a delegate reference declared to be of one of the types, we cannot assign this delegate reference to a location declared to be of the other type. This is in spite of the fact that we may be statically sure that the method encapsulated in one delegate is compatible with the other type.

It does not seem that the checks required for structural compatability of delegate types are significantly more difficult than the checks that are already in place for creating delegate values from concrete methods. Thus there is some prospect that future releases of *.NET* may provide for the required behavior. Nevertheless, in the meantime there is a problem to be solved.

Many languages specify structural equivalence for procedure or function pointer types. *Component Pascal* is one such language. There is a solution to this problem that works elegantly *almost* all the time. There are two possible attacks on the residual cases, and both are ugly but perhaps interesting. First a general observation. If all programs could agree on an algorithm for generating the names of delegate types from the signatures, then all compatible types would magically turn out to have the same name anyway. In order to make this work, the key problem to solve is that of deciding who is responsible for *defining* the class with the commonly agreed name.

Procedure Types and Procedure Values

One creative attack on the problem of implementing procedure types involves mapping procedure *types* into interface types in the *CTS*. Thus if in *Component Pascal* we have a procedure type defined in some module *A*, say —

> **type** IItoR = **procedure** (INTEGER, INTEGER) : REAL

then we declare this in the *IL* as the following interface type —

> **.class public interface** IItoR {
>   **.method public virtual abstract float64** Invoke (**int32,int32**) {}
> }

Other modules may independently define other interface types with the same method signature but with different names. For example, another module, *B* say, might declare an equivalent interface type named *IxIretD*. Variables of these two types will not be assignment compatible.

The second part of the approach is to define another type, in this case a delegate type, to hold the procedure *values*. A typical case of such a class is shown in Figure 12.5. Notice that the one *Invoke* method satisfies the contracts of all the interfaces, no matter how many of these there might be. The key observation is that when we create an instance of this class, encapsulating some particular procedure, the value will be compatible with variables of the types corresponding to *all* of the interfaces that the class implements. Thus values of this example type may be freely type-cast and assigned to variables of either of the two named interface types, *IItoR* and *IxIretD*.

```
.class private auto sealed ProcVal$1
          extends [mscorlib] System.Delegate
          implements [A]A.IItoR,  [B]B.IxIretD {
     .method public specialname rtspecialname instance
                          void .ctor (object,  int32)  runtime managed  {}
     .method public virtual instance
                          float64 Invoke (int32, int32)  runtime managed  {}
}  // end of class ProcVal$1
```

Figure 12.5: Declaration of a polymorphic procedure value

From the point of view of the compiler the process is straightforward. If a compilation unit *creates* procedure values, then it must define a corresponding class, similar to the *ProcVal$1* example. This class need not be exported but should declare that it implements *every* compatible interface that it has seen as a definition in this compilation unit or an imported declaration.

The reader might be excused for asking whether the *IL* in Figure 12.5 is legal. After all, delegate types are **sealed** and users may neither add to their methods nor even prescribe their code. The answer, for the moment, is that this construction is not rejected by either the runtime or the verifier. Even if some future release were to reject this behavior, the same semantics may be obtained by wrapping the delegate type in a user-defined class with arbitrary inheritance. This would be less elegant but hardly less efficient.

The final remaining question must be whether this particular trick is sufficient. The answer, unfortunately, is no. It is possible to encounter patterns of imports such that the compiler of a particualar module is not aware of *all* of the procedure types that a particular procedure value may end up being assigned to. This is very unusual, but it is certainly possible to deliberately write legal programs that cause it to happen. Figure 12.6 is a minimal pathological example.

There are five modules in this program. Three of them, *A*, *B*, and *C*, each define a compatible procedure type named *NoArgProc*. None of these modules imports any other module. There are two further modules, named *ModAB* and *ModBC*. The first, *ModAB*, imports *A* and *B*, and so is aware of the type *A.NoArgProc* and the type *B.NoArgProc*. The module *ModBC* imports *B* and *C*, and so is aware of the types *B.NoArgProc* and *C.NoArgProc*.

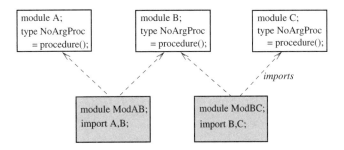

Figure 12.6: Pathological program for procedure value assignment

The limitation of the approach of this section is shown if an attempt is made to copy a procedure value from a variable of type *B.NoArgProc* to a variable of type *A.NoArgProc*. If the value was constructed in module *ModBC*, then the value will implement *B.NoArgProc* and *C.NoArgProc* but will not implement the necessary interface type *A.NoArgProc*. This is so because the compiler of module *ModBC* could not be aware of the existence of this type. The "castclass" instruction asssociated with the assignment will thus fail in these circumstances. There are plausible remedies for this shortcoming. All of these work on the principle that assignments of procedure values that cannot be statically guaranteed to be safe must be tested at runtime. As noted, the vast majority of such assignments will either be known to be safe statically or will pass the test anyway. For the exceptional cases, when the "isinst" test fails, it is necessary to take remedial action at runtime.

Construct a new delegate.   The idea behind this approach is to construct a new delegate object that is type-compatible with the destination location but still encapsulates the same method. This relies on the *reflection* or *introspection* facilities of the *CLR*. The key method is *CreateDelegate*, with the following declaration in *C#* —

```
public static System.Delegate CreateDelegate
    (System.Type type, System.Reflection.MethodInfo method);
```

This method takes an object of *System.Type*, which describes the destination delegate type, and an object of *System.Reflection.MethodInfo*, which describes the method encapsulated in the original delegate.

Let us suppose, in our particular example, that the compiler has defined a delegate type named *ModAB.PV1* that implements the two interface types *A.NoArgProc* and *B.NoArgProc*. Figure 12.7 shows the *IL* to construct the new value.[2] The *IL* starts by duplicating the delegate reference and testing whether the object implements the interface type *A.NoArgP*. If all is well, control branches to the label, and the value is assigned to its destination. If the test fails, control falls through into the remedial code.

---

[2]In this figure, occurrences of system type names have been abbreviated by the omission of the assembly name prefix " [mscorlib] " in all cases.

```
    <push delegate reference>
    dup                                         // duplicate delegate ref.
    isinst class [A]A.NoArgP                    // test against dest. type
    brtrue okLab                                // fall through on null
    castclass class System.Delegate
    stloc 'tmp'                                 // save old delegate value
    ldtoken ModAB.PV1                           // get runtime type handle
    call class System.Type
        System.Type::GetTypeFromHandle(         // get System.Type object
            value class System.RuntimeTypeHandle)
    ldloc 'tmp'                                 // restore delegate value
    call instance class System.Reflection.MethodInfo
        System.Delegate::get_Method()           // get MethodInfo object
    call class System.Delegate
        System.Delegate::CreateDelegate(        // make new delegate
            class System.Type
            class System.Reflection.MethodInfo)
okLab:
    castclass class [A]A.NoArgP                 // cast to dest. type
    <assign to destination>
```

Figure 12.7: Creating a new delegate value using reflection

The remedial code fetches the runtime type handle of the required destination type, using the "ldtoken" instruction. The corresponding *System.Type* object is obtained by a call to the *System.GetTypeFromHandle* method. The second argument for the call to *CreateDelegate* is the method information. This object is a read-only instance property of the *Delegate* type. Finally, the new delegate object is created by the call, and control merges with the usual case at the *okLab* label.

Defining a new type at runtime.   The idea of constructing a new delegate object resolves the problematic cases at reasonable cost. However, the new object that is created has a type that is statically determined by the compiler. In a really extreme situation, it is possible to have to create new delegate objects repeatedly, as delegate values are passed backward and forward.

An alternative approach that does not suffer from this limitation involves defining a new class at runtime—that is, using dynamic code generation. When a problem assignment is trapped, a runtime support method is called to define a new class. The support method is passed two pieces of information. One is the runtime type handle that would have been used to create a new delegate object in the previous approach. The other piece of information is the type descriptor of the existing delegate value. By defining a new class that implements all of the interfaces of both *System.Type* descriptors, we may be sure that the new delegate object will be compatible with all of the relevant destination locations. In the pathological case where a delegate value is passed repeatedly from location to location, the exact type of the new delegates will become more and more general until the delegate implements every compatible interface type in the program.

Of course, once we are prepared to go to the lengths of runtime *IL* generation we have other options as well. Another solution involving runtime *IL* generation implements the observation at the very start of the discussion. The idea is as follows. Whenever the compiler meets the declaration of a procedure type it automatically transforms the reference to refer to a mangled name that is derived from the signature. All compatible types will thus be given the same name. *Values* of these types are not created using constructor calls, but instead are supplied by a factory routine in the runtime system. When the factory receives a request for the first object of any particular type, it constructs dynamic *IL* to define the class, and then creates an instance. During any particular program run, the factory will accumulate references to all the dynamic classes. Subsequent requests for further objects of the same types will be met by instantiating the dynamic classes, and without further *IL* generation.

Multiple Inheritance

The *CLR* does not provide facilities for the direct implementation of multiple inheritance. In particular, the *CLR* mechanisms for virtual method dispatch and object layout are inherently tied to an execution model with single inheritance and multiple interfaces. Nevertheless, as the Microsoft managed *C++* compiler shows, it is possible to implement multiple inheritance all the same. The fundamental idea behind such an implementation is to ignore the *CLR* facilities for method dispatch and instead lay out the *v-table* explicitly. The *per-class* information will need to contain a *v-table* and information regarding the offsets between the function pointers belonging to each parent class. In a typical design there will be a single *v-table*, which contains within it the subtables corresponding to each inherited class. These *v-table* structures will be declared as data within the class objects.

In such a design, the object layout becomes the responsibility of the language implementer, just as it would be in a native code setting. So far as the *CLR* is concerned, all classes are explicitly laid out **value** classes, and all methods are **static**. A typical call sequence for such a method in *IL* will look like the code in Figure 12.8. The differences from the usual *CLR* method call are hidden away in the pseudocode that computes the function pointer. In the *CLR* supported case we would have simply pushed a copy of the method receiver and executed the "`ldvirtftn`" instruction. In this present case the execution engine cannot know how to fetch the function pointer so the pointer manipulations must be explicit.

The information that is available at compile time typically will be the offset of the method in the subtable of the *v-table* and the statically known partial type of the object. The first step in finding the function pointer is finding the location of the *v-table* pointer

```
<push receiver>
<push method args>
<compute function pointer>
calli    returnType (<arg type list>)                              // static call
```

Figure 12.8: Calling a method with explicit class layout

in the actual object. Once the *v-table* pointer has been found, the offset into the relevant part of the table is known, and an indexing operation extracts the function pointer. There are a number of different possible designs for object layout in the presence of multiple inheritance.

One other fundamental operation that the implementer must design based on the explicit object layout is the implementation of type tests. Neither the "isinst" nor the "castclass" will be helpful, since each of these presumes the *CTS* object model.

There is one essential piece of support that the *CLR* provides for languages that implement multiple inheritance. The data in the *v-table* of each class object must be adjusted at *JIT* time to ensure that the symbolically declared values in the table point to the actual addresses. The *v-table* fixup facilities of the *CLR* allow for this.

Object Layout for Multiple Inheritance

There are several different ways of laying out object and dispatch tables to support multiple inheritance. To some extent different layouts are the result of differing semantics for the implemented language. Nevertheless, even for a single language, such as *C++*, there are several possible designs.

Certainly the most obvious common feature of implementations of multiple inheritance in *C++* is the fact that casting an object pointer to one of the inherited base types may change the value of the pointer. Suppose that we have a class *C* that is derived from two base classes *A* and *B*. The layout of the object might be as shown in Figure 12.9. In the figure there are three pointers, all of which point to the same object. One pointer, *c*, is of type *C**, while *a* is of type *A** and *b* is of type *B**. The fields belonging to each of the base types are embedded in the object layout, but only one of these can share its origin with the derived class *C*.

For each of the pointer target positions within the object, the datum at the pointer target is a pointer to the shared *v-table*. The *v-table* is a data structure that is unique for each exact type. There is only one *v-table* structure for each loaded class, while every new instance of the *C* class will be a separate object structure.

The *v-table* contains function pointers for each of the virtual functions of the base types and the derived type. These are grouped in subtables, one for each type. Each func-

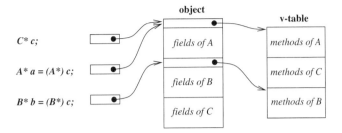

Figure 12.9: Layout of class *C* derived from classes *A* and *B*

tion has an offset relative to the starting position of the subtable that is statically known. The compiler is therefore able to emit *IL* that retrieves the function pointer by indexing from the appropriate *v-table* pointer. For example, to call the second virtual function of base type *B* the *IL* might read as in Figure 12.10.

```
ldsfld  M.B* M::b         // load outgoing this
<push args of func>
ldsfld  M.B* M::b         // load pointer b
ldind.i4                  // load v-table pointer
ldc.i4.4                  // load offset of 4
add                       // add offset to pointer
ldind.i4                  // load function pointer
calli                     // call the function
```

Figure 12.10: Calling the second virtual method of *B*

Of course if the class *C* has overridden any of the virtual methods of its base classes, then it is the new methods that occupy the relevant slots of the *v-table*. This poses an interesting problem. If class *C* has overridden a particular method of the base class *B*, then the overriding method may legally access all the fields of a *C* object, including fields that are inherited from the base class *A* for example. The problem is that the **this** of the call will point to the *B* region of the object rather than to the real origin of the object's memory footprint. What is needed is an adjustment that locates the origin of the *C* object, given a pointer to the embedded *B* object.

There are essentially three ways that the method might be supplied with an adjusted receiver, so as to reach the data of another base class. The *IL* of the method might have a hard-coded "this-adjustment" in its prolog. This is the method used by Microsoft's *Visual C++* compiler. Alternatively, the *v-table* itself might have a datum holding the adjustment. Finally, the call to the method might be indirect, going via what is sometimes called a *trampoline stub*. A trampoline routine looks just like an ordinary procedure but terminates by jumping directly to the entry point of the real method. The real method will always have the same formal parameter list as the stub. In this case, the trampoline would simply adjust the **this** argument, and then jump to the real method. In Figure 12.9, the trampoline would be called with a **this** pointing to the base of the embedded *B* object. By the time control bounces from the trampoline to the real target method, the outgoing **this** points to the base of the entire *C* object. In *IL* the "jmp" instruction supports the construction of trampoline code.

The choice between these three design styles is not at all simple. Suppose, for our example classes, that class *B* defines a virtual method *Foo* that is overridden in class *C*. We will further suppose that the offset in Figure 12.9 between the origin of the *C* object and the origin of the embedded *B* object is 24 bytes. If the "this adjustment" is built into the code of overriding methods, then the overriding method's *IL* will begin —

```
.method public instance void Foo ( <other args>) il managed {
    ldarg.0                          // get this pointer
    ldc.i4.s 24                      // load literal offset
    sub                              // adjust the this
    starg.0                          // store adjusted this
    . . .
```

A consequence of placing the adjustment within the method prolog in this way is that we must insist that overriding methods always be called with a receiver of the base type. In our example if the source code calls *Foo* on a reference statically of type *C**, then the calling *IL* must adjust the receiver by adding on 24 to compensate for the 24 that the prolog of *C::Foo* will immediately subtract off. For this design the function pointer for method *C::Foo* will appear just once in the *v-table*, in the *B* subtable.

For the other two designs the overriding method will appear twice in the *v-table*. One occurrence will be in the subtable associated with the exact type of the method, *C* in our example. The other occurrence will be in the subtable associated with the base type, *B* in our example. If the method is called on a base type pointer, the **this** will be adjusted either during the loading of the function pointer or in the trampoline stub. If the method is called on a derived type pointer, the overriding method will be called directly without any adjustment. Figure 12.11 shows how the *v-table* would look in in the trampoline case, for our example classes.

Accessing Nonlocal Variables

Languages with scope rules in the style of *Algol* and its successors allow nested procedures to access the local variables and formal parameters of their enclosing procedures. This data is not local to the procedure doing the access nor is it static data at the outer level. We call such access *uplevel access*, and such data *uplevel data*, since the data is accessed from within more deeply nested scopes. Such uplevel access presents a problem for languages

Figure 12.11: *v-table* for our example, using a trampoline stub

implemented on the *CLR*, since the activation records of inactive methods are inaccessible. The traditional methods of implementing such access have involved the use of either static links or display vectors. Both of these methods involve the taking of a base address of an activation record, and rely on the compiler being able to compute the offset of each datum in the activation record. Neither is possible for the *CLR*.

There are a number of possible methods of providing access to nonlocal variables in those languages that require it. None of these is particularly attractive. Nevertheless, there is one method that is sufficiently structured that it may be recommended over the others. This method involves the passing of one additional argument to all calls of nested procedures.[3]

The key concept in this design involves the creation of what we shall call an *explicit heap-allocated activation record* (*XHR*). If a procedure has local data that are accessed by nested procedures, then all such data are declared as instance fields in a *XHR* object on the heap. The remainder of the local data for the procedure are in the main activation record in the usual way. The point of this approach is that we may pass around references to these *XHR* objects and access the fields, even when the procedure "owning" the data is inactive.

Every time a call is made to a nested procedure, the call carries with it one additional argument. This argument is a reference to the explicit heap record of the lexically enclosing procedure. This is not necessarily the same as the calling procedure. Each *XHR* object contains a field that refers to the *XHR* of its own lexically enclosing procedure. Thus it is possible to follow the references, repeatedly, to reach the data of any enclosing procedure.

The details of the design involve the declaration of the classes that implement the explicit activation records, the rules for accessing the data, and the rules for passing the references around. We shall look at each of these in turn. As an example, we consider the procedure nest in Figure 12.12. In this example the procedure *Foo* defines two local integer variables, *i* and *j*. This procedure contains a nested procedure, *Middle*, which in turn contains a nested procedure *User*. The most deeply nested procedure accesses the

---

[3] In principle it is possible to perform sufficient static analysis to discover those *nests* of procedures that engage in nonlocal data access and avoid the additional overhead in all other cases.

local variables *i* and *j*. We shall assume that the middle procedure does not have any local variables that are uplevel addressed and does not itself access the locals of its enclosing procedure.

```
procedure Foo();
    var i,j  :   INTEGER;  (* define i and j local to Foo *)
    procedure Middle();
        procedure User();
        begin;
            <access i and j>
        end User;
    begin ... end Middle;
begin ...
end Foo;
```

Figure 12.12: Example procedure nest in module *M*

Declaring Explicit Activation Record Types

Explicit activation record types are as varied as the procedure local data that they encapsulate. One of the overheads of this design is that potentially as many new classes are defined as there are procedures in a program. Nevertheless, all these types have in common that they hold a reference to the *XHR* of the enclosing procedure. We therefore design a base type from which all *XHR* types will inherit. Because this type is used throughout the implementation, it is declared in the runtime system, as in Figure 12.13. The constructor for the type is responsible for linking the *XHR* instance to the *XHR* instance belonging to the lexically enclosing procedure. This type is not declared to be abstract since we will create instances of this type. When references to more global *XHR* are passed through intermediate level procedures that do not have any uplevel data of their own, we will not declare a new *XHR* type for the procedure but will use an instance of the base type.

Consider our example procedure that has two **int** variables, *i* and *j*, that are accessed from within nested procedures. We shall declare a *XHR* for this procedure as shown in Figure 12.14. In this case the class will contain a field for every uplevel addressed datum of its associated procedure. Of course, it will also have the inherited field *link* that chains the records together. Once again we rely on the constructor to link the new *XHR* to the *XHR* of its enclosing lexical scope. We have assumed that *RTS* is the name of the runtime system assembly in which the base type is defined.

The procedure that contains the uplevel data must call the constructor in its prolog. The argument to the constructor will be the incoming reference to the *XHR* of the lexically enclosing procedure. Conventionally this will be argument-0. In the case of a procedure at the outer lexical level, there is no incoming reference, so the link is simply set to **null**.

```
.class public XHR {
    .field public initonly class XHR 'link'
    .method public instance void .ctor(class XHR) il managed {
        ldarg.0
        call instance void object ::.ctor()
        ldarg.1
        ldfld class XHR XHR::'link'            // set initonly link field
    }
}
```

Figure 12.13: Definition of base type of explicit heap records

```
.class private Foo$data extends [RTS].XHR {
    .field int32 'i'
    .field int32 'j'
    .method public instance void .ctor(class XHR) il managed {
        ldarg.0                                      // load this
        ldarg.1                                      // load link
        call instance void [RTS]XHR::.ctor(class [RTS]XHR)
    }
}
```

Figure 12.14: Definition of explicit heap record for procedure with two **int**s

As well as defining the *XHR* type, it is also necessary to declare a local variable to hold the reference to the *XHR*. This is conventionally the first local variable—that is, local zero. The start of our example procedure with the two local variables would have the *IL* structure shown in Figure 12.15. If any of the formal parameters of the procedure are uplevel accessed, then these must be copied into the newly allocated explict activation record as part of the procedure prolog. It would be normal to allocate the *XHR* object with the very first instruction in the *IL* for the procedure. If there are local variables of reference surrogate type that are also uplevel addressed, then these must be instantiated in the normal way, but instead of copying the references to local variables, they will be stored in fields of the newly created *XHR*.

Note that procedures that do not enclose more deeply nested procedures never need to allocate an *XHR*. Thus procedure *User* in our example from Figure 12.12 does not need an *XHR*. Procedures at intermediate levels, such as *Middle* in our example, do have to allocate an *XHR*, even though they neither define nor access uplevel data. However, it is not necessary in such cases to define a new *XHR* type, since there are no fields other than the inherited *link* field. It such cases we may use the base type "[RTS]XHR" directly.

```
.method private static void Foo (class [RTS] XHR, <other args>)
                                                        il managed {
    .locals (classFoo$data, <other locals>)
    ldarg.0                                     // load link
    newobj instance void Foo$data::.ctor (class [RTS] XHR)
    stloc.0                                     // store XHR
    ...
}
```

Figure 12.15: Definition of procedure with uplevel data

Figure 12.16 shows the runtime structure of the activation records after *User* has been called. In the diagram the activation records are shown on the left, and the explicit heap-allocated records on the right. Procedure *Foo* has no incoming link from an enclosing procedure, and its ordinal-zero local variable holds a reference to its *XHR* of *Foo$data* type. Procedure *Middle* has a reference to the *XHR* of *Foo* as an incoming argument and uses its ordinal-zero local variable to hold a reference to its own *XHR*. In this case the record holds no information other than the link, so it is of the base type *[RTS]XHR*. Finally, procedure *User* has an incoming argument referencing the *XHR* of *Middle*. It does not need an *XHR* of its own.

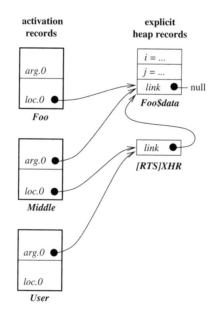

Figure 12.16: Activation record structure for example

Calling Nested Procedures

When a nested procedure is called, it is necessary to pass a reference to the appropriate *XHR*, along with any other arguments. The link that is passed must take into account the lexical levels of the procedure doing the calling and the procedure being called. There are three separate cases, depending on whether the called procedure is nested at a deeper level, at the same level, or at a shallower level than its caller.

Calling a more deeply nested procedure.   When any nested procedure is called, it must be passed a reference to the *XHR* of its lexically enclosing procedure. When a procedure calls one of its own nested procedures, the caller *is* that enclosing procedure, so the caller passes its own *XHR*. Since the *XHR* is by convention stored in local variable zero, the *IL* of the call looks like this —

```
ldloc.0                              // pass own XHR handle
<push other args>
call void M::Middle(class [RTS]XHR, <other formals>)
```

Calling a procedure at the same level.   If a procedure is called at the same level, the lexically enclosing scope of the caller and callee are the same. In this case, the outgoing reference passed as argument zero is simply a copy of the incoming reference. Here is the *IL* —

```
ldarg.0                              // copy incoming XHR handle
<push other args>
call void M::Bar(class [RTS]XHR, <other formals>)
```

Of course, the calling procedure in this case might not even have an *XHR* of its own, if it does not enclose any more deeply nested procedures.

Calling a less deeply nested procedure.   If a procedure calls another procedure that is less deeply nested than itself, it is necessary to traverse the links to find the appropriate *XHR* reference. Let us assume that the calling procedure is at lexical level N, and the procedure that we wish to call is at lexical level M. By assumption, N is greater than M. Procedures at level-1 are at the outer level—that is, at file-scope level. Such procedures do not have an enclosing scope and do not have the extra formal parameter.

In this case it is necessary to traverse $N - M$ links in the chain of static links, starting with the incoming *XHR* reference. Here is the *IL* —

```
ldarg.0                                   // copy incoming XHR handle
ldfld class [RTS]XHR [RTS]XHR::'link' // repeat this
ldfld class [RTS]XHR [RTS]XHR::'link' // instruction
...                                       // N–M times
<push other args>
call void M::Bar(class [RTS]XHR, <other formals>)
```

Of course the above instruction repeated in the *IL* may occur just once or as many times as is necessary.

Accessing Uplevel Data

Accessing your own XHR data.   Within the body of a procedure with uplevel accessed data, all access to the uplevel data becomes indirect. Thus in the example procedure *Foo*, adding the two uplevel accessed local variables would require the following *IL* —

```
ldloc.0                              // get XHR handle
ldfld   int32 Foo$data::'i'         // indirectly get 'i'
ldloc.0                              // get XHR handle
ldfld   int32 Foo$data::'j'         // indirectly get 'j'
add
```

If this data was not accessed by that pesky nested procedure, i and j would have been simple local variables, no *XHR* object would have been defined, and these accesses would have been simple local variable load instructions.

Following the links.   In order to access data from within a nested procedure, it is necessary to follow the links of the *XHR* objects. The chain must be followed for one fewer step than the difference in lexical level between the defining procedure and the accessing procedure. If we take our original example, Figure 12.12, we shall see how the *IL* in procedure *User* accesses the data defined in procedure *Foo*. In this case the difference in lexical level is two, so we shall need to follow one extra link. Here is the *IL* —

```
ldarg.0                              // Middle XHR ref.
ldfld class [RTS]XHR [RTS]XHR::link// Foo XHR ref.
castclass class Foo$data             // cast to real type
ldfld   int32 Foo$data::'i'         // indirectly get 'i'
```

You may follow these references in the *IL* in the diagram in Figure 12.16.

If the uplevel data was from the immediately surrounding scope, then the indirection in the second line would not be necessary. If the difference in lexical level was very great, then the second line would be repeated many times.

Wrapping Up

This last code fragment was the point in the whole exercise. All of the static analysis, the extra class definitions, the extra procedure arguments, and the runtime infrastructure were put there so that we could follow that chain of *link* fields.

Although the final result is relatively elegant, the overheads of the whole mechanism are somewhat undesirable. It is therefore useful to try to reduce the overheads to a minimum by avoiding unnecessary object creation. We observe the following sufficient conditions:

- A procedure must define a new *XHR* type if and only if it defines local variables or formal parameters that are uplevel accessed.

- Procedures that use uplevel data must declare an additional formal parameter of *XHR* type to receive the incoming static link.

- Procedures that lie on a path in the *calls graph* between the definer of uplevel variables and a user of those variables must allocate an *XHR* object, possibly of the base type. They must also declare an addditional formal parameter of *XHR* type.

For our model example procedure *Foo* defines its own *XHR* extension type *Foo$data*. Procedure *User* takes the extra incoming argument but does not allocate an *XHR* local variable. Finally, procedure *Middle* takes the extra incoming argument and allocates an *XHR* object. In this case, because the procedure has no uplevel addressed locals of its own, the object can be of the *XHR* base type.

Notes on Chapter 12

Chapter 1 mentioned **Project 7**. In that project a wide variety of different programming languages were implemented on top of the *CLR* by third parties. The project demonstrated that the *CLR* is a remarkably versatile platform for implementing a broad variety of languages.

This chapter has touched on a sampling of the issues involved in bending the *CLR* to the will of arbitrarily chosen languages. It has not attempted to be comprehensive, so there are plenty of challenges still out there. It is also possible that some of the tricks described in this chapter may in future be displaced by superior techniques.

Direct support for methods with covariant return types is one of those quasireligious issues. As shown earlier, implementation of this feature on top of the *CLR* is not too onerous. Structural compatability of delegate types is much less controversial. It is possible that future releases of *.NET* will directly support this functionality. That would be nice, since all of the known ways to circumvent the current restrictions are rather ugly, as the discussion illustrates.

The treatment of multiple inheritance focused on the way in which languages similar to *C++* might be implemented on the *CLR*. This choice was made because of the familiarity of the language and the ready availability of an example compiler. Nevertheless, this choice has some features that other language implementations might not have (and might not wish to have). In particular, it is quite feasible to implement a language with multiple inheritance and still be fully garbage collected. The fact that $C++$ does not do this proves nothing.

Visual $C++$ stores its *v-table* information inside **.data** declarations, and uses **.vtfixup** declarations to adjust the addresses. An alternative design might load up the *v-table* entries using explicit "ldftn" instructions in the class constructor. Of course, instance constructors would need to explicitly add to each instance one or more references to the *v-table* object.

The method described here for providing uplevel addressing in nested procedures is elegant but requires quite a bit of attribute evaluation in the compiler. All of the alternatives are at least equally complicated, probably less efficient, and much uglier.

Initialization
Analysis

As explained in Chapter 2, the program verifier performs a number of checks. The one that particularly concerns us in this Appendix is the check that all local variables are initialized along all paths in a method. The verifier performs dataflow analysis in order to make this check.

If a compiler wishes to produce verifiable code, then two alternate strategies may be used to ensure that the initialization tests are passed. The compiler might do equivalent analysis at compile time in order to ensure that source programs that will fail verification are rejected at compile time. Alternatively, the compiler may emit code that unconditionally performs some default initializations of all local variables at the start of each method.

The advantage of the second approach is simplicity, since no analysis is required. However, every other consideration argues against this approach. First, for correct programs the time spent in initialization of the locals is always wasted. Worse still, incorrect programs will remain undiagnosed both at compile time and at runtime. Truly, the worst of all possible worlds.

The advantage of performing the analysis at compile time is that incorrect programs may be rejected immediately, and no time is wasted on redundant initialization. As will be seen, there are certain other useful diagnostics that appear almost for free out of the same analysis. Of course, the disadvantage is that the analysis demands a separate semantic framework.

The *CLR* provides support for initialization of local variables in two ways. First, it is possible to set an attribute that ensures that all of the local variables in a method are given some characteristic "zero" value. This is certainly the appropriate mechanism for languages that guarantee this kind of behavior. Without this flag, the *CLR* still guarantees that local variables of object reference type will be safely initialized to **nil**. This suggests that it might be possible to only perform dataflow and emit the associated diagnostic messages for nonreference locals. This is probably a poor choice, since there is no extra cost involved in dealing with the larger set of local variables. Furthermore, from the point of view of error diagnosis, if the automatically set **nil** value reaches a used occurrence in the code, this is probably a program error.

To give you an idea of the amount of work involved in initialization analysis, in *gpcp* there are about 700 source lines dedicated to this task. Of this, a library that manipulates the *VarSet* data type accounts for about 250 lines, while about 200 lines of attribution methods appear in each of the expression descriptor and statement descriptor modules.

The remainder of this section deals with the issues involved in initialization analysis. The concrete example that is used is the implementation for *Component Pascal*. This language poses problems that are similar to those that arise in *C*-family languages. Other dialects of *Pascal* require much less work.

Dataflow Analysis

The analysis of initialization is a simple example of a forward flow, all-paths dataflow problem. Such problems are a standard part of the program analysis phase of optimizing compilers.

Dataflow problems are usually defined on the **control flow graph** (*CFG*) of a procedure. However, in the case of programs with structured flow of control we may avoid construction of a *CFG* and work directly with the *AST*. We define the problem as follows —

- a variable is *live-init* at the entry of a statement, if it is *live-init* at the exit of every statement that is a control flow predecessor of the statement

- a variable is *live-init* at the exit of a statement, if it is either *live-init* at the entry of the statement or is locally initialized by the code of the statement

This is a forward flow problem, because liveness depends on the predecessor statements. It is an all-paths problem, because liveness depends on *all* control flow predecessors.

Since the equations for each variable are independent, we may write and solve these equations by a parallel set algorithm. If we denote the the *live-init* set at the entry of statement i by the symbol $I_{i,in}$ and the *live-init* set at the exit of statement j by the symbol $I_{i,out}$, then we have the following set-valued equations —

$$I_{i,in} = \bigcap_{j \in pred(i)} I_{j,out}$$

$$I_{i,out} = I_{i,in} \cup LocalInit(i)$$

The set *LocalInit*(i) is the set of variables that are initialized by the code of statement-i. The initialization condition for the first statement, at the entry of the method is —

$$I_{entry,in} = \{v : v \in \textbf{args} \wedge v \notin \textbf{out-args}\}$$

In words, we take as initialized all incoming arguments to the method except for those marked as having **out**-mode.

Set equations of this kind, in general, do not have a unique solution. However the solution that we require is the *least fixed point* solution. This is easily computed by a bit-vector, iterative algorithm.

There is one small but important semantic detail to be decided. Suppose we wish to consistently compute a *live-init in* and a *live-init out* set for every statement type. What is the *live-init out* set for the return statement? This is important if, for example, we have the following structure —

```
if condition then
    ... (* not including a return *)
else
    ...; return; (* premature return *)
end
... (* what is live-init here? *)
```

In this example it is clear that the *live-init out* set at the end of the **if** statement is the *live-init out* set at the end of the **then** branch. Since we take the intersection of the sets that are incident at the control merge point, it is clear that the *live-init out* set of the **return** statement must be the set-intersection identity. We therefore adopt the convention that the *live-init out* from any statement that terminates the control flow is the universal set—that is, the set with all bits "on."

As we shall see later, this choice has some particularly helpful properties.

Creating the VarSet Framework

We will be manipulating bit-vectors, using the usual set operations, such as union, intersection, and various comparisons. These sets will use one bit per local variable and will thus use a variable number of machine words per set. As we have seen, in this context formal parameters are counted as local variables also.

What is needed is a framework that creates and manipulates variable length bit-vectors. As a matter of safety, we note that for any given procedure all bit-vectors will have the same length, so the operations will be well defined.

We define a module *VarSets* that exports an abstract data type implemented by a final class *VarSet*. The module defines both static and instance methods of the *VarSet* class. However, since *VarSet* is final, all of the methods will be statically bound. The instance fields of the class are an open array, *vars*, and an integer, *size*. Neither of these are public, so the sets may only be manipulated through the interface defined in Figure A.1.

```
PROC newUniv*(n : INTEGER)  : VarSet;        (* Return {0, 1 ··· n − 1} *)
PROC newEmpty*(n : INTEGER)  : VarSet;              (* Return empty {} *)
PROC (s : VarSet)newCopy*()  : VarSet;             (* Return copy of s *)
                        (* Predicates on VarSets *)
PROC (s : VarSet)isUniv*()  : BOOLEAN;                  (* s = univ *)
PROC (s : VarSet)isEmpty*()  : BOOLEAN;                 (* s = {} *)
PROC (s : VarSet)includes*(e : INTEGER)  : BOOLEAN;    (* e ∈ s *)
                (* The following modify their receiver VarSet *)
PROC (s : VarSet)Incl*(e : INTEGER);             (* s ← s ∪ {e} *)
PROC (s : VarSet)Excl*(e : INTEGER);             (* s ← s − {e} *)
            (* The following do not modify receiver or argument VarSet *)
PROC (s : VarSet)not*()  : VarSet;                    (* Return ¬s *)
PROC (s : VarSet)cup*(rhs : VarSet)  : VarSet;       (* s ∪ rhs *)
PROC (s : VarSet)cap*(rhs : VarSet)  : VarSet;       (* s ∩ rhs *)
PROC (s : VarSet)xor*(rhs : VarSet)  : VarSet;       (* s \ rhs *)
                where a \ b = (a ∩ ¬b) ∪ (¬a ∩ b)
```

Figure A.1: Interface to *VarSet* abstract data type

Computing Initialized Variable Sets

The computation of initialized variable sets according to the dataflow equations is relatively straightforward. The arbitrary flow of control possible in languages with a **goto** statement means that with such languages an explicit control flow graph will need to be constructed. In the case of well-structured languages, such as *C#*, *Java*, or *Component Pascal*, the *AST* will be enough.

For each statement in the *AST* we shall need to compute the *live-init* set attributes twice, at the entry and at the exit of the statement. In a language in which expressions may have side effects we also need to compute the *live-init* set at the start and end of evaluation of every expression.

We shall see below that expression attributes never need to be stored in the tree. Instead, we just carry a sort of a "running total" attribute around during a traversal, returning the result to caller. For statements, with just one exception that we discuss later, we do not need to store these attributes in the tree either.

As noted above, *gpcp* performs complete initialization analysis. There is a single traversal of the *AST* for each procedure, with the traversal order within the procedure mimicking the evaluation order at runtime. Two computations are involved, and both are done during the same traversal. First, we compute a *currently-known-to-be-initialized* set, which is passed around with the traversal. As variables undergo assignment, or some other initialization, they are inserted into the set. That is the first objective. The second objective is to check that all uses of local variables are correct. We thus compute the set and generate diagnostics for illegal usage during the same traversal. Figure A.2 is a very simple example illustrating the general idea. The source fragment in the figure has been decorated with the initialized set at the end of each statement. Notice that initially only the incoming parameter a is known to be initialized. One of the locals is initialized by the assignment in each branch of the **if** statement. At the end of the **if** the initialized set is the intersection of the sets at the output of the preceeding statements. In this example at the merge point we can only be sure that the parameter a is initialized.

```
procedure Bar(a :  integer);
   var b,c,d :  integer;
begin  ............................... {a}
   if a  > 0 then
      b  := f(); ..................... {a,b}
   elsif a  < 0 then
      c  := f(); ..................... {a,c}
   else
      d  := f(); ..................... {a,d}
   end; ................................ {a}
end Bar;
```

Figure A.2: *live-init* sets in a simple procedure

The loop-breaking rule.

In general, set equations of the kind that occur in dataflow analysis require a fixed-point solution to be found by an iterative algorithm. For forward flow frameworks the problem may be understood as follows.

At entry to a loop, the incident set depends on all of the predecessors. At least one of these predecessor blocks is an output block of the loop, connected to the loop header block along a back edge of the loop. In general the incident set along the back edge will depend on the entry-edge set in a recursive way. Hence a naive algorithm must iterate over the blocks until the fixed point is detected.

For *CFG*s without loops, equations of this kind may always be solved in a single pass by computing the sets in *reverse post-order*. That is, we do not compute the input set of a block until all output sets of predecessor blocks have been computed.

As it turns out, there is a subset of dataflow problems of this kind for which we can always compute the result in a single pass. The key observation is that the values of our *live-init* sets can only have elements added to them. Variables never become "uninitialized" once they are initialized. It follows that for loops with a single entry point, the set that is incident on the loop header along the back-edge is always a super-set of the set incident along the entry edge. It follows that the intersection of the two sets is always exactly equal to the entry-edge set. In effect, for this problem we may ignore all back edges of loops and compute our sets in a single pass, without iteration. Dataflow problems with the property that back-edges of loops may be ignored are said to have a *loop-breaking rule*.

Determining the VarSet size.

Initialization analysis is performed procedure by procedure. It is suggested that the traversals associated with this analysis should be done after type analysis, and only if no errors have been detected. Making this choice ensures that the trees that are traversed are well-formed and well-typed. In particular, the types and number of local variables are known.

Local variables and parameters are assigned an ordinal number, which determines that variable's position in the *VarSet* representation. This number is stored as the *varOrd* field in the *AbVar* descriptor of the variable. As it turns out, this same field will later be used for the ordinal number by which the variable is known at runtime. However we cannot persist the values between the two uses, since in *.NET* parameters and local variables are numbered independently, while in the *VarSet* they form part of the same numbered sequence.

We may conclude that the set size is equal to the number of local variables, including parameters. All sets associated with a particular procedure will use the same *size* parameter for allocation. Sets are only allocated under three circumstances. There is an initial set that reflects the semantics of the procedure signature. We also need to create empty and universal sets at particular points in the algorithm. Most sets are copied from an incoming set, where the size is determined from the size of the set being copied.

In general the dataflow algorithm works as follows. We initialize a set to denote the status of the incoming formal parameters. We then traverse the *AST* of the procedure recursively calling a (*virtual*) method *flowAttr* on each statement. The *flowAttr* methods call two methods on the statement's component expressions. The method *checkLive* tests that all used occurrences of local variables in the expression use properly initialized values. Another method, *assignLive*, returns a modified copy of the set, reflecting the effect of an assignment to the designator denoted by the receiver expression.

Initialization in expressions.

The traversal of expressions would be very straightforward, were it not for the possibility that evaluation might have side-effects. Without side-effects we could be sure that the same initialized set was passed all sub-expressions in the particular evaluation, and we would not have to be concerned about evaluation order. Consider the assignment statement —

$$a[exp_1] := exp_2;$$

The question is, does the language specify an order of evaluation of the two expressions exp_1 and exp_2? If there is no possibility of side effects, from the point of view of checking initialization, we need not care.

If side effects are a possibility, and the language defines a strict order of evaluation, then we simply traverse the expressions in that order. If the first evaluation has side effects, then we pass the result of those side effects on as a modified input *live-init* set to the second evaluation. If the language allows either order of evaluation, then the conservative choice would be to pass the same, unmodified set to each evaluation.[1]

There are at least two flavors of side effects that might be considered. First, there is the invoking of functions that have side effects. Then there are the explicit side effects of *C*'s pre- and post-increment and assignment operators. The explicit side effects of the *C* operators are tricky to model correctly, and most programmers (and textbook writers) simply do not understand the detail. The problem is that the side effects are not guaranteed to take effect until the next *sequence point*, as described in 5.1.2.3 of the *ANSI C* standard. Mercifully, we may make simplifying assumptions for this analysis. For operators which *mutate* a value, i++ for example, if i is a local variable it must be initialized before the expression is evaluated. Thus if i is not initialized by now, the program is in error, and we do not care exactly when any resulting mutation of the invalid value may take effect. Alternatively, if the variable is safely initialized, the increment has no effect on the set. The variable cannot be any more initialized than it already is! Unfortunately, this simplification does not apply to all *C* expressions. For example, it is correct to reject the *C* expression $a[i] = i = j$; as erroneous, if i is not initialized before evaluation begins.

In the case of function calls, expression evaluation is simplified by a similar consideration. Function calls may *mutate* their actual parameters in the case of reference parameters. For **var**-mode (**inout**) parameters the actual argument must be initialized prior to the call. If the value is initialized already, mutation of the value does not change the set. If it is not initialized, the program is in error. Of course, for **out**-mode parameters, if the language has them, the actual parameter need not be initialized, and the function call has the effect of initializing the parameter. Certainly, this is not a desirable programming style, but it is nevertheless legal in *Component Pascal*.

We may summarize the situation with function calls as follows. Languages without reference parameters do not mutate their actual parameters. Languages with only **inout**-mode reference parameters may mutate their parameters, but this cannot result in initial-

---

[1] This conservative computation is the safe assumption to make. But if one or both of the expressions in the example have a side effect, and this is a language with undefined evaluation order, what did the programmer think was happening here?

ization. Finally, languages with **out**-mode parameters can both mutate and initialize their actual parameters in a call.

Most *Pascal*-family languages are very simple in this regard. No expression evaluation has an initialization side effect, since there are no assignment operators and no **out** parameters. Most *C*-family languages have initialization side effects from their assigment operators, but not from function calls.

Component Pascal is different from its relatives. It has initialization side effects from function calls but no assigment operators. *C#* is also different from its close relatives. It has **out**-mode parameters, and hence has initialization side effects in function calls, as well as having assigment operators.

Having dealt with all of these somewhat obscure details, the implementation is relatively straightforward in *gpcp*. We define two methods on the *Expr* descriptor type, *checkLive* and *assignLive*. Both of these methods take the incoming *VarSet* as a parameter and return a *VarSet* that incorporates the effect of any initialization that has occurred during the expression evaluation. These methods do not modify the incoming set directly. If they return a changed set, they do so by copying the incoming set and modifying the copy. The reason is that we may need to pass the same set to several different evaluations. All refinements of these methods inherit this obligation.

The first method, *assignLive*, is an extensible method defined on the *Expr* descriptor type. The receiver is always a designator expression—that is, an "*lValue*" in C terms, and the method records the effect of an assignment to the variable selected by the expression.

In any expression denoting a variable, the variable can only occur in a *defining occurrence* if it occurs as a leaf expression. This is the case for the statement $i := exp$, where i is a variable. In all other forms of designator expression, variables occur only as *used occurrences*. This is the case for the assignment $i.f[j] := exp$;, where i and j are variables. Neither variable is initialized by this assignment, and both must already be initialized if the statement is to be correct.

The *assignLive* method computes any initialization effect of the use of its receiver expression as the left-hand side in an assignment, returning the possibly updated *live-init* set. The default case is very simple —

```
PROCEDURE  (node  :  Expr)assignLive (* invariant: lvIn is not modified *)
            (scpe  :  Scope;
             lvIn  :  VarSet)  :  VarSet,EXTENSIBLE;
BEGIN
  RETURN node.checkLive(scpe,lvIn);
END assignLive;
```

The base method checks that all used occurrences of local variables in the designator expression *node* are valid. It then returns the possibly changed set.

The only extension of this method is bound to the *IdLeaf* type and computes the effect of assignment to the variable designated by the node. Figure A.3 contains the complete code. If the identifier in the leaf is a local variable defined in the current scope but not already in the set, then we return a new set, including the newly initialized element; otherwise we return the unmodified input set *l*. Notice the way in which the new set is formed. We must respect the invariant by not modifying the incoming set. First we copy the set, then include the extra element in the copy.

```
procedure (node : IdLeaf) assignLive (s : Scope;
                                      l : VarSet) : VarSet;
  var id : IdDesc.Idnt; ord : INTEGER; tmp : VarSet;
begin
  id := node.ident;
  with id : IdDesc.LocId do              (* recall Figure 5.2 *)
    ord := id.varOrd;
    if s.defines(id) & ~l.includes(ord) then
      tmp := l.newCopy();
      tmp.Incl(ord);
      return tmp;
    end;
  else (* skip *)
  end; (* with *)
  return l;
end assignLive;
```

Figure A.3: The *assignLive* method for *IdLeaf*

Notice that in the base version of the *assignLive* method, we will recurse down to an *IdLeaf* (designators *always* start with a variable, right?). However, we recurse down with *checkLive*, not with *assignLive*. The assignment is not to the leaf, it is to some selected component of the leaf.

The second method is an abstract method defined on the *Expr* descriptor type, with the signature —

```
PROCEDURE (this : Expr) checkLive (* invariant: lvIn is not modified *)
          (scpe : Scope;
           lvIn : VarSet) : VarSet, ABSTRACT;
```

The concrete refinements of the *checkLive* method all take the incoming *live-init* set as argument. The set is passed down the tree by a dispatched traversal. The significant processing happens in the *IdLeaf* nodes, which is where use of local variables becomes visible. Figure A.4 has the code.

```
procedure (node  :  IdLeaf)checkLive(s  :  Scope;
                                     l  :  VarSet)  :  VarSet;
  var id  :  IdDesc.Idnt;  ord  :  INTEGER;
begin
  id := node.ident;
  with id  :  IdDesc.LocId do                    (* recall Figure 5.2 *)
    ord := id.varOrd;
    if s.defines(id) & ~l.includes(ord) then <notify error> end;
  else (* skip *)
  end; (* with *)
  return l;
end checkLive;
```

Figure A.4: Dataflow checks for *IdLeaf* descriptors

Another case of interest is the function call. In this case the normal unary recursion down the (designator) tree is performed, and a call is made to a procedure, *liveActuals*, that checks the actual parameter expressions. Figure A.5 has the code. The line of code containing the return statement deserves some explanation. It is possible that evaluation of the function designator has an initialization side effect, as may the evaluation of the actual parameters. However we cannot assume that these evaluations take place in any particular order, since the language specification is silent on this point. We thus compute the resulting *live-init* sets from both evaluations as though they were performed starting with the same input set. We then take the union of these two resulting sets.

```
procedure (node  :  CallX)checkLive(s  :  Scope;
                                    l  :  VarSet)  :  VarSet;
  var tmp  :   VarSet;
begin
  tmp := node.kid.checkLive(s,l);         (* recurse on designator *)
  if <node is a built-in call> then <process built-in calls>
  else                                    (* call liveActuals *)
    return tmp.cup(node.liveActuals(s,l));
  end;
end checkLive;
```

Figure A.5: Dataflow check for function call

We accept that a variable may be initialized as a side effect of evaluation of the designator or evaluation of an actual parameter expression, or by assignment to an **out**-mode parameter. What we do not accept is that the side effects of the evaluation of one argument are available to make legal the use of a newly initialized variable in another argument to the same call. Consider the following pathological example, in which a function call $f(i)$ initializes its parameter, which is then immediately used in another actual expression —

$$a[(f(i)].g(i);$$

Since we cannot assume that selection of the receiver object takes place before fetching of the argument to the call of g our algorithm rejects this expression. Pedantic?[2] Perhaps, but it is worth a little extra effort to guarantee correctness.

The *liveActuals* method must iterate over the actual parameter expressions accumulating the effect of all of the evaluations. Except for **out**-mode parameters, *checkLive* is called on each parameter expression. For an **out**-mode formal we instead call *assignLive* on the actual parameter expression, since the effect of the call is to perform an assignment to the actual parameter. In the code fragment in Figure A.5, the handling of the built-in procedures and functions such as *INC*, *INCL*, *LEN*, and so on, has been removed for clarity, at the position indicated.

Languages with predicate side effects.   For languages in which expressions may have initialization side effects and which specify so-called *short-circuit* evaluation of Boolean expressions, there is an additional consideration.

In a short-circuit Boolean evaluation, the flow of control during predicate evaluation may follow different paths according to whether the expression evaluates true or false. It follows that the initialized sets may be different in the *evaluates-true* and *evaluates-false* control flow branches. For example, in an **if ... then ... else** statement, the evaluates-true set is passed as *live-init in* to the **then** branch, while the evaluates-false set is passed as *live-init in* to the **else** branch.

We could respond with a design that ensured that our *checkLive* method would return the most conservative result, in effect only inserting initializations into the set that take place in all possible evaluations. However, it is possible to do better, by defining a new method, *BoolLive*, that returns two *VarSets*. One *VarSet* is the set of variables known to be initialized if the expression evaluates true. The other *VarSet* is the set of variables known to be initialized if the expression evaluates false. The base *BoolLive* method, defined on the abstract descriptor type *Expr*, is shown in Figure A.6. In the base case the expression evaluation does not involve varying control paths, so we simply apply *checkLive* to the expression and return the same result set as both the true and false *live-init out* set.

There are refinements of this method for several expression types. The *BinaryX* version is considered below, and others may be worked out as an exercise or looked up in the source code. However, there is one other case that is so cute that it deserves a mention. When we evaluate a leaf expression, there can be no side effect, so we normally return the same unchanged set as *live-init out* for both true and false cases. Exceptionally, if the leaf

---

[2] Actually, it is almost certain that a code generator for *.NET* will select its receiver first, but this is not guaranteed by the language definition and might not be true of other runtime environments.

```
procedure (this  :  Expr) BoolLive        (* invariant: lvIn is not modified *)
           (scpe  :  Scope;
            lvIn  :  VarSet;                              (* incoming set *)
          out tSet  :    VarSet;                          (* true result set *)
          out fSet  :    VarSet), new, extensible;        (* false result set *)
begin (* not a short-circuit evaluation *)
   tSet  :=  this.checkLive(scpe,  lvIn);
   fSet  :=  tSet;                          (* return identical sets *)
end BoolLive;
```

Figure A.6: Base method for Boolean expressions

is a Boolean constant, we return the universal set along the impossible path, as discussed on page 363. Here is an example —

> **if** P **then**   (* where P is statically true *)
>   *statement initializing variable* i;
> **end**;
> *statement using variable* i;

If the predicate were not statically constant, the compiler would reject the final statement on the grounds that the variable i was not initialized along the fall-through path. With our convention no error is generated, since it is known that the fall through cannot occur.

An example in which short-circuit evaluation is involved is the refinement of *Bool-Live* for binary expressions. If the binary operator is **and** or **or**, then we must take into account the special semantics. Figure A.7 demonstrates the general scheme of things. The processing for the **or** operator is shown. The code recurses down to the left-hand subexpression, taking the incoming set as input. The result sets are stored in two local variables. The call to the right-hand subexpression takes the false result from the first evaluation as input set, since the second expression only gets evaluated if the first expression evaluated false. In this case the result of a false evaluation of the second expression is the overall false *live-init out* set for the method. However, the overall true *live-init out* set must be formed by intersecting the true results of the two control paths. On one path the left expression evaluates true immediately, and the second is never evaluated. Along the other path the first evaluates false, and the second subsequently evaluates to true.

Figure A.8 shows an example in which a predicate calls functions with an **out**-mode parameter. The first call, $f(j)$, has the effect of initializing the local variable j, while the second call initializes k. The source fragment has been decorated with the initialized set at the beginning of each predicated branch. Along the **then** branch only the local variable j is initialized, since we cannot be sure that the second call of f was made. Along the **else** branch both locals are known to be initialized, since in this case both calls of f must have taken place.

```
procedure (x : BinaryX) BoolLive (scpe  :  Scope;
                                   lvIn : VarSet;
                              out tSet :   VarSet;
                              out fSet :   VarSet);
   var lhT, lhF, rhT, rhF : VarSet;
begin
   if <operator is Boolean 'or'> then
      x.lKid.BoolLive(scpe, lvIn, lhT, lhF)
      x.rKid.BoolLive(scpe, lhF, rhT, fSet)
      tSet := lhT.cap(rhT);                      (* set intersection *)
   elsif <operator is Boolean 'and'> then
      <similar code for 'and'>
   else
      <non short-circuit cases>
   end
end BoolLive;
```

Figure A.7: Method for Boolean binary expressions

```
procedure f (out x :   char)  :  boolean;
begin ... end f;

procedure Foo(i : char);
   var j,k : char;
begin .......................................{i}
   if f(j) or f(k) then ..........................{i,j}
      ...
   else ....................................{i,j,k}
      ...
```

Figure A.8: Example of predicate with side effects

Initialization in statements.

Traversal of statement descriptors is controlled by a set of dispatched methods, the abstract parent of which has the signature —

```
PROCEDURE (self : Stmt) flowAttr (* invariant: lvIn is not modified *)
          (scpe : Scope;
           lvIn : VarSet) : VarSet, ABSTRACT;
```

This method takes the incoming *live-init* set as a parameter and returns the *live-init out* set resulting from statement execution. The result will depend on the incoming set, and any side effects of statement execution.

The first statement type to be dealt with must be the compound *Block* statement. Dataflow analysis is about the way that information is passed from statement to statement, and the *Block* statement controls the order of evaluation for statement sequences. The code is simple —

```
PROCEDURE (x : Block)flowAttr(s : Scope;
                                l : VarSet) : VarSet;
   VAR i, max : INTEGER
BEGIN (* iterate over statements in order *)
   max := x.body.tide-1;
   FOR i := 0 TO max DO l := x.body.a[i].flowAttr(s,l) END;
   RETURN l;
END flowAttr
```

After each recursive call to *flowAttr* we update the *live-init* set l, passing the new value on to the next sequential statement. The *live-init out* of the sequence is the final value returned by the last statement in the sequence.

Assignment statements are also extremely simple, as seen in Figure A.9. In short, we must apply *checkLive* on the value expression on the right-hand side, and *assignLive* on the left-hand side designator expression. The result set is the union of the sets created by the side effects of the two expressions. We do not assume a particular order of evaluation, but we know that both evaluations will take place.

```
procedure (self : Assign)flowAttr(s : Scope;
                                     l : VarSet) : VarSet;
   var lSet,rSet : VarSet;
begin
   lSet := self.rhsX.checkLive(s,l);
   rSet := self.lhsX.assignLive(s,l);
   return lSet.cup(rSet);                         (* set union *)
end flowAttr;
```

Figure A.9: Dataflow attribution for assignment statements

Statements that involve different control paths illustrate the way in which set merging by intersection is implemented. The *Choice* descriptor is a good example of this. The flow attribution for this descriptor is given in Figure A.10. In the figure, we consider only the **if**-statement case. In overall terms, the code iterates over the predicate and statement sequences that correspond to the repeated **if** and **elsif** branches. The **with**-statement case is similar, except that the predicates in that case cannot have side effects.

In detail, the figure gives a good example of the use of the *BoolLive* method. We have two running sets. One, *nowT*, is the set that results from the latest predicate evaluating

```
procedure (x : Choice)flowAttr(s : Scope;
                               l : VarSet) : VarSet;
   var pred : Expr; ix : INTEGER;
       rslt, stillF, nowT, sOut : VarSet;
begin (* only considering the if statement *)
   rslt := VarSets.newUniv(<set-size for s>);
   stillF := l;                              (* initialize running set *)
   for ix := 0 to x.preds.tide-1 do          (* each pred. in order do *)
      pred := x.preds.a[ix];                  (* select current predicate *)
      if pred # nil then                      (* not the else branch *)
         pred.BoolLive(s, stillF, nowT, stillF);
         sOut := x.blocks.a[ix].flowAttr(s, nowT);
      else                                    (* nil is the else branch *)
         sOut := x.blocks.a[ix].flowAttr(s, stillF);
      end;
      rslt := rslt.cap(sOut);                    (* set intersection *)
   end;
   if <there was no else branch> then
      rslt := rslt.cap(stillF);               (* allow for fall through *)
   end;
   return rslt;
end flowAttr;
```

Figure A.10: Dataflow attribution for **if** statement

true. This is the set that is finally passed to the call of *flowAttr* for the selected statement. The other, *stillF*, is the set that results from all evaluations up the present evaluating false. The chaining of these sets is the critical design feature. Each predicate evaluation is passed the *stillF* set as *live-init in*, since the predicate is only evaluated at runtime if all previous predicates evaluated false. The true and false *live-init out* sets of each predicate evaluation are assigned to the corresponding running sets.

Finally, when the **else** branch is recognized, the selected statement is checked, with *stillF* as the *live-init in* set. There is also a special case when there is no **else** branch and code falls through. In this case, the *live-init out* set of the virtual "skip" statement is *stillF*, as might be expected.

The *live-init out* set for the statement as a whole is formed by taking the intersection of the *live-init out* sets of all branches. This is done branch by branch inside the loop in the code.

One exceptional case.   As a final example of flow attribution in *Component Pascal*, we must deal with the one case in which the local variables of the traversal are not sufficient to compute the result set. This need arises through the interaction of the **loop** and **exit** statements and forms a model of one way of handling more arbitrary flow of control in languages that have such things.

In *Component Pascal* the **exit** statement changes the locus of control to a point immediately following the end of the most closely enclosing **loop** statement. Since statements may be arbitrarily nested, the target of the exit is not necessarily the statement in which the local flow is being evaluated. During tree building we associate each **exit** with its closest enclosing **loop**, storing this information as a semantic attribute of the *Exit* statement descriptor. In each *TestLoop* descriptor we allocate a field named *merge* to hold the accumulated *VarSet* value. At entry to the *flowAttr* method for the **loop** we allocate and initialize a universal set and do the usual recursion on the body statements of the loop. If some of these, or their recursive children, call **exit** then the *merge* set will be mutated through the link from the *Exit* descriptor to the enclosing *TestLoop* descriptor —

```
PROCEDURE (x : ExitSt)flowAttr(s : Scope; l : VarSet);
BEGIN
   x.loop.merge := l.cap(x.loop.merge);        (* do intersection *)
   RETURN VarSets.newUniv(set-size for s);
END flowAttr;
```

This is only two lines of code, but take some care here!

We intersect the current *live-init* set with the *merge* set of the enclosing **loop** statement, using the *cap()* function. This merges the result with those of any other exits that jump to the same loop exit and modifies the eventual *live-init out* of the enclosing **loop**. However, we still need to return a *live-init out* set from the **exit** statement itself. Since control does not continue to the statement textually following the **exit**, we have to return the universal set as *live-init out* of the **exit** statement.

Some bonus attributes.   In this section we shall see how the dataflow framework provides for a few additional checks for semantic correctness of programs.

Some of the properties of the **return** statement have already been discussed. We know, for example, that the *live-init out* from a **return** is the universal set. There are some other checks that we would like to make at the same time however.

For languages with **out**-mode parameters, it is a property of well-formed programs that every *out* parameter must have been assigned a value before the procedure returns. This suggests that at every procedure return point, the *live-init* set should confirm that such an assignment has been made along every possible control flow path that reaches that point. This check is performed in *gpcp* by a method named *OutCheck*. It is called in two places. The first is whenever an explicit **return** statement is processed by *flowAttr*. The second is after the return of the call of *flowAttr* on the entire procedure body, where the implicit **return** would be located.

One other cheap check is facilitated by the dataflow framework. It is a rule that control flow in a value-returning function should never reach the end of the function without encountering an explicit **return** *value* statement. Many compilers fulfill their obligation to check for this by inserting a trap at the end of the code. Then, if by some means or another control flow reaches the end, a runtime error is notified. With the dataflow framework, we may do better and catch all such errors at compile time.

Recall that the *live-init out* set of a **return** statement is the universal set. Therefore if the *live-init* set at the end of a function is not the universal set, we may be sure that there is a sneak path to **end** that does not pass through a statement that explicitly exits the function.

Of course, we need to be sure that we do not get fooled by a *live-init* set which just happens to have all bits set "on." We can arrange for this at an entirely trivial cost. Whenever a new set is allocated, we ask for a set that has cardinality one greater than the number of local variables. The last element does not correspond to any program variable and thus cannot occur in any set that did not begin its life as the universal set. It follows that the only way in which the final set in a function can be the universal set is if all paths to **end** pass through a **return**, **throw**, or **halt**.

It is a curiosity that the following code fragment is not rejected by the compiler —

```
PROCEDURE Endless(...) : INTEGER;
BEGIN
  LOOP
  ...   (* body with no exit *)
  END;
END Endless;
```

This function has no **return** *int-value* statement, but yet the compiler says that it is correct. The *merge* field of the **loop** statement will be initialized to the universal set, and since there are no **exit** statements, this set will persist as the *live-init out* of the dataflow analysis. Strangely, the compiler is correct. There is no way of reaching the end of the function without passing through an exit, because there is no way of reaching the end of the function.

Notes on Appendix A

There are any number of books that deal with the various dataflow algorithms, and the frameworks within which compiler optimizations take place. My favorite is Robert Morgan's *Building an Optimizing Compiler* (Digital Press, 1998).

The idea of performing dataflow analysis without creating an explicit control flow graph has been an item of folklore in the structured language community. The reasons that this works have been described by Brandis and Mössenböck in "Single-pass generation of static single assignment form for structured languages," *ACM Transactions on Programming Languages and Systems*, Vol. 16, 1994.

The CIL Instruction Set

The following table contains a brief description of each instruction of the *Common Intermediate Language* instruction set. The description is necessarily brief, and surely insufficient for applications where the exact semantics of each instruction are important.

The final column in the table gives the *stack-*Δ for the instruction. Instructions marked "$\star$" have a *stack-*Δ that depends on the arguments of the call. In the case of instruction prefixes, the *stack-*Δ depends on the following instruction.

Table B.1: Instructions with no arguments

Instruction	Description	Δ
add	Add two top elements on stack	−1
add.ovf	Add two top elements and trap signed overflow	−1
add.ovf.un	Add two top elements and trap unsigned overflow	−1
and	Bitwise **and** of two top-of-stack elements	−1
arglist	Push the arglist of a "varags" method	1
break	Breakpoint instruction for debugging	0

continued on the next page

Table B.1: Instructions with no arguments, continued

Instruction	Description	Δ
ceq	Compare for equality and push **bool**	−1
cgt	Compare for greater than and push **bool**	−1
cgt.un	Compare for greater than unsigned and push **bool**	−1
ckfinite	Throw an exception if top of stack is a *NaNS*	0
clt	Compare for less than and push **bool**	−1
clt.un	Compare for less than unsigned and push **bool**	−1
conv.i	Convert top of stack to natural integer	0
conv.i1	Convert top of stack to 1-byte integer	0
conv.i2	Convert top of stack to 2-byte integer	0
conv.i4	Convert top of stack to 4-byte integer	0
conv.i8	Convert top of stack to 8-byte integer	0
conv.ovf.i	Convert top of stack to natural **int** and trap overflow	0
conv.ovf.i.un	Convert from unsigned on top of stack to natural **int** and trap overflow	0
conv.ovf.i1	Convert top of stack to **int8** and trap overflow	0
conv.ovf.i1.un	Convert from unsigned on top of stack to **int8** and trap overflow	0
conv.ovf.i2	Convert top of stack to **int16** and trap overflow	0
conv.ovf.i2.un	Convert from unsigned on top of stack to **int16** and trap overflow	0
conv.ovf.i4	Convert top of stack to **int32** and trap overflow	0
conv.ovf.i4.un	Convert from unsigned on top of stack to **int32** and trap overflow	0
conv.ovf.i8	Convert top of stack to **int64** and trap overflow	0
conv.ovf.i8.un	Convert from unsigned on top of stack to **int64** and trap overflow	0
conv.ovf.u	Convert top of stack to natural **uint** and trap overflow	0
conv.ovf.u.un	Convert from unsigned on top of stack to natural **uint** and trap overflow	0
conv.ovf.u1	Convert top of stack to **uint8** and trap overflow	0
conv.ovf.u1.un	Convert from unsigned on top of stack to **uint8** and trap overflow	0
conv.ovf.u2	Convert top of stack to **uint16** and trap overflow	0
conv.ovf.u2.un	Convert from unsigned on top of stack to **uint16** and trap overflow	0
conv.ovf.u4	Convert top of stack to **uint32** and trap overflow	0

continued on the next page

Table B.1: Instructions with no arguments, continued

Instruction	Description	Δ
conv.ovf.u4.un	Convert from unsigned on top of stack to **uint32** and trap overflow	0
conv.ovf.u8	Convert top of stack to **uint64** and trap overflow	0
conv.ovf.u8.un	Convert from unsigned on top of stack to **uint64** and trap overflow	0
conv.r4	Convert top-of-stack value to **float32**	0
conv.r8	Convert top-of-stack value to **float64**	0
conv.u	Convert top-of-stack value to natural **uint**	0
conv.u1	Convert top-of-stack value to **uint8**	0
conv.u2	Convert top-of-stack value to **uint16**	0
conv.u4	Convert top-of-stack value to **uint32**	0
conv.u8	Convert top-of-stack value to **uint64**	0
cpblk	Support for *ANSI C* "memcpy" function	−3
div	Signed division of two top elements on stack	−1
div.un	Unsigned division of two top elements on stack	−1
dup	Duplicate the top-of-stack value	1
endfilter	Return value from filter block	−1
endfinally	Return from finally block	0
initblk	Support for *ANSI C* "memset" function	−3
ldarg.0	Load the zeroth argument	1
ldarg.1	Load the first argument	1
ldarg.2	Load the second argument	1
ldarg.3	Load the third argument	1
ldc.i4.0	Load literal 0 of type **int32**	1
ldc.i4.1	Load literal 1 of type **int32**	1
ldc.i4.2	Load literal 2 of type **int32**	1
ldc.i4.3	Load literal 3 of type **int32**	1
ldc.i4.4	Load literal 4 of type **int32**	1
ldc.i4.5	Load literal 5 of type **int32**	1
ldc.i4.6	Load literal 6 of type **int32**	1
ldc.i4.7	Load literal 7 of type **int32**	1
ldc.i4.8	Load literal 8 of type **int32**	1
ldc.i4.M1	Load literal −1 of type **int32**	1
ldelem.i	Load natural integer array element	1
ldelem.i1	Load **int8** array element	1
ldelem.i2	Load **int16** array element	1
ldelem.i4	Load **int32** array element	1
ldelem.i8	Load **int64** array element	1
ldelem.r4	Load **float32** array element	1

continued on the next page

Table B.1: Instructions with no arguments, continued

Instruction	Description	Δ
ldelem.r8	Load **float64** array element	1
ldelem.ref	Load reference array element	1
ldelem.u	Load natural unsigned integer array element	1
ldelem.u1	Load **uint8** array element	1
ldelem.u2	Load **uint16** array element	1
ldelem.u4	Load **uint32** array element	1
ldind.i	Load natural integer pointed to by top of stack	0
ldind.i1	Load **int8** pointed to by top of stack	0
ldind.i2	Load **int16** pointed to by top of stack	0
ldind.i4	Load **int32** pointed to by top of stack	0
ldind.i8	Load **int64** pointed to by top of stack	0
ldind.r4	Load **float32** pointed to by top of stack	0
ldind.r8	Load **float64** pointed to by top of stack	0
ldind.ref	Load reference pointed to by top of stack	0
ldind.u	Load natural **uint** pointed to by top of stack	0
ldind.u1	Load **uint8** pointed to by top of stack	0
ldind.u2	Load **uint16** pointed to by top of stack	0
ldind.u4	Load **uint32** pointed to by top of stack	0
ldlen	Load length of array referenced by top of stack	0
ldloc.0	Load zeroth local variable	1
ldloc.1	Load first local variable	1
ldloc.2	Load second local variable	1
ldloc.3	Load third local variable	1
ldnull	Load a **null** value on the stack	1
localloc	Expand the current activation record	−1
mul	Multiply top-of-stack elements	1
mul.ovf	Multiply top-of-stack elements and trap overflow	1
mul.ovf.un	Multiply top-of-stack elements and trap unsigned overflow	1
neg	Arithmetically negate top-of-stack element	0
nop	Do nothing	0
not	Bitwise **negate** top-of-stack element	0
or	Bitwise **or** top-of-stack elements	−1
pop	Discard top-of-stack element	−1
refanytype	Extract type token from typed reference	0
rem	Remainder of two top-of-stack elements	−1
rem.un	Unsigned remainder of two top-of-stack elements	−1
ret	Return to caller, maybe with function result	*
rethrow	Rethrow the current exception	0

continued on the next page

Table B.1: Instructions with no arguments, continued

Instruction	Description	Δ
shl	Arithmetic shift left	−1
shr	Shift right	−1
shr.un	Logical shift left	−1
stelem.i	Store array element of natural integer type	−3
stelem.i1	Store array element of **int8** type	−3
stelem.i2	Store array element of **int16** type	−3
stelem.i4	Store array element of **int32** type	−3
stelem.i8	Store array element of **int64** type	−3
stelem.r4	Store array element of **float32** type	−3
stelem.r8	Store array element of **float64** type	−3
stelem.ref	Store array element of reference type	−3
stind.i	Store top of stack to natural integer pointer target	−2
stind.i1	Store top of stack to **int8** pointer target	−2
stind.i2	Store top of stack to **int16** pointer target	−2
stind.i4	Store top of stack to **int32** pointer target	−2
stind.i8	Store top of stack to **int64** pointer target	−2
stind.r4	Store top of stack to **float32** pointer target	−2
stind.r8	Store top of stack to **float64** pointer target	−2
stind.ref	Store top of stack reference to pointer target	−2
stloc.0	Store top of stack to zeroth local variable	−1
stloc.1	Store top of stack to first local variable	−1
stloc.2	Store top of stack to second local variable	−1
stloc.3	Store top of stack to third local variable	−1
sub	Subtract top-of-stack elements	−1
sub.ovf	Subtract top-of-stack elements and trap overflow	−1
sub.ovf.un	Subtract top-of-stack elements and trap unsigned overflow	−1
tail.	Prefix. Following call terminates method	*
throw	Throw top-of-stack object as exception	−1
unaligned.	Prefix. Pointer on top of stack may be unaligned	*
volatile.	Prefix. Address on top of stack is of volatile location	*
xor	Bitwise **xor** of top-of-stack elements	−1

Table B.2: Instructions with a numeric argument

Instruction		Description	Δ
ldarg	*Num*	Load the *N*-th argument	1
ldarg.s	*Num*	Load the *N*-th argument (short form)	1
ldarga	*Num*	Load the *N*-th argument address	1
ldarga.s	*Num*	Load the *N*-th argument address (short form)	1
starg	*Num*	Store the *N*-th argument	−1
starg.s	*Num*	Store the *N*-th argument (short form)	−1
ldloc	*Num*	Load the *N*-th local variable	1
ldloc.s	*Num*	Load the *N*-th local variable (short form)	1
ldloca	*Num*	Load address of the *N*-th local variable	1
ldloca.s	*Num*	Load address of the *N*-th local (short form)	1
stloc	*Num*	Store top of stack to *N*-th local variable	−1
stloc.s	*Num*	Store top of stack to *N*-th local variable (short form)	−1
ldc.i4	*Num*	Load literal *N* as **int32**	1
ldc.i4.s	*Num*	Load literal *N* as **int32** (short form)	1
ldc.i8	*Num*	Load literal *N* as **int64**	1
ldc.r4	*Num*	Load literal *N* as **float32**	1
ldc.r8	*Num*	Load literal *N* as **float64**	1

Table B.3: Instructions with a type reference argument

Instruction		Description	Δ
box	*TRef*	Create boxed copy of top-of-stack value of type *T*	0
castclass	*TRef*	Cast top-of-stack reference to type *T*	0
cpobj	*TRef*	Copy value object of type *T*	−2
initobj	*TRef*	Initialize value of type *T*	−1
isinst	*TRef*	Test if top of stack is an instance of *T*	0
ldelema	*TRef*	Load address of array element of type *T*	−1
ldobj	*TRef*	Load value of type *T* onto stack	0
mkrefany	*TRef*	Make typed reference of type *T* from top-of-stack pointer	0
newarr	*TRef*	Create array of element type *T*	0
refanyval	*TRef*	Extract pointer from typed reference of type *T*	0
sizeof	*TRef*	Load size in bytes of value type *T*	1
stobj	*TRef*	Store top-of-stack value of type *T*	2
unbox	*TRef*	Create managed pointer to boxed value	0

Table B.4: Instructions with a label argument

Instruction		Description	Δ
beq	*Lab*	Branch to label if equal	−2
beq.s	*Lab*	Branch to label if equal (short form)	−2
bge	*Lab*	Branch to label if greater or equal	−2
bge.s	*Lab*	Branch to label if greater of equal (short form)	−2
bge.un	*Lab*	Branch to label if unsigned greater or equal	−2
bge.un.s	*Lab*	Branch to label if unsigned $\geq$ (short form)	−2
bgt	*Lab*	Branch to label if greater than	−2
bgt.s	*Lab*	Branch to label if greater than	−2
bgt.un	*Lab*	Branch to label if unsigned greater than	−2
bgt.un.s	*Lab*	Branch to label if unsigned greater (short form)	−2
ble	*Lab*	Branch to label if less than or equal	−2
ble.s	*Lab*	Branch to label if than or equal (short form)	−2
ble.un	*Lab*	Branch to label if unsigned less or equal	−2
ble.un.s	*Lab*	Branch to label if unsigned $\leq$ (short form)	−2
blt	*Lab*	Branch to label if less than	−2
blt.s	*Lab*	Branch to label if less than (short form)	−2
blt.un	*Lab*	Branch to label if unsigned less than	−2
blt.un.s	*Lab*	Branch to label if unsigned less than (short form)	−2
bne.un	*Lab*	Branch to label if unequal or unordered	−2
bne.un.s	*Lab*	Branch to label if unequal or unordered (short)	−2
br	*Lab*	Unconditional branch to label	0
br.s	*Lab*	Unconditional branch to label (short form)	0
brfalse	*Lab*	Branch to label if top of stack zero or **null**	−1
brfalse.s	*Lab*	Branch to label if top of stack zero or **null** (short form)	−1
brtrue	*Lab*	Branch to label if top of stack not zero or **null**	−1
brtrue.s	*Lab*	Branch to label if top of stack not zero or **null** (short)	−1
leave	*Lab*	Exit from try, catch, or filter block	0
leave.s	*Lab*	Exit from try, catch, or filter block (short form)	0

Table B.5: Instructions with a method reference argument

Instruction		Description	Δ
`call`	*MRef*	Statically call specified method	⋆
`callvirt`	*MRef*	Virtual call of specified method	⋆
`jmp`	*MRef*	Jump from current method to *MRef*	0
`ldftn`	*MRef*	Load function pointer to specified method	1
`ldvirtftn`	*MRef*	Load virtual function pointer of top-of-stack object	0
`newobj`	*MRef*	Allocate new object and call constructor	⋆

Table B.6: Instructions with a field reference argument

Instruction		Description	Δ
`ldfld`	*FRef*	Load field of object with reference on the top of stack	0
`ldflda`	*FRef*	Load address of field of top-of-stack object	0
`ldsfld`	*FRef*	Load static field of specified class	1
`ldsflda`	*FRef*	Load address of static field of specified class	1
`stfld`	*FRef*	Store top-of-stack value to field of object next on stack	−2
`stsfld`	*FRef*	Store top of stack to static field of specified class	−1

Table B.7: Miscellaneous instructions

Instruction		Description	Δ
`ldstr`	*Str*	Load literal string	1
`calli`	*Sig.*	Indirect method call with specified signature	⋆
`ldtoken`	*Token*	Load runtime handle of metadata token	1
`switch`	...	Table switch on value (see page 39)	−1

Index

Abstract stack machine, 3, 5
Abstract Syntax Tree, 11, 135–164
Accessibility, 43, 64
Activation record, 24
Ada language, 164
Alias semantics, 55
Amman, Uwe, 18
Amortized doubling, 133, 134, 337
ANDF, see Architecture Neutral Distribution Form
ANSI C language, 3, 41, 230, 247, 285
Architecture Neutral Distribution Form, 5, 19
Array bounds checks, 7, 256
Array of arrays, 61, 239
Assembly, 2
    dynamic assemblies, 321–338
    structure of, 42
Assembly *IL* syntax, 207
AST, see Abstract Syntax Tree
Attribute evaluation, 140, 165–196
Attribute grammar, 138

Baking assemblies, 323
Bounds checking, 256
Bowles, Ken, 19
Branch instructions, 34–39
    conditional, 37
    table switch, 39
    unconditional, 36

Brandis, Marc, 377

Call instruction, 39, 221, 252
    how to choose, 253
    indirect call, 39, 349
    virtual call, 81, 82, 342
Case statement, 39, 159
.cctor, *see* Constructors
Chaining to ilasm, 210
CIL, see Common Language Runtime
    instruction set, 379–383
    textual *CIL*, 12, 199, 210, 330
Class emitter worklist, 200
Class hierarchy diagrams, 17, 142, 322
Class *IL* syntax, 62
Class member *IL* syntax, 212
Class *IL* syntax, 210
Cloning arrays, 288
CLR, see Common Language Runtime
CLS, see Common Language Specification
COCO/R, 140, 164
COM interop, 317
Command line args, 46, 48
Common Language Runtime, 1, 2, 21–52, 147, 227, 291
Common Language Specification, 22, 104–105
Common Type System, 22, 55–102
Compare instructions, 34